Fruitful Journeys

Fruitful Journeys

The Ways of Rajasthani Pilgrims

Ann Grodzins Gold

University of California Press

Berkeley / Los Angeles / London

Fruitful Journeys: The Ways of Rajasthani Pilgrims won the Hans Rosenhaupt Memorial Book Award from the Woodrow Wilson National Fellowship Foundation in 1987.

University of California Press
Berkeley and Los Angeles, California

University of California Press, Ltd.
London, England

Library of Congress Cataloging-in-Publication Data

Gold, Ann Grodzins, 1946–
Fruitful journeys.

Revision of the author's thesis (Ph.D.)—
University of Chicago, 1984, presented under the
title: Life aims and fruitful journeys.
Bibliography: p.
Includes index.
1. Ghatiyali (India)—Religious life and customs.
2. Hindu pilgrims and pilgrimages—India—Rajasthan.
3. Hinduism—India—Ghatiyali—Customs and practices.
I. Gold, Ann Grodzins, 1946– . Life aims and
fruitful journeys. II. Title.
BL2016.G48G65 1988 306'.6 86-30905
ISBN 0-520-05670-1 (alk. paper)

Printed in the United States of America

1 2 3 4 5 6 7 8 9

For Ruth Maimon Grodzins
and Morton M. Grodzins

Contents

Illustrations

Photographs

Maps

Preface

Journeys to gods and other powers, performed by Rajasthani villagers, are the subject of this study. These journeys are described, and their motives and meanings analyzed, from a particular perspective and with certain, partially preconceived, questions in mind. Most of the data that serve as sources for these descriptions and analyses were gathered in a specific locality and by a very few persons: myself, several assistants following my interests, and, in some instances, one colleague following his own. Intellectual viewpoint, personalities, and human relations influenced both the collection and the ordering of data.

In an introductory chapter I place this study within a number of simultaneous realities, all of which, to some degree, moulded its methods, styles, and conclusions. Among these "settings" I include my anthropological questions as well as my emotional quirks, both having in different ways shaped the finished product. Chapter 1 begins, then, by recalling how I formulated and refined initial problems at the University; it proceeds through narrating the ways in which I sought to answer them "on the ground" with methods more serendipitous than methodical. Through thus linking, if only sequentially, anthropological-Indological orientations with personal experience, I intended to hint broadly that they were really two sides of the same coin.

In the years that have elapsed during the metamorphosis of this work from doctoral dissertation to book, a phenomenon I described in a long footnote as a "recent current" in the literature of anthropology has swollen into a kind of torrent. This is the urge toward self-awareness—an urge compelling ethnographic introspection at a personal level even as it propels the discipline to confront its collective and individual complicities in the history and perpetuation of human inequalities. In 1984 when I defended my thesis, this trend was most evident in works that reflected descriptively on the personal involvements as well as the psychological and emotional turmoils of fieldwork, and the impact of these factors on research findings (Devereux 1967; J. P. Dumont 1978; Lévi-Strauss 1974; Rabinow 1977; Riesman 1977). The most recent voice I cited there was Clifford 1983, whose insight into ethnographic writings—as "fictions both of another cultural reality and of their own mode of production" (1983:144)—struck me as being right on the mark. Concurrent or still more recent explorations in these directions subject the process of producing ethnographies to ever more penetrating probes, giving attention to political, philosophical, and artistic as well as personal implications (for example, Dwyer 1977, 1982; Fabian 1983; Tedlock 1983).

Most recently, "writing"—the "graphy" in ethnography—has become a central target within the process of self-examination or, frequently, a projected examination of other ethnographers' selves. The anthology compiled by Clifford and Marcus (1986), classified by its publishers (this Press) as "anthropology/literary theory," provides a multivoiced manifesto for taking anthropology as literature, applying criticism to ethnographic texts, and subjecting the process of fieldwork, and the reality of its "data" to a relentless scrutiny in terms of relationships of power as well as webs of aesthetics. My original hope, embedded in that 1984 footnote, that by including the personal in this work I make my book somehow more "honest," seems a bit naive in the glare of such scrutinies.

By acknowledging Clifford's diagnosis of ethnography as doubly a "performed community of fiction," however, it was not just on the word "fiction" that I found my footing, but in the concept of performance. Understood in its creative or emergent sense (Bauman 1977), I can see this book as a joint performance by me (in the role of Ainn-bai as well as Dr. Gold), the Ghatiyalians, and a few others. If the result of my participant observation is both creative and fictional, nonetheless it arises from people and places that were and are real. If this work is well characterized as a composite of evocative fragments (Tyler 1986), these were gathered and arranged with the express ideal of maintaining as close a harmony as possible with the culture and situations where they originated.

My anthropological roots draw on Schneider's cultural analysis, on Singer's ideas about cultural performances, and on Marriott and Inden's ethnosociology of South Asia. Some basic premises that guided my fieldwork were these: record, explore and work within indigenous categories; apprehend performance as a passage to meaning; understand text and context as mobilely interlaced, substance and code as one, gross and subtle as continous, nature and all living beings as fluidly composed and perpetually transacting in qualities at once moral and physical.[1]

The research on which this book is based was shaped and informed by these orientations. In part because of their influence and in part because of my own intellectual circumspection, I have largely refrained from drawing conclusions beyond the microcosm of this study. Thus I attempt neither to argue within these pages for any overarching theoretical approach to religion nor to generalize systematically on South Asian conceptual systems. At times I speak loosely of Hindu realities or the villagers' world view—as if the two were interchangeable. Mostly I tell what people did and what they said about what they did, to each other and to me; the songs I heard them sing and what they said these songs meant and what I thought about what they said; the places I went with them and what I asked them about those places and how

1. Schneider's "cultural account" of American kinship (1968, 1977) and its underlying analytic definition of cultures as coherent systems of meanings and values constitutive of human realities (1976) directly informed my understanding of the anthropological enterprise. Moreover, Schneider's work was an acknowledged influence on some of the first attempts to analyze aspects of Indian culture in its own terms—attempts which also strongly influenced me. One important focus of these attempts, not surprisingly, was kinship (Inden 1976; Inden and Nicholas 1977); another was caste (Marriott and Inden 1976, 1979).

Marriott's transactional approach to rank and other matters (1976a) developed further possibilities for the innovative use of ethnosociological models. In his more recent and largely unpublished writings Marriott has continued to expand horizons in his work with South Asian ethnosociology and ethnopsychology (Marriott 1980; Moreno and Marriott 1981). He has also been instrumental in the organization of an ongoing series of seminars and workshops, which have stimulated many studies and continuous discourse in these areas. Years spent in the milieu of those seminars have certainly affected my work in a number of ways.

Singer (1972) gives the basis and sets the examples for using cultural performances as "units of observation" which offer access to "units of cogitation" (1972:70–71). Much to be found within the rich body of Singer's work on South Asian tradition and civilization, and more recently on the semiotics of personal and cultural identity (1984), has been a continuing source of intellectual inspiration.

they answered me and how I organized those answers around themes that also "emerged" in the course of these and other conversations. I hope thus to convey something of both the interactive nature of fieldwork and of those elusive cultural realities where this particular fieldwork did, after all, really take place through several seasons and cycles of festival, travel, and growth.

In about my second month in Ghatiyali, a young village man who had formerly assisted my American colleague, Joseph Miller, came home for a visit from his studies in Ajmer and voluntarily took the new foreigner under his wing for a night. We attended two different all-night devotional singing sessions together, and he patiently, in pure Hindi, explained the meanings of some of the hymns' verses to me in a detailed fashion such as no one had previously attempted. I was exhilarated by his lucidity, but when around 2:00 A.M. my energies began to flag, he commented that for me all the things I was experiencing in his village were "brown sugar for the deaf and dumb." This phrase, he informed me, was a Rajasthani saying—but years later I found the expression included among verses attributed to the poet-saint Kabir and intended to describe the formless Lord. What Bhoju (who eventually came to be my closest assistant) referred to, however, was the potent sweetness of his village world—his culture; *guṛ,* the brown sugar of the saying, has a flavor deeper than any known in refined American products. Not only was this sweetness inaccessible to my foreign ears (I couldn't "hear" the words of the *bhajans*), but more than this it was certain to be inexpressible through my voice. I might somehow absorb its flavor, living as I was in the midst of so many sweet impressions, but this flavor I could never convey to others, lacking language to do so. What a perfect metaphor for the anthropological enterprise! Although I accepted and accept Bhoju's verdict, I have struggled against it; in the chapters that follow, much of that struggle is crystallized.

Many different institutions and people have supported this protracted project in many ways. My fieldwork in India was funded by the American Institute of Indian Studies and the Social Science Research Council. AIIS provided far more than rupees; its institutional presence and its individual personnel gave many kinds of assistance from my first arrival in Delhi. My affiliation with the Rajasthan Institute of Folklore (Rupayan Sansthan) was a blessing, and its director, Komal Kothari, a bountiful source of practical guidance and detailed knowledge. The Committee on Southern Asian Studies of the University of Chicago and the Charlotte Newcombe Foundation contributed generous funding during the writing-up period.

My teachers at the University of Chicago saw this work coalesce from scattered ideas through numerous proposals, field reports, a thesis. Among them I especially acknowledge the continuous guidance of McKim Marriott and Milton Singer. Kim gave a close and critical reading to two drafts of the dissertation, his marginalia always illuminating my manuscript. Milton has offered steady personal support and challenging intellectual direction to my work since I took my first anthropology course with him in 1973. Other members of the academic community at Chicago contributed in important ways to this endeavor. I am especially grateful to Ralph Nicholas, who shared his penetrating enthusiasm for the study of popular Hinduism, and to Kali Charan Bahl and Joan L. Erdman. For careful readings of fragments or versions of this work at various stages of its production I am also indebted to Daniel Gold, Jack Hawley, Gloria Raheja, Sushila Zeitlyn, and the anonymous reviewers for the University of California Press. At Berkeley, Barbara Metcalf guided and cheered the revision process, and Gladys Castor's patient copy-editing added vigor as well as consistency to my language. The many suggestions of all these persons have often been incorporated without further acknowledgment.

I particularly thank Joseph Miller for bringing me to Ghatiyali and for subsequent generosities with his time, methodologies, and materials. Douglas Goodfriend and his wife, Chris Halfer, opened their home in New Delhi to me when I had hepatitis, eventually extending their remarkable hospitality to my son and to Bhoju, my research assistant, as well. I thank them deeply for this salubrious interlude which made the concluding and crucial six weeks of fieldwork possible.

My most intimate, profound, and inexpressible debts are to persons in my family. Daniel Gold, Adam Rose, Jonah Gold, Bert and Sylvia Gold, Kelly and Diana Grodzins—I thank each of you for many kinds of love and gifts that have sustained me in many different ways. My mother, Ruth Grodzins, has contributed immeasurably to this book: her professional editing polished it; her care for my children granted me the precious time and peace of mind that made writing possible; her faith and fortitude were my starting place. My father, Morton Grodzins, died over twenty years ago, yet I must acknowledge his early lessons in the craft of writing and the subtler art of paying attention to one's fellow human beings. The dedication of this book is to both my parents.

Of those who helped me in the village, I shall name only a few, but I express my enduring gratitude to all. Inder Dan Detha, Bhoju Ram Gujar, Nathu Lai Nath, Ugma Nathji, and Vajendra Kumar Sharma were paid at various times as research assistants but became much more: friends, pilgrimage-brothers, *rākhī* brothers, and partners in the production of this work. Nathu and Ugma Nath expended vast energies in patient efforts to help me understand their caste's esoteric lore. Bhoju demonstrated fine skills as photographer, interviewer, and ethnographer. A participant observer in the truest sense of the word, his voice will be heard throughout these pages, his sensibilities reflected.

The women of Ghatiyali, who pitied my drabness, were ever willing to share the color of their lives with me. I must especially thank Lila, Bhabhasa, Bari Bhabhasa, and Sohan for companionship, food, and knowledge. I have changed neither the name of the village nor those of its residents. Ghatiyalians approved my project and cooperated with me, consciously, often enthusiastically. Those I consulted about the then remote prospect of our shared work coming to print did not wish the name of their place and its special attributes to be disguised.

It is self-evident that this book would never have come into existence without the contributions of institutions, teachers, colleagues, family, and most obviously the people whose voices and values I have tried to transmit. I take full responsibility for its final shape; yet, like a pilgrim, I aver that the fruits of my journey, if inalienably part of me, belong to me not at all. At the end of chapter 1, I invoke the goddesses-and-gods of Ghatiyali and pay most particular attention to four special personages among them: Four-Armed Vishnu, King Jaipalji, Mahadev of Meditation Seat, and the Cave Baba. These oversee and protect community life, both geophysical and political, demanding unity and punishing any perpetrators of falsehood among their worshippers. I can only wish that this work fairly represents the complex sentiments of the people sheltered by these gods and reflects, however imperfectly, the deities' high standards for witnessed truth.

A Note on Translation and Transliteration

The linguistic situation during my fieldwork was complex. Some of my informants spoke only Rajasthani; some spoke Hindi; many spoke mostly Rajasthani but threw in Hindi words and syntax to varying degrees. Sometimes I had a research assistant with me interpreting from Rajasthani to Hindi, so I made notes in Hindi; sometimes I recorded and worked directly with Rajasthani. Further to compound the complexities, Rajasthani itself has numerous variants, and Ghatiyali's local language was an eclectic melange of more than one of these.

In preparing this manuscript for publication I have eliminated much of the resulting confusion by ruthlessly slashing out Hindi and Rajasthani words and passages that were lovingly reproduced in the dissertation (Gold 1984). However, a number of terms, too crucial or too awkward to translate, I have retained in the original. These terms are contextually defined when introduced in the text. Those that recur subsequently are found in the glossary, where I have, with a few exceptions, attempted to "gloss" them as concisely as possible—in order to facilitate instant comprehension rather than to convey semantic subtleties.

In general, for the sake of wider recognition, all terms existing in Sanskrit or standard Hindi appear in those familiar forms rather than Rajasthani variants; thus *bhopā*, not *bhopo; puṇya*, not *puṇ*. However, an occasional distinctive Rajasthani word is found in its original shape—for example, the infinitive *bolāṇo*. Proper nouns—names of places, people, and texts—I have left without diacritics unless they are part of a quotation or their meaning as words is also important. In the latter case I supply diacritics only once, on the name's first translated appearance. Names of texts may be found, with diacritics as provided by their editors and translators, in the references.

I have used a standard system to transliterate from Devanagari to English, with a few modifications and idiosyncrasies. I make no distinction between the Hindi consonant ड़ and the Sanskrit vowel ऋ, using *ṛ* for both, as usage of these letters allows no confusion. Both श and ष are simply written *sh*. The one letter unique to Rajasthani, ऴ or ळ in Devanagari, is rendered *ḷ*. I employ a tilde where the *candrabindu* symbol would have appeared in the original—for example, *mā̃* for माँ.

All translations of stories, songs, and printed Hindi pamphlets are my own; all translations of Ghatiyali's oral traditions were made from performances recorded by me or by Miller and transcribed by literate villagers. Whenever I have drawn from Miller's collections—which are more extensive than my own—I have noted this.

1. Introduction: Multiple Settings

A pilgrim's journey, in India as elsewhere, is usually a round trip.[1] Yet Hindu pilgrimage has most commonly been studied from that journey's destination—the riverbank, the temple town, the lake, or mountain shrine—with little attention to its closure or return lap. The student of pilgrimage, then, interviews and observes pilgrims as pilgrims in the context of their journey's goal, but not of its end. Or research may focus on the specialists in pilgrim centers who serve these transient journeyers—the bewildering hierarchies and networks of priests and other ritual experts, of guides, barbers, rest-house keepers, sweet-makers, vendors of flowers and incense. Alternatively, with still less attention to pilgrims as persons, Hindu pilgrimage may be studied as a remarkable and ancient institution sustaining a system of linked centers that helps bind together the incredibly diverse peoples of the Indian subcontinent.[2]

1. Within Hindu traditions exist two major exceptions to this generalization. One of these would be the suicide pilgrimage, mentioned in some of the classical texts both as a way of expiating heinous sins and as a means of getting heaven or release (Kane 1953, 4:596–597; 603–616; Rangaswami Aiyangar 1942:lxiv–lxvi; lxxxi). Never in the course of my fieldwork on pilgrimage did I hear such an extreme measure advocated. However, when one pilgrim was lamenting his wife's disappearance in the crowded streets of Gaya, he announced that if she was not found he too would then and there become an offering to the Ganges and receive, along with her, passage to a better existence (chapter 4). And one devout, older woman interviewed on the road spoke of the auspiciousness of death in a crossing place. She was immediately silenced by my research assistant for uttering inauspicious words which could result in her family's cursing us if they thus lost her. The second, less drastic version of a no-return pilgrimage is that made by elderly folks who choose to settle and spend the rest of their lives in a pilgrimage center, thus being assured the benefits of dying there in the natural course of events. This also was unheard of as a practice among the people I knew in Rajasthan; but see Parry 1982a for a consideration of the phenomenon in Banaras.

2. Anthropological studies focusing on centers—which usually have sections on pilgrims and on priests—would include Jindel 1976; Saraswati 1975; Vidyarthi 1961; Vidyarthi, Saraswati, and Jha 1979. Morinis (1984) offers a comparison of

Such studies cannot, nor do they pretend to, know pilgrims in their daily lives. This book, by contrast, is based in a village whose residents are much else before they are pilgrims and for much more of the time than they are pilgrims. I settled in this village with no premeditated plan of what kind of pilgrimage I would study and little prior knowledge of its denizens' pilgrimage habits. What I had premeditated were the things I might be able to learn through investigating why Hindus went on journeys to gods, rivers, and temples—any journeys at all. And I hoped to learn how their reasons for pilgrimage were integrated with or stood apart from other aspects of popular religion and the values inherent in its practices.

Chapters 3 to 5 describe and interpret three styles of pilgrimage undertaken by Rajasthani villagers, with many references back to village practices and their meanings. Chapter 2 elaborates systematically on those home practices and meanings which I found particularly relevant to my interpretation of pilgrimage. Here, in Chapter 1, I locate my understandings of Ghatiyali religion more generally in the village scene and among the local deities. But before that, I place myself—a curious apparition—among the Ghatiyalians, and—most preliminary of all—I place this work broadly within some approaches to the study of Hindu conceptual systems and unwrap a few concepts that are critical to what follows.

---

three regional centers in Bengal. Parry (1980; 1982a) is particularly concerned with funeral priests and other religious specialists in Banaras, as well as with the special attributes of Banaras in terms of Hindu cosmology. Historians of religion and students of Indian literature have also been drawn to study pilgrimage centers. Eck (1982) elaborates eloquently on the meaningfulness of Banaras's glory. Hawley (1981) focuses on the theatrical traditions of Krishna country, but in doing so conveys quite a bit of pilgrims' experience in that special domain. Vaudeville (1975; 1976) elucidates historical, literary, and legendary strands of the pilgrims' destinations of Pandharpur in Maharashtra and Krishna's Mathura.

Studies more concerned with understanding pilgrimage as a civilizational phenomenon—that survey centers, rank or categorize them in various ways, or consider their importance as integrative factors for pan-Hindu culture—include Bharati 1963; 1970; Bhardwaj 1973; Cohn and Marriott 1958.

Existing exceptions to the center-based norm have described particular pilgrimages processually, experientially, or as embedded in and explicated by other configurations of Hindu tradition (Binford 1976; E. V. Daniel 1984:245–287; Karve 1962; Stanley 1977). For a very useful, cogent, and much more extensive discussion and critique than is necessary here of approaches to South Asian pilgrimage, see Morinis 1984:233–275.

All of these orientations I call "settings." They are equally layers, angles, puzzle pieces, or interlocking circles upon which, from which, with which, and within which this study is constituted. More simply, in this chapter I present some descriptions—in sequential, linear fashion, as if they were neatly separable—of (1) the questions I took to the field and how I didn't and did get them answered there; (2) my fieldwork experience, poeticized as the sorrows of Ainn-bai with her bare head, long skirt, and heavy bangles (by Ainn-bai I mean the person I was in Ghatiyali; I hope, in fact, not only to present her experience of the "other" but in some fashion to convey those others' experience of "me"); (3) region and village as places with historical as well as present, social as well as cultural, existences (although it is on the latter terms that this study rests); (4) village divinities and an evening spent in their worship.

Finding Release through Pilgrimage: The Object of Study Conceived and Refracted

The original and lofty purpose proposed for the research that produced this book was to see the human aim (*purushārth*) of release (*moksha, mukti*) as it was valued or pursued by ordinary Hindu householders. Among the traditional four aims or ends of life—release, desire, gain, and biomoral duty (*moksha, kāma, artha, dharma*)—*moksha* is usually conceived as superior and certainly also as most remote. However, while some students of Indian society and culture have described the aim of release as subversive to the rest, and to all ordinary life (L. Dumont 1960), I argued for its continuity with normative Hindu existence. And while some Western anthropologists had found peasants seldom if ever concerned with *moksha* (Kolenda 1964:71–72; Wadley 1975:109), I agreed with others, who suggested that *moksha* is in fact an important component of a Hindu value system for all members of the culture and not just religious specialists or elite (Kakar 1978; Kaushik 1976; Marriott 1976b).

Most particularly I sought to controvert Dumont's view of *moksha* as wholly opposed to, indeed "fatal to," the other life aims

(1960:45).[3] Rather, I followed Marriott in seeing all four ends of life "as inherent in all categories of beings" (1976b:192) and found confirmation in Kakar, who asserts that "the idea of moksha is not deviant, but central to the imagery of the culture" (1978:17).

"Release" is the most literal meaning of *moksha* and is also its best translation. (Others proffered by Indologists range from "freedom" through "salvation.") This release is total and final: from all binding attachments, all futile illusions, and ultimately, conclusively, from normative cycles of rebirth and redeath, the "flux" (*samsāra*) which is the nature of creation. How might householders, typically enmeshed in family life with its affections and jealousies, and in economic toil with its hard responsibilities and vainglorious rewards, also pursue an end of detachment? Where would I search for *moksha* among Indian villagers?

For the concrete object of study I chose the practice of pilgrimage. Why this particular matching of ideology and phenomenon? I saw in prescriptive texts for *tīrthayātrā*—literally "journeys to river fords" or to "crossing places"[4] but translatable as "pilgrimages"—indications that *moksha* was numbered among, not apart from, such journeys' potential fruits (Kane 1953:585–589; 629–631). A few ethnographic accounts of pilgrimage in India (such as E. Daniel 1984:245–287) also hinted that a turning from involvement in the world on the part of participants was an important facet of such journeying.

Moksha is traditionally associated with renunciation (*sannyāsa*), whether as the fourth life stage (*ashrama*) to be entered upon by

3. The views of Louis Dumont on the linked subjects of release and renunciation are found in several of his books and articles. These views are assembled and presented most coherently, however, in the still often cited and highly influential 1960 paper, "World Renunciation in Indian Religions." One point upon which Dumont lays great stress is that, in a society where persons as actors are thoroughly embedded within hierarchically ordered social groupings, the renouncer who leaves society is the only real individual. Dumont's repeated emphasis on the creative-dynamic input of the renouncer in Hindu thought, in this context, seems subtly invidious. He considers the Indian renouncer to be structurally equivalent to a Western individual, and he also finds him more intellectually vigorous than those who function within the multiply constraining social universe of *"homo hierarchicus."* See Dumont 1960, 1965, 1972, and most recently a continuation of the same argument—renouncer equals individual—which he uses to introduce some speculations about the development of modern Western individualism (1983). Many other scholars have addressed these and related propositions of Dumont's, finding them both stimulating and arguable. See, for example, Das 1977; Heesterman 1985:26–44; Madan, ed. 1982.

4. I follow Eck 1981b:344 in usually translating *tīrtha* as "crossing place."

aged persons with married children, or as a vocation followed from youth. Chief features of a renouncer (*sannyāsī*) are indifference to both family and caste; abnegation of possessions; and a single-minded attempt to approach (unite with, become) a supreme being or reality, whether this is achieved through sheer asceticism, yogic discipline, meditative introspection, or devotional ecstasy.

The practice of *tīrthayātrā* as set forth in Sanskrit lawbooks, mythological anthologies, and the epic *Mahabharata* was explicitly designated as appropriate meritorious action for poor people, low-caste people, even women (Kane 1953:567–570; *Mahabharata* 1976:373–374; Rangaswami Aiyangar 1942:xxiv–xxv). Yet it called for ascetic modes of action and devotional credence quite consonant with those of renouncers (Kane 1953:562–564; *Mahabharata* 1976:373–374; Rangaswami Aiyangar 1942:xxviii–xxxvi), although of course for pilgrims the path was temporary, not lifelong.

For example, it was standard advice for pilgrims to practice chastity, to eat one meal a day only, to sleep on the ground, and to go barefoot—all typical of the renouncer's way of life. E. V. Daniel (1984) described modern pilgrims shedding birth-given identities, both of caste and of name—again characteristic of *sannyāsīs*. By studying householders as pilgrims and viewing pilgrims as temporary renouncers, then, I expected to be able to show that renouncers' values were far from alien to householders, and that release was in fact integral to these.

What I found out about *moksha* and pilgrimage during the course of some nineteen months of fieldwork in Rajasthan was predictably more complex than I had expected. The majority of my informants were unpretentious, unlettered farmers and artisans. To my initial dismay, they seemed at first to be just as Kolenda had characterized Indian villagers: not holding the "achievement of moksh" as a "serious goal" (1964:71–72). Thus villagers stubbornly refused to claim that they hoped for, desired, or did anything deliberately to get *moksha,* even in the context of pilgrimage. "Have you *seen moksha* at any crossing place?" one irritated man challenged me.

If, however, my research did not at once reveal that all pilgrims were ever in search of ultimate freedom, I did find an immediate and manifold connection between pilgrimage and death. Pursuing the several threads of this connection along various meandering paths, I eventually used it to structure my description and analysis of Rajasthani pilgrimage. Chapter 2 presents several conceptions of human spirits' after-death conditions that coexist in the thoughts, rituals, and realities of Ghatiyalians, and demonstrates some correlations of these with three types of journeying. *Moksha* has its place here—not the all-encompassing position I had imagined it might hold, but nonetheless a meaningful one.

In examining the motives and values of villagers, and of villagers as pilgrims, two other concepts important to an understanding of the meaning of all action—including pilgrimage—require elaboration in this first chapter of settings. One is "fruits" and the other is "fate."

Fruits (*phal*) refers to the desirable results of worthy actions.[5] As I tried to comprehend pilgrims' conceptions of "the fruits of crossing places" (*tīrthaphal*) I encountered a seeming paradox. The motto inscribed with a flourish over the front windshield of the pilgrimage bus reads "Lord make your journey fruitful [*saphal*]." The popular literature praising the greatness (*mahatmyā*) of any crossing place—readily available in cheap, simple Hindi pamphlets—promises fruits: of bathing, of viewing the gods, of making charitable gifts. According to these sources, if you even think about a powerful crossing place or say its name, you will receive health, wealth, progeny, and release. Priests conducting rites at crossing places also spoke frequently in terms of fruits. But when pilgrims were asked they consistently denied expecting to get anything from their *tīrthayātrā*s.

Outside the immediate context of pilgrimage and its rewards I found two rather divergent cultural constructions of "fruits" which help to interpret this puzzle. In the *Bhagavad Gita*—among Hindus of Ghatiyali the text that is probably read aloud and studied privately most frequently—there is a strong injunction to surrender all fruits of action to God (*Bhagavad Gita* 1973:88–89; 103), and this inner-worldly renunciation is linked to the realization of perfect devotion to a supreme deity.

Within Ghatiyali's oral tradition, however, there exists strong testimony to the effect that devoted self-disciplines and ritual ac-

5. I don't recall hearing people speak about bad fruits. The commonest phrase for bad actions and their just deserts was "sin earned" (*pāp kamāyā*), which has the dual implications of sin being the wage of past evils and earning future misery.

tions pleasing to the gods must bear fruits—from gross prosperity to subtler merit—inalienable to their originators. This is particularly true if such acts are performed without fanfare. To covet fruits openly may be considered reprehensible, but to pursue them quietly through appropriate daily routines of self-restraint and worship is righteous.

The following story illustrates this point. It is among those told by village women during the ten days of worship for Dasā Mātā (Mother of Well-Being), a form of Lakshmi who brings general well-being to the homes of her female devotees. On each day of Dasā Mātā's worship, following her own story, a tale of the "Greedy One" (*lobhyā*) must also be told.[6]

> There was a Greedy One. He would come to my house and fill his stomach. Begging and teasing, he would fill his stomach and go along his way. One day, during the month of Kartik when a religious story is read out loud in the temple every day, the Greedy One, happening to pass by, asked someone, "What is going on?"
>
> He was told, "The story for the month of Kartik is being read in the temple." So the Greedy One also went to listen. He listened and he understood the meaning; he got some knowledge. That Greedy One went into the woods and began to practice austerities. He practiced austerities for such a long time that a big termite hill was built over him with long grass growing on it.
>
> He performed such severe austerities that the throne of the king of all the gods began to sway, and the other gods and goddesses also felt that their power was diminishing. Then the great king of the gods went to Bhagvān [God] and asked him, "Who is performing such austerities on earth that my tongue won't even move? Who has such great devotional feeling?"
>
> Bhagvān answered, "It is that Greedy One. His devotional feeling is causing all of this."
>
> Then Bhagvān said, "I am going to see about this." . . . He went into the forest to look for the Greedy One. Bhagvān walked along calling, "Greedy One, Greedy One, come out!" Finally an answer came: "Lord, how shall I come out? A termite hill is built over me and long grass is growing on it."

6. Translations of other stories in these sets appear in A. Gold 1982 along with a description of Dasā Mātā's worship during the ten days following Holi. Although *dasā* means condition, and Dasā Mātā is the Mother of Well-Being, in those translations I call her "Mother Ten" because of her strong association with the number ten (*das*): ten days of worship, ten knots in her charmed string necklace, a ten-sided figure representing her presence.

Then Bhagvān gave a kick with his left foot and the hill flew away and the grass flew away and there was that Greedy One. Bhagvān said, "Speak, brother Greedy One. What do you want? I am pleased with you."

"Oh, what should I want?"

"No, speak."

"Well then, this is what I want: whenever women take meritorious baths, when they fast and keep vows and do religious duties, I want all the fruits of these actions to be mine."

Bhagvān said, "Look, Brother, some bathe without the knowledge of their husbands' sisters and their husbands' mothers; some without the knowledge of their husbands; some without the knowledge of their husbands' brothers' wives; some without the knowledge of their neighbors. They endure pain and suffering in their own separate bodies and they do fasts and keep vows. So how will you receive their fruits?"

"No, Lord, they should be mine only."

"Brother, look, it will be like this: whoever tells your story and throws your grain, then they will each get their own fruits. But those who do not give grain in your name and tell your story, their religious merit will become yours."

Hey, Greedy One! Let this grain and story's fruit be yours, and mine be mine!

As the closing prayer makes clear, and as the storyteller was at pains to explain to me, the Greedy One's tale is told just in order to secure the fruits of the rest of the worship from his clutches. Villagers often expressed the view that greed, although found in the hearts of most humans, was a trait leading to "sin" (*pāp*), causing people to forget *dharma*. The Greedy One, however, is greedy for the fruits of religious merit (*puṇya*)—not only for those which he himself accumulated through austerities, but for those accumulated by others. Moreover, he attempts to force the gods to give these fruits to him by the ancient and highly respectable means of ascetic practice, having gotten the idea from listening to a story read in the temple.

The Greedy One, in using self-denial to satiate his greed, made a brilliant but doomed try. Although there are numerous precedents in Hindu mythology where gods in situations similar to Bhagvan's in this story grant whatever boon is demanded, the Greedy One is allotted only a poor consolation prize. No matter how great the power of his austerities, he cannot win the fruits of others' vows and fasts, but he must be appeased with one story and a few grains, for he too "endured pain and suffering."

Note that the fact that women perform their meritorious acts secretively, in their own separate bodies, is the basis for Bhagvan's ultimate refusal of the Greedy One's petition. Undertaken without advertisement, without care for appearances, these acts with their inherent fruits are inseparable from those who have performed them. It is for similar reasons that anonymous donations to strangers made in distant pilgrimage centers are considered more meritorious than ostentatious charities undertaken at home.

The story's moral then appears to be twofold: (1) greed for fruits is self-defeating because (2) fruits will belong to those who have acted without seeming to claim them, but whose efforts are manifest within themselves and consequently recognized by the gods. The Greedy One can have the fruits of his own austerities only if they don't impinge on those of others.

The rationales of the Greedy One's parable and the *Bhagavad Gita's* piety are quite different. The *Gita* teaches action without regard to fruits as a way of surrendering to God: "It is sacrifice, alms-giving, and ascetic practice that purify the wise. But even these works should be done [in a spirit of self-surrender], for [all] attachment [to what you do] and [all] the fruits [of what you do] must be surrendered" (*Bhagavad Gita* 1973:103). The tale of the Greedy One teaches that fruits belong to the actor, but they belong to him all the more thoroughly if they are not publicly claimed. Both views would perhaps be conducive to consistent disavowals of any claim to fruits, such as those I heard so often from Rajasthani pilgrims. The idea of *tīrthaphal* looms so large in pilgrimage literature that I was compelled to explore it. Although I found it a difficult topic of conversation, understanding it became pivotal in my endeavor to understand pilgrims' motives, and thus thematic to this book.

The concept of preordained fate, by contrast with that of fruits, is not in the foreground of this study, but it *is* daily on the tongues of villagers. Among the terms used for this concept in Ghatiyali, *kismat* and *taqdīr,* both of Muslim origin, are probably the most frequently uttered and broadly applied. Both of these imply a fate that is whimsical and impenetrable. The term *karam,* deriving from *karma,* suggests a logical if hidden causal link between the actions of the past and the fate of the present and the future. Yet another very prevalent notion of fate is that it is inscribed on the forehead of infants by a personage known locally as Bemata.[7] This concept of fate is thus referred to as *lekh,* or something written, and *lalāṭ,* or the forehead where this writing is invisibly but indelibly penned. Still another term, *bhāgya,* is generally associated with an astrologically foretold future.

However construed, the conviction that there is a determined fate for everyone and everything may be applied to almost any conceivable situation. If a dog eats a prized sweetmeat meant for the children, then it was written in the dog's fate, but not in theirs. If a dead husband is miraculously restored to life, it is because his bride's fate was to be "auspiciously married to a living husband"—a condition for which there is one word in Hindi: *suhāgan.* Shocking tragedy and enviable good fortune alike may be received with the stock phrase "It's a matter of fate."

Pilgrimage also, of course, is subject to the machinations of destiny. An instructive, true anecdote was related to me several times to demonstrate this. Some years back a Ghatiyali man decided to go to Hardwar. As is the common practice, he consulted a local Brahman to learn the astrologically auspicious time for his departure. The Brahman, after lengthily pondering the man's horoscope in relation to the celestial almanac, unexpectedly told him that no time was suitable, because a Ganges bath was simply not written in his future. The man was stubborn, however, and went to Hardwar anyway. There he took a few steps into the river but, suddenly recalling the Brahman's words, became confused and terrified. He hurriedly stepped back to shore without ever pouring water on himself or dunking, and returned home precipitately, thus proving that he was not destined to bathe in the Ganges.

7. Bemātā (Vemātā in the *Rajasthani Sabad Kos* [Lalas 1962–1978] hereafter *RSK*) is the villagers' name for the female being who comes to all infants on the sixth night following birth and indelibly inscribes their futures on their foreheads. I was also told that Bemata gave bodily form—beautiful or otherwise—to all persons, whereas God (*bhagvān*) gave only breath. According to both the *RSK* and Hindi-speaking Ghatiyalians, Bemata is the same as Vidhata ("Destiny personified" in Chaturvedi and Tiwari 1979). The transsexuality of this equivalence—for Vidhata is masculine and also identified with the creator god Brahma—did not seem to bother anyone. For the relationship between head-written fate and *karma,* see E. V. Daniel 1983 and S. Daniel 1983.

Even a grain of wheat has a written destiny, and villagers often told me that my name must have been written on Ghatiyali's grains, for why else had I arrived so inexplicably to partake of them.

Sorrows of Simplicity: Ainn-Bai in the Village

It was pure serendipity that brought me to Ghatiyali, if not indeed *kismat.* On my fifth day in India, which happened to be the Fourth of July, a new acquaintance invited me and my son to attend the picnic and fireworks display at the American Club in New Delhi along with her and her son. There I met a number of weathered-looking scholars at various stages of their fieldwork. Among them was Joseph Miller, a Fulbright fellow from the University of Pennsylvania, Department of Folklore. His research concerned a Rajasthani oral epic, focusing on the ethnography of its performance, and he was settled in a large village in Ajmer district. On learning that I too planned to work in Rajasthan, he suggested that I consider his village as a possible research site.

As Miller described the village—Ghatiyali—it sounded extremely attractive to me, possessing all the caste variation and religious activity I sought, as well as an active curing shrine that drew a weekly influx of pilgrims. However, my prearranged affiliation was in Jodhpur district with the Rajasthan Institute of Folklore, and I was committed to go there first. Miller and I exchanged addresses and dissertation proposals but made no concrete plans. I had to settle my son in Mussoorie and then proceed to Jodhpur.

After an uncomfortable delay of several weeks caused by monsoon flood conditions, I reached Jodhpur city, and eventually Borunda, village site of the Folklore Institute. Acutely conscious of the passing of my precious time in India, I was anxious to settle on a research site as rapidly as possible. Within a few days, thanks to the efforts of Mr. Kothari, founder and director of the Borunda institution, I had begun making arrangements to live and work in a nearby hamlet. My inability to understand Rajasthani—after three years of Hindi language training—was depressing and discouraging me at this time. I was therefore not averse to remaining close to the shelter of the institute, although the hamlet was not ideal for my purposes. At this juncture, Miller appeared once more. His tales of witches and ghosts, of possessions and exorcisms, strongly tempted me to investigate Ghatiyali.

Entering Ghatiyali in Miller's wake, I heard him greeted from all sides by the simple and soon familiar formula, the rhetorical question *Ā giyā* ("You have come")? After this people gestured, not too discreetly, in my direction with questioning upthrusted hand, demanding "Who is she?" This question was not so easy to answer. Miller tried saying "my friend," but the use of the word "friend" between unrelated persons of different sexes is not neutral and was not well received.

Fortunately, one of the first personages on whom we had to call was Miller's patron in the village and his chief informant, the Gujar "priest" (*bhopā*) of Puvali ka Devji (see chapter 3). Rapidly taking in the situation, he announced definitively: "This is Jomil's father's sister's daughter." (Jomilji was Miller's common appellation among Ghatiyalians.) Thereafter we dutifully repeated this formula to all who inquired, and thus acquired a solid and convenient kinship relation.

Miller had been living in Ghatiyali for about nine months when I arrived there in early September 1979. He stayed another six months, returning to the United States shortly after Holi in March of 1980. However, as he was not satisfied that his work was complete, he was back in the village from mid-July 1980 through the end of December, when he left for good. During his second stay I was myself out of residence for a month of pilgrimage and a month of sickness. I then returned after his departure for a final six weeks of fieldwork. Out of my sixteen months spent living in the village, then, he was present for all but six. Our research aims, intellectual bents, and characters were vastly different. Nevertheless, his status in Ghatiyali, his relations with the people, and his methodology all had their effects on my own work.

Villagers' perceptions of me were, naturally, colored by their previous impressions of Jomil. I was fortunate in that they accepted and trusted me almost immediately, as they had learned over the previous months to accept and trust him. However, they soon developed a set of contrasts between us. He had fine, big, impressive-looking equipment: a video-tape-recorder system with television, two large cameras, an enormous tape recorder and two medium-sized ones, battery chargers, and endless reels of wires and cords. I had one small, pocket-sized camera and one purse-sized recorder. He was brash and pushy (which no one seemed to mind), while I was quiet and hesitant; he liked to astound and outrage, while I liked to keep a low profile. If I tried to play down my financial resources, embarrassed to have so much "government" money, he liked to boast of his. By the time I arrived, Miller had of course developed a good listening comprehension of the local language, while I often appeared, at the beginning, to understand nothing.

In sum, Jomil was cast as *hoshiyār* ("intelligent," "clever") and sometimes even as *cālāk* (*"cunning"*). I was *bholī* ("naive," "simple-minded," "innocent," "forgetful"). Now *bholī*-ness is not necessarily a negative character trait. One of the names of the great god Shiva is Bholanath, and to be simple and unconniving may be revered. But *bholī*-ness is definitely a marked disadvantage in the world—that is, the world of business, attachment, and delusion, most often referred to as *duniyā*. It extended to many matters: not knowing how to get rid of useless, unwanted company (Jomil was famous for his expertise in just that); not knowing how to apprehend liars; not knowing how to guard against cheats. The semantic content of this aspect of *bholī* is perhaps best transmitted by combining the two English terms "gullible" and "vulnerable." It also encompasses a certain lack of skills—in my case I was found wanting in the two most crucial womanly arts: cooking and dressing well.

An example of my initial discomfiture in Ghatiyali, having both personal and cultural motifs, was a series of permutations in my way of dressing. I arrived in the village wearing *kamīz-salvār* (a fitted knee-length top over loose drawstring pants) which I had had made up in Delhi as a comfortable, easy-to-wear alternative to the sari. I had known anthropologists working in Uttar Pradesh who found this dress to be convenient and acceptable there. In Rajasthan, however, *kamīz-salvār* marks the wearer as a Muslim village woman or as an unmarried college girl in the towns. Neither of these categories was appropriate for me, and I was urged by villagers to adopt a more suitable style.

Accordingly, I purchased some flowery cotton cloth, and my Rajput landlady offered her daughter's services on the sewing machine to make me some outfits. They sewed ankle-length skirts with ruffles on the bottom and loosely fitting overblouses to match. On top of these I was to wear the Rajasthani woman's most indispensable garment, the *oṛhnī,* or "wrap," which tucks into the waist in front and then is wrapped around the back and pulled up over the head. When I donned these clothes, it turned out that I looked like a Rajput, for the daughter had sewn them in her caste's distinctive style.

My Brahman women friends were quite incensed. "Wear a sari!" they cried. "This is laughable." Muslim women were also offended. Accosting me, they demanded: "Why have you taken off your *kamīz-salvār*?" With meaningful gestures they warned me that only *salvār* afforded protection against men, who could all too easily lift a skirt. Finally, the women of the peasant castes, Gujars and Malis, suggested teasingly that I dress like them in *ghāghara,* a mid-calf skirt worn with a tight-fitting half-blouse, and a wide, cooling display of bare midriff. The only general consensus was that I ought to wear ankle bracelets and bangles on my wrists.

I might have endured and weathered all this discord if I had felt comfortable myself, but the *oṛhnī* annoyed me. I detested having my head covered and tried to wear it over my shoulder, but this gave me the appearance of a shameless, distracted, or desperate woman. (When one of the goldsmiths beat his wife she ran to the bus stand with her *oṛhnī* off her head, and this event was worth a week of gossip.) It reached the point where every time I went out I was pursued by a chorus of "Ṭhīk nahī̃ hai" (It's not correct) or "Acchā nahī̃ lagtā" (It doesn't look good). One day I put on my jeans, but this was an act of bravado which I was unable to sustain. "You look like a man," was the cold, negative judgment.

Eventually I decided to adopt a dress style that did not identify me with any particular community. This was a long skirt worn with a cotton blouse of contrasting material. I refused to wear any head-covering except in the winter, when I donned a grey University of Chicago hooded sweatshirt. I never bought ankle bracelets, although I kept agreeing that I must, if only the price of silver would go down. I did wear the bright, rhinestone-studded *lākh* bangles, for without these or their colored glass equivalent, which I constantly shattered, a married woman is inauspicious.

A summary appraisal of my condition and character was formulated by a Brahman woman who was one of my closest friends in Ghatiyali. One night I had decided to please the Brahman contingent by wearing a sari to one of their wedding feasts instead of my usual skirt and blouse. However, as I had little practice in the art of sari-wrapping, and was also trying to manage camera, flash, recorder, microphone, notebook, pen, and flashlight, I kept asking my friend to readjust the sari's pleats and shoulder piece. I was feeling awkward, annoyed, and impatient. As she and a neighbor woman tugged competently at my garment, I heard her say, as if I were not present or capable of understanding, "To be so simple in the world: it's sorrow." The phrase stuck in my head. It seemed to epitomize for me the village women's appraisal of my person, which in some way I, always impressionable, partially internalized.

Through such personal experiences I was also, of course, learning things. The importance of appearance and apparel to Rajasthani women, as evidenced in their relentless attention to mine, was a theme I encountered in other contexts. A disproportionate number of the women's songs I was collecting expressed longing for so many different items of jewelry and clothing that my vocabulary cards swelled in that category. While songs addressed to husbands or brothers demanded these things, songs addressed to the deities manipulated the same images in various persuasive fashions. The goddess Mataji was wooed with promises of the same trinkets that please a village belle. Male deities were told: "I have come wrapped in a shawl" or "I have come wearing a full set of bangles"—as if prayer were complemented by the worshipper's adornment.

Often, when our relationship reached a certain level of trust and confidence, women friends would beckon me into an inner room and, extracting a key worn on their person, dramatically open up a locked tin box to display one or two fine pieces of clothing or jewelry. Perceiving how deeply important these things were to them, I came to understand why my own seeming indifference to finery puzzled and worried them.

My first several weeks in the village passed rapidly, engrossed as I was in the initial excitement of being there and in the myriad hassles involved in setting up modestly comfortable arrangements for living and working. To obtain drinking water, a good pot to store it in, bathing water and a cement *tainkī*, a cot, a table, daily milk delivery, window screens, and so forth required elaborate negotiations with experts. Nothing was easy, and I learned the value placed on things from afar long before I began to study pilgrimage. When I hired someone to bring well water I had to supply that person with a rope and bucket, but was instructed that worthy examples of these items were not available in Ghatiyali—I must send to Kekari. Even though Ghatiyali had several houses of potters, the clay pots of Sawar were superior, kept the water cooler, were less likely to crack. Even though Ghatiyali had carpenters, I ought to purchase my cot frame in Devli where it would be less costly.

This first month saw the simultaneous celebrations of Dashahara with nightly Ram Lila performances, and the goddess's "Nine Nights" (Navarātri) with intense possession sessions at her temples. A good anthropologist, one who would never sleep while drums were beating, would have had no sleep at all during this period. I also was invited to attend a number of events at different households: nightly postpartum songs for a new mother, and the festive ninth day, which involves cleansing plus sun worship; all-night men's *bhajan* sings; afternoon ladies' *bhajan* gatherings that were also tea parties; and twelfth-day funeral feasts, which seemed to occur all too frequently. An early funeral-feast experience exemplifies my fragile state of mind during those first weeks and also shows how I managed to enhance my reputation for softheadedness; it was an episode not easily forgotten by anyone.

The feast was a lavish Gujar affair in the nearby village of Nadi (about a half-hour walk through the fields from Ghatiyali). The crowd was dense, and the majority were not from Ghatiyali and were therefore very curious about the white-skinned woman with a camera. I was accompanied only by two girls, Lali and Bali, whose ages were probably fourteen and eleven respectively. It was a very hot sunny day in late September. We had spent many hours sweating among the milling groups of peasants in a festive mood, after observing the early morning worship of Path Mother and the bringing home of Ganges water (see chapter 4). In mid-afternoon the time for feasting arrived, and women (who, in an inversion of domestic routine, are always served first at these affairs) were seated on the ground in long curving lines with leaf plates set before them.

The feast consisted of the most prestigious and expensive fare encountered at such events: "five fried treats" (*pānc pakvān*) of which three were sticky sweets. I had already attended more modest twelfth-day celebrations, with only one sweet, where servings were generous but not beyond normal eating capacity. Here, however, I was taken aback to see the quantity of food slapped down by the servers on their first rounds—far more than anyone could comfortably consume. I noticed that many women were carefully wrapping up most of this in squares of cloth and only then beginning to eat, but it did not occur to me to do the same. After all, I had no square of cloth and no family waiting at home for their share. Seeing others eating, and feeling hungry, faint, dehydrated, and desalted, I tried to begin myself several times, but Lali and Bali stayed my hand, scolding and advising me rapidly in the rough Gujar dialect, which at this moment I could not understand enough to obey. I only knew that for some reason they thought I should not eat.

Clearly I was making some dreadful mistake, but I didn't know what it was, and I began to feel panicky. Then the girls decided to solve the problem: they picked up the excess food (treats soaked in a lot of oil and sugar syrup) and attempted to wrap these up in the end of the long scarf worn across the shoulders with the Muslim clothes I was still using. I sensed or imagined sticky stuff on my hair and neck attracting flies and my clothes stained with oil. Standing up abruptly, I angrily shook out the scarf and began to cry, walking blindly away from the food line and back toward the house of the chief mourner where I could shelter in some shade.

The point was, as I later understood, that if I had started to eat, the masses of food would all have become *jhūṭā,* polluted by saliva and unfit to carry home. The point for me was that I was not able to stand up to crowds, sun, teasing, and incomprehension. But I did not leave the funeral feast. A young Brahman woman whom I knew as a neighbor in Ghatiyali and whose schoolbook Hindi was balm to my ears, appeared and literally held my hand, guiding me for the rest of the long hot day.

By inexplicably crying in public, however, I had not only dismayed the Gujar girls—it took them weeks to regain their nonchalance in my presence—but startled and upset the whole community. For weeks afterward, everywhere I went, people, whether acquaintances or total strangers, would call out to me: "Why were you crying in Nadi?" I improvised several answers according to my limited means: "Heat struck me"; "Dizziness affected me"; "I got confused." The latter (*ghabaṛā gayā*), a common village expression, I found to be the most acceptable and perhaps the most truthful as well.

In fact, my confusion at Nadi was symptomatic of a period of confusion, an existential impasse that lasted several weeks. During this time I was unable to write, and, retrospectively, I can only attempt to reconstruct its mood. As I recall, the source of despair was a series of linked realizations, whose truth I still cannot wholly deny: I was unfit for this work; I had gravely erred in choosing anthropology; my advisers had gravely erred in encouraging me; institutions had gravely erred in funding me; I was not the kind of person who could go around exposed and intrusive among total strangers asking absurd questions and, in fair return, being myself mocked, toyed with, and intruded upon. I thought, very rationally, that I might as well go fetch my child from boarding school, where he was not happy, pick up my return ticket, which I had prudently stored in Delhi, and leave India. Only the difficulty of travel in the rainy season and a deep embarrassment (toward those who expected better of me) kept me from acting on these, in some ways valid, impulses.

The funeral feast episode is an apt model for the larger tale. Instead of fleeing, I found support in the company of a few people who had become familiar and intelligible. Guided by them, I was able to begin to work toward my aims. My techniques of gathering data and retaining my equilibrium developed conjunctively.

My home in the village was with a large joint family, and participation in their activities was a continuing source of education. These ranged from singing five songs promised for a boon-giving goddess to picking debris out of wheat before milling it into flour; from daily worship at domestic shrines to rare and joyful excursions: to the fields for roasted corn, to the uncultivated areas called "jungle" (hardly dense with trees) to gather *boṛ*, a prized red berry.

From one older woman within my household, who was much preoccupied with religious matters, I collected stories and songs about deities, as well as all sorts of ritual knowledge, techniques of healing, and ready exegesis on these. From her sister, who was more earthy and without pretensions to religious virtuosity, and from the numerous daughters and daughters-in-law who were closer to my own age, I absorbed other kinds of village lore: child-rearing practices, food preparation, yearning for absent husbands or natal homes, fear of loneliness and darkness, jealousies, conflicts, and general gossip. Although I lived with sequestered, high-caste Rajput women, I also moved freely in the village, as they did not; indeed I came to serve them on occasion as a source of information and as a messenger.

A few Ghatiyalians sought me out in order to develop a connection for reasons of their own. Sometimes this worked to our mutual advantage, and sometimes of course it did not. Among those with whom it did, the most important was a woman in her early twenties of the Damami ("royal drummer") caste, who was estranged from her husband, had lost her only child, and lived with her parents. She was seeking, certainly, material gains to be extracted from keeping company with a foreign woman. But more than that, she was drawn to me because my existence suggested the possibility of a woman's life other than the, for her, fatally circumscribed one that she knew.

Her mother was the oldest literate woman in the village, having been forced to learn to read and write as a girl at her in-laws' house while, as she told it, she wept and begged to be allowed to cook instead. Lila, the daughter, had passed sixth grade and had then been married to a man who scorned her for her dark skin and the fact that her family still fulfilled their role as drummers while his practiced only farming and herding. Her husband had beaten her, and she had fled his house, refusing to return, although all her dowry wealth remained there. Unlike the other lower castes, Damamis practice neither widow remarriage nor second marriages. In this they proudly follow the custom of the Rajputs, claiming a special affinity with their royal patrons, whose lineage names they often share.

Drummers, although no one will take food and water from them, mix easily at all levels of the caste hierarchy, from untouchable Regar to Brahman. Drumbeats summon not just worshippers but gods, and thus drummers play a vital role in many village rituals. Because of her drum's indispensability, Lila always knew of significant happenings in advance. Rapidly discerning my interests, she became a guide for me in many situations where no one else among my circle of acquaintances could have led me. Lila once dreamed of me as the goddess, riding a white horse on the hilltop, but, alas, in the end I could do nothing lasting to better her plight.

Among the advantages of working in collaboration with Miller was that we were able to pool our resources in hiring assistants. Each of these men had unique qualities, and we shared their time and talents. The assistants worked at the transcription of recordings; the logging of photos, slides, and tapes; and a house-to-house census. They also became adept at taking notes in Hindi during complex events. Only one among them had a college education; the rest had reached various levels of higher secondary. Only one spoke English, and his period of employment was brief and largely spent on map making. All, however, were masters of lucid Hindi, and their work frequently involved explaining Rajasthani passages to us through the medium of Hindi.

As it happened, the research assistants came from a number of different castes. During the course of my fieldwork we had working for us, at various times, a Nai (barber), a Brahman, a Gujar (cowherd), a Mina (settled tribal) and a Nath (yogi-magician)—all native-born Ghatiyalians, as well as a Caran (royal bard) from Borunda who stayed just two months. Because of their different backgrounds, the network of close personal connections developed through these assistants extended into diverse realms of village life. The Brahman, for example, was closely related (through his sister's marriage) to Ghatiyali's three chief Sanskritic ritual experts. He was the main priest (although his widowed mother did much of the work) for the Shri Nathji (Krishna) temple. The Nai's parents were intricately involved in weddings and all other life-cycle celebrations. The Nath's uncle was a long-haired, ochre-clad renouncer who lived at and tended the Mahadev Temple at Meditation Seat; his father, now deceased, had been a famed practitioner of good magic, still often remembered and praised in the village.

Through our connections with these men we not only got to know their communities' distinctive roles in village society but were inevitably drawn into major events among them: births, first haircuts, marriages. We also lived with them through crises—a child's convulsive fever, the sudden death of a young niece's husband—and from these shared experiences discerned much about ways of coping with adversity and understanding fate.

Many of the research methods I found most productive allowed me a lot of time indoors, out of the public view, working with a few people with whom I felt on easy terms. During my first four months I spent many hours a day just reading transcripts of Rajasthani recorded in Ghatiyali. These included comic, improvised interludes from the Ram Lila (the formal dialogue was in Hindi); women's worship stories; semiformal discourse on religious knowledge (*gyān carcā*). My tutor would paraphrase in Hindi the Rajasthani lines, and I would then question him as to exact meanings and grammatical nuances until we were both satisfied that I understood. He boasted widely of the enormous patience and verbal skill demanded of him by this job; of how he split his head for my benefit.

Even when language acquisition was no longer my foremost aim, I continued to spend many hours translating songs, stories, *bhajans,* rituals, and conversations from transcribed texts. Going over these materials word by word, often with several informants, was painstaking, time-consuming, but ultimately fruitful work. Long, illuminating discussions, and sometimes bitter arguments, enlivened translation sessions. The texts themselves have become, as the following pages will reveal, certainly the chief embellishments of this book and occasionally its prime inspiration.

When I participated in public events, which I learned over time to do selectively, I found it was usually better to attend in the company of either an assistant or a woman companion such as Lila. In the same way, when I went to conduct interviews in situations where I had had little previous personal contact, I always took someone with me, largely to explain me and my purposes sufficiently to appease the interviewee's curiosity. If I went alone, I too often found myself engaged inextricably in a total anthropological role reversal, answering questions ("Do they have cows in America?") instead of asking them. When I went on pilgrimages, long or short, I also normally had someone with me, whether friend, paid assistant, or a blurred composite of the two.

Eventually I succeeded in gathering a great deal of material, both on my proposed twin subjects of pilgrimage and release and on many other aspects of village life. I also attained a measure of personal contentment. But—and this is my major point here, the justification for including this self-portrait—my methods and consequent results developed directly out of my initial shock, as ways to propel myself beyond the first black impasse. I didn't turn into the kind of "good" fieldworker I could imagine my more extroverted classmates becoming. Rather, I developed a style of doing things which allowed me to function within the limitations of my disposition.

I was happiest among people who took my presence for granted. Thus, when I was told that Ghatiyali's grain was destined to be eaten by Ainn-Bai, I was pleased. It was still more comforting to hear, as I sometimes did, that, rather than an arbitrary stroke of Bemata's hand, it was good impressions or mouldings (*samskāras*) from previous lives that had fetched me from so far, away from kin, into this alien clime to view its gods and learn the ways of their pilgrims.

Rajasthan and Ghatiyali

The land called Rajasthan and the village of Ghatiyali have characteristics and histories that matter to the pilgrims whose ways I portray in this book. By the sketchy treatment of region and village which follows here I intend to orient readers within the places from which these pilgrims set forth on their purposeful quests and aimless wanderings. Whereas geographers, historians, and politicians have been at times much occupied by the identity and problematic unity or nonunity of Rajasthan as a region,[8] my concern here is less with state or region as bounded entity and more with a culturally tangible Rajasthaniness. Similarly, in portraying village society I aim to suggest ambience more than to elucidate social structure. Nonetheless, these sketches can hardly evoke Rajasthan and Ghatiyali except as productions of history and environment, of wars and water resources, of strictures of caste and shifting alignments of power.

When Ghatiyalians sojourn outside Rajasthan they are readily recognized and labeled by others as Rajasthanis; it is written in the

8. The regional identity of Rajasthan is approached from many perspectives in the new, interdisciplinary volume edited by Schomer et al. (1987). Two other recent publications which illuminate various aspects of Rajasthani history and culture are the collected essays of Rudolph and Rudolph (1984) and Erdman's study of performance and patronage in Jaipur (1985). Lodrick (1987) manages to argue persuasively both that the modern state of Rajasthan was derived from an arbitrary construct of British origin and that it comprises an area whose distinctive culture and regional identity are indisputable. Jinavijaya (1966), Plunkett (1973), and Stern (1977) all also present strong evidence of distinctive characteristics in Rajasthani politics and society.

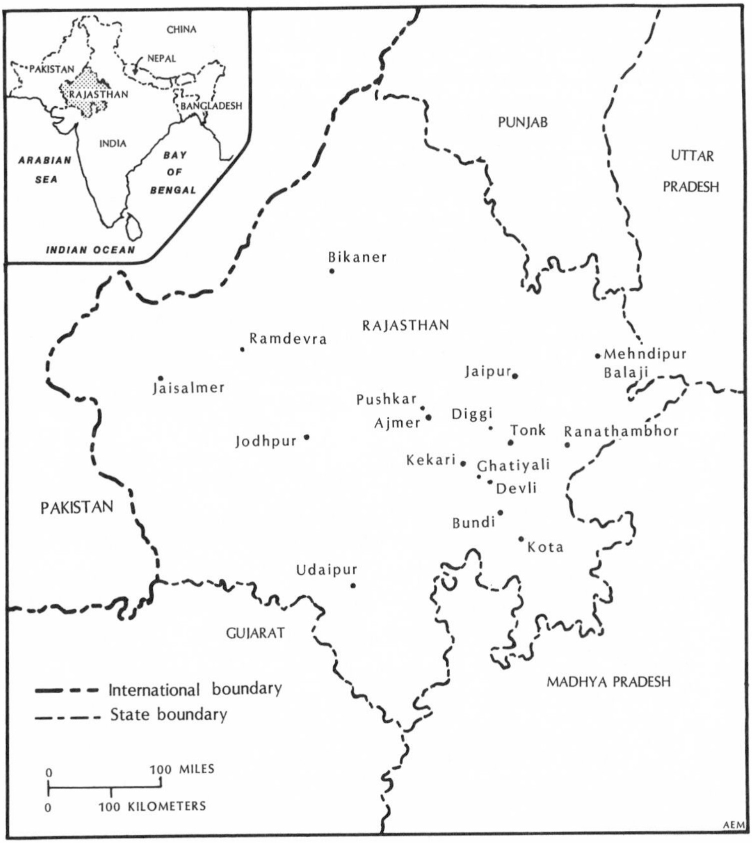

Map 1. Rajasthan, with inset of Rajasthan in India.

colors and styles of their garments even before they begin to speak. Sometimes they are politely directed as guests to rest houses and eating spots catering to their regional tastes. Sometimes they are rudely singled out as uncouth bumpkins, unwelcome because of their known predilection for finding their early morning "latrine" in the open fields. Sometimes they are sinisterly marked (or warned) as likely victims, with their heavy silver jewelry, for highway robbery. Moreover, outside of Rajasthan I found that Rajasthani pilgrims speak of their homeland with affection, praising its communal attributes of love and hospitality, its dry salubrious air, its nourishing wheat, corn, and *ghī*. All these traits are contrasted, with homesick fervor, to less trustworthy human and climatic environments.

Joan Erdman suggests that "as a geographical area and as a political state Rajasthan makes sense to its inhabitants" (1985:24). This simple statement accurately reflects the rather low-key identification with the place Rajasthan held by most Ghatiyalians. But what are the cultural components of Rajasthan's common-sense reality? Deryck Lodrick mentions three factors contributing to the region's genuine internal coherence: language, caste structure, and the Rajput heritage (1987). Among these it is the Rajput heritage that has most captured the interest of scholars past and present who have focused on various facets of this tradition.[9]

James Tod, whose nineteenth-century *Annals and Antiquities of Rajasthan* recognized and, some say, invented the historical reality of the region, located its chief homogeneity in religion:

> The same religion governing the institutions of all these tribes operates to counteract that dissimilarity in manners, which would naturally be expected amidst so great a variety, from situation or climate; although such causes do produce a material difference in external habit. Cross but the elevated range which divides upland Mewar from the low sandy region of Marwar, and the difference of costume and manners will strike the most casual observer. But these changes are only exterior and personal; the mental character is less changed, because the same creed, the same religion (the principal former and reformer of manners) guides them all. (1978, 1:100)

By religion, it is fair to surmise from the content of his volumes, Tod meant Rajput *dharma*—a birth-given code for conduct.

Lloyd and Susanne Rudolph have characterized the "Rajput ethic" as "valor without regard to consequences" (1984:4), although much of their work has been concerned with highlighting an alternative "practical norm of conduct" also existent in the region (1984:44). Besides being imprudent, "martial Rajputs" have been described as cherishing images of themselves as rulers and warriors "by birthright and natural endowment" (Hitchcock 1959:11). Appropriate to the violent nature of their *dharma* as killers of men for honor and glory, Rajputs are stereotypically and

9. For studies of Rajput history and ethos, see, for example, Hitchcock 1959; Rudolph and Rudolph 1984; Saran 1978; Ziegler 1973, 1978.

often actually meat eaters, liquor drinkers, hunters. John Hitchcock finds that "martial Rajputs" reject for themselves the possibility of other Hindu life styles, including those of farmer, shopkeeper, and wandering ascetic (1959:13–14).

Within traditional Rajput ideology, however, there does exist a conjunction of the martial and ascetic modes. This is manifest at the moment, described by Norman Ziegler among others, when "the Rajput adopted the saffron turban and saffron robes of the *sannyāsī* in order to show his unreserved commitment to battle and to death in battle. Death in battle was itself seen as a salvation" (Ziegler 1973:69).[10]

Today's Rajputs no longer have the option of becoming warrior-renouncers, and it seems likely that the modern Rajput ethos is subtly undermined by this loss, even as land reforms since Independence have grossly undermined Rajput political and economic dominance. Any study of Rajasthani attitudes concerning release and renunciation should, however, remain cognizant of warrior ideals even if those ideals have lost most of their foundations in action. Many of the most important village deities, as well as innumerable minor ones, find the source of their divinity on the battlefield.

If the state of Rajasthan is, as Ziegler describes it, "a transitional frontier zone" (1973), the part of Ajmer district where I worked was itself, although geographically centered within the state, in many ways a borderland. The situation of Ghatiyali would indeed invite neither historian nor linguist looking for a clear case, and anthropologists working in Rajasthan have also tended to choose sites squarely within defined subregions.[11]

10. The nature of this alleged "salvation" is unclear. In modern Rajasthan, the heroic dead are worshipped, not because they have received *moksha,* but because they have not; their spirits linger—demanding worship and offering boons in exchange—near the scenes of their violent deaths. See chapter 2.

11. Miller came to Ghatiyali through a chain of connections that led him from the study of *paṛ* painters in Bhilwara town to familiarity with the *bhopā*s who perform the recitation of Dev Narayanji's epic during the Kartik Purnima fair in Pushkar. There he met the priest who eventually introduced him to Ghatiyali. Of the relatively few ethnographies set in rural Rajasthan, several are clustered in Mewar (Atal 1968; Carstairs 1961, 1975, 1983; Chauhan 1967) and near Jaipur (Chakravarti 1975; Srivastava 1974). G. R. Gupta (1974) worked in Kota. Linguists and historians (Bahl 1972, 1980; Saran 1978; Ziegler 1973, 1976, 1978) have been attracted to modern Jodhpur, traditional Marwar, whose bardic chronicles are lush and whose language is distinctive.

Ghatiyali was located, but just barely, inside Ajmer-Merwara, an area appearing on maps of the Raj period as a small island of British sovereignty in a sea of princely states.

Villagers' awareness of having lived on an arbitrary boundary is memorialized in the existence of a minor deity, Tax Sati (*Ḍāṇ Satī*). According to informants, this goddess's icon is set at the place, on the road to nearby Sawar town, where taxes were collected from passersby in both directions as they traveled from the jurisdiction of the British (Ghatiyali side) into that of the Rana of Mewar, and vice versa. No one could tell me who had installed the featureless icon at that exact spot (not the actual borderline) or why it was called *satī*—a title normally reserved for monuments to wives who have voluntarily burned on their husband's funeral pyres. Tax Sati received only minimal worshipful attention from villagers, but her presence and her name serve as reminders of history not long past.

To the southeast of Ghatiyali were the small principalities of Bundi and Kota; to the south and southwest, Mewar (Udaipur), the kingdom most perfectly epitomizing the nonpragmatic standards of Rajput valor; to the north and northeast, old Dhundar (Tonk and Jaipur); to the northwest, beyond the extent of Ajmer-Merwara, the western desert kingdoms of Marwar (Jodhpur) and fabled Jaisalmer. These major surrounding areas—former princely states—are still important, named subregions within modern Rajasthan. Ghatiyali, sharing the confusion of Ajmer's past, belongs to none but has ties with many—ties forged and sustained not only on the battlefield but through trade, marriage, and pilgrimage.[12]

The history of Ajmer and its immediate environs is one of conquest and turmoil, lacking the continuities and strengths provided by a relatively stable ruling house that allowed other parts of Rajputana to retain a kind of integrity through similar vicissitudes.

12. The oral traditions of Ghatiyalians contain many references to other parts of Rajasthan. I recorded songs which praise Sanganer shawls and Jaipur wraps, and which speak of getting lost in the Kota bazaar. Shri Kalyanji of Diggi in Dhundar (today's Tonk) and Ramdevji in Marwar (today's Jodhpur) are the subjects of many praise songs, and their shrines are important goals for pilgrims. Dev Narayanji's epic makes villagers intimately familiar not only with the scenes of his birth, battles, and death within Rajasthan but with a legendary Malva, part of today's Madhya Pradesh, where Devji spent his youth in a pastoral exile similar to Krishna's Vrndavan idyll.

According to Har Bilas Sarda, one of Ajmer's few English-language historians, that city "attained the highest prosperity that it ever enjoyed" (1911:34) during the reign of Prithviraj, who was defeated in A.D. 1192 by Sultan Shahabuddin Ghori.

After this "the prosperity of the town declined" (Sarda 1911:35) until the time of the Mughal emperors. Akbar began to build in Ajmer in 1571, deeming it an important city because of its powerful saint's tomb, today a major pilgrimage attraction for all South Asian Muslims. With the degeneration of the Mughal line, Ajmer became, in the late eighteenth and early nineteenth centuries, "a bone of contention, first between the Mughal kings of Delhi and the Rathors; and then between the Rathors and the Marhattas" (Sarda 1911:38). In 1818 the city was ceded to the British.

While Muslim and British overlords dominated Ghatiyali's area for centuries, village "lords" (*ṭhākur*s) appear to have operated much like local rulers of the surrounding Hindu princely states, manipulating their fortunes and fates through alliances, both martial and marital, and through good works such as temple building, tree planting, and pilgrimage.

From a pamphlet (Mathur 1977) published by a present scion of the royal house of Sawar, I gathered a certain amount of documented local history. The record begins in 1627 when Badshah Shajahan gave the "dominion" (*riyāsat*) of Sawar to Gokal Das of the Shaktavat "clan" (*vansh*) of the Sisodiya "branch" (*khap*) of Rajputs. Gokal Das, according to the pamphlet, was descended through two cadet lines from Maharana Uday Singh of Udaypur; thus the lineage of local rulers derives its ancestral glory from Mewar.

The grant that Gokal Das received included 1,444 villages among which 27 were known collectively as the villages of Sawar-Ghatiyali. The pamphlet goes on to chronicle the successors to Gokal Das, noting monuments built, battles fought, and women who became *satī*. This descent finally arrives at the most shining personage of the line: Vansh Pradip Singh (whose name means "Lamp of the Lineage"), born in 1892, who succeeded to the Sawar throne in 1914. Vansh Pradip's memory is very much alive and deeply venerated among Ghatiyalians today. As the pamphlet tells it, and as people readily confirm, he was a man of well-rounded and appropriately royal interests. He liked horses and hunting; he constructed buildings and water reservoirs; he planted shade trees and gardens. In the Sawar Fort he made many improvements—most significantly, a new temple and the installation of electric light. A devotee of Four-Armed Vishnu, he funded many meritorious fire oblations; an exemplary master of royal largesse toward Brahmans, he made gifts of cows, clothing, and grain.

Despite all his good works, however, this benevolent ruler died (in 1947, the year of India's independence) without a male heir. His queen adopted the elderly *ṭhākur* of Chosala, Vrajraj Singh, as her son, and the courts legitimized his succession. Vrajraj Singh, born in Chosala in 1882, ascended to the throne of Sawar in 1951. Although the pamphlet praises his religious activities (a devotee of Shri Kalyanji, he and his wife performed a barefoot walking pilgrimage to Diggi and had a book of Kalyanji's *bhajan*s printed), public opinion affords him nothing like the respect given Vansh Pradip. He is, however, the father of the present local *ṭhākur*s.

Vrajraj Singh's numerous sons were each allocated villages. Although the role of today's *ṭhākur*s is quite ambiguous and varies from case to case according to their personalities and public spirit, they are minimally a presence—with occasional surprising residual potency. Ganaraj, who received Ghatiyali, appeared to me at first to be aloof from, and insignificant in, village affairs. Owning both a motorcycle and a jeep, the only private motorized vehicles in the village, he could be heard, when petrol was not too scarce, zooming in and out at odd hours.

After I had been in Ghatiyali for some time I began to perceive that the stone Fort (*gaṛh*) on the central hill where the *ṭhākur* and his family lived was neither so remote nor so powerless as I had at first thought it to be. For example, when my drummer friend Lila's enraged husband wanted to drag her back to his parents' village against her will (he was living in town with another woman and only wanted Lila to do chores for his family), and her own parents and brother were unable or unwilling to assist her, she fled to the Fort. Her husband, bold as he was, would not attempt to remove her from that shelter and, losing face, was forced to board the next outbound bus. Lila returned home complacently.

Having passed from the royal ethos of Rajasthan to Ghatiyali's own royalty, it remains to describe the village itself. Hills rise on two sides of Ghatiyali, but except for the central fort, most of the village lies on flat terrain. It is perhaps a two-minute descent from Ganaraj's stone ramparts to Ghatiyali's dusty lanes.

Except at the height of a good monsoon season, the main impression given by the physical nature of the village and surrounding countryside is aridity. Vegetation is sparse; through the double depredation of women gathering firewood and goats and sheep feeding, most surrounding trees are reduced to grotesque stubble. This deforestation, according to villagers, is a recent phenomenon, its causes perhaps a combination of population growth and the post-Independence degeneration of local authority. Whereas the righteous *ṭhākur* Vansh Pradip Singh protected and planted trees, his heirs sinfully sold them off for lumber.

Only the fields, patiently irrigated, show whole patches of green. The area's staple food crops are wheat and corn, although barley and millet are also grown. Chickpeas are widely cultivated and eaten in numerous forms (fresh roasted or stewed; dried, hulled, and split for *dāl*; ground into flour, which is the basis for most fried treats both spicy and sweet). Mustard seeds, sesame seeds, and peanuts are oil-yielding crops. Cotton is also produced. The vegetable gardeners cultivate tomatoes, spinach, eggplant, cucumbers, and green beans. One enterprising Muslim has planted a small orchard and successfully grows papayas and lemons, among other luxuries, which he vends to the *ṭhākur*'s family and the resident schoolteachers. This man practically lives in his garden, however, in order to keep it watered and protected from animals and thieves. Other villagers say frankly that it is not worth such sacrifice.

Ghatiyali boasts a prosperous dairy business: goat, buffalo, and cows' milk are all abundant. Each morning large cans of milk are taken by bicycle to Sawar, the nearest town, and eventually reach Ajmer markets. There are also herds of sheep, and thus trade in wool and mutton. Another important factor in Ghatiyali's economy is a stone quarry. Carved by "stone-splitting Malis" (a branch of the gardening caste that no longer gardens) into pillars and ornamental latticework for houses as well as icons for shrines, Ghatiyali's high-quality stonework is in demand throughout the surrounding area.

Ghatiyali has a post office, a lower school, and a dispensary.

There are several electricity-powered flour mills, innovations of the past decade which have transformed the lives of women who formerly rose regularly, several hours before dawn, to grind the day's supply by hand. Worship of the grindstone is still part of the prenuptial rites for both bride and groom in their respective homes. Electricity itself came to the village some twelve years before my arrival, and its benefits are by no means universally or steadily enjoyed. Only the well-to-do can afford to wire their homes, and the supply is extremely irregular.[13]

Jain merchants vend certain essentials of life: raw sugar, white sugar, tea, oil, matches, soap, low-quality incense, dry coconuts for offerings, multicolored string (*lacchā*) essential to most rituals. Villagers buy these things in small quantities from one of several local shops when the need is pressing. When large amounts of goods are needed, as for a funeral or a wedding feast, most Ghatiyalians prefer to shop in the nearby market towns of Kekari, Devali, or even Sawar, where they find a wider selection and better rates. One advantage of trade within the village, however, is that it is transacted in grain, wheat being the standard medium. Little children come running to the merchant's shop with a grubby pocketful of wheat and receive in exchange a few garish hard candies. But any goods in the shop may be bartered for amounts of grain, carefully weighed on the merchant's balance scales.

Gardeners also regularly balance their wares against grain, most often taking the equivalent weight, although for special items they may ask double. Some of the least sophisticated gardeners refused to deal with me because I had no wheat to trade—not, I suspect, because they didn't want coins (most everyone did), but because they were uneasy with the complication of setting a rupee price. Peddlers from outside occasionally appeared, their cycles laden with bulging saddlepacks of bananas, cauliflowers, or guavas. They would be rapidly surrounded by women eager to purchase these welcome additions to a monotonous diet, and they, too, normally accepted wheat.

13. This description of modern amenities in Ghatiyali is based on conditions existing during my stay there in 1979–1981. Changes—improvements—certainly continue to take place; today, for example, there are two lower schools on different sides of the village.

Near the central square, in front of Four-Arms Temple, which is also the bus stand, a bicycle rental store and three tea stalls dignified by the name "hotel" did business. There were several other shops in the "bazaar," a narrow stretch at the heart of the neighborhood known as Solahpurī ("Sixteen-city") because it was inhabited by sixteen different castes. These bazaar shops were operated by Muslims and displayed goods known collectively by the borrowed English word "fancy": bangles, buttons, braid orna-

Table 1. *Jāti*s of Ghatiyali by Number of Houses

Jāti	Number of Houses
Mālī (gardener)	66
Regar (leatherworker)	53
Gūjar (cowherd)	42
Brāhmaṇ (priest)	40
Lodā (farmer)	36
Camār (leatherworker)	20
Rājpūt (landlord, warrior)	18
Mīnā (settled tribal)	17
Khātī (carpenter)	15
Mahājan (Jain merchant)	10
Musalmān (Muslim)	10
Balāī (weaver)	7
Dhobī (washerman)	7
Kumhār (potter)	7
Harijan (sweeper, pigherd)	6
Nāth (yogi-magician, guru)	5
Vaishnav Sādhū (priest)	5
Lohār (ironworker)	4
Mahātmā (Jain guru)	4
Bhīl (tribal, gatherer of honey and herbs)	3
Nāī (barber)	3
Sunār (goldsmith)	3
Damāmī (drummer for high castes)	2
Lakhārā (bangle maker)	2
Chīpā (cloth printer)	1
Darjī (tailor)	1
Dholī (drummer for low castes)	1
Telī (oil presser)	1
Total	389

ments, plastic tea-strainers and metal flour-sifters, cheap toys, pens that rarely worked, and pencils with flawed leads—all in all, a motley selection. The owners of these shops did much of their business by setting up stalls at fairs and large funeral feasts throughout the surrounding area. One of the shopkeepers, a successful entrepreneur, also did a brisk business in tattooing at fairs, as well as running a flourishing loudspeaker rental service.

The bazaar also housed several cloth shops, owned by Jains, and a number of craftspersons: goldsmiths, potters, tailors. Elsewhere in the village other artisans—high-ranking carpenters, lower weavers, and untouchable leatherworkers—still practiced their caste-linked arts. The single family of cloth printers, however, no longer printed cloth, and the oil pressers, put out of business by mechanization of their industry, have turned to agriculture. During my residence in Ghatiyali, one of the two bangle-making families moved to Devli where they set up a bangle shop at the bus stand, but were in the process of educating some of their children for a different future. It was often the case that within one household some family members followed traditional occupations and others did not.

Table 1 lists the twenty-eight *jāti*s resident in Ghatiyali,[14] ranked according to number of houses surveyed in the census attempted by Miller and me. The census was a difficult, time-consuming, and in the end statistically unsatisfactory enterprise. Nevertheless, all resident castes are included here and, for the most part, the relative numerical strengths of the castes are correctly reflected.[15]

14. I introduce caste names with diacritics and, in parentheses, provide traditional occupations or other identities. The *jāti* names given in table 1 will be used throughout as proper nouns, without diacritics, and occupational identities are repeated only if these are particularly important and not obvious in context. Some subdivisions within the twenty-eight *jāti*s recorded here should be noted. The category Brahman includes six endogamous subcastes of which two, Gujarati Brahmans and Gujar-Gaur Brahmans, are numerically important. The remaining four are represented by one or two houses each. The Mahajan or Jain merchant category includes houses from the two endogamous Jain sects, Svetambar and Digambar.

15. According to the 1971 rural primary census abstract, Ghatiyali had 469 households containing a total population of 2,390 divided equally between the sexes (a strikingly unlikely coincidence). The house-to-house census which Miller and I undertook in 1980, however, allows us to sympathize readily enough with census-takers' misperceptions. To mention only one of several pervasive confusions: the ideology of the joint family versus the reality of separated brothers fre-

My own first and lasting connections in the village were among Brahmans, Rajputs, and Gujars. During my last few months there I worked most extensively with Naths. Of course I also knew well one or two persons from a number of other castes, and shared short and long pilgrimage experiences with many of these. But I never felt that I was interacting with the majority of villagers, or even with a fair sampling of the social spectrum. A series of lengthy and highly illuminating interviews with a group of Regar and Camar pilgrims just returned from Ramdevji was the closest I got to these untouchables. It was a function of my disconnection from their communities that I had not learned of this journey in time to join it. As my fieldwork goals did not directly concern demography, rank, or politics, I made no concerted effort to perfect the census, to study the niceties of village hierarchies in terms of food transactions, or to follow the ongoing power plays and shifts in the panchayat.

In the course of one and one-half year's residence, however, I did see the full cycle of seasons and festivals more than one time around. From scattered instances I was also able to observe most ceremonial markers of life-cycle passages, especially the rites following births and deaths and weddings. During the wedding season of 1980 I spent most of the auspicious, hot month of Baisakh (April–May) following the elaborate and prolonged events surrounding the marriages of one Brahman and two Mina grooms and a Rajput bride. I assiduously recorded and translated oral traditions, documented rituals and festivals, and kept a daily journal that included humdrum events, juicy gossip, interpersonal crises

---

quently resulted in double entries. Thus a father would list and get recorded all his sons as living with him; then the same sons would be found recorded on another form as heads of separate households.

This problem, however, cannot explain our arriving at a tally of 389 for total households—a figure considerably lower than that given by the government census. It was obvious from house construction patterns that Ghatiyali was expanding, and some of our discrepancy is probably the result of overlooking a number of homes. Our total figure for village residents, however, is much closer to the published data, being 2,192 to their 2,390. This would, of course, indicate a higher number of persons per household and be in keeping with patterns of general population increase for the seventies. It is likely that the present population, then, is considerably greater than either census indicates. The village tax-collector and record-keeper, who was engaged in organizing the 1981 "people count" at about the time I left, estimated over 500 houses and a population near 5,000.

(my own and other peoples'), and a variegated array of random anecdotes and lore.

Most of this "village ethnography" does not appear in the following chapters, at least not on the surface. However, my initial decision to study pilgrimage from a village rather than a crossing place was founded on the conviction that pilgrims must be understood first as householders. Transformations of their persons or life aims in the pilgrimage process would only be intelligible from that foundation. Thus my extensive participation in many aspects of village life, especially those connected with worship, vows, and other attentions to the gods, underlies most of what I have to say about pilgrimage. I made a systematic study of powerful places within Ghatiyali's perimeters, and the final setting to be presented in this layered chapter is that of village deities' domains and their worship. For Hindu villagers there is a way, both profound and practical, in which, although charity may not, pilgrimage does indeed begin at home.

Ghatiyali's Own Places of Power and Protection

Just as temples are like mountains, the approach and entry into a temple by a worshipper who may not have traveled any significant distance is like a pilgrimage. He ascends the temple as mountain to reach the inner sanctum as divine peak (Eck 1981a:47).[16] One of Ghatiyali's respected elders, Madhu Mali, composed a *bhajan* praising the village's *cār dhām,* or "four established deities' spots." He thus deliberately and worshipfully finds the supreme goals of Hindu pilgrimage within his own village.[17]

Madhu's *bhajan* named Meditation Seat, Jaipalji, Bhairuji of the Tank, and Sundar Mata of the Mines—where members of Madhu's branch of stone-splitting Malis work and worship. Although the idea of the village having "four spots" was wide-

16. Eck makes this observation in her small introductory book on *darshan* (1981a), but it should be noted that her fieldwork and resulting monograph (1982) concerned pilgrimage and the meaning of Banaras as a pilgrims' center at various levels of cosmic reality. See also Beck 1976 for other temple homologies.

17. The famed *cār dhām* of India are located at remote extremes of the subcontinent in the four cardinal directions. Although many Ghatiyalians had been to Puri in the east, some to Dwarka in the west, and one or two to Kedar in the north, I knew of none who had visited or even aspired to visit all four.

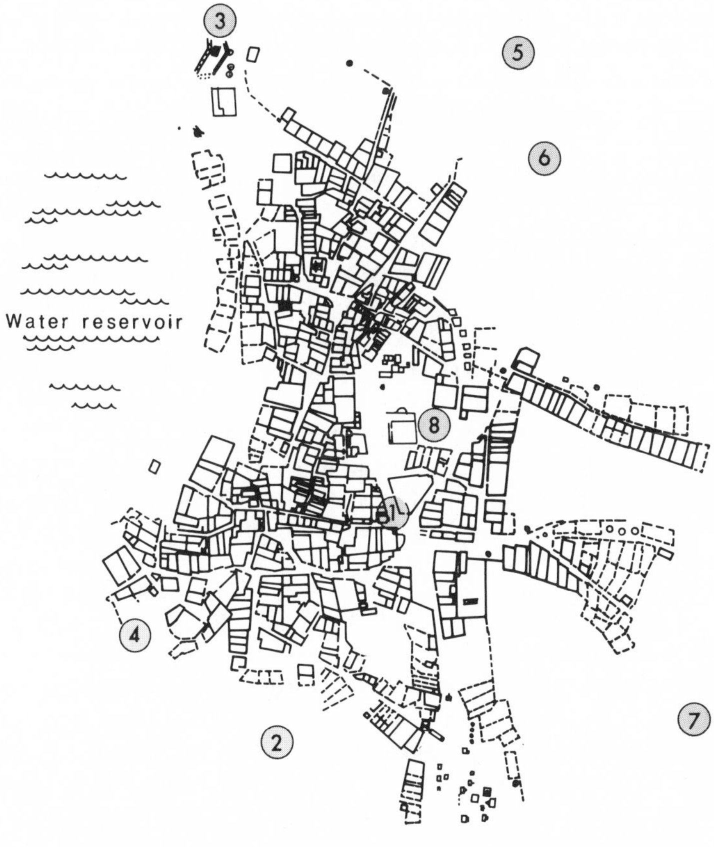

1. Temple of Four-Arms
2. Hill of Jaipalji
3. Meditation Seat
4. to the Cave
5. Cremation Ground
6. Path Mother
7. to Puvali Ka Devji
8. the fort

—— house walls
----- manure pile boundaries
• wells

Map 2. Ghatiyali.

spread, I found, at first to my disappointment, that the places enumerated varied from informant to informant. Some, for example, substituted the Cave for Sundar Mata; some preferred Four-Armed Vishnu or Hanuman to Bhairuji.

Obviously the selection of Ghatiyali's "four spots" depended in part on the chosen deities as well as on the caste and neighborhood affiliations of the selector. More important than who are named is the popularity of the concept. In the context of discussions about journeys to faraway gods, several persons remarked, "Ah, why go there when we have *cār dhām* right here in the village?" This was only one among many arguments used, not to deride the practice of pilgrimage as such, but to question the religious valorization of wandering.

There follows a brief survey of the kinds of deities' places found in Ghatiyali. Then I focus in detail on four gods whose spots are my own candidates for the village's *cār dhām*—a selection congruent with that of a number of informants. These places include one temple centrally located in village space and society, the Temple of Four Arms (Cār Bhujā kā Mandīr); and three outlying sites: Jaipalji, Meditation Seat (Asān), and the Cave (Gufā). Among these four places exists a dynamic of powers important to village welfare particularly in times of drought or other geophysical crisis. To demonstrate this I narrate an event, Inder Puja, or worship of the shrineless rain god Indra. This worship was an attempt to mobilize the forces of these four shrines in order to bring desperately needed rains at a critical moment in the agricultural cycle.

Through portraying some of the variety, scope, and interplay among Ghatiyali's own powerful places, types of pilgrimage centers and modes of worship beyond the village boundaries are also foreshadowed. Knowledge of how to treat the gods and what to expect from them, primary experiences of *darshan,* ritual, and prayer, are all locally founded. They are thus fundamental to a study of how and why persons move beyond familiar places to petition or gaze upon distant deities and bathe in distant waters.

The category "village temples and shrines" expresses a valid geographic identity but is very much a catchall. It encompasses a wide range of powerful places which vary along more than one axis of differentiation, including style and grandeur, spatial orientation, community served (range of effectiveness), who performs what kind of priestly duties when, and more still. Terminology used for shrines and temples varies from locality to locality and speaker to speaker. The general word for "places of the gods" is literally that: *devasthān*. Other Rajasthani words of more restricted usage include *devaro, deval,* and *thān*.[18] Hindi *mandīr* for "temple" normally labels a limited category of deities' abodes.

The prevailing usage of *devasthān* (as well as *devaro* and *deval*) clearly indicates the main characteristic of such places: the god or gods (*deva*) who dwell there. In ordinary conversation shrines may be referred to simply by the deity's name ("I am going to Path Mother"). They may also be called "place" or "platform" ("I am going to Path Mother's place"; "I will leave this grain on Bhairuji's platform"). The words "place" and "platform" are commonly heard in many contexts outside the domain of deities' abodes. Just as most village gods are not set apart from life concerns, their shrines are thus frequently designated in the same ways as other village spaces.

Ghatiyali's places of the gods number approximately fifty-eight,[19] among which several distinct sorts may be described, although a total and exact classification is not possible. The most

18. See Kothari 1982 for a discussion of several sorts of Rajasthani shrines. His definitions and descriptions, based largely on research in other parts of the state, do not tally exactly with mine and provide interesting comparative material.

19. A caveat is certainly in order regarding the actual numbers of shrines reported here. My survey was guided by informants' opinions and can be taken to enumerate with fair accuracy those deities who have some public as opposed to purely domestic recognition. However, there is also a sense in which any count is arbitrary. For example, hardly a house or field exists which does not have its *jhūjhārjīs*; no well is dug without the installation of a Bhairuji.

Map 2 indicates the approximate locations of some of Ghatiyali's shrines, temples, and other landmarks. This map was paced off and painstakingly drawn on a large scale, over a one-month period, by two research assistants—Inder Dan Detha from Borunda and Mahavir Nai, a native Ghatiyalian—working for Miller and me. Unfortunately the original was unwieldy, its scale seemed untrustworthy, and its penciled lines began to fade even as its paper began to tatter. So much effort had gone into drawing it, however, that it seemed important to preserve. In Chicago Kali Charan Bahl kindly photographed the map and I then had it drawn—in the form appearing here—by a cartographer working from the photo. Not resembling the kind of schematic map that usually accompanies ethnographies, map 2 shows houses rather than the streets and lanes between them. Although it may appear needlessly dense and complex, it does reflect two Rajasthani villagers' own notions on how to represent their environs systematically. For example, the inclusion of manure piles, distinguished from houses by dotted boundary lines, says something for the importance of compost (and cow dung). As the enumeration of deities' places may be accepted with qualifications, the map should similarly be viewed—not as a perfect rendering of what's really out there, but as one shared indigenous version of that setting.

strikingly contrastive category is that of temple versus all the rest. There are ten structures in the village which most people would agree to call temples: five Vaishnavite, three Shaivite, and two Jain. What distinguishes then from other places of worship? The criteria given combine mythological, architectural, and social factors.

First, temples tend to enshrine a form of the pan-Hindu "Lord" (*bhagvān*), while other places are dedicated to particular entities among the legions of lesser regionally or locally identified "goddesses-and-gods" (*devī-devatā*).[20] This means, generally, that temples are dedicated either to Vishnu or to one of his "descended incarnations" (*avatār*); or to Mahadev (as Shiva is usually called), worshipped in the form of a *lingam*. The Jain places of worship with their meditating Tirthamkaras are also always called temples.

While popular Rajasthani hero-gods such as Dev Narayanji, Ram Devji, and Pabuji are considered to be incarnations (of Vishnu, Krishna, and Lakshman, Rama's brother, respectively), they more often are established as localized deities in *devaro* or *deval* than as *bhagvān* in temples.[21] The goddess Mataji, in her many manifestations, also unites the qualities of a minor, restricted power and the all-conquering energy of the great demon-slayer Durga. Her places may range from open-air platforms called *thān* to elaborate temples, although there are no examples of the latter in Ghatiyali.

Temples are roofed buildings—more ponderous structures than other *devasthān*—and should, according to informants, incorporate certain architectural features. Chief among these features indicative of temple status are two: a crowning orb (*kalash*) on the dome or spire and a path for circumambulation. A *kalash* is ideally covered with gold leaf, and is "raised" or "offered up" atop the roof or dome of a temple. It should be situated directly above the primary deity, and is spoken of as God's "crown."[22] Circumambulation may be performed at any shrine, whatever its structure or lack thereof. Within a temple complex, however, there ought to

20. See Wadley, however, for continuities here as well. One of her informants states that "*bhagvān* is the biggest *devatā*" (1975:119).

21. Little has been published, although several research projects are under way, concerning Rajasthani hero-gods and their epic traditions. See, however, Joshi 1976; Kothari 1982:17–22; Miller 1980; and Smith 1977, 1979.

22. *Kalash* is also used regularly to refer to a clay pot when it is employed in ritual, usually to contain some powerful substance or being.

be a special pathway, designated for this purpose, encircling the central space of the reigning deity.

Temple worship may also be characterized by the kind of priests performing it, as well as the service (*sevā*) they perform. *Bhagvān* is attended by members of priestly specialist castes, Brahman or Vaishnav Sadhus or—for Mahadev—Naths. Shrines of the goddesses-and-gods, on the other hand, have attendants drawn from the general population of their worshippers, or another middle-to-low-caste group. (Ghatiyali's Jains have their own system of rotating service, which does not fit either pattern.) Whereas shrine deities' regular fare in the way of smoke is *dhūp* (*ghī* on smouldering cow-dung coals), temple worship is distinguished by the exclusive use of perfumed incense.

Vague but significant factors in the application of nomenclature to places of worship are the community that is served, its location, and who's talking about it to whom. Thus I was told that the untouchable Regars' shrine of Ramdevji in Ghatiyali might quite properly be called a temple, as it possesses the requisite architectural features and enshrines an *avatār* of Vishnu. Yet few people conversationally apply the term "temple" to this structure; the Regars themselves hesitate, because of their low status in the village, to appropriate the "higher" designation, and members of the upper castes would not gratuitously bestow that dignity on a place of worship belonging to untouchables.[23]

As a final point, it is not irrelevant to note that when talking with an ignorant foreigner, like me, people used *mandīr*—a respectable, easily understood Hindi word—more often than the Rajasthani variants to refer to all deities' places. Thus, during the early days of my research, one of my assistants consistently called the open-air shrine of an ancient Hanuman "Hanuman's Temple" (Bālājī kā Mandīr), even though it possessed none of the qualifications for temple mentioned here. This did not reflect common usage, as I eventually discovered, but it does show the facility with which the blurred types sketched here can become

23. A current trend among the middle- and low-caste communities of Rajasthan who either cannot or dare not build temples in their separate villages is to construct them collectively in Pushkar—a regional and pan-Hindu pilgrimage center. There these modern edifices, much adorned with glass and gilt, are showpieces for their builders' communities, hopeful markers of self-respect and upward mobility. I toured Pushkar's elegant low-caste temples during the 1979 Kartik Purnima fair under the fine guidance of Komal Kothari.

blurrier. Anywhere a deity dwells, or any "pure" place, can be a "temple"—whether it be the human body or the alcove where drinking water is kept.

The places of power and worship in Ghatiyali which are not called temple I have heuristically categorized by types of deity and counted—just in order to indicate broadly the range of powerful beings within and around the village. Eleven shrines honor the Rajasthani hero-gods of epic fame: Dev Narayanji has four places, Ram Devji has four, Tejaji has two, and Pabuji has one. Nine spots are dedicated to Matajis—goddesses who may manifest threatening or benevolent aspects of *shakti,* or female power.

There is one place of the pan-Hindu god Ganesh and there are two of Hanuman. Others enshrine beings known only in the immediate locality: Pathan (a Muslim spirit), the Cave Baba, Jaipalji. There is hardly a shrine without its contingent Bhairus, but six places in Ghatiyali are especially built to house particular named, singular, or multiple icons of that complex deity.[24] Like Bhairu, Sagasji, a sort of Rajasthani "unknown soldier," often has his stone at others' shrines, but he also possesses two separate places of his own. There are many small shrines built to honor and appease the heroic dead of a caste, a lineage, or a family: nine female Sati Mas and five male Jhujharjis. The former are dedicated to the spirits of women who burned alive on their husbands' funeral pyres; the latter, originally, to spirits of brave warriors who perished nobly in battle. Nowadays, however, although there are no wars, Jhujharjis continue to make themselves known, displaying power and demanding worship (see chapter 2).

With a few major exceptions, all the village temples and shrines are neighborhood- and often caste-linked institutions. Each has its atmosphere and character, derived in part from the locality or community it serves. However, a deity's range of influence has no prescribed dimensions. As a general rule, when a god builds a reputation for performing cures or other miracles his place inevitably begins to draw worshippers from a wider spectrum of the population. The converse of this is also true: a deity of little potency receives only perfunctory *dhūp* on special holidays from his nearest

24. Bhairuji's mythological nature and active character are discussed in chapters 2 and 4.

"kin" or neighbors. Even this residual recognition may eventually be lost as the shrine crumbles out of memory.

Among those temples and shrines located within the settled part of Ghatiyali, surrounded by dwellings, only one is pointed out by villagers as serving the community as a whole, rather than particular groups. This is the Temple of Four-Arms situated at the crossroads heart of the village. A number of outlying shrines, however, are involved in functions which crosscut caste and neighborhood interests. These include Sitala Ma, the goddess presiding over smallpox and other fever and rash diseases; Pathvari Ma, who protects the pilgrims' path (see chapter 4); and Bicala Vasa Bhairu, or Middle-Dwelling Bhairu, who is worshipped on the way to the main cremation ground by all the castes who burn their dead there.

Outstanding among the outlying shrines, however, in functioning to promote general well-being, are Jaipalji, Meditation Seat, and the Cave. Associated with Nath magicians and wandering renouncers, these three places are said to give protection to the whole village. They are resorted to in times both of sudden disaster, as when hailstones fall, and of gradual dismay, as when rains are late or sparse, crops wilt, and future famine looms. Mustered into unison, they allow worship of the shrineless rain god, Inder. This triadic peripheral unit is not, however, fully effective without invoking the reigning Lord of the central temple: Four-Arms. The structure of Inder Puja might be equated with a *cār dhām* pilgrimage performed within Ghatiyali's boundaries though reaching powers far beyond.

The Temple of Four-Arms

Located near the Temple of Four-Arms today, significantly enough, are other "public" places, all additions of modernity. Thus, the door of Four-Arms faces the bus stand; close at hand are the village panchayat and cooperative society buildings, the school, and the post office. Four-Arms overlooks these innovations within his realm quite impassively, it seems, for they have hardly affected his dominion, which extends into numerous facets of Ghatiyali's ritual and social life.

The temple's history is obscure. Informants stated only that *bhagvān*—a marble, four-armed "form" (*rūp*) of Vishnu—was installed here by the forefathers of Vansh Pradip Singh, without estimating how many generations back. In the same fashion, they told that the service of the temple was given into the family of the current *pujārī* (a Parashar Brahman) "generations ago." Prior to Rajasthan's post-Independence land reforms, the temple was well endowed with a land grant from the court of Sawar; the priest's stipend of food, and money for repairs, were all provided by royal largesse. Today, however, the village panchayat must support Four-Arms and its priest out of much more limited resources.

Consonant with its spatial centrality and logical contiguity with modern public institutions and services, Four-Arms has several central functions in village life. One is as witness to important political decisions. If the whole village wishes to pass a resolution or consider a special matter concerning general welfare, people will gather in front of Four-Arms to do this. Such meetings are held at this site, villagers asserted, because no one will speak falsely if God is observing. Moreover, whatever work is decided here, its outcome should be good because God has participated in the community process. In private as well as public affairs, Four-Arms acts as a witness for truth. Anyone whose word is challenged may, if he has the nerve, enter the temple and swear an oath before Four-Arms. He will then certainly be believed, for those who swear falsely are rapidly punished by God.

The space around Four-Arms is appropriate for any public performance of a cohesive nature. Ghatiyali's Ram Lila, an annual event for the past twelve years, is staged here. When a wandering renouncer was invited to stop in the village and perform a public reading of the Hindi *Ramayana,* each nightly session took place on the outer porch at Four-Arms.

Another event which takes place in the vicinity of Four-Arms, under its auspices so to speak, is a major annual livestock-protection rite. Once a year, on the day called "Village Outside Cooking" (*gā̃v bāhar rasoī*),[25] all the animals from one side of Ghatiyali must be driven in the dusty dawn, before milking and before any housework is done, underneath a charmed rope sus-

25. The remainder of the day is devoted to cooking and feasting. Although, as its names indicates, this day's feast was traditionally cooked picnic style outside the village, people nowadays find it more expedient to prepare the same picnic fare at their home hearths.

pended across the path in front of Four-Arms.[26] Auspicious objects and bundles of powerful substances dangle from the rope, the entire thing further infused with potency by a specialist's spells.[27]

Four-Arms has a part to play in the personal as well as the community life of most villagers (excluding the unclean castes). Many occasions that demand prostration and an offering at one's neighborhood temple or at the place of a chosen deity also involve similar attentions to Four-Arms. For example: departing and returning pilgrims pay respects there before and after the worship of Path Mother; brides and grooms stop there on their prenuptial processions round the village; mourners stop at Four-Arms after the group bathing that immediately follows cremation, to be sprinkled with *caraṇāmṛt* (the icon's bath water) before returning to their homes. Four-Arms' bath water is purifying and auspicious and lightens the danger ensuing from contact with the dead. It also may be given to the dying in the same way that Ganges water is given.

Four-Arms, then, is a place for establishing consensus, for hearing about and benefiting from *dharma*. It is also a place for conducting protective rites that crosscut lines of caste and neighborhood. The deity, in Vishnu's traditional role, is a protector: of social harmony against deceitful self-interest and of the living against the potentially malevolent dead. Four-Arms is rarely a resort for specific private complaints, except when he functions as some person's favorite god. The public role of Four-Arms might be said to concern above all the community's moral well-being.

26. For the sake of logistics, because the size of Ghatiyali and its animal population are both large, two such ropes are in fact employed. While one is raised in front of Four-Arms, the other is placed near the shrine of Pabuji, on the other side of the village. Pabuji is hero-god of the Rebaris, a camel-herding caste not present in Ghatiyali. His greatest eminence is in Marwar, but the itinerant Rebaris founded shrines to their deity in many villages along their travel routes, as Ghatiyali once was. Pabuji is considered a deity with particular protective powers over herders of all types and their beasts.

27. The substances bound up in small cloth parcels and suspended from this rope include charged debris from various village shrines and icons: dust from the Four-Arms floor; "body grime" scraped from Hanuman (actually the residue of oily red pastes applied during worship); ashes of burnt offerings to Tejaji and Sagasji. Other traditionally auspicious items hung on this rope include a clay pot lid and five kinds of grain. A hereditary expert, not a Brahman, works all night making magical passages over the rope to infuse it still further with protective powers.

Moral welfare, however, is interwoven with bio- and geophysical welfare, as will become more evident when the three outlying shrines are described.

Jaipalji

Jaipalji, also called Ajaipalji, is built into a slight indentation on a rather steep hill (the hill of Jaipalji) that lies just to the west of the village, rising immediately behind the neighborhood belonging to the Nath caste. Despite its peripheral location (actually no more than a hard ten-minute climb), no one remains unaware of Jaipalji after nightfall. From almost any point in the village the god's oil lamp can be seen burning, a steady glow in the midst of solid darkness. It used to be, I was told, an "unbroken lamp," continually fueled day and night. The ruler of Sawar maintained this flame with a generous donation of pure sesame oil every year. Now, however, such largesse is no longer forthcoming, and owing to economic considerations the lamp goes out sometime in the middle of the night. Nevertheless, it is faithfully rekindled each dusk by one of the Naths among whom attendance on the shrine rotates systematically.

Jaipalji is a featureless stone. Ranged about him are other deities accumulated over the years—Sagasji, Sitala Ma, Hanuman, Kala-Gora Bhairu, Mahadev, and the Cave Baba—also in the form of unprepossessing stones. But who is Jaipalji? The name belonged to an ancient founding king of Ajmer. He is mentioned in Tod as "a scion from Macaouti, named Ajipaal, [who] established himself at Ajmer" (1978, 2:358–359). Tod adds in a footnote that the name Ajmer is said by tradition to derive from "the humble profession of this young Cauhan," who was a goatherd, "Aja meaning a goat in Sanskrit" (1978, 2:358). Illiterate village informants who knew nothing of Tod's *Annals* (their Hindi edition is, however, a favorite source book for local literati) also told that Jaipal was a goat-herding king of Ajmer of the Cauhan lineage—stressing that they were Gujar, not Rajput, Cauhans. It was because of his unhappy, poor goatherd childhood that Jaipalji the king became worthy of worship; he did not forget his lowly beginnings.

Several much-repeated stories revolve around Jaipalji's commanding magical potency. I condense the most popular of these here because it effectively evokes the mystique of Ghatiyali's shrine. Jaipalji's power as portrayed in the story accords well with

1. View of Ghatiyali from Jaipalji, as some Nath women ascend for a morning ritual.

reputed powers possessed by the living Naths who tend his shrine.

> Once messengers came from Ravana, the demon monarch of Lanka, demanding that King Jaipalji pay a tributory tax. Jaipalji did not accept Ravana's claim on him. He drew a picture of "golden Lanka" on the earth and then broke—in the picture—five of the ornamental pieces which topped the city's walls. His response to the messengers, then, was that if Ravana's real wall in Lanka also had five broken pieces, he, Jaipalji, would refuse to pay the tax.
>
> Another time when Ravana's messengers threatened him with extortion of tribute, Jaipalji scattered a lot of grain for the birds. When they arrived to peck at it, he told the demon messengers; "If you command all these birds to stop pecking in King Ravana's name and they stop, then I will send the tax. But if they don't stop, then I won't send it."
>
> The birds kept on pecking despite the command in Ravana's name. But when Jaipalji commanded them to halt, they all immediately ceased pecking and remained standing still on one foot. All, that is, except for the *ḍekaṇ* [a small, cooing, pigeon-like bird, populous in the environs of Ghatiyali]. The *ḍekaṇ* was deaf, and failing to hear the king's command, just kept on eating. Then Jaipalji hurled his discus at the *ḍekaṇ* and sliced through its neck. Later, however, he restored it to life, but ever since then the *ḍekaṇ* has had a visible black line encircling its throat.

Needless to say, Ajmer never sent tribute to Lanka. These episodes show Jaipalji to possess certain magical faculties: control through diagrammatic replication of distant objects and command over dumb creatures. In his treatment of the *ḍekaṇ* he displays the ability to take away and to restore life.

How did this great king of Ajmer, this wielder of effective powers which bested even the arch-demon Ravana, arrive at Ghatiyali's hillside? No one could really say. All that people told was that there was a great battle in which Jaipalji fought very bravely but was killed. His feet are worshipped in a village called Pagara ("feet"); there is a shrine for the trunk of his body in Ajmer; and his head became Ghatiyali's deity. How or why this far-flung dismemberment occurred is obscure. When I pressed my Nath informants to give me some solution to these mysteries they

2. Jaipalji himself, receiving worshipful attentions.

only asserted that the head reached our hillside "of its own accord"—no one put it there.

Jaipalji is resorted to when animals are sick or when drought or hail threatens the village. The control of hail (and locusts) is the special art of the Naths, to whom the service of Jaipalji's shrine was given by a pious ruler of the past. But to bring rain requires a combination of several other powers with Jaipalji's. Nonetheless, his shrine is where Inder Puja must begin, and we will return there; for the present it is enough to keep in mind that Jaipalji is a being of royal and magical command, having influence over weather and the health of livestock.

Meditation Seat

"Meditation Seat" (*āsan*) has a secluded atmosphere although it is actually not far from the gregarious scene at the village water reservoir. The spacious, walled grounds belonging to Meditation Seat include some choice agricultural land. Within them are a Mahadev temple (rebuilt and rededicated since my departure from the village),[28] living quarters for the attendant, and a number of old *samādhi*s—stone memorials erected upon the burial spots of renouncers.

The temple's chief icon is a Shiva *lingam,* very old in appearance, which is said to mark the place where a particular renouncer took "living samādhi" (had himself buried alive while deep in meditation) about seven hundred years ago. This man, whose name was Sundarnath, had lived for some time at Meditation Seat and performed various wonders in the village. The names and stories of the other old *samādhi*s outside the temple building at Meditation Seat are not remembered.

The current resident and priest of Meditation Seat, Ogarnathji, was born in Ghatiyali into the Nath caste of householders. He was a sickly child, and hoping to save his life even if it meant losing him to the lineage, his mother took him to Meditation Seat's temple and dedicated him to service there—to a nonhouseholding life

28. This rededication was apparently a grand affair in which villagers competed with one another to spend money and demonstrate their devotion to Mahadev. There was a procession around the entire village and a great feast (personal communications from Nathu Nath and Bhoju Gujar).

3. Mahadev of Meditation Seat (the stone *lingam* behind the offering flame).

of celibacy. For this reason he was given the name Ogarnath. According to the *Rajasthani Sabad Kos, ogar* means "a fully self-realized *sannyāsī,*" and according to village informants it is understood as "one who always stays by the *dhūnī* (renouncer's fire)"—that is, one who spends his whole life outside of society in ascetic pursuits.

As a young man, following the death of his guru, Ogarnath rebelled against this enforced vocation and fled to Marwar, where he lived with Rajputs, worked, and possibly married. However, for reasons he never disclosed, after seventeen years he came back to Ghatiyali. Accepting at last the life which fate had decreed for him, he began to perform the service at Meditation Seat. He wears long hair, rudraksha beads, and ochre robes.

Like Jaipalji, Meditation Seat offers a recourse when there is some threat to the village crops: when too much rain or hail falls, or when rain is needed. Thus, in the complex surrounding Meditation Seat, as in that surrounding Jaipalji, Naths, control of geophysical forces, and a founding history involving magical feats are all present.

The Cave

The "Cave" (*gufā*) is located much farther out than Jaipalji or Meditation Seat. To reach it from the village center takes a good half-hour to forty-five minutes and requires a much more difficult climb than Jaipalji's hill. No priest resides there, nor is daily service performed. However, on the bright second of every month a renouncer, Marya Maharaj—formerly a Gujar villager—spends a day and a night at the Cave. Those who wish to make offerings will usually go while he is there, although the place always remains open for worship. For persons who lack the time or physical capacity to make the hike, it is also possible to seng *ghī* or a coconut up with the goatherd boys who range their flocks in the surrounding terrain.

Even less is known about the "Cave Baba" (Gufāvālā Bābā, as he is normally called, although his name was Balaknathji) than about Sundarnathji of Meditation Seat or Jaipalji. While informants estimated Sundarnathji's time as seven hundred years ago, they ascribed double that age to the Cave Baba. Like Sundarnath,

4. Balaknathji's "renouncer's fireplace" in the Cave.

he is said to have taken living *samādhi*. The place of his final meditation inside the Cave is marked by sculpted stone "footprints" thickly covered with the remains of flower offerings. Close to one side is his hearth with iron tongs implanted in it. Both these items are standard appurtenances at any shrine dedicated to a renouncer. Near the hearth are several pairs of wooden sandals and a few strings of prayer beads—both appropriate gifts to please a saint. Hanging from the roof of the Cave are a few straw "cradle-baskets," common thank-offerings at any shrine when a child is born by the grace of that place's deity.

The Cave Baba is traditionally worshipped at weddings as well as in times of natural crisis, as are Jaipalji and Mahadev of Meditation Seat. However, although the site has been one of Ghatiyali's powerful places since an ancient past, it was Marya Maharaj who gave it its present tidy physical appearance and established regular worship there. To quote him:

> When I [first] came here, there was no one. There was much garbage and filth. There was a lot of bat shit. People used to take it away [for fertilizer]. On both sides [gesturing] was bat shit. . . .

> And people, very few, if they came to give *dhūp,* they would push aside the bat shit and offer it there and leave. There was nobody here; it was completely deserted, desolate.

If in one way Marya Maharaj reestablished the Cave by cleaning and ordering it and making his regular, monthly pilgrimage there, in another way his own story demonstrates that the Cave's power was an ever-felt presence in Ghatiyali. As a child growing up in the village, Marya must have been attracted by the stories he heard about the place.

Unlike that of Ogarnathji, Marya's life as renouncer was not preordained for him; rather it was a sudden decision taken as a young man for reasons he would not divulge. What he did relate was that on leaving his home forever, during the goddess's festival of Nine Nights, he went directly to the Cave. He says that the Cave Baba is the only guru he ever had, thus claiming direct discipleship of a being deceased fourteen hundred years back.

In recent memory the Cave Baba performed one well-known miracle in Ghatiyali on behalf of his disciple Marya Maharaj. This was on the occasion of Marya's father's funeral feast—the only time Marya reentered his home village after becoming a renouncer. According to popular accounts, there was a shortage of money and therefore of food in his family's household at this time and a danger that they would be disgraced by a lack of provisions to feed the crowds of invited guests. However, Marya Ram sat in meditation for three days in the household grain-storage room, and during this time everyone feasted; there was never any shortage of foodstuffs. After this satisfactory affair, Marya once again quit Ghatiyali, this time for good.

Another Gujar villager of the same *gotra* as Marya Ram also claims the Cave Baba as his guru. This is the priest of Puvali ka Devji, whose history and character are described in chapter 3. Although I was unable to obtain the details of their feud, I was told that bitter enmity existed between Puvali's priest and Marya Maharaj despite their being both *gotra*-brothers and guru-brothers. Some hinted that in part this enmity might be the result of Puvali's stupendous success and profit in recent years, whereas the Cave remains only infrequently attended by petitioners. However, although not too many persons bring their separate problems there, the Cave is one of the prime village protective shrines and has in that way an enduring eminence quite different from Puvali's present boom. Moreover, Marya emphatically expressed a genuine dislike for dealing with pilgrims.

Inder Puja

Inder Puja is a ritual undertaking which unites the powers of Ghatiyali's major protective spaces in order to address the ancient and remote Vedic rain god, Inder, who has no place of worship of his own. Although his blessings are wholly crucial to their welfare, villagers have no way to approach Inder directly. Jaipalji, Mahadev of Meditation Seat, and the Cave Baba, with their magical powers derived from heroism and renunciation, may mediate with Inder to promote village welfare if they are properly entreated to do so. This endeavor to secure communal well-being also requires the assistance of Four-Arms, public deity par excellence.

It was the second year in succession that the late monsoon had failed in parts of Rajasthan, including ours. Good early-June rains had brought the earth to life, and it was all the more heartbreaking to watch once-promising crops withering in the fields. Only those lucky enough to have deep, full wells and industrious enough to spend day after day tediously irrigating by means of bullock-powered water wheels would have a decent harvest. Many would reap next to nothing.

The whole village, therefore, was hoping and praying for rain, and Inder Puja, it should be noted, was not the only means resorted to in this crisis. One man of the Mali caste attempted single-handedly to get the gods' attention by taking up residence in his caste's Mahadev temple, where he fasted and sang *bhajan*s day after day. Many consulted and implored a whole range of oracles and deities. Some sought a scapegoat, blaming the drought on some sinister purpose of a visiting renouncer—such beings lending themselves to dark suspicions. Inder Puja should be viewed, then, not as an isolated attempt to influence the heavenly powers, but rather as one movement within a community's response to a critical situation.

Just as he lacks a shrine, the god Inder has no fixed time appointed for his worship. The decision to perform it on this night—the bright twelfth of Sravan only a few days before the auspicious full moon holiday of Raksha Bandhan—apparently was taken quite by happenstance. A prestigious and senior Brahman had encountered a member of one of the farming castes, who lived in Jaipalji's neighborhood, as the latter was on the way to his field that morning. The Brahman suggested to the Loda that Inder Puja be performed. This, at least, was the scenario later recounted to me by the participants in the ritual. Except for a single boy, whose Brahmanic presence and rudimentary Sanskrit skills were utilized, no Brahmans participated in the event. Nevertheless, the initial motion was ascribed to a Brahman elder.

Once the decision was firmly taken to worship Inder that night in order to bring rain, a house-to-house collection was made to defray the costs. This yielded thirty-five rupees, three or four kilograms of grain, and some *ghī*. Most of the cash was used to purchase more *ghī*, required for burnt offerings. At twilight a drum began to beat in the Nath neighborhood to inform the village that men were gathering at Jaipalji in order to perform Inder Puja. Besides the Camar drummer, those participating in the night's worship included Khatis, Lodas, Naths, the Brahman youth, and at first a lot of children from Jaipalji's neighborhood.

At the shrine, *dhūp* was offered to all deities present. One worshipper declaimed: "We should think within ourselves that we suffer famine and that there should be much rain from today until tomorrow night." Everyone shouted "Victory!"—the children with their usual boisterous enthusiasm. Then one of the Nath men, a sincere devotee, addressed Jaipalji with a personal touch: "There must be rain by tomorrow night because in my fields the flies are causing me and my oxen much annoyance as we irrigate."

A fire was then prepared for *ghī* oblations and people called for a "speaker of mantras." After several shy protests, the one Brahman present—a boy about thirteen years of age—was prevailed upon to chant some Sanskrit lines, whatever he knew that might be appropriate. *Ghī* was poured into the fire as each chant concluded with "om svāhā." The boy's audience was pleased to find that his limited repertoire did include a line or two about Inder and rain, as well as mention of "all the gods." Everyone praised him for a job well done.

After this Sanskritic interlude, Jaipalji was again alternately beseeched and cajoled by his worshippers in Rajasthani: "Listen, listen! We are all standing in front of you, O Jaipalji, and we have come because of our sorrow. By tomorrow, take our sorrow away!" There was much loud and pointed talk, clearly to impress Jaipalji, about spending lots of money to fix up his shrine. They would build a permanent cement platform and a stone floor; they would beautify it with red clay. All of this was of course contingent upon the prompt delivery of rain.

As this second round of prayers and promises ended, the group of men discussed their next step. The party would not venture out to the Cave in the night, but would send its allotted *ghī* early the next day with the goatherds. Now, minus the children who were sent home to bed, everyone trooped to Meditation Seat, located at the opposite extreme of the village.

The petitioners entered Mahadev's temple, presented their offerings to the renouncer-priest, Ogarnathji, and squatted or sat facing the shrine to pray for rain. They asked Ogarnath to perform a simple divination procedure with their grain offerings. He plucked up a random small quantity of grain from the pile and counted to see if an auspicious number had been received. If it had, this would mean that the god looked favorably on their request. However, the first pick was not good. There was some consternation. Everyone prayed again: "Hey God, we ought to have bliss, we ought to have rain."

A second time the priest picked up grain on their behalf, but once again it was an inauspicious number. Someone among the party of worshippers then noticed that they had been praying sitting down. Everyone hastily rose and repeated their prayers once more. At last the grain count turned out well. But it is better to get it right on the first try, and some worshippers continued to repent their poor behavior: "Why should he give rain if we laze around at our ease?"

Calculations in *ghī* and cash followed. A decision was reached to raise more money the next day to purchase one-half kilogram of *ghī* to be divided equally between Four-Arms and the Cave

Baba. That freed the remaining cash on hand, which was immediately required to buy items needed for the worship of Inder himself: raw sugar, red powder, colored string, and incense. One person went to obtain these supplies by rousing a shopkeeper, for by now it was about 1:00 A.M. The rest of the party proceeded directly to the appointed place for Inder Puja. This was behind the Fort at a crossroads. I was told that this location was in the direction from which rain comes.

In order to worship any god without an icon, five stones may be set together, upon which five men jointly place their hands, thus empowering the stones with the installation of a chosen deity. In this case the god invoked was Inder. Red paste was applied to the stones, and incense was lit for them. In order, by a kind of sympathetic magic, to encourage rainfall, water from a full pitcher was poured all at once onto the stones, simulating a sudden and powerful cloudburst. The Brahman boy then tied colored string on the five men's wrists—this being part of the conclusion of any ritual.

One of the Naths, addressing Inder humbly, said, "There should be many big men here, but we are only a few, and just as the pandit is a child, so are those with him." Then he added a final prayer for rain: "This pitcher is now empty; you fill it up." With that, the evening's work was complete. It remained the next day to see to the *ghī* for the Cave Baba and Four-Arms. Although the group performing the worship went directly only to Jaipalji and Meditation Seat, they were greatly concerned with the equitable distribution of *ghī* among all four spots.

Alas, no rain fell. But my own sense of embarrassment was not shared by those who had instigated and performed the ritual. Previously, I was told, Inder Puja took place every year, but now villagers were lazy, apathetic, and took action only when it was too late. Previously, in a better, more moral time, the prayers took instant effect. People would be drenched even as they descended Jaipalji's hill. This current failure could be explained in a variety of ways: from the particular mistake of sitting down in front of Mahadev to the cover-all condition of the present age of decadence, the Kali Yuga, when all communication and interaction between men and gods is flawed and problematic.

Those powers whose conjunction is dramatized in Inder Puja are the same ones that generally provide protection of the whole village's well-being as embodied in its main sources of livelihood: agriculture and dairy herds. The three outlying shrines have several things in common: (1) association either in their origins or in their current service with Naths as a caste or as renouncers; (2) control over weather and animal diseases (powers often attributed to Naths); (3) association with unusual deaths (Jaipalji's in battle and the living *samādhis* of Sundarnath and Balaknath). By contrast, the centrally located Temple of Four-Arms is connected with the ruling Rajputs,[29] its priest is a Brahman, and its chief functions involve not nature but society: life-cycle rites and village-wide ceremony and decision-making. It is, however, the location of a major livestock protection rite on a day that celebrates the unity and uniqueness of Ghatiyali.[30] The conjoined worship of these four places in the event of Inder Puja, then, brings powers—deriving from ascetic feats and royal charters, yogi-magician and Brahmanical influences—simultaneously to bear on the community problem of drought.

The concerns and techniques of Inder Puja, as well as the kinds of power-sources it gathers to its purpose, foreshadow some themes encountered in the following chapters dealing with four conceptions of death and the dead in the village and three styles of pilgrimage beyond it. For example, the worship of spirits of the lingering dead in households and the link between that practice and journeys to regional deities, often deriving powers from heroic or ascetic deaths, have a clear resonance with the stories and potencies of Jaipalji, Meditation Seat, and the Cave. All three of these places indeed are sometimes the goals of pilgrims' journeys practiced by non-Ghatiyalians. Such journeys are most often made to get relief from specific problems, just as Inder Puja seeks to alleviate drought with rain.

29. The identification of Four-Arms with the nobility is further attested by the practice of greeting high-born Rajputs with "Victory to Four-Arms" instead of the familiar "Ram Ram."

30. A day designated as Village Outside Cooking is held by many other villages of the region, but each selects its own day every year by an astrologically informed communal decision. It is a day to display hospitality across family, caste, and neighborhood lines.

Four-Arms plays a part in the funeral sequence and associated Ganges pilgrimage intended to give final peace to spirits of those who have died at a ripened age. As a form of Vishnu, Four-Arms may be equated with supreme gods, like the Lord Jagdish of Puri, that are visited on extended pilgrimages—gods who hold in their hands, as villagers put it, the ultimate life aim of release. The aim of release is also evoked by the ancient *samādhi*s of the Cave and Meditation Seat, commemorating the spots where detached renouncers took the inner, meditative way to perfect freedom.

2. Responses to Mortality

Beyond the elementary fact of movement from one place to another, the diffuse meanings of *yātrā,* translated here as "pilgrimage," are united by a common involvement with death. Also pervasive among pilgrims' concerns, and complexly linked with the ideas and actions surrounding death, are the birth of living sons and the rebirth or non-rebirth of deceased kin.[1] Therefore, as prelude to considering the aims and fruits of different kinds of journeying, I consider the different but often intermeshed results of mortality and their implications for life and life cycles.

Death (*mṛtyu, maut,* in Hindi and Rajasthani) is defined in the *RSK* as "that time, condition or situation when some breather's breath leaves his body," or "the end of life." It is also "illusion" (*māyā*) and "time" (*kāl*). Awareness of death, both as separation from perishable flesh and as the basis for this world's illusory nature, is a dominant theme in Hinduism; a common name for earth is *mṛtyulok,* the "realm of death," that world where mortality uniquely prevails among many where it does not.

For Hindus, the end of life in the fleshly body, although it is certainly recognized and ritually marked as a significant passage, is by no means the end of existence for the "spirit" that was embod-

1. Several scholars have recently pointed out in various contexts that the Hindu world view posits essential cyclical continuities as well as structural parallels between death and birth. Nicholas, in a recent article on *shrāddha* (faithful offerings), has demonstrated that "in the *shrāddha* rites for the departed, the paradigmatic action is birth or rebirth" (1982:378). Others (including Das 1979:98; Parry 1982a:358, 1982b:85–86) have also shown that conceptions of death are modeled on, or imaged as, birth. Although the primary focus here is on mortality rather than procreation—because much of the data most directly concerns death and the dead—the theme of birth as a model for, and an antidote to, death will be a recurrent one throughout this and the following chapters.

ied there.[2] There are at least four distinct ways in which Rajasthani villagers conceive of and treat both the immediate and the far-reaching aftermaths of breaths leaving bodies. These aftermaths involve both the condition of spirits of the dead and the ways in which that condition affects and is affected by the living, especially kin. Kinship—for South Asian Hindus both founded in and defined by bodily and nonbodily sharing and exchange (Inden and Nicholas 1977)—does not cease with the loss of the gross body. But the ways in which the sharing and exchange are construed and sustained (or severed) are certainly altered by the fact of death and variously reconstituted, depending on death's various outcomes.

A number of deaths took place during my time in Ghatiyali. They occurred among different castes and ages, with corresponding differences in reactions and rituals. Not surprisingly, those deaths which evoked the most heartfelt sorrow and required meticulous ritual attentions were of persons, both male and female, struck down in their prime. A death which left behind a youthful spouse and small children was considered particularly grievous because of both the loss for the living and the perilous after-death condition of the deceased. Those who die in the midst of engrossing involvements and attachments, at the peak of the "householder life-stage" (*gṛhastha āshrama*) will find it most difficult to quit the locality of their unfulfilled life span and loosen the binding ties to their household members. Their spirits are potential lingerers, who may afflict the living out of resentment or out of a simple craving for attention.

In contrast to these most unacceptable deaths, the loss of the very young or the very old is less problematic, although in different ways. Infants are buried in the jungle with almost no ceremony. When referring to the death of a newborn it is common to say flatly, "It went back." Unmarried older children are cremated, but not at the main cremation ground, and with minimal pollution observances and little subsequent ritual. The spirits of infants

2. I use the English word "spirit" to represent roughly Hindi and Rajasthani *jīv*, which might be rendered more precisely but ponderously as "life-essence" or "living being's consciousness." I also use "spirit" to translate the term *ātmā-rūpī-jīv*, or "spirit-in-the-form-of-a-soul," employed by some Ghatiyalians to refer to that which does not die with the body. This allows me to talk generally about "spirits of the dead," as well as to describe the varying attributes of these spirits in different contexts. *Ātmā* when unmodified I render either as "soul" or as "self."

and children often return to their homes as domestic "deities" (*devatā*), requiring worship, but this eventuality is neither so dangerous nor so upsetting as the identification of an adult's lingering spirit, which is less easily appeased.

The death of an old person with mature, living progeny (ideally including a son's son) requires elaborate mourning and mortuary rites, but in the complex process there is a sense of fulfillment and ultimately of celebration. Given the usual ritual assistance, the spirits of such deceased persons should go compliantly to join the lineage ancestors in "ancestor-realm" (*pitṛlok*), for their days are "fulfilled," or "ripened."

A secret "path" (*panth*), or cult, active in Ghatiyali, holds peculiar death rites that claim to give immediate release to the spirits of deceased cult members. Study of this cult's teachings reveals an acceptance of death through somber and thorough denial of value attached to familial and social connections in the ephemeral world of mortality. However, a very different set of values is expressed on certain village-wide festive occasions, whose chief participants are often women, where the meaning of death is blatantly opposed by a rowdy sexuality evoking consequent fertility. These public demonstrations affirm continuities within family, caste, and wider social groupings and elevate rather than reject such groups' cohesiveness and perpetuity.

In the following pages I first consider spirits of the dead who do not go away but take up residence in their former homes. Once they are recognized and their wishes are understood, these invisible family members can be reembodied in icons and enter into regular symbiotic relations with their living kin. They may impose their needs and whims upon the domestic circle, but they also give advice and grant blessings. Poignant and numerous among household deities are those who died in infancy or childhood. They reside on their parents' or siblings' necks, feed on rice pudding, and are soothed with lullaby-like songs that speak of swings, gardens, milk, and attentive, loving kin.

One old man's demise, at the end of a full lifetime, is then followed from sickbed to funeral feast. Both the social ambience of death and the ritual reembodiment of the person as ancestor are highlighted here. The activities of the twelve days following death include, for those who can afford it, a pilgrimage to "sink flowers" (*phūl boḷāṇo,* "flowers" being the regular euphemism for bones of the dead) in the Ganges. The subsequent Celebration of Ganga (Gangotsav; Gangoj) is performed as part of the twelfth-day ceremonies.

The ideas of death expressed in the secret rites, *nirguṇa bhajans* (hymns praising God without qualities) and legendary traditions of the Nath caste may be described as having an orientation toward release. The rites promise quick and perfect liberation, and the *bhajans*, whose texts will be closely examined, exhort humans to recognize the harsh finality of death in order to achieve freedom from illusory attachments in the world. Complementary to the *bhajans*' didactic stance is the tale of King Gopi Cand, sung annually in the village as part of the Naths' public performance tradition. Hounded by his mother (or his destiny) to abandon the world, Gopi Cand's pathetic progress toward man's highest aim dramatizes the conflict posed by the *bhajans*—family attachments versus freedom—and offers sympathetic insights into the vast difficulties of perfect detachment.

Finally, I report a fourth approach to the subject of death and renewal of life through analysis of women's rites and play on the day of Calf Twelfth (Bach Bāras). These are less concerned with the after-death existence of separate persons than with community life and its continuity, less with the release or lingering of spirits of the dead than with a general antidote to death itself. Calf Twelfth and other similarly bawdy occasions offer, I suggest, an important view coexisting with the rest, which is significantly sustained by women but benefits the village as a whole.

The organization here prefigures in part the organization of the subsequent chapters and also follows a logical geographic sequence from near to far (and, in two different senses, back again). The first three sections below—on harboring, transforming, and releasing the spirits of the dead—thus describe three aspects of the meaning and nature of Hindu death, each stressed in, although certainly not exclusive to, one of three kinds of pilgrimage.

The identity and wishes of spirits of the dead who take the form of household deities are often identified through short journeys to nearby shrines (chapter 3). Relations with these lingering spirits of the dead may also be subsequently ordered through repeated consultations with shrine deities, as represented by non-Brahman priests (*bhopās*), whether through possession or divination.

The spirits of those who die at a ripe age are normally transported, embodied in their "flowers," to the Ganges. There they receive peace when those bodily remains are submerged in the river, and the power-filled water of that place is carried home by the living (chapter 4).

The message of Nath funeral *bhajans*—that release is attainable only through detachment, divine grace, and inner knowledge—is consonant with an ambivalent ideology described for protracted journeys made to wander, to view the gods, and to bathe in "crossing places" (*tīrthas*) (chapter 5). One part of Hindu cultural ideology defines such "journeys to crossing places" (*tīrthayātrā*) as renunciative motions toward the pilgrim's own release. However, most Rajasthani pilgrims expressed real skepticism concerning the soteriological pretensions of distant pilgrimage. Just as *cār dhām* are within the village, the most worthy and difficult-to-obtain spiritual goal, as villagers understand it, is ultimately found within oneself. Striving toward this inner, subtle realization, however, may be aided by the loosening of bonds and the emptying of wealth that a long pilgrimage entails, and is also readily imaged as a microcosmic journey. This bent toward inner realities is one kind of return to the pilgrim's origins.

An orientation that has more to do with what goes on at home than with journeying, but is of a quite different nature, is explicated in the fourth section below. Rather than withdrawal from relationships, this orientation stresses mixing; rather than asceticism, fun; rather than emptying, filling—impregnation. Although it is directly aligned with neither a single type of pilgrimage nor a corresponding chapter, the valence given to fertility in this exuberantly physical approach to mortality permeates the others to varying degrees.

Care and Feeding of Lingering Spirits of the Dead

The houses, lanes, fields, and wastelands of Ghatiyali are inhabited by the spirits of many kinds of dead persons whose presence affects the living. Some of the more exalted dead—Sati Mas, Jhujharjis, Sagasjis—have shrines that are essentially public if parochial. Three major protective places of the village described in chapter 1, Jaipalji, Meditation Seat, and the Cave, derive their powers from persons who led extraordinary lives and long ago died exemplary deaths. There is also a host of nameless "ghosts" (*bhūt-pret*) who may grab anyone who is so imprudent as to walk alone at night in uninhabited places.

The focus here, however, is on the undeparted spirits of named persons, usually fairly recently deceased, whose lives were not of particular note. While the ghosts of unknown dead persons generally can only be avoided and expelled, some of these lingering spirits may, under the right circumstances, be identified, appeased, welcomed back into the family that they left in abrupt or untimely fashion, and nourished there. These are the spirits of the dead who play most intimate roles in domestic life. They are called by two terms: *pattar* and (again) *jhūjhārjī*. Both are included by villagers among the large category of "goddesses-and-gods" (*devī-devatā*), beings of limited but definite powers.

The main criterion contrasting *pattar* to *jhūjhār* that most informants cited is marriage: if a person dies before his marriage, and the spirit lingers, it will manifest as a *pattar;* the undeparted spirit of a married person may manifest as *jhūjhār*. While *jhūjhārjī* generally prefer to reside in carved stone icons placed in house or field, *pattar* normally choose to be "seated on the neck" of their mother, brother, or other designated natal kin, in the form of metal pendants. In this penchant for clinging to the bodies of the living, as well as most of their other desires and tastes, they resemble small children, whose deaths gave most *pattar* their origins.

Before looking at the roles the spirits of these deceased persons play in their families' lives, a brief consideration of the significance and ambiguities of the terms by which they are designated is in order. *Jhūjhār* was first defined for me by informants as one who had died in battle (*jujh; yuddh*), had not received release, and therefore caused trouble.[3] More educated and literal-minded informants told me that the current usage of *jhūjhārjī* in the village to refer to any adult person's spirit which lingered after death was a mistake. The word, they felt, should be reserved for heroic war-

3. The *RSK* supplies a more positive explanation of the same phenomenon, giving as the primary meaning a person killed in a battle fought "for the benefit of others" and who is later worshipped. It gives as second defintion anyone killed in war. Ziegler, characterizing the Rajput of middle-period Marwar, includes among his descriptive terms *jhumjār*: "an individual of great strength and power who fought until death in battle in the assistance (protection) of others and who was afterwards worshipped for his deeds" (1973:67–68).

riors only. However, there are no wars nowadays, and yet new *jhūjhārjī* continue to manifest themselves and insist on being worshipped. Moreover, they emerge among washermen as well as Rajputs. Some of them are even female. Those who argued against the term's correctness could not dispute the fact that in popular usage *jhūjhārjī* no longer implied a noble warrior's death.

The origin of the term *pattar* (also spelled *patar* and *patra*) presents a far more puzzling configuration. *Pattar* is in fact the Rajasthani equivalent of Hindi and Sanskrit *pitṛ*. Monier-Williams (1899) gives the prime meaning of *pitṛ*, from the *Ṛg Veda*, as "a father," and his further glosses include "forefathers" and "ancestors" who inhabit "a peculiar region," that is, *pitṛlok* ("ancestor-realm"). Thus, the chief fact about *pitṛ* is that they are progenitors, predecessors, who dwell in a distinct realm. The chief fact about village *pattar* (which are sometimes referred to by educated villagers as *pitṛ*), on the other hand, is that they are unmarried children—virgins and therefore categorically without progeny—who far from residing in their own separate realm, linger persistently about the house. Ancestors (*pitṛ*, but also pronounced *pattar* by most uneducated villagers) are also worshipped in Ghatiyali, receiving Sanskritic "faithful offerings" (*shrāddh*) during the dark half of the month of Ashoj (called the *shrāddh paksh*) and, in certain castes, special attentions at Divali.[4] What are the possible explanations for this homonymy, this terminological merger of two distinct categories?

Two plausible rationales occur to me. The first is that the term is used euphemistically and prospectively. Just as the virulent, fever-heating, smallpox goddess Sitala's name means "cool," and her special day is marked by extinguished hearths and the use of cold foods, so potentially intrusive, malevolent, resentful dead children are dubbed "ancestors," with all the implications of peaceable and distant benevolence that term implies. Moreover, the condition of lingering, though it may continue for lengthy spans of time, is not conceived of as permanent. Eventually, the

4. An unfortunate gap in my data resulted from my arriving in Ghatiyali just after the 1979 *shrāddh paksh* and being absent on the one-month bus pilgrimage during that period in 1980. The bus tour was planned so that pilgrims would be able to make offerings to their ancestors in Gaya during those special days. Communal water-offerings, called *chānt bārhno* (to proffer drops), are made by Gujars and Balais to their ancestral *pitṛ* at the village water reservoir on the second day of Divali.

cravings that have trapped them here will subside, and these spirits of the lingering dead will, like most human spirits, be recycled. They may be reborn, live full lives, and become ancestral *pitṛ*. The merged usage might then be interpreted as wishful prophecy.

A second possibility is that the term's dual usage reflects those notions of metempsychosis existing within Hindu thought which posit reincarnation within the family. Jonathan Parry, for example, mentions the "idea that the great-grandfather comes back as his own great-grandson" (1982b:85). This he surmises from the ritual moment when the chief mourner's wife, if barren, may eat the grain-ball dedicated to her husband's father's father.[5] Any infant might then be viewed as *pitṛ,* and such a perspective could underlie the identity of ancestors with the lingering spirits of juvenile dead.[6] Whatever validity these two hypotheses may have, it is certain that Ghatiyali's *pattar* do not act like placid, benevolent ancestors.[7] Their demands and treatment are rather those of powerful, invisible children.

Turning now to the nature and needs of *jhūjhār* and *pattar* as household deities, why they linger and how they make themselves known are the first two points to clarify. Informants of various castes, ages, experiences, and education displayed a remarkable consensus on the question Why does a dead person become *pattar* or *jhūjhār?* All stated, using similar language, that for whatever reason at the time of death that person's "desire" remained "in the house."

5. Kane writes: "We have already seen . . . that the middle one of the three *piṇḍa*s for paternal ancestors was to be eaten by the wife of the performer of the shraddha if she was desirous of a son" (1953:480). Manu provides that "the . . . [wife] should eat the middle *piṇḍa* . . . and then she gives birth to a son who lives long, secures fame, is intelligent and obtains wealth and progeny and who is of a good and righteous turn of mind" (Buhler 1969:124).

6. There is also a belief that the spirits of dead infants who don't linger and become *pattar* may be rapidly reborn, sometimes to the same mother. A baby who dies shortly after birth may be marked by its mother with a smear of *ghī* or oil so that she will be able to recognize it in its next life—if born with a similarly placed birthmark—as a "deceiver."

7. See Steed 1972:140 for a case, in rural Gujarat, involving "restless ancestors," called *pitruns*. Among other things these ancestors when angered afflict living descendants with impotence, therefore preventing the continuity of the line. Both their involvement in affairs of the living and their characterization as "restless" make these "ancestors" appear to me more like Rajasthani *pattar* and *jhūjhār* than like those spirits of the dead who dwell in remote ancestor-realm and receive *shrāddh*. Kolenda reports an "irony" in the worship of *pitar*s, or "fathers," in an Uttar Pradesh village. "These are men among their patrilineal ancestors who never had a son. Thus, *pitar*s are really 'failed fathers'" (1982:240).

For example, a young Gujar man provided this definition of *pattar:* "For some reason his desire remains in some thing or person of the house; then his soul keeps wandering, his release doesn't happen, and if he takes worship (*pūjā letā*), then he is called *pattar.*" This definition might apply equally to modern *jhūjhārjī.* Another villager, an old Damami woman, however, found the source of cloying desire in the attribute of virginity. "Especially virgins become *pattar*— those who are married don't—because virgins' desire remains very much in the home." When asked to explain her statement she only elaborated on it: "Their spirit keeps clinging (*laṭaktā*) to the house; for example, to Mother, Father, Brother, Sister, places; or it remains clinging to their land." The distinctive characteristic of virgins stressed here as producing *pattar* derives then from a childish "hanging on" (the literal meaning of *laṭaknā*) to the domestic circle.

It is, in a sense, natural and predictable that the spirits of dead children should be prone to remain attached to the home in this way; unfortunately, their untimely deaths are tragically commonplace.[8] The death of a married adult, struck down in his prime, is by contrast always shocking, and the unfulfilled desires of such a mature person are apt to be more acute. Snakebite and drowning are the classic cases mentioned by informants as examples of precipitate, unexpected deaths, likely to produce *jhūjhār.* However, the one *jhūjhār* I saw enshrined during my time in Ghatiyali resulted from a youth who had wasted away with tuberculosis. His demise was neither speedy nor unexpected, although certainly grievous and untimely. His death rites, like all those for adults in their prime, were carried out carefully and elaborately, in the hope of facilitating a reluctant departure. When it was determined that he wished to be worshipped in the home as *jhūjhārjī,* this revelation came as no great surprise. There is a definite sense that after such a death the spirit will not go readily, if it goes at all.

Neither unmarried girls nor married women often become *pattar* or *jhūjhār,* although both may occasionally do so. One type of female whose death very often results in a household deity is a

8. I have no statistics on infant mortality for the area, but my impression from living in the village and also from information that emerged during the house-to-house census was that it was a rare household which had not suffered the loss of one or more children even in the currently reproducing generation. Few women did not wear around their necks the medallions enshrining *pattar.*

young wife whose widower soon remarries. The first wife's spirit is usually enshrined in a neck ornament, worn and worshipped by her successor, and is called by the special name *agalī* ("the one who came first"; "the preceding one"). Sati Mas, of course, represent women whose exceptional, self-sacrificial deaths, like those of the warrior *jhūjhārjīs,* have made them posthumous wielders of power.[9]

All accounts of *pattar* and *jhūjhār* are in concordance concerning how their presence is first known. As one informant put it, "They give blindness, they make stomach pain, and they give sickness." Another stated more succinctly, "They give disturbances" (*vighnā,* also translatable as "interference," "meddling," "obstacle"). These disturbances may take the form of ill health, bad luck, or madness.

There does not seem to be any resentment toward spirits of the dead for causing such problems. As one man, afflicted by the *jhūjhār* of his father's brother with violent and painful episodes of crazy behavior, expressed it, "They will strike you, what else can deities do? Can they drive the plough?" A living uncle, who was supervising his mad nephew's cure at Ghatiyali's Puvali ka Devji shrine, added, "They will eat us [afflict us] according to our fate [*karam*], bad-good-bad, they strike oneself and they also strike others nearby." He is making two important points here: (1) The afflictions meted out by spirits of deceased kin who take the form of household deities may be tied into a more general framework of causality; (2) although such spirits, when seeking recognition or some specific service from the living, may single out one family member on whom they inflict disturbances, the whole household is inevitably implicated in the ensuing troubles.

9. Other malevolent, invisible feminine powers may originate within a living practitioner of evil arts, but continue to exist, and indeed increase in danger, after they are no longer restrained by a body. The *ḍākaṇ* is a living woman who has, through the use of spells, acquired extraordinary power (*shakti*), allowing her—among other things—to see and eat the liver of other women's children and thus destroy their lives. After an accomplished *ḍākaṇ* dies she is known as *meḷī,* and it is much harder to remove her from her victims because she has no body of her own to which she can return. An expert shrine priest may, however, confine and bury her in a clay pot. Such evil female spirits, known to have deliberately pursued powers during their embodied careers, contrast with *pattar* and *jhūjhār,* who apparently attain their measure of influence in the world of the living only through the hapless accident of leaving it in untimely fashion.

Occasionally, *pattar* and *jhūjhār* who wish to get attention from the living announce themselves straightforwardly in dreams, stating their immediate requirements. More often the process of identifying and appeasing them is a prolonged trial-and error venture that involves interpreting ambiguous clues. For example, one may see a snake in a dream and suspect that this is some *pattar* who wants to be worshipped, but to trace that spirit's specific identity then demands other divinatory techniques and often consultation with experts.

Perseverance in questing for a spirit's identity is crucial, however, because only when it is recognized and satisfied will that dead person's spirit cease to afflict, to strike, and to impose obstacles, and become instead beneficent. Having a specific recognizable identity is, of course, the determinative difference between *pattar* and *jhūjhār,* on the one hand, and the kind of eternally nameless and threatening *bhūt-pret* that dwell in the jungle, on the other. Unlike ghosts of the jungle, *pattar* and *jhūjhār* need not be homeless wanderers and malevolent powers forever.[10] If they find pleasant shelter and satisfaction among their kin and take up residence as household deities, they may be persuaded to protect and aid their families, for they share the same interests as the living.

A *pattar* or *jhūjhār* should never be installed in an icon, however, without its wishes having been consulted. As one woman bluntly expressed it, "We have seated them after asking them; if we seat them according to our desire then they make us sick." Once the spirit's explicit wishes have been understood, the accepted way of celebrating its installation involves some public expenditure and becomes a social event (which is also true of almost any major undertaking in village life). The most common way to honor new *pattar* and *jhūjhār* is to hold a night-long singing session. This may be a "night-awake" (*rāti jagā*), in which only women participate, or a "wake" (*jāgaraṇ*)—an all-night session of *bhajans* performed by men, during which women may also cluster to sing their own songs. Invited guests and singers must be served tea and raw sugar to sustain them through the night. A large pot of sweet rice is also prepared, offered to the deities at dawn, and served to the company as *prasād.*

10. See Rosin 1983:24 for an interesting discussion of how "dread" in rural Rajasthan arises when a person is "unable to identify and relate to power."

Divinatory techniques to determine the identity of *pattar* and *jhūjhārjī* may be performed in the home, but the most common resort for those who suspect the presence of an unidentified lingering spirit is to visit deities' places. On the principle that it takes one to know one, the deities enshrined in such places are able to reveal the names and wills of spirits of the dead who wish to become enshrined as deities in households.

It may take more than one conference with more than one shrine deity, however, before adequate results are achieved. People often related to me their fruitless peregrinations from place to place which preceded an ultimately successful pronouncement. My Gujar research assistant's mother was periodically ill for four or five years (throughout his late childhood and early adolescence). During a bad spell she could neither eat nor speak, sometimes for days on end. The only effective remedy for this condition was large doses of strong country liquor, which her brother fed her almost daily. Consultations with the family's chosen god (Dev Narayanji) were of no lasting help.

Finally the concerned brother visited a famed Sagasji shrine in a nearby village where—an unusual circumstance—a husband and wife priestly team (*bhopā-bhopī*) work together. Their specialty is identifying the afflicting dead through possession by Sagasji. They ascertained that the spirit causing the problem was that of this woman's father's elder brother, whose only daughter had always treated her with great respect and kindness. This personal connection was stressed in relating the story. It made sense that the afflicted woman owed respect to her father's brother's spirit because his daughter gave respect to her.

After the *jhūjhār* was named by Sagasji, the family held an all-night *bhajan* sing in its honor, and it then possessed my assistant's mother and stated its wish to be seated on her neck in gold.[11] The family complied with this wish and established a shrine in their house for good measure. They continue to worship this deity on

11. This example demonstrates that *jhūjhār* may on occasion choose to reside on the neck, like *pattar*. However, as spirits of mature persons, in the pattern of warriors, *jhūjhārjī* normally prefer extradomestic enshrinement. Ramanujan's discussion of the Tamil categories translatable as "interior" and "exterior," and their implications for poetry (1970:101–104), may be relevant to an understanding of the locational difference usually existing between *pattar* and *jhūjhār*.

dark-moon nights and bright elevenths with offerings of rice pudding, boiled grains, and raw sugar. The mother's sickness has never recurred, and liquor is forbidden now in her house as part of the added purity required by the presence of the *jhūjhār*. When the family has a question or a problem to solve, they may summon this domesticated *jhūjhār* to possess its former victim and give them advice through her mouth.

Wearing a *pattar*'s icon on one's neck or having a *jhūjhārjī*'s icon in the house imposes certain duties and limitations on the persons and families involved. Besides the niceties of periodic worship, these deities require various kinds of specific behaviors demonstrating respect. An example of this would be forbidding the consumption or presence of liquor in the home after enshrining a *jhūjhārjī*, as was just related. Another woman I knew, who was resisting her mother's notion that her deceased son's spirit wanted recognition as a *pattar* (based on the young woman's dreams about snakes and her perpetual quarrels with her estranged husband and in-laws), said that wearing a *pattar*'s icon caused too much annoyance. You must always step into your skirt (instead of pulling it on over the head), for the proximity of a woman's skirt would be offensive to the deity. Moreover, you must remember to remove it from your neck when having sexual intercourse.

Once relations between spirits of the dead and their living kin have been made to flow harmoniously, it is still possible to upset this balance through violation of some restriction or general negligence. One might embark on some important undertaking (a new house, a well, a land deal, a marriage) and forget to consult one's *jhūjhārjī* or *pattar*. The spirit might then become angry and affronted, engendering a new cycle of afflictions, consultations, and divinations. Eventually a "sin of omission" (*dosh*) against a *pattar* or a *jhūjhār* will be determined and appropriate appeasements undertaken. These deities, moreover, have whims of their own and may cause troubles purely in order to gratify such whims. For example, one man was caused a great deal of misery by a *jhūjhār* that had taken a notion to move from the house where it had received worship for years to a well in its former fields.

Even when they don't perpetrate major difficulties, *pattar* may still be mischievous, like children. An example of this occurred one dark-moon night when I was recording women's songs for *pattar*. One of the singers began to suffer from such loud outlandish hiccoughs that, gasping for breath, she became unable to participate and indeed disturbed the others' singing. Between songs she continued to hiccough while she and the other women explained to me that her *pattar* was causing this embarrassment, deliberately obstructing her singing. The same thing had happened before; it was just a meddlesome *pattar,* which for reasons of its own did not appreciate her efforts to please it. These explanations were given with animation and apparent good-humored indulgence for the *pattar*'s idiosyncrasy.

Although pacification of a lingering spirit depends on identification of its origin in one particular deceased person, it is not afterwards worshipped by that person's given name. Instead, it is called by the general name of *pattar* or *jhūjhār*. As categories of beings, these spirits do seem to have collective presences. Indicative of this is that a group of unrelated women can sing "songs for *pattar,*" which appear to address them as a class and yet be pleasing to each woman's own. In songs for *jhūjhārjī* a "lineage" (*gotra*) name is sometimes given; if *jhūjhārjī* of different lineages are relevant among the company singing, identical verses are repeated inserting each lineage name.

The texts of songs sung to please *pattar* and *jhūjhār* are revealing of these deities' natures. Songs for *pattar* are performed on the dark-moon night, usually by a small gathering of neighbor women invited by the hostess to join her. Five separate songs will be sung on such occasions. One song each for *pattar* and *jhūjhārjī* must also be rendered when women methodically sing songs for all the goddesses-and-gods, including Ganeshji, Hanumanji, Sati Ma, Sagasji, Bhairuji, and others. The night before a wedding ceremony or a celebration of postnatal bathing are events that call for such serial homages.

These five songs for *pattar* were recorded in a single consecutive session at a wealthy Kumhar's house, a few doors from my own.

Song for Pattar 1

[Refrain] A cradle of green bamboo was made
and hung in the joining room.
Pattar swings in the cradle.

[1] His[12] father came and pushed the swing,
His grandfather pushed the swing,
His grandmother gave him milk to drink,
Pattar swings in the cradle;
His mother gave him milk to drink,
Pattar swings in the cradle.

[2] His mother's brother came and pushed the swing,
His brother came and pushed the swing,
His mother's brother's wife gave him milk to drink,
Pattar swings in the cradle;
His brothers' wives gave him milk to drink,
Pattar swings in the cradle.

[3] His elder sister's husband came and pushed the swing,
His mother's sister's husband came and pushed the swing,
His sister gave him milk to drink,
Pattar swings in the cradle;
His father's sister gave him milk to drink,
Pattar swings in the cradle.

Song for Pattar 2

[Refrain] Kept on roaming, kept on drinking milk,
Kept on roaming, kept on drinking milk,
Oh, turning, turning they gave a blessing;
Among banana trees pattar are pleasantly roaming.

[1] Father planted sweet flowering vines,
Grandfather planted sweet flowering vines,
His grandmother watered banana trees where pattar are pleasantly roaming;
His father's younger brother's wife watered banana trees where pattar are pleasantly roaming.

[2] Mother's brother planted sweet flowering vines,
Elder sister's husband planted sweet flowering vines,
His mother's brother's wife watered banana trees where pattar are pleasantly roaming;
His mother's sister watered banana trees where pattar are pleasantly roaming.

12. Throughout this and the following songs the third person pronouns refer to the *pattar* or *pattars*.

[3] Elder sister's husband planted sweet flowering vines,
Father's sister's husband planted sweet flowering vines,
His sister watered banana trees where pattar are pleasantly roaming;
His father's sister watered banana trees where pattar are pleasantly roaming.

Song for Pattar 3

[Refrain] For his bathing a fine, fine bank,
To please him many Gujaris.[13]
For sitting in shade, a coconut tree,
To please him many Gujaris.

[1] Your [14] father asks, "Where has pattar gone?"
Your grandfather asks, "Where has pattar gone?"
"I have gone, gone to Ganga's bank to graze the cows."

[2] His father's younger brother asks, "Where has pattar gone?"
His brother asks, "Where has pattar gone?"
He has gone, gone to Ganga's bank to graze the cows.

[3] His father's sister's husband asks, "Where has pattar gone?"
His elder sister's husband asks, "Where has pattar gone?"
He has gone, gone to Ganga's bank to graze the cows.

[4] His mother's brother asks, "Where has pattar gone?"
His mother's sister's husband asks, "Where has pattar gone?"
He has gone, gone to Ganga's bank to graze the cows.

Song for Pattar 4

Beneath mother's father's castle, where do you play, O pattar?
Beneath father's father's castle, where do you play, O pattar?

We play in the rooms, we play on the porch.
Drink milk from a golden cup, O pattar.

Beneath sister's husband's castle, where do you play, O pattar?
Beneath brother's castle, where do you play, O pattar?

13. Gujaris are women of the Gujar (cowherd) caste.
14. In this first verse, "you," like "his" in the other verses, refers to the *pattar*. When directly addressed as "you," he answers "I."

We play in the rooms, we play on the porch.
Drink milk from a golden cup, O pattar.

[In my recording this song repeated with "mother's sister's husband's castle," "father's sister's husband's castle," and "sister's husband's castle."]

Song for Pattar 5

Their uncle went to milk the cow,
Their grandpa went to milk it too,
Their grandma raced to catch the calf,
Their mother raced to catch it too.
    Come my pattar on the dark moon night!
Seated in the doorway, the pattar said,
"O Grandma, take a look at me;
"My mother, take a look."

"With what ornament, son, shall I take it?
"With what shall I take a look?"

"With gold, Mother, make the ornament.
"Hold it in your hands and look."

In a new clay pot the yogurt thickened;
Invited pattar will feast.

[This song also repeats, substituting other kin terms.]

To sing these songs is to worship the *pattar,* to appease them, to pray to them, and to reassure them of continued love and care from the living. All the songs indicate that the *pattar* are in every way content, and the second one suggests that being thus content they bless their benefactors, their living relatives. Certainly the most striking feature of the texts is the litany of kin terms recited in each. Women explain that it is important when singing to name all the basic categories of relation on both the mother's and the father's side. Despite each *pattar*'s residing on a particular family member's neck, no *pattar* should ever feel slighted by anyone. More than once I have seen women apparently finish a song and be in the midst of chatting, or even embarked on the next song, when suddenly one among them recalls an omission. They will return abruptly to the uncompleted song and rectify the slight. Thus, what to us in transcription and translation seems so repetitive as to call for ditto marks and etceteras, is to them the distributive essence, the real intention of the song.

The fifth song is most poignant, creating a dialogue between the departed child and its mother and grandmother. He asks them to look at him, using a local equivalent for *darshan,* or viewing a powerful being. When they ask how to see him he explains that they must make a gold ornament, take it in their hands, and look. The song thus evokes the bereaved mother's desire to touch and to see her child and explicitly points to the gold or silver medallion in which *pattar* are usually enshrined as a medium of contact with them. It is just this enshrining which transforms the *pattar* from invisible threat to benevolent deity, as well as from vanished loved one to a constant presence. Touching and viewing may imply both mutuality and intimacy, a two-way flow between the *pattar* and his worshippers.[15]

All the offerings mentioned in these songs are such as would please an infant or a young child; swings, milk, a pleasant garden, nursemaids. Gujar women were traditional wet nurses to noble Rajput infants, and so the pleasing Gujaris in Song 3 may suggest breast milk of royal quality. This emphasis on infantile enjoyments is unique to songs for *pattar* and confirms their existence as beings quite unlike ancestors.

By contrast, songs dedicated to mature deities, including *jhūjhārjī*, speak of temples, clothing, jewels, and foodstuffs richer than the simple milk and yogurt suggested for *pattar*s. Two extracts from songs for *jhūjhārjī*, one recorded at a prenuptial night-awake and one at a postpartum bathing celebration, exemplify the sort of extradomestic blandishments addressed to them.

Song for Jhujharji 1

[Refrain] Jhujharji, come stroll in the jewel-like court,
Jhujharji, whose line produced you?
Jhujharji, whose brave youth are you?
Jhujharji, come stroll in the jewel-like court,
Jhujharji, come play in the wide square.

[1] Jhujharji, I'll build you a platform of gold.

[2] Jhujharji, I'll boil up delicate pudding,
Jhujharji, I'll add a whole handful of sugar.

[3] Jhujharji, I'll milk the cow's extra-rich milk
Jhujharji, I'll milk the buffalo's extra-rich milk,
Jhujharji, I'll boil up thick milk-rice pudding.

15. See Babb 1982 and Eck 1981 for some dynamic aspects of *darshan*.

Song for Jhujharji 2

On the true jhujharsa, pearls are pleasing,
On the true jhujharsa, a golden chain also looks good.

Covered with colored foil,[16] jhujharsa looks lovely,
Jhujharsa's lineage is ______.

On the true jhujharsa, metal arm bands are pleasing,
Jhujharsa's long gown also is pleasing.

Both songs have references to familial origins. The first does not name but clearly claims the *jhūjhārjī* as one of the lineage's own brave youths; the second calls the deity by *gotra* title. Other than these particularities of identity, there is nothing greatly to distinguish songs for *jhūjhārjī* from songs for other male deities, such as Bhairuji and Sagasji, who also appreciate adornment and good food.

The lingering attachment of *pattar* and *jhūjhār* to their homes or villages is obviously not only recognized but at least temporarily fostered, despite a strong emphasis in other contexts on the torment and futility of just such binding affections. Some persons attempt to reconcile the two views by stating that these deities resulting from lingering spirits of dead kin will surely not remain forever. Eventually they too may be released, if not from cycles of birth and death, then at least from their condition as minor deities haunting the scenes of a past lifetime. One informant confidently asserted that this release would happen inevitably after a period of twelve years, but it is clear that such an arbitrary limit is not in effect. Certain public *jhūjhārjī* in the village date from distant past generations. The fact that ancient women are to be seen wearing icons for the *pattar* of their lost infants also testifies to a duration well beyond twelve years.

The third of the songs for *pattar* depicts them as having gone to the Ganges, but not in any permanent way. If they have left to graze the cows, the implication is that they will return home. However, the song may evoke the occasional practice of attempting to take *pattar* or *jhūjhār* to powerful crossing places in order to release them (and oneself) from their clinging condition. Before embarking on such a journey the *pattar* must be consulted, either through possession of a family member or through a shrine priest.

16. Thin sheets of foil decorated with colored patterns may be applied to most stone icons of the gods to enhance their beauty.

One woman told ruefully of trying to take her *pattar* on pilgrimage "by force" without their approval. They afflicted her quite violently along the way, causing her to drop things and to trip and fall herself. In this way they would not permit her to take *darshan* in the temples until she relinquished her intention of leaving them at Gaya.

Sometimes, however, a *pattar* or a *jhūjhārjī* does sign his agreement to go and stay in a crossing place, most commonly by speaking through a possession vehicle or in response to asking with grain. If there are no bone-remains (as in the case of a buried infant or someone whose remains were previously disposed of), "silver flowers"[17] representing that deceased person may be taken on the pilgrimage. These are treated in identical fashion to real bones of the dead. After a dead person's remains are submerged in the Ganges, that person's spirit supposedly loses its position in the house: "After entering *tīrtha*s they have no right to eat."[18] Nevertheless, living kin may continue to make offerings.

In fact, there is a healthy skepticism among villagers as to the efficacy of transporting locally attached spirits to abandon them at distant river banks. Many stories are told of such attempts ending futilely with the *pattar* or *jhūjhārjī* "jumping back" either on the road home or shortly after the pilgrim's return. If pilgrimage to pan-Hindu sites on the Ganges is sometimes attempted as a last-ditch resort for getting rid of the spirits of housebound dead, it is much more common to negotiate with them at local shrines.

The routinized worship of *pattar* and *jhūjhār* as a way of living with the dead might be interpreted as making the best of a bad situation. Ideally, spirits of dead relatives should go away (whether to ancestor-realm, heaven, rebirth, or release are further issues). But if these spirits are too attached to their homes to leave them, then it is imperative for the living to convince the spirits of the dead to continue to share an interest in familial well-being.

17. A Sonar (Goldsmith) will be commissioned to fashion silver flowers by replicating in silver the fragments of bone that are gathered from the cremation ground on the third day after death.

18. In this statement, "Tīrth mẽ jāne ke bād vo khāne kī koī hakadār nahī̃ hai," the use of *khāne* is ambiguous. It might be a noun meaning "food"; or it might be the verb "to eat," which also very commonly means "to afflict." However, the same logic underlies all these possible interpretations: once spirits of dead kin acquiesce to being transported to some crossing place, their bones are submerged there, and flour balls are offered; they should then have no further claim on the living.

A major factor in this well-being is, of course, fertility, especially the birth of sons to carry on the lineage and perform rites for deceased members. Both *pattar* and *jhūjhār* may prevent or permit fertility. *Pattar,* by definition the spirits of unmarried children—most often infants—are both inherently and subtly linked with procreation. The term "flower" (*phūl*) nicely embraces all the implications of birth and death surrounding *pattar*. *Phūl* is always used to refer to the bone remains of all deceased persons, sometimes used to signify the medallions enshrining *pattar* (which, like bones on pilgrims, are worn around the neck) and occasionally means a boy-child. Moreover, according to the *RSK* (although I did not record this usage myself) *phūl* means womb and menstrual blood, the very place and stuff of birth.[19] Turning next to the rites and processes that transform spirits of the dead to ancestors, further continuities of death with fertility and birth emerge in the celebration for returned pilgrims who have "sunk flowers" and brought home Ganges water.

Death at a Ripe Old Age

The death of Mangilal Mishra, a Brahman of the Gujar-Gaur subcaste, occurred in the household where my colleague Joseph Miller was living and where I frequently worked in the day and always took my evening meal. Miller and I were thus able to observe and record the entire sequence of events. Moreover, it was a death demanding full ritual attentions befitting a household head, though not one inspiring the kind of anguish that would have made our photos, tapes, and questions rude or unfeeling. The old man had lived a full life and was survived by a grown son. In his last days he had grown terribly frail and feeble, and no one felt

19. Real flowers are themselves ritually meaningful—pure offerings to the gods, signs of joy and life. The goddess who presides over Ganges pilgrimage, Path Mother, has only flower-growing Malis (gardeners) for her priests. Her place—a place of auspicious departures and joyful reunions—is traditionally described in song, if rarely seen in fact, as "covered with flowers." Any kind of swelling is referred to as "flowering"; the belly, of course, flowers in pregnancy. The same verb "to flower" is used in one of the most vehement antiwordly *bhajans* to be discussed below to describe the human mind's useless meanderings in an illusory world of perishable attachments. Flowers and flowering may thus ambivalently stand for both prized vitality and devalued life cycling. See Egnor 1978:11–22, 140–156 for flower imagery in Tamil culture.

that his passing was untimely, except for his widow. Her grief was certainly the most acute. She repeatedly reproached God for not taking her first, as all women desire the favor of dying before their husbands.[20]

In describing Mangilal's death I do not propose to present every ritual and social detail. Such thoroughness would require space disproportionate to my purposes here. Rather, I will highlight these major events in order to shed further light on the meaning of death in the village: (1) dying, cremation, and immediate aftermath; (2) gathering and sinking flowers; (3) preparations for the twelfth day; (4) the twelfth day.[21]

Dying, Cremation, and Immediate Aftermath

The indication of the old man's decline which first drew serious attention was his refusal of, or inability to eat, solid foods. His daughter-in-law dutifully prepared several special dishes commonly served to the sick and weak, *daliā* (cracked-wheat porridge) and *khicaṛī* (boiled rice and lentils) being foremost among these. Despite her best efforts, Mangilal consumed less and less and finally refused even tea. This was taken as a grave sign, later to be dramatically evoked during endless recountings of the old man's decline to friends and relations.[22]

20. In fact, Mangilal's wife outlived him by only thirty days, passing quietly away on the day of his one-month-after-death rites, thus starting a whole new round of observances. I was unfortunately unable to record these completely, owing to family obligations that took me out of the village on the seventh day following her demise. It is interesting to note that my son, then ten years old and present throughout these occurrences, became upset about the old woman's situation shortly after the end of Mangilal's funeral ceremonies. He said to me, "They're killing her!" without being able to explain what he meant with any concrete evidence. He had perceived, without any prompting, the cultural if not the normative truth (Schneider 1976:199–203). The old woman was passively encouraged to die, and she did not wish to prolong her own life. After so many years joined in auspicious wifehood, it was intolerable to her to exist as a disjoined widow. Although *satī* is no longer practiced, the widow's will to die is still condoned as virtue by her family and by general public opinion. Her death appeared to have no cause other than old age, grief, and near refusal to eat.

21. For other descriptions of death rites in Rajasthan, see Chauhan 1967:221–223; Srivastava 1974:125–150; Zeitlyn 1986.

22. See Parry for a discussion of the refusal of food by the dying person "in order to weaken his body so that the 'vital breath' may leave it more easily; and in order to make himself a worthy sacrificial object free of foul faecal matter"

When it seemed apparent that Mangilal's hours were numbered, Gam Shyamji, a Sanadhya Brahman and priest of the Niranjani temple, was summoned to read the *Gita* aloud to the dying man, who at this time was still stretched out on a cot. As Gam Shyamji read, others present occasionally shouted, "Listen, old father, listen!" To hear the *Gita* as death approaches is said to ensure instant release. So is the ingestion of a few drops of Ganges water and a small piece of basil leaf (*tulsī*), which Gam Shyamji also administered. These measures are only the first in a long series of actions aimed at that very distant end, all claimed to be, but none really accepted as, foolproof.

Later that day, according to custom, Mangilal was lifted off the bed and laid on the floor.[23] As the news of his imminent departure spread, relatives and friends of the dying man and his family quietly gathered outside the room, having come to greet him for the last time. None lingered too long, and there was constant traffic of a strikingly mixed-caste composition. Not only fellow Brahmans of several subcastes but Gujars, Rajputs, Vaishnav Sadhus, Naths, an untouchable Regar, and several Muslims were among those who came and went. The Regar was Mangilal's land-partner; the Muslims were some of his son's fellow schoolmasters.

Only two days after the initial stir about his loss of appetite, early on the morning of December 22, 1979, Mangilal was dead. Preparations for his cremation began immediately. A bamboo "bier" (*arthī*) was constructed just outside the house while within it, simultaneously, the corpse was readied for its final *samskāra* ("polishing"; any life cycle ritual). The men who prepared the bier were a mixed-caste group of friends and neighbors, but the more intimate work requiring contact with the corpse was done by closely related caste brothers of the deceased man. Throughout

---

(1982b:82). Refusal of food is thus appropriate behavior for the dying, but no less appropriate are the concerted attempts by the living to encourage consumption.

23. According to villagers, there were two explanations for this practice (a pan-Hindu one; see, for examples, Bouillier 1979; Kane 1953; Stevenson 1971). They said that a raised bed was suspended midway between heaven and earth and was therefore not a good place to be—presumably because of its indeterminate nature. They added that earth herself is pure. As Marriott has suggested (personal communication), the "purity" of earth in this context may derive from its capacity to process dead, decayed, polluted matter and revitalize it.

these preparations women spent their time wailing in the company of Mangilal's stricken widow. Their loud mourning cries faded at intervals into muted comforting phrases but resumed at full pitch with each new arrival.

After washing the body the men dressed it in an undergarment over which the shroud was wrapped. When the bamboo bier was ready it was spread with special *dob* grass and raw cotton. Then the corpse, borne outside by the same men who had washed and dressed it, was laid upon the bier. A skein of cotton thread was used to tie the body firmly to the bier. Round balls of barley flour (called *lāḍūs* by some informants and *piṇḍa*s by others) were placed at the dead man's hands and feet. Then *gulāl,* a red powder which figures significantly in Holi-play[24] and on the occasions of long-term festive departures, was applied liberally to the corpse.

Now six men lifted the bier, and the procession moved into the village streets, all present chanting the usual funeral *mantra*: "Rām Nām satya hai, satya bolyā gata hai" (The Name Ram is truth, truth spoken is passage). One man carried a pot containing fire to ignite the funeral pyre.[25]

The procession halted briefly in front of the Temple of Four-Arms in order that the deceased might give his final prostration to God. It then proceeded toward the cremation ground (*shamshān*), stopping only once more en route about halfway between the edge of village settlements and the burning ground itself, at the shrine of Middle-Dwelling Bhairuji. Here the barley-flour balls were offered to Bhairuji, along with *dhūp,* by one of the Vaishnav Sadhu neighbors of the deceased.

The bier with all its attendants then passed directly on to the burning ground. An oxcart filled with wood and dried cow-dung

24. Miller has suggested (personal communication) that Ghatiyali's Holi is funereal in several ways—among these, of course, the grand burning itself that recalls cremation. Another strong hint is given during the parade that carries Holi's *"badshāh"* (Muslim ruler, a part actually played by a poor Brahman), crowned with manure and thorns and garlanded with shoes, around the village streets. The funeral *mantra,* "Rām Nām satya hai," is chanted at this time.

25. Women do not attend cremations, and the following account is based on personal communcations from Miller as well as on his tapes and photographs that were logged by assistants actually present at the event. I stayed with the women, and the narrative returns to my own observations when the men return from Four-Arms. I did defy sex-role limitations by attending one adult's cremation at the burning-ground and one child's cremation in the jungle during my stay in Ghatiyali, so I also have my own general impressions.

cakes for the fire had preceded them there, and the men rapidly unloaded it. One member of the party of mourners started a small fire fueled with some of the cow-dung cakes. Others began arranging more cakes on the ground as the foundation for the pyre. Wood was laid on top of the dung cakes.

A single clockwise circumambulation of the pyre was performed by the pallbearers,[26] who carried the bier with head toward the village. Then the body was removed from the bier and placed on the pyre. Little by little the shroud was peeled down and the corpse simultaneously covered with cow-dung cakes. Finally the shroud was freed (an untouchable would receive it) and the nude body fully covered with fuel. A coconut was then placed over the stomach, and it also was concealed beneath dung, followed by a final, overall layer of wood.

The only son of the deceased man, Ladu Ram, was the first to ignite the pyre. He was openly weeping at this moment of final severance. Several other members of the party also touched the pyre in different places with grass torches, and then most of the men sat quietly to one side to wait out the burning.

One of the village's three chief ritual-expert Brahmans, using a spoon attached to a long bamboo pole in order to avoid the flames, performed the *havan,* or "fire sacrifice," a term usually used in Ghatiyali to refer to pourings of *ghī* into a sacrificial fire. Equipped with a manual entitled "Last Rites Fire Sacrifice Performance," this presiding Brahman read Sanskrit verses to accompany each oblation. At the appropriate moment, chief mourner Ladu Ram, using the same long-handled spoon, poured *ghī* into the skull after it had cracked in the heat. To accompany this oblation a nephew to the deceased added items from a *pūjā* tray: sesame, barley, and a special incense powder.

Throughout these events the rest of the group of men had remained seated. Now they rose, and one by one each tossed a piece of cow dung on the fire and made the respectful hand gesture called *pranām,* palms pressed together in final salutation to Mangilal. Last of all, Ladu Ram, again weeping, gave this respect to the mortal remains of his father.

26. See Das 1977 and Parry 1982b for treatment of the precremation dead as pure and auspicious—thus the circumambulation in an auspicious direction before the skull cracks and the soul escapes, leaving a polluted carcass.

All now returned to the village and bathed together at a large step-well. They then continued as a group to the Temple of Four-Arms, where the priest sprinkled them with the deity's "foot-nectar," and returned to the house of mourning. From there the men dispersed to their respective homes.

Meanwhile some women had been busy thoroughly cleaning the room where the death took place and freshly plastering the floor with cow-dung paste. At a spot near the place of death they strewed flour and covered it with an inverted brass tray. After the men returned, they looked beneath the tray to see if a symbol had appeared in the flour. This symbol may be read as an indication of a future condition for the deceased person's spirit. An OM, for example, as was found in this case, suggests a good outcome—heaven or even release. Other shapes may signify certain animal births.

The women also bathed, in the house, and, wailing all the way, went to the Temple of Four-Arms for their own *caraṇāmṛt*. During the remainder of the day there was a constant flow of visitors at the house of the deceased. Women squatted inside with the widow, comforting her and one another with talk of God and fate and with caresses on the face. As before, with each visitor's arrival new howls of grief broke out, then slowly and gradually subsided. Men sat on the curb just outside the widow's room, conversing in subdued fashion. Again and again the sequence of events that led to Mangilal's death was rehearsed, and the efforts made by son and daughter-in-law to preserve the old man's life were stressed.

Over the next two days similar activities continued, with more relatives collecting from other villages. The subject of conversation turned from the context of death to the practical business at hand, the funeral feast. Lists were made for invitations to be delivered; necessary quantities of supplies were calculated and arrangements made to purchase them.

The issue of whether Ladu Ram should go now to Hardwar with his father's bones, or wait for his mother's death and take both parents together, was much debated. In making his choice to go now, Ladu Ram was clearly acting under some pressure from his caste society. They advised an immediate pilgrimage, both for the sake of increased prestige deriving from the display of willingness to spend cash for the sake of duty and to avoid legal difficulties with the funeral feast (a consideration whose logic will be explicated shortly). However, Ladu Ram eventually claimed that he went only to give peace of mind to his mother so that she might herself go to rest knowing her husband's bones had been sunk in the Ganges. In stressing the service of his still-living parent, Ladu Ram was claiming higher motivational sensibilities according to villagers' consensus on what is truly moral. To serve living parents was universally considered more difficult and more worthwhile than to treat dead parents' bones to rituals (see chapter 4).

Gathering and Sinking Flowers

Ganges pilgrimage to sink the bones of the dead is the subject of chapter 4. Here a schematic outline of the main events will suffice to place them within the processual context of the twelve days immediately following a death. This summary must be prefaced with a note of explanation concerning the inclusion of Hardwar pilgrimage within this period. The practice is in fact of quite recent institution and continues to increase in popularity, for reasons both of expediency and of "fashion."

Before modern transportation, it was of course not even possible to make a round trip to and from Hardwar between the death of a relative and the twelfth-day feast. In those days, bones were regularly saved in the house for years, sometimes generations, until a company from the village decided to make the slow and arduous journey to the Ganges. Today postponed submersion of bones is still a perfectly acceptable practice. However, according to villagers (this may well be a folk interpretation of the legal situation), the Indian government has instituted legislation which makes a distinction between feasts given for "social" reasons and those given for "religious" ones. The former are forbidden, the latter permitted (although I'm told that the police still have to be bribed not to take note of them). Therefore, if an important elder family member dies and one wants to legitimize a lavish funeral feast (considered "social"), one hurries to Hardwar, brings home Ganges water, and calls the event Celebration of Ganga (considered "religious"). Thus, death and pilgrimage, which have always been closely associated, are now even more intimately linked.

Early in the morning of the third day following Mangilal's death, Ladu Ram, accompanied by a Barber, returned to the cremation ground.[27] There they gathered up a few pieces of bone—never called *haddi* ("bone") but always *phūl* ("flowers")—from the site of Mangilal's pyre.[28] The other remnants of the cremation were sprinkled with water and pushed into a mound; a small amount of rice was cooked on the spot and offered, along with warm milk, as *dhūp* to the spirit of the deceased. The flowers were then placed in a small clay pot with a lid. Ladu Ram and the Barber proceeded together to the water reservoir, where they bathed themselves; Ladu Ram also "gave a bath" to the flowers. He then returned to his house with the pot, which was carefully placed in a protected and pure wall niche. Such pots with flowers remain in the house until a family member undertakes a Ganges pilgrimage. In Ladu Ram's case, he embarked the next day, but sometimes years may pass before the flowers are moved.

On the morning of the fourth day Ladu Ram prepared for his pilgrimage to Hardwar, having taken the decision to go at the last minute after several vacillations. While his father's brother's daughter sewed a new, red-cloth drawstring bag in which to carry the flowers, Ladu Ram washed them in milk and gave them offerings of *ghī* and cooked food. He prostrated himself before the remains of his father's mortal body as he had before the living man during his father's lifetime. Ladu Ram then carefully placed the flowers in the new bag, but did not yet put it around his neck. First he sat to eat the traditional prepilgrimage meal of cracked wheat cooked in raw-sugar syrup with a little white rice on top, bread with plenty of *ghī,* and a sauce of hot buttermilk, spiced and thickened with chickpea flour. This special rich food, having been previously offered to the spirit of the deceased and other household deities, was eaten by family members as a kind of *prasād.*

After his repast and a thorough washing, Ladu Ram secured the bag of flowers on a string around his neck. Carrying his father's walking stick in his hand, he went first to his neighborhood temple (Sitaramji) to bow before the deities. Accompanied by a small circle of friends and relations, he then proceeded to the place of Path Mother, the presiding goddess of Ganges pilgrimage.

27. The gathering of Mangilal's flowers was witnessed by neither Miller nor me. My description of the actions at the cremation ground on the third day is based on Ladu Ram's own brief account and a detailed, generalized report on these actions kindly supplied by Bhoju Gujar.

28. Prescriptively, the bones that should be gathered are from five parts of the body: the head, both hands, both feet. But, to quote my informant, "No one pays attention to this. Any large bone, like a rib, or any strong big bone is taken."

There the same Brahman who had officiated at the cremation ground helped Ladu Ram to perform the worship of Path Mother. After this he went directly to the bus stand, in time to catch the mid-morning run to Devali, a point of connection. He would have made this pilgrimage alone, but was not averse to having me and my current assistant, Vajendra, as company. The latter was a Brahman of a different subcaste who had a long-standing relationship to Ladu Ram as a "younger brother."

Reaching Hardwar by mid-afternoon of the following day, we picked our way through the clamor of touts at the station and went by tonga to the *dharmashālā* (pilgrims' rest house) kept by *paṇḍā*s (pilgrims' priests) serving our area of Rajasthan. The next morning Ladu Ram had his head shaved in the *dharmashālā,* and the efficient *paṇḍā*s took him through the essential rituals at the river: "worship of Ganges" (*Gangā pūjā*) and "offerings of flour balls" (*piṇḍadān*). He placed his father's flowers in the river along with the walking stick and obtained a sealed pot of Ganges water, white-sugar-candy *prasād* supplied by the *paṇḍā*s, and a handful of cheap *mālā*s (prayer-bead necklaces) made of yellow straw. He also purchased two new walking sticks. That and a pledge of grain to the *paṇḍā* (to be collected later in the village) finished his business at Hardwar.

Before returning home, however, Ladu Ram needed to bathe and worship in Pushkar (pan-Hindu crossing place in Ajmer district, Rajasthan), a detour obligatory for all returning pilgrims from our area. There he gave one of the two new walking sticks to a beggar. This, he explained, made the stick, given in Mangilal's name, available to Mangilal's spirit in heaven.[29]

On reaching Ghatiyali, Ladu Ram should have repeated Path Mother's worship, but he omitted this step, proceeding directly to his house after bowing perfunctorily at the Temple of Four-Arms.

29. This demonstrates the chronological and locational confusion involved in performing pilgrimage to sink flowers within the twelve days following death. During this period the ghost-soul of a deceased person is expected to linger near its former home. Ritual immersion of remains in the Ganges and flour-ball offerings made at a crossing place, however, are supposed to remove the lingering presence of a dead person's spirit from his home forever. The modern fashion of precipitate pilgrimage seems not to affect the traditional notion of a twelve-day period of lingering for all spirits. Rather, the results of this pilgrimage might be said to have a delayed action, going into effect only after the normal time lapse, when the usual rites in the village are complete. On the return lap of his pilgrimage, Ladu Ram thought of his father's spirit as having reached heaven, but back in Ghatiyali he treated it just as he would have if the Hardwar journey had not been accomplished.

Once home, he stored the sealed pot of Ganges water in his domestic shrine, where it remained until the eve of the twelfth day.

Preparations for the Twelfth Day

The "ghost-soul" (*pret-ātmā*) of a deceased person is thought to remain about the house until the ritual intended to unite it with the lineage ancestors is performed on the morning of the twelfth day. It is that ritual which puts an end to death pollution, thus allowing the household once again to offer food to others, dramatized by the grand funeral feast. However, the achievement of that final purification is not abrupt. Rather, it follows a serial course of bathings, shavings, anointings, and housecleanings, beginning, as was described above, on the day of cremation.

The tenth day is appointed for the collective shaving of head, beard, and underarms—required of all close male relations to the deceased, including young boys. This took place near a public step-well and was followed by bathing. The women also bathed collectively, at another well, vigorously washing their hair and putting on clean clothes. The women's bath was followed by an informal ritual in which each took a piece of special green grass in her hands, poured a water-offering to the deceased onto the ground, and threw the grass on the same spot. Retrieving these grasses, the women returned to the house of the deceased, where they placed them in the lap of a little girl who was Mangilal's classificatory granddaughter. Finally an oil lamp was lit and placed, along with the grasses and a pitcher of water, in the household drinking-water niche.[30]

For several days Ladu Ram's wife, aided by several of her own female relatives as well as her husband's assembled kinswomen, had been occupied with the vast labor of cleaning wheat and split chickpeas for the funeral feast. On the tenth day, cooking pits were dug in an unused animal corral belonging to Ladu Ram's neighbors. Soon the sweet-maker would arrive from the nearby town of Sawar and the great work of preparing "five treats" (*pānc pakvān*)[31]—the most elaborate, extravagant, and prestigious feast

30. I failed to elicit an explanation for this tradition, but it seems to replicate the life-out-of-death theme that is, here as in many other contexts, engineered by females with greenery and water. See the last section of this chapter and chapter 4 for the development of this theme.

31. Although one or two items may vary, these five treats are usually enumerated as (1) *pūṛīs,* small, round, fried wheat breads; (2) *sev,* very hotly seasoned,

menu—would commence. Thus most peoples' attention during the eleventh day was focused on the cooking pits. Men and women alike took long turns rolling out an endless collection of *pūṛīs*, flat bread to be deep fried.

That night, the eve of the twelfth day, witnessed several important actions. A *jāgaraṇ* (all-night singing of *bhajans*), such as precedes almost any significant occasion, was kept by the men in the neighborhood temple of Sitaramji. Before the *bhajan* party began to sing, Ladu Ram went to worship briefly in front of the temple icons. He then placed before them both the sealed brass pot of Ganges water which he had brought from his recent pilgrimage to Hardwar and a much older brass pot which once had contained Ganges water or now contained a small amount (a fact never made clear to me). People said that this pot might just miraculously be filled in the night, and it was used as a source of "Ganges water" in the next morning's ritual. Shortly after this, the men's singing began.

Women also gathered to sing in the house across the street from Ladu Ram's. Around 9:00 or 10:00 P.M., well after dark, a select group of them slipped off without fanfare to go and give an "invitation" to the Bhairuji at the place of Path Mother. They performed a very brief worship there by lamplight, without the help of a pandit. Most important, they applied multicolored string (*lacchā*) to Path Mother and her Bhairu, known as Ganga's Bhairu. They then tied more string on the left wrist of each woman who planned to carry Ganges water on her head during the next day's Celebration of Ganga. String is a common ritual-participation marker and protective device; this string was also a special sign of the wearer's desire to be possessed by the deity Ganga's Bhairu. She is supposed to invite him silently within her heart at this time.

The Twelfth Day

The twelfth day had four major movements: (1) uniting flour balls (*sapiṇḍī shrāddha kriyā*, "act of faithful offerings [resulting in]

---

crisp-fried, chickpea-flour batter in noodle-shaped pieces; (3) *būndī* or *nukatī*, small, extremely sugary, fried chickpea-flour droplets (these three constitute the minimal funeral feast); (4) *cakkī* or *besan kī barfī*, squares of a sweet, turmeric-yellowed chickpea-flour dough; (5) either *jalebī*, squeezed-out pretzel-shaped treats made of white flour first fried and then soaked in sugar syrup, or *mākhan-bharā* (full-of-butter), a white-flour preparation with a crumbly texture, somewhat sweet and, as its name implies, very rich.

shared *piṇḍas*"); (2) Celebration of Ganga (*Gangotsav*); (3) turban-tying (*sāfā bandānā* or *pagrī bandhan kī pūjā*); (4) the feast (*nuktā*). This day witnessed the culmination of mortuary rites for Ladu Ram's father, ideally effecting a final transformation of the spirit of the deceased man from "ghost" (*pret*) to "ancestor" (*pitṛ*), thus removing his presence from the house and simultaneously lifting the strictures of death pollution. The twelfth-day rituals also effect the combined legal and ritual assumption by the surviving son of the position of head of the family and heir to the property and community status of the deceased.

Uniting Flour Balls. The *sapiṇḍī shrāddha kriyā,* as it was called in Ghatiyali, more commonly known as *sapiṇḍikaraṇa* or *samyojana shrāddha,* has been frequently and thoroughly described and discussed by historians of religion and by anthropologists.[32] As its various names indicate, this ritual act involves "faithful offerings" (*sharāddha*) to the spirits of the dead, which effect a "joining" (*samyojana*) resulting in the recipients becoming "sharers of *piṇḍas*" (*sapiṇḍī*).[33] By uniting the *piṇḍa* belonging to the ghost-soul with the *piṇḍa*s of the ancestors, this ritual, if successful, unites the spirit of a recently deceased person with previous generations in his patrilineage, and thus with the ancestors in ancestor-realm.[34] It

32. For descriptions and analyses of this ritual, see, for example: Bouillier 1979:151–152; Kane 1953:520–525; Knipe 1977; O'Flaherty 1980a; Pandey 1969:267; Parry 1982b:84–85; Stevenson 1971.

33. According to Monier-Williams's dictionary (1899), *sapiṇḍa* means having the same *piṇḍa, sa* being a prefix expressing junction, conjunction, possession, similarity, and equality. To be made *sapiṇḍa,* then, refers not only to the merging of *piṇḍas* in this ritual but to the fact that the three generations of ancestors, with whom the spirit of the deceased has now been ritually united, will share future *piṇḍa* offerings from their descendants.

34. According to Kane (1953:523), the *sapiṇḍī karaṇa* rite is actually composed of two kinds of *shrāddha,* for the ancestors and for the ghost-soul, which accounts for the repetitious nature of the offerings and the general density of the event. While its heart is the merging of the *piṇḍas*—the transformation of four into three—Kane tells us that the moment in which the actual union is accomplished is *not* when the balls are reformed but when the *dakshiṇā,* or honorarium, is made to the presiding Brahman. It is that act which marks the disappearance of the ghost (1953:523). Stevenson's ethnographic account, on the other hand, places particular emphasis on the perfect seamless modeling of the three new *piṇḍas* (1971:186). Kane's comment is consistent, however, with several recent arguments in anthropological literature on Hindu death. Parry (1980), Raheja (1985), and Zeitlyn (1986) have all pointed to the importance of gifting in removing the inauspiciousness of death, and to the ambivalent nature and function of Brahmans as the recipients of these marked gifts. Raheja most specifically and convincingly details and demonstrates how inauspiciousness is removed along with *dān.*

thereby effectively removes the spirit of the deceased from his former home's environs to another realm and neutralizes his specific nature, simultaneously transforming a hovering threat of inauspicious interference into part of a peaceable and generalized source of potential benevolence.

All this is achieved through a substantial merging: the *piṇḍa* representing the ghost-soul is sliced into thirds, and each piece is then carefully moulded by the chief mourner into one of the three *piṇḍa*s representing the three previous generations of ancestors. This merging blends the identity of the deceased into the class identity of ancestors. In striking contrast to the spirits of the lingering dead, who become household deities and for whose pacification it is critical to know their particular identities, ancestors appear to shed all personal traits and are prescriptively worshipped only as a class.

A summary of salient features in the two-hour *sapiṇḍī shrāddha kriyā* held for Mangilal Mishra follows:[35]

1. The ritual was performed in the room where Mangilal died.
2. Assembled paraphernalia included thirteen brass pots called *ghaṛiyā̃* and a large brass tray on which ritual items were laid, including barley, a coconut, raw sugar, rice, sesame seed, betel nut, red powder (*rolī* or *kumkum*), turmeric powder, a clay oil lamp, cotton wicks, multicolored string, *dob* grass, a skein of unspun cotton yarn, sacred threads (*janeū*), and a small bottle of honey. There were also a number of leaf cups—some empty and some containing *ghī,* milk, and yogurt—and a brass platter with wheat flour for making the *piṇḍa*s.
3. The same Brahman who had performed the cremation rites oversaw all the preparations of materials.
4. The Nāīn (female barber) came and prepared the *guhālī̃,* a rectangular area on the floor painted with thin cow-dung paste on which the ritual action would take place. Such a purified space is required for most household rituals, even those performed only by women and without Sanskritic components.
5. Salagramji,[36] a rounded pebble-like stone which is accepted

35. Sources for the following description of this complex ritual are my own notes; my Brahman research assistant's notes: Miller's photographs, color slides, and tape recordings; and retrospective discussions of all of these with participants in, and observers of, the event.

36. Madan reports that, according to some of his informants, "Hindus worship the black stone *sāligrāma,* the symbol of Visnu, the preserver, which resembles the

as a form of Vishnu, was brought from the Sitaramji temple next door by its priest, one of Ladu Ram's Vaishnav Sadhu neighbors.

6. Ladu Ram's wife's brother fetched back from the same temple the unsealed, old pot of Ganges water which Ladu Ram had placed there the previous night. (The sealed Ganges water which Ladu Ram brought from his recent pilgrimage was not to be opened until the Celebration of Ganga.)

7. The pandit softened the *dob* grass in water and knotted several strands each into two kinds of rings called *cit* and *pavitrī*.[37]

8. Ladu Ram put on one of the grass rings called *pavitrī;* he also placed one on his waistband, one underneath his low stool, and one under the tray containing flour for the *piṇḍa*s.

9. Some Ganges water was added to turmeric and "Ganges clay" to make a paste, power-charged and purifying, that was used to mark Ladu Ram's forehead.

10. Ladu Ram, instructed by the ritual-expert Brahman, made a dough out of the wheat flour to which milk, sesame, honey, yogurt, and, lastly, sufficient water were added. Once the dough was formed he divided it into two parts. Out of one half he fashioned three round balls; of the other half he made a single, slightly elongated oval shape which informants consistently described as having the "form of a coconut."[38] The coconut-shaped *piṇḍa* represented the newly deceased person; the three round *piṇḍa*s, identical to one another, were for the three generations of ancestors: grandfather, great-grandfather, great-great-grandfather.

11. A series of respectful offerings were made to each of the four *piṇḍa*s in turn. These were followed by libations to the three

---

womb in shape" because "the mother is the feeder and preserver of the foetus" (1982:230). The presence of Salagramji at the rite of *sapiṇḍī shrāddha* would then provide yet another link between death and birth. For a different perspective on *sālagrāmas* and their worship among South Indian Srivaisnavas, see Narayanan 1985:58–61.

37. The use and meaning of these grass rings is somewhat obscure. According to Monier-Williams 1899, *cit* means thought, intellect, spirit, soul. The primary Sanskrit meaning of *pavitra* is "means of purification," such as a filter or a strainer, and from this a prayer or *mantra* to purify the mind. Monier-Williams also mentions, as does the *RSK,* a ring of grass worn on the fourth finger on particular ceremonial occasions.

38. Coconuts in Hindu thought seem to represent persons in numerous ways. The most obvious, perhaps, is the use of the word *khopaṛā* for "coconut" and "head" or "skull," particularly in slang expressions. When women seek progeny at shrines in Rajasthan, the priest will fill their "pouch" with a coconut wrapped in red cloth, clearly representing the desired child (see chapter 3).

ancestor-*piṇḍa*s only, upon which the grass rings called *pavitrī* had been placed.

12. Four clean leaves were then set out and on each leaf one *cit* ring was placed. The four *cit* then received the same honors and offerings as had just been given to the three *piṇḍa*s with *pavitrī,* as well as sacred threads.

13. At about this time the focus of the ritual turned temporarily away from the *piṇḍa*s to the thirteen pots and the apportionment of feast food. The thirteen pots were wrapped three times round in a clockwise direction with white thread, and Ladu Ram gave them offerings of water and incense. Seven plates of "five treats" were set atop the pots. Another plate was offered to Salagramji, and four more were set out "for the four *pitṛ.*" One "special portion," to be eaten by a caste-fellow in the dead man's name, was also prepared.

14. Ladu Ram announced the "gift" (*dān*) he would make to the Brahman performing the ritual.

15. Now came the climax: Ladu Ram cut the coconut-shaped *piṇḍa* into three equal parts. Then he made a small dent in the first part and added *ghī*, sugar, and sesame, after which he kneaded it into one of the round ancestor-*piṇḍa*s, which he carefully rounded once more and replaced on its leaf. He repeated this with the other two pieces and the other two *piṇḍa*s, and then made further offerings to the three newly formed balls representing the three generations of ancestors with which the spirit of his deceased father was now fully united.

16. Ladu Ram then distributed the four plates of food "for the four *pitṛ.*" The distribution for these is supposed to be this: one to the crows, one to a dog, one to a cow, and one to a guest, but as no guest will eat a plate dedicated to a *piṇḍa,* this last one was also fed to a cow.[39] The "special portion," however, also called the *ant-kāl thālī,* or "plate of the time of death," will be eaten without any protest by a member of the deceased person's caste.

17. Men and women of Ladu Ram's lineage and extended family made resolutions over the new *piṇḍa*s to give certain amounts

39. The plates "for the four *pitṛ*" were originally dedicated to the four *piṇḍa*s, before their transformation into three. This is the only time when four rather than three *pitṛ* are mentioned, and the most likely explanation seems to be that it is a polite way of including the *pret,* who is, in any case, soon to become a *pitṛ*. The explanation for not eating the plates of food, which was explicitly that they belonged to *piṇḍa*s, would support this interpretation.

of money to the Brahman (again called *dān*), and prostrated themselves to the ancestors.

18. Ladu Ram made final salutations to the three *piṇḍa*s. Then he put them back in the platter along with all the other paraphernalia of this elaborate ritual.

19. Seven women of the deceased's caste came to take the thirteen pots and perform the action called *ghaṛiyā̃ ḍholnā* "spilling out pots."[40] They emptied them of water outside the room and turned them upside down (later to be repossessed by various owners, as most were borrowed). Each woman took home one of the seven portions of food which had been set upon the pots. The priest of Sitaramji took Salagramji's plate.

20. Ladu Ram now left the house and went to the water reservoir, where he emptied the contents of the platter filled with ritual debris. He then bathed himself, and this bath marked the end of his death pollution.

21. The women at home ceremonially wept and cleansed the room where the ritual had taken place. Then one who was literate wrote on the floor in white paste: "Rām Nām satya hai," the same *mantra* that was chanted on the way to the cremation ground. When Ladu Ram returned from his bath the women wept once more, but this was the last mournful moment of the day.

Celebration of Ganga. After a brief rest, Ladu Ram, his household and helpers prepared for the Celebration of Ganga (see also chapter 4). Led by the village drummer, a procession moved from Ladu Ram's home to the place of Path Mother. Five women were carrying on their heads covered vessels of well water with which the precious Ganges water would be mixed. Ladu Ram himself carried the still-sealed brass pot of Ganges water inside his pilgrim's basket, and the second of the two walking sticks that he had purchased in Hardwar. The women sang songs of Ganges Mother and Path Mother as they walked slowly along.

After performing the worship of Path Mother and her Bhairu,[41] the priest pierced the sealed pot of Ganges water with a penknife.

40. Why are thirteen pots spilled out on the twelfth day? It might be a condensation of acts once performed daily following a death and now inserted into the *sapiṇḍī* process. Elsewhere in Rajasthan (and India) *piṇḍadān* and feasts are offered on the thirteenth rather than the twelfth day following a death. Women's association with pots of water—and this is the only part they play during the elaborate *piṇḍa*-joining ritual—should once more be noted.

First offering a few sprinkles onto the icons of Path Mother and Bhairuji, he then poured a small amount of the precious liquid into each of the five vessels already filled with well water. At this time Ladu Ram's wife took some green mung beans from the *pūjā* tray and placed them in a fold of her wrap, indicative of her desire to bear another child (she had no son and only one daughter).

Each of the women who had invited Bhairuji on the previous night received a covered vessel on her head, containing the admixture of well with Ganges water. Balancing the vessels, these women circumambulated Path Mother's shrine, as did Ladu Ram, who had taken the original brass pot of Ganges water on his head. The crowd now watched expectantly to see if Bhairuji would possess the women carrying vessels. Usually, two or three of the maximum number of five women will become possessed. On the occasion of Ladu Ram's Celebration of Ganga for his father there were two who did. Once a woman is clearly possessed, onlookers refer to her as *bhāv,* and I will also use the term, as it is succinct and untranslatable. It means the "feeling" of the deity, which is at the same time all that controls the possessed person, who remains without consciousness of her own during the episode, and without recall afterwards.[42]

The *bhāv* holds her vessel with both hands clasped tightly over the lid, in sharp contrast to the normal village woman's effortless style of balancing full open pots while her hands swing free. Sometimes a *bhāv* goes backwards, sometimes she leaves the road and strays into a field, sometimes she plants herself in one place with legs somewhat apart and sways from side to side, making small rhythmic breathing sounds. Her face is completely hidden by her wrap. The water in the vessel sloshes out when she sways violently. I was told many times that a sure test of the *bhāv*'s "truth" (that is, whether it was really Ganga's Bhairu, rather than somebody's *pattar* or *jhūjhārjī* or only "intoxication" caused by the drumbeat) was that, despite the loss of water proved by the

41. Chapter 4 presents some detailed descriptions of rituals performed at Path Mother's shrine.

42. In the Rajasthani language the word *bhāv* is highly polyvalent. The *RSK* gives over fifty glosses for it, ranging from "any thing, situation or being's existence" through condition, devotion, belief, imagination, idea, mind, love, honor, soul, birth, root, etc. Meaning 46 comes closest to the usage here: "Some deity's presence being experienced in the body, according to which there are manifestations of moving limbs and sounds." *Bhāv* in the context of shrine pilgrimage will be discussed in chapter 3.

woman's soaked clothing, the vessel would remain brimful. However, when the *bhāv* reaches the house at last the vessel is invariably taken immediately into an inner room and no one announces or displays its content.

The *bhāv*'s seemingly erratic but in fact patterned and predictable behavior is encouraged by female onlookers with several special songs of Bhairuji (see chapter 4). All these songs are sung with great enthusiasm and a distinctive rhythm. The possessed women themselves do not sing or utter any intelligible sounds. The celebrant has various prescribed techniques he may use to coax the *bhāv* to move in the desired direction (toward his home). Ladu Ram swept the road in front of one of the *bhāv*s with the end of his turban, an extremely humbling act generally performed only for a deity's vehicle during a temple procession. He prostrated himself and offered *dhūp*. The ultimate recourse, however, is to stand before the *bhāv,* split open a coconut, and lure her to move by placing pieces of coconut in her "pouch" (*johlī,* a receptacle formed in the front of her wrap which, before becoming possessed, she arranged by tying it in a special way).[43]

Coconut pieces, offered by Ladu Ram, did get one *bhāv* to proceed on her way; but more than once, after moving forward a short distance, she stopped again, and all of the worshipful acts had to be repeated. When she reached the house at last, on the threshhold, just as the vessel was lifted from her head, she fainted and sank to the ground. Women pulled and carried her inside, loosened her clothing, fanned her, and put a little water in her mouth. As commonly happens with this type of possession, she revived within a few minutes and saw at once to tidying her disheveled clothes and hair.

If there are several *bhāv* to coax along, close relations assist the celebrant by also bowing, sweeping, and offering coconut pieces. Depending on the number and capriciousness of the *bhāv,* it may take some time to get all the Ganges water safely into the house. On this occasion, since only two women had become possessed, both *bhāv* had arrived and been relieved of their precious burdens by about 2:30 P.M. It was possible now to begin serving the feast, although there was still other ritual work to be accomplished.

43. There are clear implications and explicit evidences that this act may be interpreted as impregnating. These will be discussed in chapter 4.

Turban-tying. The confirmation of Ladu Ram's assumption of Mangilal's position as property owner and head of household took place in the same neighborhood temple, Sitaramji, where the previous night's *bhajan* party had sung. The *pūjā* ingredients featured Mangilal's old turban and several auspicious signs of prosperity such as piles of grain and coins. A fairly simple worship directed in part at the turban itself was conducted by the brother of the exhausted pandit who had overseen the morning's events. Next all the men present—mostly Ladu Ram's caste-brothers—with arms raised above their own heads passed Mangilal's old turban from hand to hand until it had moved full circle and been touched by each of them. In this way they affirmed both their respect for the deceased and their recognition of his son's succession. Now Ladu Ram could tie his father's turban on his own head.

Most of the participants then filed up to wind gaudy new gift turbans over the original, rather shabby old one, and some contributed token amounts of cash. Occasionally Ladu Ram politely but firmly rejected the gifts of inappropriate donors, including his Vaishnav Sadhu neighbor who, as a servant of god, was classified as a permanent receiver and an unsuitable giver.

As each turban was wound on top of the previous one, Ladu Ram's head swelled enormously and a little grotesquely. Wearing the multiple turbans, and accompanied by a small group led by the drummer, he walked to the Raghunathji temple.[44] There he removed all the turbans in a single lump and placed them upside down before the shrine. He made an offering, received a forehead mark and *caraṇāmṛt* from the priest, and replaced the giant multiple turban on his head. On returning to his own house Ladu Ram bowed to his household deities, including his "clan goddess" (referred to as Diyāṛī Mā̃ or *kuladevī*), and then to his actual mother, the deceased's widow. He received from her blessings and loving caresses, as well as two rupees and a coconut. His wife then pressed the feet and lower legs of all women in the caste older than herself and received in turn their blessings.

Feast and Conclusion. The twelfth day now reached its fit finale as the invited guests consumed an apparently endless supply of

44. This temple is located in the Brahman neighborhood, where Ladu Ram did not live but where he had caste affiliation.

"five treats." Guests of honor, including the elected head of the village council (*sārpanc*), the tax collector (*paṭvārī*), the two Americans, and various other dignitaries, were served in elevation on the roof and thus were able to survey the impressive scene. Ladu Ram, exhausted but far from able to rest yet, circulated among the company making sure everyone was eating well and distributing sips of the Ganges water mixture brought home by the *bhāv*s. Many deities had been invited, worshipped, and fed this day as guests; human guests, whom villagers always say should be treated as deities, were also well served and fed at the funeral feast.

Reaction to and aftermath of an ideal demise like Mangilal's are orchestrated harmoniously within village and caste communities. Coming gently at a ripened age, Mangilal's death contrasts starkly with sudden deaths that are violent, accidental, untimely. When the pregnant niece of one of my research assistants lost her schoolmaster husband in a senseless mishap due to a malfunctioning kerosene stove and a flammable synthetic shirt, reactions approached violence and terror, and the aftermath was disordered and discordant. Although the funeral did not take place in Ghatiyali, I heard enough about it to absorb an impression of an ambience altogether different from that surrounding the rites for Ladu Ram's father. And the scene at the home of the pregnant widow was one of overwhelming, uncontrolled grief.

There was little doubt among Mangilal's family about the fate of his spirit: having received the proper rites it would be at peace and would participate in vague ancestral beneficence. Sometimes it was spoken of as having reached "heaven" (*svargalok*). For the spirit of the schoolmaster who died on the verge of fulfilling the householder's great aim of parenthood, and who died, moreover, involved in the trivial, worldly act of preparing tea, there was little hope that the rituals would have such a successful outcome. His surviving relations might well anticipate his lingering claim on their attentions and resources. He might cause afflictions and ultimately demand and receive worship as a *jhūjhārjī*.

In Mangilal's case the group easily refilled its ranks; the son replaced the father and was recognized by his associates as doing so. This smooth transition is again in clear contrast to the aftermath of the young schoolteacher's sudden death. The wife's side, in Ghatiyali, soon became totally estranged from the husband's and spoke bitterly and aggressively of future lawsuits. The husband's family, against the stated wishes of the wife's family and obviously unrighteously, had precipitately tied the turban on a younger brother of the deceased without waiting to see if the unborn child would be a son and heir, which indeed he turned out to be.

These contrasts between appropriate and inappropriate deaths further exemplify the contrasts between the funeral materials just presented and the special handling of spirits of the dead previously detailed. However, from a broader point of view, the spirits of the dead who linger about their former homes and those of the dead who have been smoothly joined with the ancestors are both still trapped in the perpetual cosmic flux of rebirth and redeath (*samsāra*). Neither may be said to have received release, although ancestral spirits may be said to have "peace" (*shānti*). *Pattar, jhūjhār,* and ancestors alike remain connected, if to different degrees, with the places and relations of their previous births, and most will inevitably experience further births and deaths. In order to be truly released, human beings, if not themselves renouncers, must at least understand the world as renouncers do, and a major component of this understanding is the perishability of bonds between kin. I next describe a cult largely concerned with rites that claim to grant complete release to the spirits of dead initiates. Its expressed ideology wholly denigrates family and social positions and attachments, yet it weaves its own net of binding obligations.

"What is the Connection?" The Meaning of Death in *Nirguṇa Bhajan*s and the Hard-won Immortality of King Gopi Cand

The materials to be presented and analyzed here have their source among a caste of householder Naths. While these materials represent a set of attitudes toward the process of dying and the fact of death which differ in several ways from those characterized earlier, nonetheless they compose an alternative response to the same issues. Naths certainly share other villagers' familiarity with and fear of lingering spirits of the unhappy dead. They also share a strong concern for sustaining the continuity of families and community, both by ensuring the peaceful condition of ancestors and by conducting funeral feasts and succession ceremonies such as those just described for a Brahman group.

However, in their rituals, songs, and legends Naths also maintain a vital concept of total release and how to get it. Their ideas seem to derive in part from the heritage of early Nath yogis, whom they claim as their lineage ancestors, as well as from the related tradition of the medieval Hindi Sants—devotional poets and gurus. Nath lore also contains clear references to the terrifying afterworld cosmology detailed in the *Garuda Purana*.[45] An awareness of all these strands of Hindu tradition is important in approaching the teachings of Ghatiyali's Naths. However, most of the explanations and interpretations advanced here were supplied by villagers.

Ghatiyali's Naths have the status of a middle-level, clean, farming caste; they are landowners and successful agriculturalists. However, they are also known to possess special powers, chief among these being the ability to ease scorpion stings and ward off locusts. Naths often act as gurus to the peasant castes: sometimes they also serve as priests in Mahadev temples and other shrines. The practice which, of all traits, distinguishes and separates Naths from other clean castes in the village is the way they dispose of their dead. They, and the small population of Vaishnav Sadhus who also have an ascetic ancestry, are the only castes in Ghatiyali that do not cremate their adult dead but instead practice burial. This practice is certainly connected with the prescriptive burial of all Hindu world-renouncers who are the legendary forebears of both these castes.[46]

The Naths' cemetery is quite close to their homes, in this contrasting with the common cremation ground and the Vaishnav

45. For Naths, see Briggs 1973; Dasgupta 1969:191–225; and for Naths in relation to Sants, see Vaudeville 1974:81–119. For Sants, see D. Gold 1987; Hess 1983a; Schomer and McLeod, eds. 1987; Vaudeville 1974. The *Garuda Purana* exists in both a full form concerning many different topics and a short "handbook," which condenses all it has to say about death. The latter is popularly known in its Hindi version and often read aloud and discussed in Rajasthani villages, including Ghatiyali. I have consulted two poor translations of the unabridged Purana (*Garuda Purana* 1968; *Garuda Purana* 1979), an old but better translation of the condensed form which includes the Sanskrit text (*Garuda Purana* 1911), and a Hindi pamphlet version of the condensed form (*Garuda Purana* n.d.).

46. See Das 1977, *Garuda Purana* 1911:96, and Parry 1982b for noncremation of renouncers. For a religio-historical approach to the problem of householders with an ascetic heritage, see Gold and Gold 1984; and for the ethnography of a similar Nepalese case, see Bouillier 1979.

Sadhu burial spot—both located well away from settled land. It is not far from a frequently traversed path, leading up to the Nath-tended shrine of Jaipalji. As this burial ground is confined to a very limited space, it is not unusual for old remains—most often bones and silver jewelry—to be uncovered during a new interment. This does not seem to disgust or upset the Naths, who told me about it as an occurrence of somewhat startling interest. It does, however, as I learned, disgust and upset other villagers when they stop to think about it.

Although a Nath research assistant had been working for me for several months, and I had become acquainted with most of his family, I was unaware of the Nath caste's peculiarities regarding their dead until the opportunity (I thought) arose for me to attend an all-night *bhajan* sing on the eve of the twelfth-day feast for a deceased Nath woman. Until then I had freely attended many such affairs in Ghatiyali and neighboring villages with full approbation from my circle of acquaintances. Now, I was surprised to find my Rajput and Brahman friends, and even my low-caste Damami companion, all sternly admonishing me not to go.

The gist of their objections, as far as I could make out, lay in the Naths' ghoulish practice of keeping their dead in the earth near their homes. Behind this was an innuendo that I would not only be behaving in an inappropriate fashion but courting personal danger if I went. They chided me as hopelessly stubborn and ignorant to continue to insist on going. With rare self-assertion I did persist in my intention to accompany my Nath friends to their *jāgaraṇ,* but was ultimately blocked by the Nath guru himself, who had come from another village to conduct the night's ritual.

For the Naths and other members of the *panth* over which they preside, the eleventh night's event is not just a preliminary *bhajan* sing, as was the one for Ladu Ram's father. It is rather an esoteric rite, replacing the twelfth morning's flour-ball offerings. To be present at this event is to be automatically implicated in the cult, and one's own death is then affected.

Although I was ready to be initiated into this *panth,* whatever it might involve, as my Nath friends assured me that by doing so I would receive superior teachings, the guru refused. He argued that I was a foreigner and that I would presumably return to, and eventually die in, my own land. If I were a member of the *panth* it would be utterly essential that these same secret rites that I now so desired to observe be performed on my behalf. But in America who would do this work? And if it were not done, my unsatisfied spirit would become a wandering ghost, tormenting my son and perhaps even afflicting the guru, who by initiating me would take upon himself in part the burden of my release or nonrelease.

I offered to arrange to have a wire sent him upon my demise, whenever it took place, and promised that my family would defray the expenses of the ritual by a transfer of dollars, but he astutely placed no stock in such long-distance assurances and, to the satisfaction of all but my Nath friends, flatly barred me from attending the night's event. My tape recorder, being soulless, was allowed to be present, however, and it went on to several subsequent such gatherings, so that I obtained a large collection of *bhajans* sung on these occasions. These are *bhajans* of the *nirguṇa* genre[47]—that is, they praise the Lord without qualities, or Niranjan Nirākār ("Spotless Shapeless"), as villagers frequently call that mode of the supreme deity. Their subject is often death.

Before seeing what these texts reveal of the Nath response to mortality, we may glimpse a bit more of their performance context. Fortunately, one of the *bhajans* supplies these fragments of a mystery. There is danger to both teller and hearer in divulging the Nath cult's eleventh night's mysteries to noninitiates, and I never pressed my reticent associates beyond their self-imposed limits of candor.

The ritual of the eleventh night is referred to as a *pūjā* to Hing Laj Ma. This exotic goddess, whose original shrine and icon are located in the hills of Pakistan,[48] is worshipped by the Nath cultists only in the form of a flame. The flame is produced in a large cotton wick kept burning all night long—according to infor-

47. The division of *bhakti* into *nirguṇa* and *saguṇa* traditions (devotion to the Lord without qualities versus devotion to the Lord with qualities) is reflected in two basic types of *bhajans* performed in Ghatiyali. Whereas *nirguṇa bhajans* such as those we'll examine here speak of the supreme power as the Master or the Guru or the Name of Ram, *saguṇa bhajans* describe the gods—Radha and Krishna, Shiva and Parvati, Ram Devji, Dev Naryanji, Tejaji, and so forth—and relate mythological episodes concerning them. There is in the village a kind of rivalry between *nirguṇa* and *saguṇa bhajan* parties, and most persons, whether singing participants or not, will express a definite preference for one or the other.

48. Hing Laj Ma, also spelled Hingalash Ma, is noted in the *RSK* as a special icon of Durga, whose shrine is located north of Karachi in the hills of Sindh and Baluchistan, on the Hingol River. This place is numbered among the Shakta *pīṭhas*—those sites where bodily parts of Shiva's consort Sati, dismembered by the other gods in order to halt Shiva's destructive dance of grief over her demise, fell

mants, who couldn't resist boasting about this chief miracle of their secret rites—in a jar of pure water. Unfed by *ghī* or oil, the flame is sustained through the power of "verbal spells" (*mantra-tantra*) wielded by the guru.

The first four verses of the descriptive *bhajan* as well as its refrain speak of this magical and powerful flame, inviting the assembled company to view it, praise it, and have *darshan* of the saints within it. Verse 4 mentions the three great Hindu gods as praising this flame alone. The fifth verse summons up the founding Nath gurus, Gorakh and Macchindar (Matsyendra), who are spoken of as the first kindlers of the flame.

Bhajan of Hing Laj Ma Puja

[Refrain] The flame begins to burn, O Sants, take darshan;
The flame begins to burn, O Sants, take darshan now.

[1] All beings in the world should contemplate this flame,
recite its name,
Praise this flame's great power.

[2] A Sant lit this flame; in it are many Sants,
You see them, you see many in this flame.
It's filled with diamonds and with precious pearls:
remember this!

[3] From this flame the imperceptible is made: remember it,
In this flame will man be made: remember only this!
In this flame are palaces and beauty.

[4] Yes, great seers and munis praise it alone,
The greatest seers and munis praise it alone,
See Brahma, Vishnu, and Mahesh praise it alone.

---

to earth (Sircar 1973:5–7). The place of Hing Laj is the *pīṭha* where fell the goddess's *brahmarandhra,* or "the suture on top of the skull"—that is, the fontanel. Significantly, in relation to Ghatiyali's rite, one Hindi source describes the shrine as a place where "from the earth a flame spontaneously keeps emerging" (Gupta 1979:277–278; I thank K. Erndl for this reference and for other tidbits of information on Hing Laj). Crooke notes that Hing Laj's shrine is the site of an "oracular well" (1924:716), but he does not mention a flame. Tod tells of the Rathor king "Oogra-Prebhoo" making a pilgrimage to the shrine of "Hinglaz Chandel, who, pleased with the severity of his penance, caused a sword to ascend from the fountain, with which he conquered the southern countries" (1978, 2:5)—testifying to early Rajasthani affiliations with the goddess. However, no one in Ghatiyali could tell me any stories about Hing Laj Ma, and to the extent of my knowledge, she is worshipped there only in the context of the Nath-led death rites described in this chapter.

[5] Gorakh Yogi lit the flame.
Remembering Macchindar, Gorakh lit the flame,
O Crazy Ones,
See and recognize the true word, mingle flame in flame.

The next three verses refer more directly to some other practices of the *panth,* which my informants were reluctant to clarify. The vine of verse 6, they said, indicates the linking of hands by all participants, but they offered no explanation of the "one sound"—perhaps a *mantra* recited in unison. Another set of actions involving hands and sound is elaborated in verse 7. Verse 8 refers by name to the presiding guru (the one who excluded me) and his special work of making an elaborate grain design called *pāṭ*.[49] The last verse is the customary "signature" (*chāp*) in which the composer identifies himself.

Bhajan of Hing Laj Ma Puja (continued)

[6] Form the true word's vine; hold singleness,
Yes, form this true word's vine and hold one sound.
Seize the essence of all Sants, and having understood, recite the name.

[7] Three persons place their hands and hold a single sound,
Yes, three persons place their hands and hold a single sound, release their hands, move back, recite the name.

[8] Goradhan Nath is my guru, yes Goradhan Nath is my guru,
He made the *pāṭ* fully, that true guru, deeply,
Yes, he made the *pāṭ* fully, that true guru, deeply.

[9] Ugma Nath said, "Pay attention to this thing."
The flame begins to burn, O Sants, take darshan.
Praise it, O Crazy Ones, remember the guru.
The flame begins to burn, O Sants, take darshan.
Victory to Hing Laj Ma!

49. The use of *pāṭ* for ritual grain design is not found among the word's many dictionary meanings. These definitions do include "throne" and "square stool such as may serve for a seat of honor." In this context, then, the *pāṭ* may be understood as a throne of sorts for the goddess whose presence in the form of a flame graces the ritual occasion. In and around Ghatiyali, *pāṭs* are usually constructed by Brahman experts in conjunction with fire oblations. I never saw the *pāṭ* of Hing Laj Ma Puja, but my Nath informants considered it to be one of the most powerful and secret aspects of the rite.

As was mentioned above, this ritual of the eleventh eve is said to replace for Naths or other members of their *panth* the twelfth-day flour-ball offerings made among most castes to unite the spirit of a deceased person with his lineage ancestors. It was pointed out to me by my cautionary friends that what other castes do in the daytime the Naths were doing at night, and what other castes did in open rooms, the Naths did behind closed doors and shutters.

Beyond such evident distinctions, a contrast in purposes was also striking: whereas the rite of joining flour balls promised to make the spirit of the deceased an ancestor and give him peace, Hing Laj Ma Puja was said to grant immediate *moksha,* or release (although the meaning of release to villagers is in certain contexts not greatly distinguished from the meaning of peace; see chapter 4). The rites were truly equivalent in one important sense, however: if they were neglected or poorly performed, the result would be a lingering and unhappy ghost.

The Naths' integration into village society, despite their esoteric calling, is well demonstrated by their twelfth-day funeral feast, which seems no different from those of any other caste and may, moreover, be heartily eaten by the same persons who shuddered at the very thought of Hing Laj Ma Puja. Despite the secrecy surrounding the ritual, there is no similar taboo on the *bhajans* (witness the permitted tape recording). Naths are members of other mixed-caste *nirguṇa bhajan* parties that sing in many homes and temples around the village and area. Thus, excepting the "flame" *bhajan* just cited, their repertoire may be known by noninitiates and performed on any appropriately serious occasion. Non-Naths, especially persons from the peasant castes, are frequently initiated into the cult of Hing Laj Ma.

Although *nirguṇa bhajans* are regarded as "deep" and said to be understood only by those who can perceive their "essential meaning" (*bhāvārth*), they are by no means wholly inaccessible to general village society. They are often subjects for public "discussions of knowledge" (*gyān carcā*). The point of view which they take is not only appreciated for its wisdom but shared to a certain extent, although recognized as difficult to act upon. The Naths also propagate their cult importantly through the oral text of the story of King Gopi Cand, to be discussed below. This tale is traditionally sung yearly in the village by a Nath bard who moves from neighborhood to neighborhood as he strums, sings, and interprets the legend. Most villagers are thus familiar with that basic story, too.

The texts of nine *bhajans* will be presented and discussed here.[50] They were selected from a collection recorded on three different occasions of night-long Hing Laj Ma Puja and are numbered for analytic purposes only. There appears to be no given order for the *bhajans* sung at a single session; the leader of the singing, a role that will switch several times in the course of one session, simply follows his inclinations.

The title of this section, "What Is the Connection?" is taken from the refrain of a *bhajan* criticizing the infatuation of the *man,*[51] the egoistic human mind, that tarries frivolously and dangerously in the illusory world of appearances and attachments.

Nirguna Bhajan 1

[Refrain] The mind flowers, turns in the world,
What is the connection?
Yes, what kind of connection remains in the world?
What is the connection?

[1] The mother says, the son is mine;
the sister says, the brother is mine, O Brothers!
The brother says, this arm[52] is mine;
the woman says, this man is mine.

[2] Grabbing her stomach, the mother cries;
the brother grabs his arm.
"Alas," swaying, swaying the woman cries;
the swan-soul goes alone.

[3] Yes, four persons meet and decide to take the wooden bier,
Hey Ram, to take the wooden bier.
On all four corners fire is lit,
blown into flame like Holi.

50. Rajasthani *nirguṇa bhajans* are not easily translated. Their style is highly elliptical and their content full of allusions ranging from Hindu myth to tantric yoga and metaphors based on local agricultural, botanical, and zoological lore. I have attempted to stay as close as possible to the original text and literal meanings without totally sacrificing resonance and rhythm. I do supply missing words, without clumsy bracketing, when English grammar demands them.

51. This *bhajan* and several others to follow have the signature of Kabir. Hess sums up "what Kabir means by 'mind'" by citing from his verse: "The mind is a nervous thief, / the mind is a pure cheat. / The ruin of sages, men and gods, / the mind has a hundred thousand gates" (1983b:326).

52. "Arm" here means "brother" because a brother, I was told, is like your other arm.

[4] Bones burn like wood, hair burns like grass,
O Brothers, that hair burns like grass.
The gold-like body burns up; no one comes back.

[5] The woman of the house begins to search,
searching she turns in all four directions;
O Brothers, searching she turns in all four directions.

According to informants, the meaning of this final verse is that the deceased's wife is already looking for a new man. Such heartlessness effectively represents the cruel transience of human bonds.

On two occasions when the meaning of this particular *bhajan* was our subject of discussion, my two Nath assistants summed up its message with the phrase "Nobody is anyone's." They then went on to drive home the point by relating the following story (retold in my own words from notes, since it was never recorded):

At the time [hundreds of years ago] when the Cave Baba was alive [see chapter 1] there lived in our village a well-to-do merchant's son who, although a married householder, would daily attend discussions of knowledge held by that renouncer-guru. This merchant's son listened carefully but refused to accept the guru's statement that, in the world of flux, "nobody is anyone's."

"Look," the merchant's son would argue, "my mother and father are certainly mine; my wife is certainly mine. I know this."

The guru wanted to show him the truth, so he suggested an experiment. He gave the young merchant an herb that would make him appear dead while actually retaining consciousness. Then he could easily see and hear what his family might do.

The merchant's son ate the herb and appeared suddenly to sicken and die. His family began to weep and mourn for him loudly. Then the Cave Baba appeared at their house and told them to stop weeping because he knew a remedy to restore their son's life. They simply needed to wash the corpse with water, and collect the water in a vessel. If one person among them would voluntarily drink it, the son would be alive and well again, but that person who drank the water would die in his place.

The family was quite taken aback. The father said, "But I have my business to attend and I must take care of it." The mother said, "I have my husband here and it would be sinful to leave him." The dead man's wife said, "If his own birth-givers won't sacrifice their lives for him, why should I who am the daughter of another house?"

> The guru then offered to drink the water and the father enthusiastically encouraged him to do this, vowing to perform a big sacrifice and build a fine temple in his memory. The father was more than willing to spend money but would hardly give his own life to redeem his son's.
>
> When the guru duly revived the merchant's son, the young man decided to renounce the world and follow the Cave Baba's detached life-style, readily agreeing with his master's adage that "nobody is anyone's."

This story makes explicit the view, hinted at by the *bhajan,* that the snares of familial attachments are in fact doubly false. That is, they are not merely ephemeral in the face of time and mortality, but also hypocritical façades even for their limited duration. The fact of death's parting loved ones, then, denotes not a painful severance of real bonds but an unmasking of false ones. This is a viewpoint which, of course, might make the renunciation of such bonds easier. It is not consistently held in the Nath teachings, however. The story of King Gopi Cand, as we shall see later, finds the ties of husband to wife and brother to sister far more serious and difficult to loosen.

The next text, which interestingly enough bears the signature of Gopi Cand and his companion-in-renunciation, his mother's brother Bharatri, shows little sympathy for the foolish mortal who has chosen to enjoy earthly comforts and neglect good works. When his time comes he can only beg futilely for a reprieve and then, made aware of the consequences of his wrongly spent life, for a second chance. This *bhajan* is composed of dialogues, with interspersed narration, and is one of the few I have seen that lacks a repeated refrain. To make it clearer, I have parenthetically identified the speakers as [S] "Swan-soul" (*hamsā*);[53] [D] "Death's messengers" (*yamadūt* in Hindi but here, in colloquial Rajasthani, *jam bhāīṛā*); [L] "the Lord" (*sāībā,* an Urdu term); [N] narrator.

53. The equation of the human soul with the majestic wild goose (*hamsā*)—which some translators, myself included, prefer to call swan—goes back to Sanskrit. Rajasthani villagers like to contrast the rare swan, who eats only pearls, showing both discrimination and nonviolence, with the common heron, equally white and graceful in appearance, whose attention is fixed on hunting and consuming fish.

Nirguna Bhajan 2

[D] Let's go, Brother, let's go, Swan-soul, your Lord is calling you.

[S] Stay where you are, Death's messengers, I will meet a bit with my mother.

[N] Death's army comes and stands there and will shut the ten doors of the body.
Brother, at the final time death comes, death comes to take you.
What's the use of herbal potions? Not one medicine does the trick.

[S] Stay where you are, Death's messengers, I will meet a bit with my household.

[N] But the Swan-soul had to comply, and left, and the household began to cry.
Those who had served him went crazy, those whose master was taken away.
He went to the Ruby Square and God asked him more than once:

[L] Hey, Swan-soul, what did you eat and what did you wear and what dharma did you perform?

[S] O Lord, I ate well, I dressed well, but I did not an iota of dharma.

[L] Well, throw him into a deep pit of insects and let loose crows on his head!

[S] Lord, heed me now, give me a chance, I will build your temple.
Lord, I had no floating gourd,[54] no means to swim.
Lord, heed me now, give me a chance, I will do your dharma.
Lord, I will build your temple in the center of my heart.

Gopi Cand and Bharatri spoke: Don't anyone become immortal. We became immortal and suffered sorrow and just keep wandering in circles.

54. Gourds are used by ascetics as water carriers, so this line might imply a regret for not having become a renouncer. My informants, however, simply said that the meaning of gourd here was "devotion" (*bhakti*).

There is an ambiguity in this signature line which will become clearer when Gopi Cand's story is summarized. It appears that the ceaseless wandering of the two great immortals is almost as agonizing a fate as that awaiting the hapless, improvident human at death. The body of the text, however, contains a straightforward message: to live with your attention fixed on worldly pleasures will condemn you, not just to death's painful separation as so vividly sketched in Bhajan 1, but to further retribution. This *bhajan* thus takes seriously the *Garuda Purana*'s prognosis of hell and tortures for those who don't practice *dharma* in their lifetimes.

It is worth mentioning that these images and ideas sometimes receive different twists in popular interpretation. A very old Loda woman, a neighbor of mine in the village, was lying down in her home when she *saw* (not in a dream) Death's messengers ready to take her. She asked them to wait until her scattered children could be called to come to her side, and in fact, they obliged her. She died peacefully a few days later, having greeted and blessed her loved ones once more. People related this as an altogether satisfactory outcome. Thus, what Bhajan 2 clearly intends to depict as futile and vain—the attempt to stay death's advent—in her case became a worthwhile ploy.

Such a death steeped in familial affection is hardly what the *bhajans* mean to promote. Moreover, in the *Garuda Purana,* which is the major source for *yamadūt* lore, the fearful harbingers above all personify the ruthlessness of mortality, sweeping away with their clubs and pitiless punishments all wordly-oriented delusions of life. They hardly seem the types to show compassion for a dying peasant woman's sentimental longing. The message of the *Garuda Purana,* in fact, is very like the combined messages of Bhajans 1 and 2, as a line cited by Wendy O'Flaherty reveals: "His relatives turn away and depart, but *dharma* follows him" (*Garuda Purana uttara khaṇḍa* 2.22–25, cited by O'Flaherty 1980a:16).

Bhajans 1 and 2 both devalue family ties, but while Bhajan 1 treats death as total annihilation, Bhajan 2 pictures the judgment, suffering, and remorse that may come to a person's soul after disembodiment. While Bhajan 2 suggests temple-building as a way of improving one's lot after death, Bhajan 3 presents a quite different remedy. This is the remedy of the Lord, or the guru,[55] who

55. D. Gold (1987; 1988) gives illuminating religio-historical analyses of the joined identity of Lord and guru in the Hindi Sant tradition.

opposes Yama's dominion over man's fate, and who is to be approached with inner devotion rather than external demonstrations.

Nirguna Bhajan 3

[Introductory couplet]:
If you meet the true guru, it's good;
If not, then they say, you become a ghost of the jungle,
or a piece of livestock.

[Refrain] Take, O my life, that day's remedy.
Take, O mankind, that day's remedy.
That day's remedy, Madman, that day's remedy,
Take, O mankind, that day's remedy.
Take, O my life, that day's remedy.

[1] King Yama came to take the person who didn't keep faith, the person who didn't keep faith.
They beat him with clubs and took out his life; eyes flowed water.

[2] Yes, a beautiful woman's in the house, and mother, son, and brother; mother, son, and brother.
Goods mined from the world don't go along; neither does a body.

[3] When King Death threw me in the pit my body lost its wits, my body lost its wits.
Grant me now a chance, I won't forget you, Raghuvir.[56]

[4] Break from all, join the guru, keep a share in bhajan.
Then Yama's force won't move you, says the slave Kabir.

Bhajan 3 evokes the saving power of the Lord or guru as antidote for the terrors, loneliness, and helplessness of the journey after death, which in *Garuda Purana* cosmology includes the crossing of a frightening river and numerous pits for torture.[57] Bhajan 4 is more of a praise song for the bright hope offered by total devotion to that saving power. However, it also proclaims a triumph over Death's messengers.

56. Raghuvir is a name of Rama.
57. For a vivid and frightening description of the "way of Yama," the cruelty of the messengers, the "terribly horrible Vaitarani River, which when seen inspires misery, of which even an account arouses fear" (*Garuda Purana* 1911:11), see chapters 1 and 2 of *Garuda Purana* (1911, English) or *Garuda Purana* (n.d., Hindi).

Nirguna Bhajan 4

[Refrain] Four Vedas, eighteen Puranas cannot describe the bounds
of Brahm.
Formless essential current.
Has neither parts nor shape.

[1] Within this jug a breathing creature speaks.
Yes, this road is not apparent.
The ocean of Ram's Name is full,
This ocean is limitless.

[2] The Lord is unto himself
With neither lineage nor family.
Turn the prayer-beads of his name
And Death's messengers can't fall upon you.

[3] The Bright One's sheet is colorfast,
His sheet is threadless,
His sheet wraps up the world of flux.
Those who forget do not have faith.

[4] Kabir says, the guru's song is deep,
In singing there's some real worth.
From his lotus feet like this,
Those without glory got darshan.

Bhajan 5 is a plea for the guru's help in crossing over. While *pār utāro* ("take me across") is a very common petition in Hindi verse,[58] that which is to be crossed in this *bhajan* is called *badh* ("slaughter") rather than the more common ocean or whirlpool. However, water, whirlpools, and shores also figure in the imagery of the verses. With its juxtaposition of mass slaughter and human frailty to the guru's potent truth, this *bhajan* sums up the themes of 3 and 4, laying equal stress on the terror of man's plight and the access to release found only in the guru's world.

Nirguna Bhajan 5

[Refrain] Guru-god, take me across this slaughter,
Hey, take me across this slaughter, Guruji,
take me across this slaughter.
Guru-giver, take me across this slaughter.

58. Wadley in her analysis of divine powers and deliverances in North Indian village Hinduism, discusses several different kinds of crossings and the role of God as boatman (1975:91–125).

[1] The deep water's boundless, the shore unseen,
Moved by the wind, waves are up to my head.

[2] Our manners ruled by unknown fate,
our hearts give no support.
Within the body an arrow struck, guru, savior.

[3] Crocodiles of delusion follow behind,
In the fearful whirpool fallen.
Beaten with clubs, the breathing creature's dwelling is left deserted.

[4] Know the guru's word is true,
O soul, seize the Name's true goodness.

[5] Kabir says, listen, Brother Sadhus,
Easily reach the shore.

The remaining four texts are a little more obscure, but it is worth attempting to penetrate their allusions, for each contributes a unique piece to the puzzle of death's meaning for singers and hearers of *nirguṇa bhajans*. Bhajan 6 is one of the most popular in the somber *nirguṇa* repertoire, probably because it uses such homely metaphors to evoke the terror, mystery, and "remorse" (*pachtāy* of mortality. The refrain is a mournful plea addressed, according to my Nath informants, by a human "consciousness" (*suratā*) to the "Swan-soul" (*hamsā*). *Suratā,* as they explained it, belongs to a single life span. But the Swan-soul is *ātmā* ("soul" or "self"), also called *ātmā rūpī jīv* ("spirit in the form of a soul"), undying and ultimately one with God.

In the verses the finite consciousness speaks to the perishable body (*sharīr*) with which it was once knit together; but without the animating Master, the Swan-soul, both consciousness (*suratā*) and body (*sharīr*) remain useless. The Swan-soul is thus the swimmer, eater, lighter, sleeper of verses 2, 3, 4, and 5, and also the Master of the refrain. My informants were not able to say precisely what the regretful water, plate, oil, and cot represented. One might speculate that, as media for the embodied person's acts, they are the illusory world itself, which becomes bereft and desolate without human vitality.

This is a *bhajan* not of hope for salvation but of nostalgic mourning for the loss of life. Its portrayal of very ordinary human acts, unfulfilled because cut short by death, may move singers and listeners to tears. Recorded on two occasions, it was given two different signatures, once of Kabir and once of Gorakh, testifying to the intertwining of the Sant and Nath traditions in these Rajasthani folk renditions.

Nirguna Bhajan 6

[Refrain] Master of my body, Swan-soul,
Don't leave me on this earth and go.
Master of my body, Swan-soul,
Now's the time of separation, and we'll not meet again.

[1] On the riverbank, Brother, stands a tree,
whose tiny leaves are falling.
Listen, tree of the forest, Swan-soul,
Now's the time of separation, and we'll not meet again.[59]

[2] You were the tank and I the shore.
The water remained remorseful,
The swimmer went away.

[3] Swan-soul Brother, you were rice and I was mung.
We were boiled up in one pot,
But the plate remained remorseful, Swan-soul,
The eater went away.

[4] Swan-soul Brother, you were the lamp and I the wick.
But the oil was left remorseful, Swan-soul,
The lighter went away.

[5] Swan-soul Brother, you were the quilt and I the mattress.
But the cot remained remorseful, Swan-soul,
The sleeper went away.

[6a] Swan-soul Brother, your slave Kabir petitions the guru.
Please listen, devotees, servants of the self,
Now's the time of separation, and we'll not meet again.

[6b] O Swan-soul, Guru Gorakh Yogi spoke, who dwells in
paradise:
Swan-soul, don't leave me in this bad land and go.
Now's the time of separation, and we'll not meet again.

Bhajan 7 is of interest because it effectively links the horror of death with that of birth. Thus it juxtaposes the folly of carelessly

59. This refrain is one of the few lines from a Rajasthani *bhajan* with Kabir's signature for which a close parallel can be found in an English critical edition of Kabir's poetry: "The leaves as they fall are crying: / 'Listen, O great Tree, Lord of the forest! / Parted from thee, we shall never meet again, / far away from thee we shall fall!'" (Vaudeville 1974:252).

losing a "diamond-birth"—that is, a chance for salvation—with the benighted situation of the hapless unborn in the womb. A lost birth leads to more birth, and man is shown trapped in the circular forgetfulness of life cycles, of *saṃsāra*. If the Hindu view often likens death to birth in a positive sense, here we find that birth may be like death in a negative sense, entailing loss, diminishment, lapse of memory, and abandonment even by God. This attitude toward the evils of the womb is clear in classical texts as well. O'Flaherty, referring to the *Brahma Purana,* notes that "the *jīva* becomes deluded as the embryo develops inside the womb" (1980a:20).

Nirguna Bhajan 7

[Refrain] Given a diamond-birth, you lost it, Man,
    lost a diamond-birth.
In all three life-stages defeated,
What use taking warning now?
Given a diamond-birth, you lost it, Man,
    lost a diamond-birth.

[1] Hung inverted in the womb's darkness, Ram's Name,
Head and arms below, feet up, feet up, feet up.
No Lord to cross you over the ocean of experience,
    your name forgotten.

[2] You'll be, Ram's Name, withdrawn from the womb,
The promise belongs to others.
Your heart will harden: forgotten Ram's Name,
    Ram's Name, Ram's Name, Ram's Name.
Forgotten will be Ram's Name, forgotten in wandering.

[3] Childhood lost in play and laughter,
Betrothed in marriage a full-grown youth;
When old age came, besieged by affairs of
    "yours" and "mine," death devouring came.
For the sake of profit stored abundant goods,
    but lost the source.

[4] Yes, the saints crossed over and attained paradise,
    attained the essential spot.
Sings Purush Ram, remember, Brother,
Ram's Name, Ram's Name, Ram's Name, Ram's Name,
Ram's Name.
With open palms you'll go.

Bhajans 8 and 9 are very similar in theme. Men (and other conscious actors, such as deities and demons) are vain and self-aggrandizing fools without knowledge of reality. Both the natural images in Bhajan 8, such as pretty parrots and raucous monkeys, and the mythological examples in Bhajan 9, such as the demonic brutes Bhasamasur, Harnakush, Ravana, and Bali,[60] serve to make the same point: man is deluded and ultimately defeated by a profound and grasping selfishness whose source is ignorance.

Bhajan 8 is one of the few oral texts which I collected in the village in which the word "release" (*mukti*) actually appears. Significanctly, it takes an approach to this human aim identical with the most common one elicited in the course of many interviews on the subject: such matters are in God's hands.

Nirguna Bhajan 8

[Refrain] Release won't be had for the asking, Brothers.
Release will stay in the Master's hand,
And the mad bee's stuck in the mind.

[1] If gold is sown, Brothers, it sprouts,
and diamonds, pearls, and rubies grow.

[2] Crazy man's deluded, O my guru,
Just a paper marionette whose string's
in the hands of the buzzing bee;[61]
He dances as he's made to dance.

[3] Green-feathered parrot sits on the Campa Tree's branch.
The parrot grasps the branch;
It doesn't grasp the essential root.

60. Bhasamasur, or "Ash-Demon," had a magic armband which gave him great power because anything over which he circled his arm was reduced to ash. In the popular story referred to here, Parvati, in order to rid herself of his unwanted attentions, asks him to dance for her. He circles his arm over his own head—a common dance movement—and thus thoughtlessly destroys himself. King Harnakush (Sanskrit Hiranyakasipu; see Dimmitt and van Buitenen 1978:76–79) was the wicked father of the great Vishnu-devotee known as Bhakt Prahlad. The king had an unrealistic sense of invulnerability, having received a boon listing numerous conditions under which he could not be killed. Neither man nor beast, for example, could kill him, nor could he be harmed by any weapon. In response to Prahlad's devotion, Vishnu took his Man-Lion (Narasimha) incarnation in order to destroy the demon-king, using claws. Ravana's lust for Sita is of course part of the main plot of the epic *Ramayana*. The story of the two brothers—evil Bali who attempted to supplant good Sugriv—is also part of *Ramayana* lore.

61. "Buzzing bee" (*bhãvarjī* in Rajasthani or *bhramar* in Hindi) has specific connotations in the *saguṇa* devotional poetry of Lord Krishna. It is the name by which

[4] Monkeys spoiled the garden, Brother,
Obtuse fools spoiled society;
Greedy covetous ones spoiled devotion,
Just as idiots mix dust in saffron.

[5] Kabir Das petitions his guru:
Listen, please, Creator!

Although Bhajan 9, like Bhajan 8, demonstrates and derides weakness and folly, it also takes the popular view that preordained "fate" (*karam*) is the real victor over unenlightened, egotistic aspiration. Like the prelude to Bhajan 3, it predicts the disastrous result of becoming a ghost after a misspent lifetime. Here not even a saving guru is called upon, so that the postulated bad ending appears inevitable. However, the signature verse states that, if these stories are not heeded, then there will be no passage—implying perhaps a slight hope of learning from bad examples and thus improving.

Nirguna Bhajan 9

[Refrain] Beaten by fate he'll be, without understanding.
Beaten by fate he'll be; at his last moment
what will he do?
He'll die and become a ghost;
Without wisdom after death he'll be a ghost,
without understanding.

[1] Whoever tries to gather the bees' food won't eat,
they won't let him eat.
The robber gets robbed,
without understanding.

[2] Ash-Demon, he did this, chased after Parvati,
Took his charmed armband and burned himself up,
without wit.

Krishna's cowherd girl lovers, the Gopis, refer to Uddhav—the messenger Krishna sends to persuade them to give up their passion for his person and to practice a restrained yoga instead. Here it would seem that the bee represents the futilely busy mind (*man*); perhaps this is some underlying reflection of the Gopis' scorn for Uddhav, who intellectualizes and does not appreciate their ecstatic devotional awareness. (In the end, however, he is converted to *bhakti*.) See Hawley 1984:47–49; 98–114 for Sur Das's bee songs; see also McGregor 1973 for a translation of Nand Das's "Uddhav's message," a verse dialogue between the Gopis and Uddhav.

[3] Harnakush was king, he gave sorrow to Prahlad;
Without weapons Prahlad had him killed,
without understanding.

[4] Ravana was proud, he carried off Sita,
But his whole lineage was made to weep,
without understanding.

[5] Bali had strength and stole Sugriv's house,
But Rama came whose arrow struck him,
without wit.

[6] Atma Ram says, without understanding these stories,
there will be no passage.
So many men were destroyed,
without understanding.

The *bhajans* all depict death—more or less bluntly (as in 1) or poetically (as in 6)—beginning with irreversible disembodiment. Their portrayal of the human condition after death, however, varies quite widely. Some speak of the road to hell in the clutches of Death's messengers (2, 3, 5) and the subsequent judgments passed on a soul by God or King Death according to its past works (2, 3); one vividly portrays agonizing rebirth in the dark womb (7); two mention the evil fate of a wandering ghost (3, 9); several stress shelter or salvation offered by the formless Lord or the true guru (3, 4, 5) with a faint hope of release, through grace, for foolish man (8); some seem simply to view death in terms of its finality (1, 6). How then may these texts be shown to demonstrate a response to death which is in some way both unique and internally consistent? And if such a response is found here, how does it relate to those set forth earlier in this chapter?

All the Nath *nirguṇa bhajans* (and I include in this generalization the thirty-five or so in my collection, not just these nine), whatever outcome they envision for the spirit of mortal man, consistently stress an absence of connection between that spirit and living persons. Death must be recognized, in their view, as a final removal from all that was known and cherished in life. This is a lesson that decidedly countervails the presuppositions underlying the kind of continuing relations between living persons and the spirits of their dead kin which we have already seen are maintained in village expectations and practice. The *bhajans* never speak of ancestors. If they speak of lingering ghosts, then it is as *bhūt,* the unidentified jungly villains, rather than as domesticated *pattar* and *jhūjhār.* Both the establishment of *jhūjhār* and *pattar* as household deities to be subsequently worshipped, coddled, and consulted, and the making of faithful offerings to benevolent ancestral spirits, sustain the very connection that these Nath *bhajans* repeatedly assert is broken forever by death.

In the *bhajans* the soul or self (most often *ātmā* or *hamsā*) is of central importance and its fate is ultimately a solitary one. They assert that the only help available to it comes, not from rituals or gifts dedicated by the living, but from the compassionate guru or Lord without qualities. That powerful aid can be summoned only when the soul takes cognizance of its aloneness: hence the *bhajans*' repeated harping on the ephemeral nature of affective attachments in the world of mortality. Some of these texts, indeed, appear as the obverse of songs for *pattar,* reciting a litany of close kin relations only to deride them as unreliable rather than to make them a charm for comfort and security. However, the *bhajans*' very insistent derision of familial bonds is a sign of those bonds' depth and the difficulty of uprooting them from the heart. The knowledge that "nobody is anyone's" comes hard to man.

The story of King Gopi Cand, like *nirguṇa bhajans* part of the Nath caste's lore, is an object lesson in just how slow and painful the renunciation of family bonds may be when it is attempted within life instead of at the inexorable disjuncture of death. The story as sung and told by Madhu Nath of Ghatiyali is a very long praise-song rich in detail but also highly repetitive.[62] Here I shall give only its bare skeleton, but even this outline demonstrates a more sympathetic approach to emotional attachments in the world than the *bhajans*' harsh didacticism offers.

62. The following discussion of Gopi Cand draws only on the Rajasthani oral tradition as I recorded it in Ghatiyali; hence the peculiar spelling of names such as Bharatri, who is more commonly known as Bharthari. The tale was completed in four recording sessions and fills approximately fifteen hours of tape and 465 legal-size pages of *devanāgarī* transcription. The story, however, is not as long as this bulk would suggest, because the bard first sings each segment in Marwari—the more literary western Rajasthani language—and then gives an explanation in the local language which essentially repeats everything he has just sung, embellished with colloquial color. King Gopi Cand is a widely known figure throughout North India. Hansen (1986) reports on Gopi Cand traditions in popular Hindi theater. The Panjabi rendition of his story may be found in Temple 1962, 2:1–77; a Bengali version in Grierson 1878, 1885. The Bengali tale is discussed in Dasgupta 1969:224–228 and Mahapatra 1971.

Gopi Cand was born only because his mother, after much fruitless worship and good works, exacted a boon from Shiva, despite the fact that there was no son written in her fate. Through Shiva's mediation she is granted the *loan* of a son from among the disciples of the accomplished yogi Jalindarnath. The terms of this loan, however, require that, after ruling his kingdom for only twelve years, her son be returned to the Nath guru as a disciple. From this difficult renunciation, Gopi Cand would receive an immortal body-soul (*kāyā*). If, however, he should refuse to sever his ties to the world, he will die (literally, "time will eat him").

The story opens with the arrival of the appointed year for Gopi Cand to give up his kingdom. Jalindarnath duly arrives on the outskirts of town and makes camp, along with his numerous disciples, in the palace gardens. He sends a message to Gopi Cand's mother that he has come to reclaim his loaned disciple, who was in fact his former favorite. Gopi Cand's mother then breaks the news to him of the circumstances of his birth and the necessity of the moment. He questions her closely and, having understood the situation, acts at once. What does he do? Accompanied by some trusty courtiers, he goes straight to the yogi's camp in the garden, throws his former and future guru down a deep well, and pushes in a huge stone after him. For good measure he then conscribes peasant labor to fill carts with the dung of his 750 royal horses and to dump this on top of the stone, tamping it down thoroughly.

Needless to say, this crude tactic gets him nowhere. As was prophesied, Death's messengers come and start to drag him away with them. But just as they are pulling him through the sky, Jalindarnath, whose yogic powers were unaffected by Gopi Cand's maltreatment, comes storming up behind them and challenges the servants of King Yama: "Hey, sister-fuckers, where do you think you're going with my disciple?" Yogic authority prevails, and Gopi Cand, even while he is mourned in the palace, returns to his body. His miraculous revival is greeted with great joy by his mother, his 1,600 slave girls, and his 1,100 queens. However, chastened by this close encounter with mortality, he admits that he must now do as his mother had told him at the outset: renounce the world.

Now renouncing the world is no mean feat for Gopi Cand, because his possessions are multiply seductive. Besides the thousands of women, among them a favorite who has borne him a daughter, he must part from his mother at home in the palace and his still more beloved sister, who is married to a king of distant Bengal. Nor is he immune to the lure of his marble buildings, his cherished horses and elephants, his retinue of bards and nobles. Not least among all his regrets is that which he feels for the loss of his personal luster, his beauty, which must be buried beyond recognition beneath a yogi's ash paste and rough garments.

All in all, Gopi Cand's transformation from vainglorious, pleasure-loving raja to immortal yogi is a prolonged, painful, tearful process. Long after he puts on the outer look of an initiated wandering renouncer, he is inwardly full of carping regrets for his lost kingdom and endless self-pity for his unchosen destiny. Only the vigilance of the guru sees him through. Jalindarnath recognizes that Gopi Cand is not yet a "firm" (*pakkā,* also "ripe" or "cooked") disciple. He takes him on a long pilgrimage during which Gopi Cand must carry a tray of fire on his head. After this, believing that the former king is now sufficiently prepared for the ordeal, Jalindarnath demands that Gopi Cand present himself as a beggar for alms at his own palace, and that in the course of doing so he call his chief wife "mother."

This episode and the similarly structured episode of Gopi Cand's farewell to his sister are equally replete with misery. Moreover, when the guru reproaches him for his lack of concentration and his perpetual ensnarement in the "net of illusion" (*māyājāl*), Gopi Cand replies rudely, "What do you know of such things? You fell from the sky and have no mother and father." The truly unattached guru's advice, then, is seen by Gopi Cand as lacking in value because it is not based on experience. No one who has not directly known it can appreciate the torment of renouncing family bonds.

Whenever Gopi Cand collapses during his trials, and this is not infrequently, Jalindarnath saves him as he saved him from Death's messengers. In one instance Gopi Cand, having washed off his renouncer's ashes and been recognized by his weeping queens, is seated in their midst. His chief wife enters and dramatically tosses their little daughter into his lap. At this moment the pressure on the former king, husband, and father is so great that Jalindarnath can save him only by reducing him to ashes and then reincarnating him in another locality.

It is clear that Gopi Cand would have failed repeatedly as a yogi without his indefatigable guru's grace. Eventually, however, he does become immortal, along with his mother's brother Bharatri, who had formerly undergone an equally painful set of partings from the world (and who is the subject of another lengthy song of praise in the Nath tradition). Ironically enough, Gopi Cand and Bharatri, nephew and uncle, often spoken of as a paired unit by villagers, end up meditating in caves in one another's company, each thus maintaining at least one kinship bond from their prior lives.

Although Gopi Cand, ever weeping and vacillating, may seem to be a definite anti-hero, self-indulgent and spineless, he is revered as a great religious exemplar in Rajasthan. Yet his immortality and that of his mother's brother are problematic. Theirs is said to be an immortality on earth, a bodily immortality. The term body-soul, or *kāyā,* used in the tale's stock phrase "his body-soul will become immortal," is the same word used in Bhajans 1 and 6 for that which perishes and is burned. Even today the pair of Gopi Cand and Bharatri, still embodied, are said to be wandering somewhere, anomalies in this world where everything else dies. Their hard-won immortality seems in some ways a poor prize, a less than enviable condition, actually quite close to the plight of the homeless, lingering ghost, as is suggested in the signature verse of Bhajan 2. The rationale for this ambiguous outcome may have been lost in the legend's historical permutations. Here it can only be said that if today Gopi Cand is venerated, he is also pitiable, and that few or none would actually aspire to an immortality such as his.

While some of the *bhajan*s mock and disparage kin ties, Gopi Cand's legend offers a balancing version of their profound penetration into the human heart. What is the connection between "mind" and the world? Gopi Cand reveals it, unashamedly: he adores his station in life and his kinfolk. He would far rather keep them even for a brief spell than gain a lonely immortality, and this is true, I suggest, of most villagers, despite their appreciation of the world-renouncer's values. Gopi Cand's fate runs directly counter to his inclinations and makes him a holy man willy-nilly. Listeners appreciate his apotheosis because they readily empathize with the sufferings, deprivations, and humiliations he endures along his way.

Yet both *bhajan*s and legend have the same moral: all connections will be severed one way or another. It is here that the response to mortality expressed in these Nath oral traditions differs radically from the responses enacted in funerals and worship of *pattar* and *jhūjhār,* both of which allow the living to sustain relations with the dead. In place of that nourishment tendered hopefully by families to their dead through faithful offerings to ancestors or worship of household lingerers, Nath lore offers the guru, the spotless, shapeless Lord, as sole protector and savior. He may carry souls across the fright and loss of dying if they surrender wholly to him. Such a surrender is difficult for infatuated humans, however, and most villagers know quite well that it would require at least as powerful and forgiving an ally as Jalindarnath to untangle their own selves from *māyā*'s well-woven net.

Thus the Naths, too, lest we forget the context of our texts, sing of death's unbinding in the midst of an elaborate ritual that binds all present in deadly secret complicity and is sponsored by living persons on behalf of the spirit of a dead kinsman. The modern Nath guru is not an accomplished master yogi-magician like Jalindarnath; still less does he resemble the remote savior praised in the *bhajan*s. Rather, he is a farmer who has inherited certain spells and techniques; their adept manipulation contributes to his livelihood. Moreover, the performance of Hing Laj Ma Puja to release the dead is known to fail from time to time, producing Nath *jhūjhārjī*s and resulting in Naths making pilgrimages to Hardwar carrying "silver flowers."

Goat Play: Women's Jokes and the Sexual Reversal of Death

The data used to consider here another response to death which exists in the village come not from rites dealing directly with the dead but from the activities of a festive day, Calf Twelfth (Bach Bāhras), which falls on the twelfth day of the dark half of Bhadra, the fourth and final month of the rainy season. The themes of Calf Twelfth, to anticipate, may be simply stated: sexual reproduction—that is, the organic fertility of man and nature—gives a continuity to life which prevails over the grief and finality of death.

The motif of fertility is not absent from any of the approaches to mortality already described. Lingering spirits of the dead may hinder or permit progeny, and their reincorporation into the family is often a way of ensuring their forbearance from hindrances in these matters. The term for the flour balls used to embody and unite ancestors, *piṇḍa,* also means embryo, and a wife of the lineage may eat such a flour ball in order to get a son. The Celebration of Ganga in the context of funeral rites will be interpreted (in chapter 4) as promoting fertility through women's possession by the lusty deity Bhairuji. Spanning both the complex that surrounds lingering spirits and that which surrounds ancestors is a homology suggesting identity between icons embodying spirits of dead children, bone remains of cremated adults, womb, and unborn child expressed in the world "flower," which may be used to refer to any of these.

The Nath approach to death, entailing disassociation from *samsāra* and devaluation of its connections, would not seem likely to harbor fertility motifs. Yet several deep *bhajan*s recorded in the same setting as those already presented were interpreted by informants as subtle sexual analogies, referring to procreation as if it were an esoteric miracle. One of these is built on an elaborate agricultural metaphor; its refrain contains the line "Now you plant your cool seed." A renowned *nirguṇa bhajan* expert in Ghatiyali (not a Nath himself but a leading adherent of their cult) interpreted this for me as "When man and woman's gazes meet, then the cool seed is released."

The same person was asked to explain a line in another *bhajan* about juice flowering in the "crooked channel" (*bank nal*) and drop by drop watering the "plant-bed" (*kyārī*) of the *sushumnā,* or central "conduit" (*nāḍi*), of the subtle body. What sounded to me like pure Tantric physiology (see Eliade 1969:236-245; Woodroffe 1964) was in his view a veiled description of the act of sexual procreation.[63] Thus, according to him, the plant-bed was the "oyster," or "female organ." He said, "The drop falls into the female organ and from this the family flowers; then the 'embryo' (*piṇḍa*) is made."

On Calf Twelfth, the linked themes of sex and fertility are neither subtle nor hidden but quite outspoken. This has to do in part with their expression in a segregated feminine context, a context

63. It is also true, of course, that sexual intercourse may become in yogic teachings or Tantric practice a model for or an experience of divine realization. See, for example, Dimock 1966; Eliade 1969:254–273; O'Flaherty 1973:255–292; Varenne 1976:143–177.

that does not demand demonstrations of prescribed "modesty" (*sharm*).[64] I was alerted to the advent of Calf Twelfth several weeks beforehand by women who, giggling or slyly smiling, told me that I must be sure not to miss the fun that day, when they would all go to the banks of the water reservoir for "joking," "exuberant dancing," and "speaking goat talk" (*bakrā bolī bolnā*). Divining potential mischief in their insistence that I join them, I was both curious and apprehensive.

The morning of Calf Twelfth was decorous enough. It is the occasion for "cow worship" (*gāy pūjā*). Two cows fulfilled this function for the whole village, circulating in their respective moieties. Led by an untouchable Regar, in the case of my side of the village, the cow arrived at a meeting place near a temple or a well, and the women of the neighborhood one by one worshipped her and her calf, giving forehead marks and treats to both. The cow then moved on, and the women proceeded to tell the story of the day of cow worship and four other stories of the gods. During these story-and-song sessions they decorated their hands with henna, as is done before weddings and other celebrations. Everyone then returned home, and special foods appropriate to this day were eaten: spicy, dry-roasted chickpeas, cornbread, and yogurt or buttermilk. Neither wheat bread nor sauces of cooked vegetables or lentils are prepared on Calf Twelfth.

By afternoon the women's mood was altered as, dressed in holiday finery, they began to gather in their neighborhoods once again. Groups of women stopped at nearby homes where a death had occurred over the past year, persuasively encouraging the reluctant female denizens of these homes to join them. In colorful clusters they then proceeded toward a general assembly place near the water reservoir, just beyond the last houses of the village. Here was a gathering and mingling of women from Brahman and Mahajan with those of peasant and artisan castes. Secluded Rajput wives do not participate.

The drummer's daughter, Lila, performed a solo dance to her

64. I qualify this statement with "in part" because there are other verbally unrestrained, if physically slightly more restrained, occasions when women play in proximity to men. Notable among these are Holi and weddings. At weddings "insults" are directed by female relations of the bride against the groom and his female kin, although the latter are not present. See A. Gold (1987b) for an analysis of Rajasthani women's sexuality and fertility as expressed in folk songs.

mother's drumbeat. Soon more spontaneous singing and dancing began to break out among the rest of the women. One of the crowd, an old toothless woman notorious for her lewd talk even on ordinary days, began to wield a long stick. As the mood became properly giddy, she would thrust this stick from behind between the legs of other, younger women, slightly lifting their skirts. The "*Bā bā bā bā bā*" of "goat talk," an imitation of male goats' mating cries, was heard. All of this frolic was good-natured, but men are reputedly and probably truly afraid to come near. I was told that they were afraid of being beaten by the women if they did. (Miller and our male research assistants, however, who sometimes seemed to wear cloaks of invisibility, were not molested.)

After perhaps an hour of this sport, the women who had arrived in separate groups returned to the village en masse, goat play continuing on the way with added vigor. Many women repeated over and over again the "joke": "Lots of babies will be born after this day." On the road they caught Ainn-bai with the stick, and after her Patvarinji, the wife of the tax collector, a Mahajan with so many children she hardly needed to join in a fertility rite.

The whole procession now ascended to the Fort, in order to greet the *ṭhakurānī,* wife of the village's hereditary lord. Reclining royally on her cot, she received them coolly, not appearing particularly glad to have this rare intrusion into her monotonous "curtained" existence. Respecting village traditions, however, she politely greeted those who could fit in her chamber while outside the rest enthusiastically sang risqué songs. After leaving the Fort the women dispersed and the day's fun was over.

How shall we interpret the events of Calf Twelfth? Clearly they have to do with domestic animals, with sex, and with reproduction. Less clearly, from what has been revealed thus far, they have to do with sacrifice and death. In order to begin to elucidate these underlying themes I present a synopsis of the story of cow worship. I heard it told several times that day, each with some slight variations.

> In the whole region it was raining, but in our place there was no rain. Then some teller, some Brahman seer, said, "There is a merchant here with five sons, and if he will bury his eldest son in the

village water reservoir, then it will rain within this place's boundary, but if he will not, then there will be no rain."

The villagers all began to mutter that he should do this, and finally he agreed to put his eldest son in the water reservoir. But he kept delaying. Jeth passed, Asarh passed, Shravan passed [the first three months of the four-month rainy season] and there was no rain and people began to die. Finally in the month of Bhadra [the month in which Calf Twelfth is celebrated] he buried his son in the water reservoir. Then much rain fell: the reservoir, the gutters, the ditches filled with water.

The day of Calf Twelfth came and women were going to the water reservoir for their play and they called to the merchant's family to join them, but the merchant just answered, "If only our son were here!" The rest of the world had no grief, but the one who put his son in the reservoir had much grief.

Then the son's wife, who didn't know what had happened, arrived from her parents' home for the occasion of Cow Worship. She dressed herself and ornamented herself and was waiting for her husband. Her in-laws didn't dare to tell her the truth. Instead they told her, "He's just coming." She went to the water reservoir and her husband emerged from it alive, his head covered with mud. He bathed and dressed and they worshipped together. The merchant's wife praised her daughter-in-law for her good fate in being auspiciously married to a living husband.

The storytelling ends with a prayer: "Hey, Mother of Calf Twelfth, as you kept her honor, so keep the world's! As you brought him back to life, so bring the world!"

There are two striking themes to this story. One is that of life (rain) coming from death (sacrifice). This is effected by males: the Brahman seer, the merchant, and his victim son. The other theme is the reversibility of death, exemplified in the restoration of the buried youth only slightly muddied from his ordeal. This is effected by females: by his wife whose good fate makes his death impossible, by his mother who recognizes this, and by the goddess to whom the closing prayer is addressed.

By putting the story of cow worship together with the sexual implications of goat play, the meaning of this day's activities as a whole becomes clearer. One of the customs of the day, as was mentioned above and alluded to in the story, is for women on the way to their gathering by the water reservoir to make a special stop at homes saddened and reduced by death during the past year and to insist that female mourners participate in the celebration. Their bawdy joking is thus ribaldry in the direct face of death; a communal fertility is evoked which effaces separate losses.

What does the placid mother cow have to do with all this? It is worth looking at the "standard" version of Calf Twelfth's story, translated from a simple Hindi manual of holidays published in Uttar Pradesh, because the cow's role is highlighted here, and the logic of the Rajasthani transformation is thereby somewhat illuminated.

> There was a king who had seven sons. He had one grandson. One day the king thought that it was necessary to dig a well. He had the well constructed but no water came into it. Then the king called the pandits and asked, "What is the matter? Why is there no water in my well?"
>
> One Brahman answered, "Maharaj, if you offer up your grandson and make a sacrifice then water will come." The king said, "Do so." The preparations for the sacrifice were completed and the child was given as an offering. As soon as the child was sacrificed, it began to rain and the well was filled with water. The king no sooner heard this news than he went to worship at the well.
>
> That day, there being no vegetables in the house, his servant girl slaughtered a calf and made sauce. When the king and queen came back from worshipping, the king asked the servant girl, "Where is the cow's calf?" Then the servant girl said, "I slaughtered it and made sauce." The king said, "Sinner woman! Why did you do this?"[65]
>
> The king buried the pot of meat in the ground and said, "When the cow returns from the woods then how will I explain to her?" In the evening when the cow came back she went to the place where the meat of the calf was buried. In that place she began to dig with her horn. When the horn struck the pot then the cow brought it out, and from the pot the cow's calf and the king's grandson emerged. From that day on, that day's name was "Calf Twelfth" and cows and their calves began to be worshipped. (Singh n.d.:85)

This story differs from Ghatiyali's version in several ways. The latter omits the butchering of the calf by the stupid servant girl and replaces the mother cow with a virtuous wife as agent of re-

65. The king's revulsion against curried calf meat may be the source of the interdiction of "sauce" on Calf Twelfth in Ghatiyali, even though this part of the story is absent from Ghatiyali's lore.

suscitation. There is no hint in the Hindi story of the goat play that follows cow worship; the Rajasthani version does mention the women headed to the water reservoir for their sport.[66] Whereas the Hindi text concerns a king who must sacrifice his son's son to fill his own well, Ghatiyali's is about a whole community suffering drought, and the sacrifice is demanded of a merchant's house rather than of royalty.

The two counterpoint themes identified in Ghatiyali's story, however, remain the same here: a precious human life, an eldest son or an only grandson, must be sacrificed by males, according to directions from Brahmans, to get water (on which all nourishment and growth depend). But the very sacrificial finality of death may be intuitively undone by females. The wanton calf-killing by the female servant in the Hindi version appears to be a mocking echo of the males' intentional and instrumental sacrifice rather than of any inherently female significance.

Wendy O'Flaherty, in discussing the "sacred cow" and the "profane mare," has observed a consistent unlinking of sex from fertility in Indian culture. Her account of the development and transformation of the symbolic complexes surrounding mares and cows from Vedic times to the present is very intricate and historically contextualized. In the course of this development she finds that "the persistent separation of eroticism and fertility in Hindu myth is reflected in actual behavior patterns that in turn resonate in the myths." Ultimately, "erotic, nonfertile female energy—mare power—came to be contrasted with nonerotic, fertile energy—cow power" (O'Flaherty 1980b:248-249).[67]

On the day of Calf Twelfth, however, women having paid their tribute to mother cow, gather together in an uninhibited demonstration of "goat power." The domestic well-being embodied in the cow is nothing without progeny, and that can only be

66. I have little data concerning other places in Rajasthan where goat play occurs as part of Calf Twelfth's activities. According to Zeitlyn (personal communication), Brahman women in Pushkar perform cow worship on this day and tell a variant of the story, but do not indulge in any kind of ribaldry. Pushkar is in Ajmer district, only a half-day's travel away from Ghatiyali.

67. Bloch and Parry (1982) suggest a cross-cultural disjunction between erotic sex and fertility and a corresponding association of sexual reproduction with death. However, the universal validity of their observations seems far from demonstrable. In a recent lecture O'Flaherty (1986), drawing on folkloric as well as Sanskritic sources, significantly revises the terms of her previous dichotomy.

obtained, the village women well know, through erotic engagement. In mimicking the mating cry and actions of billygoats, Ghatiyali's matrons revel not only in their own female sexuality ("mare power," as characterized by O'Flaherty), but they also, even more boldly, appropriate male eroticism—goat power—the randy goat being a famed emblem of unflagging promiscuous sexuality. Yet the avowed if joking purpose of the day's play is that "lots of babies will be born."

The action of Calf Twelfth, then, despite its division into morning cow worship and afternoon goat play, represents not the separation of eroticism from fertility but the conjunction of both in opposition to death. Thus mourners are cajoled into participation, and the meaning of death is reduced to a temporary matter in the face of exuberant, playful sexual engagement and its promise of new life. The day's story shows that women possess a creative power different from that perpetuated by men through sacrifice. The merchant's son emerging from the water with his muddy head is surely an image evocative of birth. To make it even sharper, another version of the story has him emerging with the ring of a broken clay pot around his neck, the same image that is used for the potter woman's genitals in a popular song.[68]

If all the events of Calf Twelfth are considered in conjunction with its story, then the loosenings inherent in sexual play and general female revelry may be viewed as complementary to the strictures of Brahmanic sacrifice. For in the story, before the intervention of devoted wife or mother cow, sacrifice appears as a closed system in which life must be paid for with death. But this system cannot truly prosper, is insufficient, without the infusion of female energy, whether as the cow mother or the good-fated wife (and the apparent interchangeability of the two here is itself of interest). Calf Twelfth, then, celebrates the disorderly mixing of intercourse and evokes the mess of birth as vitally complementing the sacrifice's perpetuation of life even as they counteract its perpetration of death.

68. "The potter woman's vagina's like a broken jug's rim; a rolling mouth, all that's left is the hole." Such verses are sung particularly during the days preceding Holi and those that follow it through Gangaur. These songs include barbs at numerous castes (in terms of their sexual attributes) but are sung communally by mixed caste groups of women with great esprit de corps. They display a sexual imagination that is little credited to South Asian peasant women and evoke an eroticism that is explicitly linked to fertility, if also to infidelity (A. Gold 1987b).

Calf Twelfth poses the simplest, most organic, and most diffuse response to mortality (and natality) among those described in this chapter. Rather than treating particular deaths within families, it addresses death as a communal problem. Unconcerned with the fate of any particular spirit-in-the-form-of-a-soul, Calf Twelfth affirms the endless cycling of all human spirits. Rather than being seen as illusory snares, these life cycles are praised as the valued gifts of a responsive deity. Nor are bodies and wombs devalued here; their reproductive potential is celebrated as cosmically beneficient. The devotion of wives is not a hollow farce but a power for miracles.

Generative meanings such as those expressed on Calf Twelfth are also present in the worship of lingering spirits of the dead as household deities and in funeral rites and festivities. In funeral rites, as on Calf Twelfth, it is explicitly women who enact these meanings, particularly in their ritual uses of water and green sprouts and grasses, and in their deliberate intake of seeds and seed substances (as mung beans and coconut pieces). Those lingering spirits who are children usually must be pacified by their female kin in order to persuade them to allow subsequent offspring to live in health and peace.

The Nath tradition, geared toward release, is at times vividly misogynous and depicts birth as an ugly, degenerative process. But sexual reproduction can also appear in Nath lore both as metaphor for inner development and as the mystically valued result of inner knowledge. The female organ becomes then a pearl-making oyster or a fruitful field rather than a place of darkness and pollution.

The four responses of Ghatiyalians to the universal human phenomenon of breath leaving the body coexist in the village world view. Each may be stressed or deemphasized according to many factors of contextual appropriateness. Villagers experience no cognitive dissonance from such shifting cosmological perspectives. Each response in its ritually performed moments is taken as a whole truth; all are readily acknowledged to be but partial representations of a larger, unfathomable reality.[69]

69. See Ramanujan 1980 for context-sensitivity as an "Indian way of thinking." For other pertinent observations on ambiguities and multiple perspectives within South Asian culture, see S. Daniel 1980, 1983; and Egnor 1978, 1985.

In the following three chapters the same concerns that have been shown to underlie various ways of dealing with spirits of the dead and comprehending or overturning the reality of death will be shown as motivations of relative weight for different kinds of pilgrims' journeys. Hopeful petitioners attend regional shrines for cures and divinations, to identify and appease spirits of dead kin wishing for worship in their houses, and to obtain the desperately desired boon of healthy sons. Close relations transport bone remains of deceased kin to the Ganges river, sink them with appropriate offerings to spirits of the dead as ancestors, and return carrying pots of powerful water to be ritually opened and shared in a celebration with pronounced fertility motifs. People travel, often in their old age, on chartered bus tours "for the sake of wandering." Such external journeys are sometimes said to help loosen worldly ties and lead to release from endless life cycles.

3. Dealing with Deities: Vows, Trips, and Transactions in the Rajasthani Countryside

Small shrines dedicated to local deities are found throughout Rajasthan (and all of India) near water tanks and wells; on hillsides and hilltops; in village streets, fields, pasturelands, and wastelands; and by the roadside. Such shrines may be nearly deserted, drawing only a few worshippers on a few special days of the year, or they may be regularly attended by crowds of petitioners. To put it in very broad and overly simple terms, they draw pilgrims in lesser or greater numbers, from smaller or wider catchment areas, according to their reputations for accomplishing "work," fulfilling prayers, and demonstrating "wonders" (*camatkār*) or "proofs" (*parcyā*).

The regional shrines of Rajasthan have been characterized by Komal Kothari as the rural peoples' "court of justice, their hospital and mental home, their guidance clinic as well as the focus of their faith" (1982:5). In describing the functions of these shrines, Kothari uses pragmatically oriented secular service institutions as his chief metaphor, and relegates any purely "religious" experience of shrine pilgrimage to a distinctly secondary place. Journeys to local and regional shrines are in fact most often made to obtain some kind of concrete boon or assistance from the presiding deity or deities. They are motivated responses to specific problems as varied as snakebite, infertility, madness, unemployment, and domestic disharmony, to mention only a few.

Shrines are patronized, not indiscriminately but selectively. People will tick off certain shrines whose powers they acknowledge, while others for them may be useless, mercenary, or simply irrelevant. Their choices are based on a combination of factors, including the general reputation of the shrine; ways it has benefited them, their families, neighbors, or acquaintances in the past; visionary direction received in a dream or divination by a specialist. Moreover, a person may discriminate among place, icon, god, and priest, putting faith in one or more of these and excluding others. Another sort of discrimination may be made among the works of a particular shrine. Thus villagers often assert that a place which claims to cure barrenness, snakebite, madness, stomachache, skin disease, and so forth in fact only cures stomachache, and one should go to this or that other deity for this or that specific affliction.

The general precipitating factors for villagers' journeys to shrines were all kinds of physical and mental anguish, preeminent among these being the related sorrows of infertility and infant mortality or disease. Mental disorders causing aberrant behavior were another major cause of resort to regional pilgrimage. In the domain of shrine deities such griefs are often found to be perpetuated by intrusive, wholly malevolent, nonkin beings ("witches" and "ghosts") or the spirits of unappeased, potentially benevolent deceased kin (*pattar, jhūjhārjī*). The former thus need to be conquered and expelled, the latter identified and served.

Treatments for the problems brought to shrines are varied, multiple, and often successful. Causes and treatments crosscut many differing afflictions: an offended household deity might be the cause of sick children, madness, or poor business; and the remedy for any and all of these might involve certain offerings, acts of worship, and applications of powerful substances. Following the proper execution of prescribed remedies, healthy babies, the cessation of disturbed behavior, or financial success should ensue; and following such reversals of difficulty, satisfied pilgrims revisit shrines to affirm, celebrate, and perpetuate the boons they have received. Such celebrations naturally increase the deity's fame and are thus considered extremely pleasing to him.

People go to shrines because they are suffering from troubles and seeking the physical and material attributes of happiness. They go out of faith as well as sorrow. As one informant put it, when asked about his constant recourse to gods' places during his son's long-term, undiagnosed, incapacitating illness: "Squirrels run to the pipal tree." My assistant explained his use of this Rajasthani saying to me as follows: "Whenever he is in some trouble or danger, the squirrel is able to run and climb the pipal tree; he can go no further than this. In just this way, when M's son became sick, he came straight to the deities [that is, to shrines]." As the pipal tree traditionally offers shelter to a frightened animal who has no other place to go, so the gods of shrines offer relief and solutions to men under all kinds of stress; and, as the saying implies, beyond them there is no readily conceivable recourse.

Whereas the following two chapters trace in temporal and geographic sequence the routes and actions of particular pilgrims, the order of this one is thematic, jumping from place to place for examples and demonstrations. The logic of these contrasting organizations is consistent with the logic of indigenous practice and exegesis: a *tīrthayātrā,* such as those treated in chapters 4 and 5, is a major enterprise set apart from and involving a definite break with ordinary life patterns; most trips to local shrines are, on the contrary, utterly commonplace and well integrated into normal existence. Thus, *tīrthayātrā* is apt to be recollected as a single unitary experience, its events related in more or less linear sequence, and its totality disconnected from daily village life. Journeys to local shrines, on the other hand, are spoken of in many different contexts, and informants are apt to skip from one to another, associatively mentioning their respective virtues, miracles, favors, and sights. Sometimes, if a shrine is nearby, a pilgrimage to that place may be squeezed into a day's or at least a half-day's work by going before dawn or after dusk. Even if several days away from house and fields are required by a round trip, such sojourns are not marked, like *tīrthayātrā,* with exit and entry rites, but are undertaken as casually as any business expedition.

By way of introduction to the practice of regional pilgrimage, I will first consider the basis, in villagers' conceptualizations, for the distinction between shorter journeys and those which reach more distant regions, gods, and goals. Based on motivations as well as practices, these contrasting types of journey will be illustrated with examples from women's songs typifying both extremes and suggesting an intermediate range as well. Hindi-educated persons enunciate the contrast with a differential usage of Sanskrit and Hindi *yātrā* and Rajasthani *jātrā.*

The second portion of this chapter concerns pilgrims' reasons for visiting regional shrines and portrays in some detail the activities that characterize these visits. "Pouch-filling," or impregnation through a shrine deity's grace, is described as one of the ways that shrines deliver "happiness" to pilgrims. A description of Ghatiyali's own popular curing shrine, Puvali ka Devji, and its operations follows. Three case studies of severely troubled petitioners at Puvali are examined in order to exemplify pilgrims' concerns, to show the response of shrines and their deities, and to call attention to the kinds of transactions that flow continuously at shrines. It is through multiple exchanges in substances, works, and knowledge, in promises and proofs, that the beneficent results of shrine pilgrimage are effected.

The Distinction between *Yātrā* and *Jātrā*

The transformation of *yātrā,* meaning journey and commonly used for pilgrimage, into *jātrā* is one instance of a phonetic change common in many colloquial North Indian tongues: Sanskrit *ya* into *ja*. This change is not ordinarily accompanied by a change in meaning. However, among my Rajasthani-speaking informants a fair number, most often school-educated in Hindi, retained both words and insisted that each carried distinct semantic content, although both shared the sense of travel to places of power.[1] According to these informants, *yātrā* indicated pilgrimage to a *tīrtha,* or "crossing place," such as the Ganges River at Hardwar or Gaya, the temple of Jagannath Puri near the ocean shore, or the Himalayan peak of Shri Badrinath. *Jātrā,* on the other hand, implied a trip to any of countless shrines dedicated to "goddesses-and-gods," most often of very local origin and fame.[2]

Informants pointed to two factors as most significantly distinguishing *yātrā* from *jātrā*. First was the "rank" of the deity or dei-

1. A similar meaningful distinction of *jātrā* from *yātrā* occurs in Madhya Pradesh and Maharashtra as well as Rajasthan (Marriott, personal communication).

2. In his book *Hindu Places of Pilgrimage,* the geographer Bhardwaj has described two "patterns of pilgrim circulation" which he calls "merit," or "general," and "specific." These patterns correlate broadly with journeys to pan-Hindu and journeys to regional or local shrines respectively (1973:168–172). Strikingly, the usage of *yātrā* sketched here corresponds with the "merit" pattern of Bhardwaj's scheme and *jātrā* with the "specific"; Sanskritic pronunciation denotes extraregional participation in pan-Hindu culture, whereas vernacular phonetics have become associated with local practice.

ties involved. *Yātra* concerned places of *bhagvān*, vast and omnipotent, to be approached with selfless devotion. *Jātrā* took pilgrims to lesser gods and goddesses, many of whom had once been human and whose powers were more susceptible to manipulation than to adoration. The second differentiating factor was found in pilgrims' objectives. *Yātrīs* pursued "merit" (*puṇya*), "removal of sins" (*pāp dūr karnā*), "biomoral duty" (*dharma*), and even "release" (*moksha*); jātrīs had work to be done or vows to fulfill.

In keeping with these differences, *yātrā* is set apart from the particularities of village social life by ritual prerequisites and aftermath. An auspicious time for departure must be determined by a Brahman; the path goddess (Pathvari Ma) must be worshipped both going and coming (see chapter 4). When pilgrims return imbued with substantial residues acquired in divine crossing places, even their superiors in age or caste may touch their feet. *Jātrā* is not hedged in this fashion by ritual attention nor regarded as transforming social identity. A decision to petition a local shrine deity may be taken at any time and accomplished without public fanfare. Illiterate informants did not always enunciate the distinction between *yātrā* and *jātrā*, but they conceptualized it in quite the same manner. They readily contrasted both the powers and the fruits of "crossing places" (*tīrthasthān*) with "deities' places" (*devasthān*).

One way to elucidate the difference between *yātrā* and *jātrā* is to look at some texts of songs appropriate to each. Women's songs are an important part of almost every ritual and social event in rural Rajasthan, and journeys are no exception. The following song of Badrinath, a form of Vishnu, was recorded among a mixed-caste company on a month-long bus pilgrimage to major Hindu centers outside of Rajasthan. Badrinath's site in the Himalayas is the northern node of the *cār dhām*, or four established points of Hindu pilgrimage, each located in one of the cardinal directions and composing in their circuit a complete subcontinental tour.

Song of Badrinath

[Refrain] Listen, Brothers, Sadhus, Saints, he is beloved;
The high mount is Badrinath's.
Master of the Poor, his ford is difficult.

[1] Praise Ram of Dwarka;[3] by the Lord's Stairs[4] Ganga
measures deep, my lord Ram.
Atop the mountain of three worlds expansive Badri
reigns.

[2] O Ram, midway to the peak it's very steep, I cannot
climb, my Ram.
Let Badrinath grab either hand and take me.

[3] Ram, whoever sings of vast Badri will not suffer birth
again, my Ram.
Woman becomes man, all the company will cross over.

Note that the journey to Badrinath is hard, just as classical lawbooks say that *tīrthayātrā* should be. The weary and humble devotee struggles to reach his goal and expresses his dependence on God's help to do so. Indeed, the refrain praises Badri just because it is difficult to attain.

Badrinath's pilgrim offers devotion demonstrated in the arduous effort he makes to reach the *tīrtha*. His pilgrimage is a kind of self-sacrifice, and the fruit sought is the ultimate Hindu goal: freedom from rebirth expressed here as "to cross over" (*pār karnā*). Informants told me that what was to be crossed was the "ocean of existence." The transactional pattern portrayed in the next song is quite dissimilar. It is a praise song for the goddess, here named only Mother (*Māījī*), recorded during a procession culminating her special festival of Nine Nights. Sung as a question-and-answer dialogue, the song is understood as an interchange between devotees and the goddess herself. They are asking about her distinguished pilgrims from afar.

Song of the Goddess

[Each line begins "O Mother" and each line is immediately
repeated once.]

Where have the gentlemen come from, where have the pilgrims
come from?
The gentlemen came from Bundi, the pilgrims came from Kota.[5]
How did the gentlemen come, how did the pilgrims come?

3. Dwarkanath in Gujarat is the westernmost of the *cār dhām*, and the final home of Krishna.

4. The Lord's Stairs (*har kī pairī*) is the name of the chief bathing *ghāṭ* at Hardwar, a place usually visited by pilgrims on their way to Badrinath, as it lies on the route.

5. Bundi and Kota are two major cities to the south of Ghatiyali.

The gentlemen came in trains, the pilgrims came by bus.
Where did the gentlemen disembark, where did the pilgrims disembark?
The gentlemen stopped at the station, the pilgrims stopped at the food stall.
What did the gentlemen bring, what did the pilgrims bring?
The gentlemen brought grain,[6] the pilgrims brought sweets.
What do the gentlemen ask, what do the pilgrims ask?
The gentlemen ask for jobs, the pilgrims ask for sons.
What do the gentlemen offer, what do the pilgrims offer?
The gentlemen offer feasts, the pilgrims offer goats. [recorded by Miller]

The goddess is glorified because her *jātarī*s are sophisticated and wealthy enough to come by train and bus. This also implies, of course, that they have traveled a fair distance; such greater scope and wider fame increase any deity's prestige. The events schematized here actually represent a rather typical sequence for regional shrines. On a first visit, petitioners are likely to present a small quantity of grain, which may be designated either for the priest or for scattering as pigeon-feed. These grains are also employed in a simple divination technique: the shrine priest takes up a few from the pile and counts them to see if an auspicious number shows that the deity looks favorably on the pilgrim's enterprise.

Offerings of milk sweets are always appropriate and carry more prestige than simple grain. They might be expected from the "classy" city pilgrims portrayed in the song. What do the *jātarī*s ask for? Jobs and sons are certainly high on the list. The word "proof" (*parcyā*), occasionally inserted in the song here, covers a whole range of miraculous feats. Finally, when proofs have been received, jobs secured, sons born, then major thank offerings are expected: feasts and goats.[7]

Many other songs of the regional shrines consist largely of lists of promised offerings.[8] One of this genre is particularly relevant

6. The word used here is not the common *anāj* but *maṭaṛī*, a term applied only to small quantities of grain placed as offerings on shrine platforms and often employed for grain-pick divination.

7. Not all the local deities of Rajasthan appreciate animal sacrifice, which is largely reserved for the goddess and Bhairuji.

8. All the songs of Devji that follow here were recorded by Miller among groups of pilgrim women keeping nightlong vigils at Devji shrines or at the homes of Devji's devotees. Many other gods and goddesses (particularly Mataji and Bhairuji) are sources of fertility and objects of worshipful songs quite similar to

here because its theme is the opposition between journeys to distant crossing places and worship at local shrines. A woman says to the Rajasthani hero-god Dev Narayanji that had her in-laws *not* gone traveling on a pilgrimage to foreign lands, she would have served him with the finest gifts and honors offered at regional shrines.

Song of Dev Narayanji 1

Husband's Mother and Husband's Father, O Narayan, went to *tīrtha*.
If not, I would sponsor your fair, O Dev.
I would sponsor your fair, I would build your shrine,
I would make fire-oblations from the pot of *ghī,* O Dev.

Husband's Elder Brother and his wife went to *tīrtha*.
If not, I would have built your dome, O Dev.
I would have built your dome, I would have raised its crown,
I would have made fire-oblations from the pot of *ghī,* O Dev.

Husband's Mother and Husband's Father, O Narayan, journeyed to foreign lands.
If not, I would have built your eaves, O Dev.
I would have built your eaves, I would have lit a flame,
I would have sponsored night-long hymns and feasted your pilgrims. [recorded by Miller]

Left behind, without resources, the singer implies that her own faith in a regional deity is more worthwhile than her husband's family's motivations for pilgrimage in "foreign lands." There, presumably, they are squandering the money that she would have used to make these grand offerings to Devji if she had had her way.

Numerous other songs show women's devotion to local deities, such as Dev Narayanji, and their shrines opposed by and opposing the authority of male in-laws. The singer's point of view in these may be seen as characteristic of a young woman's stereotypical estrangement from her husband's family where, especially until the birth of a male child, she has little status, voice, or comfort. Unspoken in the preceding example but often made perfectly explicit is the core of many young married women's heartfelt devotion: the desire to receive a son through the deity's grace.

---

these. The emphasis on Devji here is a function of Miller's interest in that deity's tradition, and Puvali ka Devji's prominence in our area as a child-granting place.

The birth of a son will vindicate the woman's devotion in the eyes of her in-laws, as is shown in the following verses.

Song of Dev Narayanji 2

Father-in-law, don't forbid me to go and bow to Devji;
Father-in-law, those who forbid are marked with fault.
I will go to the brave Lord.

Daughter-in-law, what is your proof of brave Devji?

Father-in-law, to one hundred barren cows he gave calves;
Father-in-law, to me he gave a god-like son.
That is my proof of brave Devji. [recorded by Miller]

In contrast to the preceding two songs, the final example here shows the singer trying a different tactic and identifying the god's authority with that of her husband's male kin. Her wish, however, remains the same. Two versions of this song were recorded, and there follow samples from each. In the first a woman describes her own attractive apparel as she approaches Devji with prayers and promises. The second set of verses proposes explicit bargains: you do this and I'll do that.

Song of Dev Narayanji 3a

[1] I am wrapped in a shawl, I have come to Narayan.
Established-by-five Devji, will you hear my plea?
Worship-established Dev, will you hear my plea?

[Refrain-a] If you hear my request, then hear me like this:
On the sloping roof a long-tailed peacock.[9]

[2] I have put on a nose-ring, I am wrapped in a shawl.
Established-by-husband's-father Devji, will you hear my plea?
Established-by-one-hundred Devji, will you hear my plea?

[3] I have put on a full set of bangles, I have put on a forehead ornament.
Established-by-husband's-elder-brother Devji, will you hear my plea?
Established-by-husband's-younger-brother Dev, will you hear my plea?

9. A peacock on the roof is an auspicious sign and a rather common sight in Ghatiyali and its environs.

[Refrain-b] If you hear my plea, then hear me like this:
Give sons to barren women.

Song of Dev Narayanji 3b

[1] Established-in-bricks Devji, will you hear my plea?
Shadower-of-the-priest Devji, will you hear my plea?
If you hear my plea, I will build your dome,
Atop the dome I'll raise up a crown.

[2] Banjyari's[10] true Devji, will you hear my plea?
Ghanti's innocent Devji, will you hear my plea?
If you hear my plea, then I'll offer a throne;
After that I'll present an iron cane.

[3] Puvali's true Devji, will you hear my plea?
Ghanti's innocent Devji, will you hear my plea?
If you give a son, then I'll give a big feast;
At Puvali I'll raise up a flagpole. [recorded by Miller]

Apparent here is one of the most important distinctive characteristics of *jātrā* (absent in *yātrā*) associated with its expectations of tangible results. This is the *bolārī* or *votanā*—literally something which is spoken—both of which may be translated as "pledge" or "vow." Pledges are often made at home when some distress or problem is at hand. Placing faith in a chosen deity, a person will say something like this: "If my daughter recovers from this illness, I will cause her to bow at your shrine and I will hold a feast there"; or "If my son's marriage arrangements are satisfactorily completed, I will come to your shrine and offer fifty-one rupees"; and so forth.

Especially in the case of sickness, such pledges may be marked by tying a piece of raw-cotton string or a strip of cloth torn from a turban onto the afflicted person's body while taking the chosen deity's name. Later, when the vow of pilgrimage is fulfilled, the string or strip is unknotted at the shrine and usually tied onto a convenient pillar or tree there. Eventually, as these accumulate, they become visible evidence of that particular deity's effectiveness, as do many thank offerings, such as iron tridents, one-room rest houses, golden domes.

10. Banjyari and also the following place names (Ghanti, Puvali) are sites of locally important Dev Narayanji shrines.

The pattern of pledge and fulfillment involves explicit bargaining, just as in the song: "If you give a son, then I'll give a big feast." Correspondingly, if no cure is received, if the marriage arrangements fall through, if no child is born, then no subsequent pilgrimage and offerings are forthcoming. By the same token, however, a person who gets what he asked for and does not pay up is inviting punishment—at least the loss of his coveted boon if not greater disaster. Such negotiations and deals are appropriately entered into with lesser gods and goddesses. They would not be suitable in approaching the Lord in temples or crossing places. Thus vows are paradigmatically associated with *jātrā* but not with *yātrā*.[11]

There also exists a pilgrim's journey that seems to stand intermediate to clear-cut *yātrā* and *jātrā* types. Informants indeed sometimes could not agree upon whether such journeys should be called *tīrthayātrā* or *jātrā*, and plausible supporting arguments for each interpretation might be made. Once again, the praises sung by devotees can serve to highlight the qualities of their pilgrimage.

The following song does not speak of bargains, though it does tell of miraculous cures. It was recorded inside the temple of Shri Kalyanji at Diggi in Tonk district where I had accompanied a busload of pilgrims from Ghatiyali. Although Diggi is a most unenchanting, dusty little town, quite lacking in the natural beauty associated with most major Hindu pilgrimage sites, its temple and deity have widespread fame in the area surrounding Jaipur and Ajmer, and many Rajasthanis accept the site as a crossing place.

Song of Shri Kalyanji

[Refrain] Grain-giver, truly look upon me,
Kalyanji, hear me wholly!
The king of Diggi in Dhundar land is a great Lord.

[1] Crippled and lame your many pilgrims come.
Remove the lepers' leprosy.[12]

11. Bhardwaj also mentions "vows" as strongly associated with his "specific" pattern (1973:154–162). *Yātrā* often begins with a "resolution" (*samkalp*), but this is more an inner dedication of the pilgrim to his journey than a deal with a god.

12. In the temple's founding myth, Kalyanji's first miracle is to cure a king of leprosy caused by a heavenly nymph's curse.

[2] Yes, the crested turban on your head is lovely,
rings in your ears so pleasing.
And in that beard twinkle and twinkle
the rays of diamonds.[13]

[3] Yes, thrice-daily glimpsed, your temple's wondrous
beauty[14] removes the sad folks' sorrows
And gives eyes to the blind.

[4] My boat in the whirlpool lurches and tilts,
swirling me from the shore.
My boat is caught midstream, Kalyanji,
cross me over, Lord.

It is immediately apparent that the desires of Shri Kalyanji's pilgrims combine elements of *jātrā* and *yātrā*. First, the deity is called upon to cure cripples and lepers and lauded for giving sight to the blind—curative functions typical of regional shrines. Ultimately Kalyanji is implored for help in "crossing over" just as is Badrinath, the high deity who can be reached only on a difficult *tīrthayātrā*. Moreover, the pilgrim to Kalyanji humbly expresses his own helpless inadequacy at reaching the goal, as do Badrinath's pilgrims. But Diggi is not a distant *tīrtha,* and no metaphorically apt mountain need be climbed to get there. Most of Shri Kalyanji's *jātarī*s probably manage the trip in less than a day by bus.

The identity of Kalyan with Dhundar land is an important part of his appeal. In that sense, he is a localized, rooted Rajasthani deity whose scope is far narrower than Badrinath's atop the "mountain of the three worlds." But he is, at the same time, a "form" of the Lord,[15] the high god Vishnu, and not a *devatā*. For this reason many informants wanted to call Diggi a crossing place. As *bhagvān,* Shri Kalyanji was himself a remover of sins (as well as other troubles), and thus a pilgrimage to his feet was cleansing in

13. The icon of Shri Kalyanji has diamonds set into its chin.

14. Shri Kalyanji's *darshan* is given three times daily, and there is a miraculous aspect to it. In the morning the icon appears as a child, at midday as a man in his prime, and in the evening as if aged.

15. Marriott has pointed out that high gods with regional shrines and identities, like Shri Kalyanji, are of course found in other parts of India as well. Vithoba in Maharashtra and Vyankateshwar in Telugu-Tamil country are examples supplied by him (personal communication). Morinis' recent study of pilgrimage in Bengal (1984) considers three such deities, all of whom may be approached for material as well as "spiritual" reasons.

the same way as a bath in the Ganges. Nonetheless, pilgrimage to Shri Kalyanji at Diggi is often made to fulfill vows or to seek help in a fashion absolutely typical of *jātrā* to local, lesser deities. Pilgrims negotiate with the king of Diggi just as they do with any other *devatā* of more circumscribed scope.

Within the regional pilgrimage complex, Rajasthani villagers recognize and describe a type of journey made neither to ask for boons nor to fulfill vows but for more diffuse reasons of dedicated devotion. The common colloquialism for such a pilgrimage is *kānkarī gūndabā,* or "to press down pebbles"—that is, to place one's feet deliberately on the grounds of a deity's shrine. Although the term may be applied to a single journey, its usage more often implies a high frequency of periodic visits. Thus, "I go every Saturday, just to press down pebbles." The term may be used in opposition to having particular work or vows.

One woman had made the pilgrimage to Ramdevji, whose place in western Rajasthan is the best known of all pan-Rajasthani shrines, for twelve consecutive years. She firmly contrasted, however, the first seven years made to fulfill a vow with her current practice of an annual pilgrimage "to press down pebbles."

Pilgrim: Now there is no necessity, we go for pleasure. We ask only for happiness and peace.

Interviewer:[16] This time when you went what prayer did you make?

Pilgrim: "We have come to your door; keep us in happiness and peace."

Interviewer: Did you ask for release?

Pilgrim: Happiness and peace, no sickness, enough!

Her goals are thus neither specific nor soteriological. The diffuse objective of "happiness and peace" is all she will allow, and she is firm and proud on this point. There is a way in which having no

16. Here and frequently in the pages that follow I reproduce in translation the tape-recorded and transcribed texts of interviews jointly conducted by myself and Bhoju Gujar or, less frequently, Nathu Nath or Vajendra Sharma. The voice of "interviewer"—abbreviated "I"—is sometimes my own, sometimes an assistant's representing in local dialect a question I expressed to him in Hindi, sometimes an assistant's formulating his own question in general congruence with what he understood to be my interests. Except when such a situation becomes a three-way conversation, or when the person being interviewed addresses him or herself specifically to a fellow Rajasthani and not to me, I do not distinguish the identity of "interviewer."

specific motivation elevates the act of pilgrimage. "Pressing down pebbles," countrified as the phrase and its usage may be, is a way of turning *jātrā* into *yātrā*.

The triadic results of deliverance identified by Susan Wadley (1975:107–125) in her study of village religion in Uttar Pradesh help to illuminate the Rajasthani case. Wadley's three kinds of deliverance—salvation, shelter, and rescue—correspond rather well with the various goals of Rajasthani pilgrims that have been discussed. Salvation is release—a final crossing over—the high goal of *yātrā*. Rescue is relief from immediately disastrous situations and thus applies to the pursuits of *jātrā* associated with having work and vows. Shelter, the middle term, implies several things: protection, removal of sins and sorrows, and thus the potential attainment of happiness. It is also strongly associated with an enduring, mutually satisfying relationship between deity and devotee. The configuration of meanings denoted by shelter fits well with that which underlies journeys made "to press down pebbles."[17]

Rather than dichotomous, the *jātrā* and *yātrā* typology may be better characterized as a continuum with the journey for shelter—to press down pebbles—at some intermediate position between instrumental and diffuse. There is also an apparent correlation between this intermediate style of pilgrimage and shrines like Ramdevji's and Shri Kalyanji's—shrines of more than local, but of distinctly regional, significance. Such pilgrimage spots are ascribed the higher rank of crossing places but retain the effective wondrous powers wielded by deities who do pilgrims' work and expect compensation. The rest of this chapter will focus on *jātrā* in the broadest sense. Its scope thus includes journeys made for happiness, shelter, or "pressing down pebbles," as well as for sons and many kinds of healing.

Troubles Relieved, Well-being Procured: What Happens at Shrines

When bluntly approached in the environs of a shrine and asked the reason for their presence, many Rajasthani pilgrims will reply

17. See Moreno 1984:199 for a progression in a style of South Indian pilgrimage from need to obligation to love—thus from specific to diffuse reasons for pilgrimage, from rescue to shelter, from *jātrā* to "pressing down pebbles."

expressively, "sorrow and trouble." One priest of a powerful place of the goddess informed me that from pleasing her, "every single sorrow of the body (*sharīr*) is removed." By his use of *sharīr*—the term linked with perishable body, rather than *kāyā,* the ambiguous "unitary body-soul," or *ātmā,* the undying, transmigrating self—he frankly conveyed both the dominion and the limits of the powers of shrines and their gods.[18]

Pilgrimage to Rajasthani shrines, *jātrā,* indeed has little if anything to do with the *ātmā,* its accumulation of merit, or ultimate release. It is also largely unconcerned with future births. The work of the shrines is for this life and on this body. Correspondingly, the spirits whom these shrines sometimes help to identify and properly locate are those of the dead who have lingered in this world (*pattar, jhūjhār, bhūt-pret*), unable to relinquish the attachments accumulated in their most recent lives.

In the following discussion of the nature of well-being as sought from and granted by shrines the data come from a number of different places, and the focus is less on shrines themselves than on pilgrims' prayers and their fulfillment. One particular shrine and some of its more afflicted pilgrims will be described in an attempt to unravel the sorrow-and-trouble complex, or at least three specific instances of it.

Well-being is, of course, the collective opposite of the sorrow-and-trouble from which people take refuge in the gods.[19] The complex of well-being includes health, prosperity, and progeny, which taken together produce a mental ease that is the highest and most diffuse goal usually claimed by *jātarīs*.[20] All the components of well-being are notably "this-wordly" in the sense that they

18. This distinction should not suggest an opposition between body and soul or physical and spiritual such as characterizes Christian binarism. Rather, it is a difference, contextually posed, between the person living and coping in the world of flux and the person as eternal, unchanging self.

19. By "well-being" I gloss the total implications of several adjectival pairs applied to the human condition. Although each might be more poetically translated, all do, I believe, amount to the same thing. Among these are *rājī-khushī* (joyful-and-happy) and *harī-bāṛī* (replete with greenness). The noun pair most commonly used to refer to the state that I call well-being is *sukh-shānti* (happiness-and-peace).

20. In an interesting discussion of the uses of temples and temple-worship in Tamil Sri Lanka, Pfaffenberger shows that the well-being or human vitality achieved there through temple-building is equivalent to that effected elsewhere through Vedic sacrifice. Citing a medieval Orissan Sanskrit text on temple architecture, the *Silpa Prakasa,* Pfaffenberger tells us that it "asserts that the patron will, in this world, always have 'peace, wealth, grain and sons,' which are precisely the objects of the Vedic Sacrifice (Kaulacara 1966:122)" (Pfaffenberger 1982:79). Here we may add that these same goals are precisely those of Rajasthani *jātarīs*.

concern comforts of one's current birth, although the yearning for sons certainly has a strong soteriological component (see chapter 4).

In a series of interviews with pilgrims recently returned from Ramdevra, the hero-god Ramdevji's special place northwest of Jodhpur,[21] I asked them in different ways what prayers they had made to Ramdevji on their pilgrimage. These peasant pilgrims' replies were individually worded but homogeneously construed.

Interviewer: When you went and had *darshan,* what did you think in mind?

Pilgrim: Keep me flourishing and happy and I will come and offer fifty-one rupees.

Interviewer: When you were taking *darshan* of Ramdevji, what feeling did you have?

Pilgrim: Just give me food and strength, what else do you want? Let me remain good-looking and disease free.

Interviewer: While you were making your prostration, what were you thinking?

Pilgrim: At this time I was thinking nothing, except that, if in this year I get two thousand rupees income, I'll come again to Ramdevji.

Interviewer: What were you thinking when doing *darshan?* Did you make another vow? [This pilgrim had just fulfilled a vow for a snakebite successfully cured in Ramdevji's name.]

Pilgrim: Yes, I thought, if I have a grandson, I will send my son and his wife both to prostrate themselves.

Interviewer: When you were taking *darshan,* what was your feeling, what were you thinking?

Pilgrim: Brother, leader, for you I have come wandering one hundred *kosh* [one *kosh* equals approximately two miles]. Keep me happy, keep my wealth and oxen, mine and everyone's!

Interviewer: When you were taking Ramdevji's *darshan,* what was your feeling?

Pilgrim: What would I think? Give me food and strength and keep me happy!

Interviewer: When you were in the temple looking at the icon, what were you saying in your mind?

21. See Binford 1976 for an account of one pilgrimage to Ramdevji, and a good description of the shrine itself—its lore and atmosphere. Bishnoi 1979 gives Ramdevji's legend in detail.

Pilgrim: Nothing, but the first time I went I thought, "If my garden flowers,[22] then I will offer up twenty-one rupees." This time I just thought, "Give me cash and bread, keep me happy, enough!" What else could you want? Now the family has flowered; now only wealth and happiness are needed. As long as I live I will keep pressing down pebbles there.

This sampling of responses clearly demonstrates that the pilgrimage to Ramdevji is made by most *jātarīs* for specific boons, or out of allegiance generated by boons previously granted. Very evident, moreover, is the frankly transactional nature of the pilgrims' relation to the god. They often phrase their wishes in the form of bargains: you do this for me and I'll do thus and so for you—offer money, make another pilgrimage, send others to prostrate themselves.

These seven responses, representative of all those received from Ramdevji's *jātarīs*, clearly set forth all the components of this-worldly well-being which a deity like Ramdevji can bestow: grain, food, cash, healthy livestock, a strong and disease-free body, plenty of sons and sons' sons. All these more marked items are contained in the less marked, more nebulous "happiness."

Some problems with health will be considered in depth later. Wealth, although everyone wants it, is less sought after at shrines than health and children, and will not be a particular focus here. I turn, then, to the getting of progeny, a pivotal them of *jātrā*. This subject, how babies are made through the power of shrines and their deities, affords a more circumscribed field of inquiry than do the other components of happiness. Although I made no statistical survey, in my experience it was numerically, as well as emotionally, one of the most powerful rationales for shrine pilgrimage.

A common sight at many of Rajasthan's local shrines is clusters of wide straw baskets hanging from tree branches or rooftops. Some appear new; others are weathered by wind, sun, and rain to various stages of disintegration. These baskets, called *pālanā,* or "cradles," are placed there as thank-offerings from pilgrims who have received the boon of a living child's birth. Each basket thus stands for a child born, and a shrine with ample quantities of these baskets on display possesses indisputable testimony of its power to grant fertility.

22. A flowering garden is a popular image of fertility in the family; her meaning is "if children are born."

In the following song, when Devji promises his plaintive pilgrim that he will "cause her to offer an undying cradle," he is promising her a child. (Although there are three speakers in this song—the barren wife, the taunting father-in-law, and Dev Narayanji—it is sung in unison by a chorus of women.)

Song of Dev Narayanji 4

Father-in-law taunts me, my Lord Ubi,[23] in your fine place,
Father-in-law taunts me:
    Daughter-in-law, they play, they play, the sons of
        your husbands' brothers' wives.
    You have remained a barren woman since your birth.

Lord, why do I bring shame to my mother and father?
Why did they feed me milk, a barren woman?
    Girl-child, you come, come to my shrine!
    Girl-child, come, come to the Devji of Ghatiyali!
    I will cause you to offer an undying cradle. [recorded by Miller]

Inside the baskets when they are offered are coconuts swaddled in cloth, and these are the same tokens used in the rite of "pouch-filling" (*jholī bharnā*) which women seeking children undergo at many shrines. At Ghatiyali's Puvali ka Devji, pouch-filling involves more than one trip to the shrine. On the first visit the pilgrim explains the situation. A shy young bride will rarely speak for herself when petitioning for a child, but will stand before the deity, her face completely covered with her wrap and her head lowered, while her husband, an older female relation, or some other connection presents her case. More seasoned married women, however, may address the god quite boldly.

The deity (that is, the priest possessed by Devji's agent Bhairuji) then tells his petitioner to bring "pouch ingredients" on a specified date. He will often name the next upcoming festival, or *melā,* day when there is bound to be a bigger crowd than usual at the shrine. A number of pouch-fillings on such a day of maximum exposure will increase the place's prestige. These days are also, of course, usually auspicious ones (astrologically and calendrically) for beginning any undertaking.

A literate devotee or bystander (both Miller and I found ourselves pressed into service on occasion) will be asked to make a

23. Ubi is another name of Dev Narayanji.

list of necessary things which the pilgrim should bring on the appointed day.[24] When that day arrives, the woman and her accompanying kin present themselves at the shrine, bearing the specified items including rice, sugar, oil, incense, a small bottle of perfume, and a small amount of hard cash. They also bring two coconuts and lengths of red and white cloth. One coconut, swaddled in the red cloth, is placed prominently upon the shrine's platform.

The woman desiring a child wears her hair newly washed and unbraided beneath the customary wrap, which she has arranged in a special fashion so that a secure "pouch" is formed in the front.[25] When her turn comes to stand before the god, the red-clothed coconut is "caused to bow" before the icons just as the infant will be on his first visit if the outcome is successful. Then, while the drum beats a power-summoning rhythm, the possessed priest places the coconut in the pilgrim woman's prepared pouch. Obviously this is a gesture of impregnation, the coconut representing the child-to-be, and the red cloth evoking the blood of birth as well as the vigor of life. Rather than presaging the perilous embryonic state, the coconut seems to stand for the fully developed and safely birthed baby. One evidence for this is the bowing routine; another is that the same coconut, carefully preserved, returns

24. The full list of *jholī* ingredients includes one and one-quarter kilos of rice, one and one-quarter kilos of sugar, one and one-quarter "pints" (literally one-quarter liter) of oil, one and one-quarter "pints" of wine, one and one-quarter hands of red cloth, one and one-quarter hands of white cloth, good quality perfume, two coconuts, five lemons, one packet of incense, one and one-quarter rupees' worth of *sindhūr* (red powder), and one and one-quarter rupees "for pouch-filling." The number one and one-quarter (*savā*) is not peculiar to pouch-filling and is frequently used in shrine offerings. Raheja's research in Uttar Pradesh has shown that there *savā* is associated with removing inauspiciousness or transferring it with gifts (1985:132).

25. In chapter 2 I described the Celebration of Ganga where a woman receives coconut in a prearranged pouch. Note some interesting contrasts between that event and this one: In that case the woman is possessed by the deity (Ganga's Bhairu), and a man offers the coconut, splitting it on the ground as he crouches before her, and putting broken coconut pieces in her pouch. The fertility motif of this act is not explicitly stated (except in one verse of a rowdy women's song that forms a background to the occasion; see chapter 4). In the case of shrine pouch-filling, of course, the wish to receive a child is quite explicit; the priest, not the woman, is possessed by Bhairuji (or another god, or not possessed at all but simply representing the deity); the coconut is never broken. This pouch-filling coconut, rather than an offering to the pouch-wearing woman, is more like *prasād,* taken back from the shrine where it was placed before the god. On both occasions, however, the women receiving coconut wear their hair significantly unbraided, open.

to the shrine in the cradle-basket hung as a postpartum thank-offering.

At the time of pouch-filling no major cash offering is presented to the god, but the woman and her family members speak vows to return with considerable amounts (fifty-one or one hundred and one rupees are typical) or to finance some construction at the shrine, should a healthy child be born. Sometimes, though not always, they specify a boy-child. This pledge should be fulfilled shortly after the birth, when the cradle-basket is hung and the infant made to give its first obeisance to the deity who should now be its lifelong protector.

At Ramdevji's shrine, pouch-filling has developed into an event that not only promises miracles but demonstrates them. Unfortunately, I was never able to observe this for myself, but according to everyone I spoke to who had been there, it was an everyday miracle to be "seen with the eyes" at that place. There the candidate for pouch-filling sits by the shore of the lake on the temple grounds. The priest tosses her coconut into the lake. The coconut then, witnesses state, bounces back "of its own accord" into the woman's pouch—if she is destined to bear a child. Sometimes it takes a couple of tries, which are interpreted as intervening miscarriages before the full-term birth of a living child.

In some cases pouch-filling may be accompanied by exorcism. As one informant described an incident witnessed at Ramdevra, it appears that there is no room within the female pilgrim for the auspicious coconut-child and the destructive "ghost." One comes in and the other, raucously admitting defeat, departs. When I asked my informant whether she had ever seen any "wonders" (*camatkār*) in her several visits to Ramdevra, she related this incident:

Pilgrim: Yes, this very time. With us was a woman, Ram Nath Regar's wife, Kamala, who was sick when we left and got well there. She had a "dirty heart" [euphemism for possession by witches or ghosts]. They sat her down on the bank of the water and threw the coconut in the Ram Sagar, and it came back and landed in her pouch. It came back from the water with speed, *saṛṛāṭ* [sound effect] right into her pouch.

Interviewer: All at once?

Pilgrim: Yes, and it was completely dry.

Interviewer: They threw it in the water and still it wasn't wet?

Pilgrim: It was not wet. After that it [the ghost] began to play: "Hey Ramdevji, I'm going, I'm going, don't beat me!" Then we all bathed and went back to the temple. When we were going in the door, it began to play again. Two men grabbed her arms and it cried: "O Baba, I'm going, I'm going!" Then, as she was entering the temple it left her body, saying, "You have me under control so now I won't come." It had not been controlled by any other deity.

The simultaneity of pouch-filling and exorcism is also indicated in the case of a "witch" treated at Puvali ka Devji (which will be described below). The possessed priest agreed both to fill a pouch for this woman and to exorcise her "witch." The two processes were two sides of the same coin, as he had diagnosed the witch's responsibility for the stillbirths of this woman's previous children.

At other shrines, especially when ghosts and witches are not involved, the work of giving children may be effected much more quietly. Perhaps what is required is neither priest nor coconut but only an inner vow. One man I knew well was an only son, born late in his mother's life, who had himself fathered one daughter and remained without further progeny for seven years. His elder sister, proud wife of a prominent Brahman, heard from some peasant women of the great powers of a local Sagasji. Mocking the deity and his devotees, she challenged it to do the impossible—to give her brother a son. Scornfully she vowed allegiance to the shrine if her wish should be fulfilled. Almost immediately following her skeptic's vow, the brother's wife conceived.

On the occasion of the ensuing boy-child's first prostration I accompanied the women of this family to Sagasji's out-of-the-way place. We were a small troop of women and children, our goal a lonely but tidy platform-shrine far from any habitation. The shrine-priest, a hardworking farmer, had not been summoned for this ceremony. The Brahman women thus performed Sagasji's worship without benefit of male priestcraft, employing a young boy (aged seven or eight) to climb up on the platform in order to anoint the icon and offer *dhūp*.[26]

26. Women are forbidden, except in rare cases, to mount a shrine platform because of their inherent uncleanliness, often explained as the possibility that they are wearing a skirt which at some time might have come into contact with menstrual blood.

The infant, eyes heavily daubed with protective *koyal* (soot), and dressed in bright new clothing, was briefly laid howling on top of a pile of grains offered on the platform. He was considered to have been given by that god, and thus was received as *prasād* on this occasion by his mother and his father's mother. The grains were left, presumably for the absent *bhopā* to collect if livestock or birds did not consume them first.

In this simple rite, then, the pouch-filling process was in a sense replicated after the fact of birth. Just as the coconut for pouch-filling is placed upon the shrine and then returned to the woman's waiting pouch, or thrown in power-filled water to bounce back, so this child was placed on the shrine and reclaimed by the women. All children who are "given" by deities, and this is a large percentage, are referred to as belonging to the god rather than to their parents. Often the answer to the question "Is that your child?" is "No, it is God's." A child given by God continues to belong to him and thus to command his attention and partake of his shelter.

Conception and birth are hardly the final necessity of parenthood. Children must also be safely reared, and this process is fraught with danger at every stage. After they survive to maturity, they should be peacefully married, gainfully employed, and themselves become the producers of male progeny. All these connected phases of the worldly cycle may be enhanced by resort to shrines. Two of the three cases of affliction to be closely examined below involve fathers seeking relief for a grown son's problems. The third is that of a woman whose children are born but do not survive.

Puvali ka Devji: Sources and Outlets of Local Power

The whitewashed platform shrine of Puvali ka Devji with its tall flagpoles flying the god's triumphant colored pennants imprinted one of my first and strongest impressions of Ghatiyali; indeed, it was among the main attractions leading me to choose that field site. Here was a village where I could find not only residents traveling out on pilgrimages but pilgrims streaming in, at least up to the outskirts where Puvali was located. I was assured from many sources that this shrine weekly drew scores, at least, of *jātarīs* from all over the surrounding area, some from as far away as Kota and Jaipur. And in fact, with the exception of its priest's core of followers, few Ghatiyalians chose to solve their problems so close to home. Most of the worshippers who crowded Puvali on Saturday afternoons came from other villages.

Although it was an immediate point of fascination from the very beginning of my research in Ghatiyali, I found myself constantly postponing the confronting of Puvali as a main subject of study. There were several reasons for this, foremost among them the fact that its priest was Miller's chief informant, the man who had first introduced him into the village; and its god, Dev Narayanji, was the hero of the epic that was Miller's thesis topic.[27] Moreover, Miller was already well known in the area as a "devotee" of Devji and was gradually contributing what came to several thousand rupees toward improving the shrine at Puvali. I wanted to stake out independent territory for my own work. Nevertheless, ineluctably, I went to Puvali every week, but without camera, recorder, or research assistant.

Usually I sat to the side under the *nīm* tree among the female pilgrims clustered around my landlady, known as Bhabhasa (honorific "Grandmother"), who was deeply involved in the shrine's operations in ways mysterious to me at the time. Rajput devotee of a Gujar god, she showed all the weight, royal bearing, and golden ornaments of her caste, and I privately dubbed her "Queen of the Cowherds." Most of the pilgrims at Puvali, although by no means all, were peasants: Gujars, Malis, Minas. Many of their women held whispered consultations with Bhabhasa before presenting their cases to the deity, and sometimes she would herself rise and intercede with the possessed priest on their behalf. She advised, directed, and consoled these troubled women with a brilliant style composed of just the right admixture of authority and intimacy. The authority derived from her caste status, age, and religious knowledge as well as her privileged access both to priest and deity; the intimacy flowed from an organic shared understanding of the female concerns that brought these women to Puvali. Often the most embarrassed and tongue-tied among them

27. Miller is currently at work on a fully annotated Rajasthani text and English translation of the oral epic of the Bhagaravat Brothers and Dev Narayanji, as he recorded it in Ghatiyali from Devji's *bhopās*. Unfortunately, this work is not yet available.

5. Priest of Puvali ka Devji, seated on the shrine platform with the *bhāv* coming to him. Photo by Joseph C. Miller.

suffered from menstrual disorders referred to categorically as "curtained illness" (*parde kī bīmārī*).

Attending Puvali week after week, I continued to struggle with a sense that it would always remain impenetrable and unintelligible. Not only linguistic but psychological barriers prevented me from accepting the situation at face value: that the priest was possessed by Bhairuji acting for Dev Narayanji, and that these people had come, some from considerable distances and some with very grave problems, to seek that deity's aid. The chief priest, about whose person all the shrine's activities revolved, was one of the first characters I met in Ghatiyali. It was he who had facilitated my entrée into village society by announcing my relation to Miller as "father's sister's daughter" (see chapter 1). Thus on our first encounter he had demonstrated his perspicacity simultaneously with a lightning aptitude for appropriate fabrications. When I watched him become possessed and deal with his pilgrims, I could not help recalling his ready penetration and solution of my own problem, effected without the help of Devji or Bharuji.

The priest's antics while he was possessed did not seem to me to manifest divinity. His eyes bulged; he trembled and gasped and blurted out phrases or syllables, sometimes gesticulating madly. It was the reverence which earnest pilgrims displayed toward his person that eventually allowed me to begin accepting the scene at Puvali on its own terms. When I turned my eyes to the *jātarīs*' faces I was often strongly moved by a sense of the presence of power.

Because I was unable to understand much of what was said by pilgrims or priest, my strongest initial impressions of Puvali were nonverbal. There was a sensual richness to these impressions. The background atmosphere included a monotonous, almost stupefying combination of perpetual birdcalls, wind, and a pervasive olfactory haze mingling sweet incense and acrid *dhūp*. Then there would be a sudden awakening shock of sound as the possessed priest violently roared or clanked an iron tool, and the drum beat a prescribed climactic rhythm; or a tactile shock of flying cow-urine drops against the skin. The shrine itself was bright with colors, metallic glitter, and flame. Even taste was involved, for when the possessed priest ordered his assistant to honor me with *bhabhūt* (ashes of *dhūp*), I dutifully ate the ash as I saw others do, wiping the remainder from my palm onto my forehead with appropriate respect for its potency and purity.

Still functioning largely on a nonverbal level, I began to observe that much of the shrine's operations could be crudely categorized as bringing and taking away, giving and receiving, obeying and commanding. I saw pilgrims pour large piles of grain onto the shrine. The possessed priest would later pluck up a precious few of these and, after carefully counting them, hand them to the pilgrim. If the count was an auspicious one (5, 7, 9, or 11), the deity would favor that pilgrim's work. If it was not (3, 4, 6, 8, 10), frequently the priest would simply take another pick. Pilgrims carefully tied these grains up in clean pieces of cloth, often along with a pinch of *bhabhūt,* and carried them home to preserve permanently in a pure place as tangible evidence of a hopeful answer to their prayers.

Also heaped on the shrine platform were small glass bottles filled with pure country *ghī* which pilgrims brought for *dhūp*. If the deity favored their petition, a bright flame would rise from the cow-dung coals in Devji's *dhūp*-holder when the priest added this *ghī,* and the flame was understood, like the auspicious grain-count, as a "proof" (*parcyā*) from the deity of his attention.

Another form of give-and-take was visible in various kinds of motions. Full prostrations on the part of worshippers were frequent. Children, invalids, and recalcitrant mad persons were all caused to prostrate themselves if they were too young, weak, or crazy to do so voluntarily. There was clearly something vital to the workings of the shrine in this gesture of submission, which was also one of incorporation, similar perhaps to the way family members routinely "take the foot dust" of their elders. Circumambulations were also prescribed for pilgrims—this clockwise encircling of deities being an ancient Hindu gesture expressing auspiciousness and respect.

The most common and the simplest curing technique in use at Puvali was "lifting off with the *dhūp*-holder" (*dhūpeṛo utārṇo*). After hearing of some localized physical complaint (stomachache or headache, for example), the possessed priest would command his assistant to take the clay *dhūp*-holder from its place before the icons and make a number of passages with it around the whole afflicted person or the ailing part. During these moments the drum would deliberately beat a compelling rhythm associated with evoking the presence of deities and their powers. Again, some transmission was occurring. The *ghī* that fueled the burning cow-dung was offered by pilgrims, but the healing power that was carried in the flame and smoke surely emanated from the god. The priest and his assistants, using their expertise to manipulate the shrine's sources of power, appeared simply to orchestrate a beneficial contact between deity and pilgrim in such cases.

Frequently a grateful pilgrim would sponsor a nightlong sing and subsequent feast at Puvali, and I attended many of these events. All the participants donated their wakefulness and their tireless songs of praise, while the sponsor expended a fair amount of goods and cash. The god obtained glory through this public recognition of his accomplished works and appeared well disposed toward new pilgrims' cases presented on the day of a feast. The priest often advised clients to attend his nightlong sings and asked that feasts be pledged by pilgrims seeking difficult cures or boons. The *prasād* dispensed at dawn after a nightlong sing was white rice cooked in sugar water, slopped stickily from right palm to right

6. Removing a malign intrusive spirit from a woman pilgrim with Devji's offering flame; Puvali. Photo by Joseph C. Miller.

7. Puvali's priest administers the deity's healing powers through his foot. Photo by Joseph C. Miller.

palm without leaf or serving utensil. Those who had kept the wake received this gooey grace after morning *āratī* and were thereby perhaps made more fit to receive boons from the deity when he summoned them to state their cases later that day.

The feasts that followed nightlong sings were usually held between a special morning and the regular afternoon possession session. They were called *savāmaṇī,* or "one and one-quarter maunds," referring to the amount of wheat flour (approximately fifty kilograms) that was conventionally used in their preparation, along with proportionate accompaniments. The flour was always made into fried bread, served most often with heavily peppered potato stew and a sweet—generally the relatively inexpensive *lapsī* (cracked wheat boiled in raw sugar syrup), but sometimes a more prestigious preparation involving *ghī* and white sugar. Anyone present at the shrine on the day of a *savāmaṇī,* even strangers to the feast donor, would be invited to eat. The food was the same as that served at feasts marking weddings and funerals, but such affairs involved careful calculations according to past obligations and anticipated returns. The *savāmaṇī,* on the contrary, was an expression of largesse—of giving without expectations—performed in the deity's name.

As a Saturday afternoon regular, I ate at many such feasts (and got sick from some) long before I approached a feast sponsor to ask him what he was doing and why. As with my other Puvali experiences, then, nightlong sings and feasts were physically assimilated long before they were anthropologically examined. It seems to me very possible that my initial nonverbal apprehensions of Puvali suggested and moulded to some degree my subsequent interpretation of this place (and all Rajasthani *devasthān*) in terms of substantial transactions both gross and subtle: cash for a protective armband; *ghī* for powerful ashes; faith for blessings. The patterns that I intuited there began to make sense on a wider scale, however, as I pursued my fieldwork more systematically on other fronts. Visits to many other shrines in the surrounding area, where there were less flamboyant priests, fewer sources of power, and generally less chaotic activities, helped me to notice those patterns repetitively common to all deities' places.[28]

28. See A. Gold (1987a) for a detailed analysis of transactions at the shrine of Shri Lakreshvar Mahadev in Rajasthan.

Eventually, with the help of a few patient informants, several assistants, and transcriptions of Miller's tape recordings, my understanding of the motivational concerns of Puvali's pilgrims grew. Finally I pieced together some crucial fragments of the shrine's history—hardly ancient but already imbued with a blurred and mythic quality. Entwined with it, of course, is the history of the chief priest and his followers and backers. A sketch of that vital background follows here, along with a less subjective presentation of the place itself as deities' domain and pilgrims' goal.

Puvali is a brisk ten- to fifteen-minute walk from Ghatiyali's center (that is, from the bus stand or Four-Arms Temple). It lies to the side of an unpaved road, which is a daily bus route to and from Devli town during the eight months of the year when buses ply. Thus, except during the rainy season, pilgrims may come and go by that convenient means. Many, however, arrive by oxcart, by bicycle, or on foot, and some occasionally by the truckload. Puvali's domes and flags are just visible from the road, but the shrine is set well back from it, requiring a short hike through fields.

According to a venerable Rajput informant who was himself much involved in the shrine's recent revitalization, Puvali was a very old place of Devji, but little tended or attended, lacking even a cement platform. Devji's traditional brick icons were there, however, and a hereditary *bhopā* from a nearby village performed minimal service for them and made Saturday rounds in Ghatiyali, asking grain for his efforts.

Then, between thirty and forty years ago, a few miraculous cures were associated with Puvali's Dev Narayanji, leading to renewed interest in the place. This Rajput informant himself received one such cure—learning in a dream that its source was Puvali's Devji. The shrine was rebuilt, and a new stone icon of Devji was made ready for installation. The men involved in this project were Gujars, Rajputs, and Naths, and significantly, members of these three castes today still figure largely in the shrine's operations. While the story thus far is vague and undetailed, my Rajput informant's description of the actual event of installing the icon was by contrast very sharp, for he himself had done it.

As this man told the story, a Brahman pandit had been consulted to determine the auspicious time for installing the new icon at Puvali. A small group of devotees then assembled there in the dark of night to await this moment. However, seeing some eerie-looking light approaching them, most of these men fled in fear to a safe distance while my informant, being unafraid, held his ground. His equanimity proved reasonable and rewarding. The light was a lantern carried by a member of the householding Nath caste. The Nath instructed the Rajput to install the icon as planned, despite the absence of the other men. I give the climax of this narration in my informant's words:

> This Nath came near and said, "Prince?" [a standard polite address term for any Rajput male] I said, "Yes?" He said, "Get up. The auspicious time to install the icon has arrived." I said, "This is not work for me alone, it is the work of five men; only they can do this. The pandit also will come." Then he said, "No, there is no necessity for any Maharaj [Brahman], for any kind of pandit. You do it yourself right now."

Thus the new icon of Dev Narayanji was installed by the hand of a Rajput, under the authority of a Nath. That night's events engendered a further restructuring of authority at the shrine. The hereditary priest had been summoned but had failed for some reason to present himself, and soon afterward the service at Puvali was "given" to the current priest, who had undergone a series of extreme personal trials by which Devji made it known to him that he was to become his *bhopā*.

The sources of power at Puvali are not restricted to Dev Narayanji, and a brief look at the shrine's major icons and their uses will help to clarify the curing processes that are implemented there. The primary icons of Puvali are installed at the back of a large raised platform. These are Dev Narayanji's "bricks" (*īṇṭ*), as well as a carved icon of Devji riding his famed mare Lila Ghori. The flat stone plank directly beneath these is said to belong to Pipal De Rani, Devji's wife. Behind the bricks are stones representing the couple's twin son and daughter known as Bila-Bili (born after Dev Narayanji placed two crushed leaves of the *bīl* tree in Pipal De Rani's "pouch," a significant precedent for pouch-filling). The "essential" shrine is also embellished with framed colored pictures of the gods, and small, ornate, silver umbrellas donated by pilgrims to shade and honor the icons. The bricks themselves are kept nicely "dressed" with sheets of colored, patterned foil. Overspreading the shrine from its right side is a *nīm* tree,[29] beneath which resides one of the compound's several Bhairujis.

Despite the preeminence and centrality of Dev Narayanji's icons at Puvali, many detractors of the priest's enterprise and several realists among his followers asserted that his actual miracle-working power did not come from Devji at all. Facing and somewhat to the side of the main shrine is the renouncer's fireplace of Balaknathji, Ghatiyali's legendary Cave Baba (see chapter 1). Puvali's priest counts this village deity among his chief gurus. It is at Balaknathji's shrine, and not Dev Narayanji's, that the protective metal armbands (*kaṛā*), which many pilgrims obtain from Puvali, are empowered.

In order to charge these bands with their potency, they are placed in a red "pouch" (*jholī* again) and deposited in a niche over the fireplace. The priest then recites "spells" (*mantra-tantra*) over them, after which he removes them from the pouch and worships them with raw cow's milk and cow urine. Finally, the armbands are turned briefly in smoke and flame from Dev Narayanji's *dhūp* and stored beneath a *dhūp*-holder on the main shrine platform. For full effectiveness, the charging process must be repeated every year, just like renewing a passport, as one informant explained it. The Cave Baba's manifest part in Puvali's complex is also testified to by a newly constructed "umbrella-dome" raised over stone

29. On this *nīm* tree hang not only cradle-baskets but a tale. During the latter part of my stay in Ghatiyali, owing in part to Miller's magnanimity, shrine-improving construction was going forward apace at Puvali. A Muslim master-workman was engaged, and he presented an elegant design for three crowning domes over the main shrine's icons. His plan, however, would have necessitated cutting off a large branch from the *nīm* tree. Puvali's priest while possessed forbade this violently and tearfully: "Don't cut my *nīm* tree!"

An alternative design, somewhat less pleasing aesthetically, was devised to accommodate the deity's whim, but the master-workman was not happy with it. Construction was already under way, however, when the "Pushkar Maharaj" visited our village. This imposing personage, an ochre-robed renouncer, had a kind of authority over all of Dev Narayanji's temples in the area. He did not like the second plan, which kept the tree intact, and by his authority the branch was cut after all and the original design accomplished. The deity wept once more over this desecration of his beloved tree.

After I returned to America I heard through letters that the Pushkar Maharaj was experiencing great personal and financial difficulties. This was shocking news, as he had always appeared to be a pillar of strength. My correspondent suggested, almost two years after the *nīm* episode, that these unaccountable developments were a direct punishment inflicted by Dev Narayanji because of the branch.

8. Priest of Puvali ka Devji performs spells to empower protective armbands (in square pouch) at the Cave Baba's fireplace; Puvali. Photo by Joseph C. Miller.

"footprints" representing him. This edifice was erected at the expense of the Rajput woman devotee and accomplice of the shrine, Bhabhasa, to honor Balaknathji.

Somewhat more distant from the main platform are the small separate places of Bhairuji and Gailaji. These are vital to the workings of the shrine. Although all pilgrims first address themselves to the priest as he sits beside Devji's throne, difficult cases of malign possession or madness are brought to these discrete places, where cures are effected by their respective deities.

Bhairuji, who is often associated with the control of ghosts and spirits of the ill-doing dead,[30] is an ubiquitous, multiplex deity in Rajasthan. In the form of Kala-Gaura Bhairu, he has his place in Dev Narayan's mythology and is present at all his shrines. He is, at Puvali as elsewhere, considered Devji's agent and the one who actually possesses the priest, since Dev Narayan, as *avatār* of the high god Vishnu, would not engage in possession. Bhairuji's wor-

30. See Kakar 1982:53–88 for the description of a powerful Rajasthani shrine where another Bhairuji, in conjunction with Hanuman, deals very effectively with violent and restless intrusive spirits. This place, Mehndipur Balaji—the main deity being Hanuman—is also briefly encountered in chapter 5.

ship at this subsidiary shrine, however, is distinctly separate from Devji's. For example, Bhairuji craves and receives offerings of home-brewed liquor. Dev Narayan, on the other hand, abhors all use of alcohol, demanding strict temperance. When liquor is offered, then, Devji's view of Bhairu's shrine must be blocked with an improvised curtain.

Gailaji, whose name means "crazy," is a deity whom I have encountered only at Puvali. He is not connected with the Dev Narayan epic. Significantly enough, Gailaji's special place, his original shrine, is located near the natal village of Puvali's priest's mother. While staying there over a protracted period of time, long before taking up his role at Puvali, the priest had been intermittently sick and crazy. This Gailaji cured him and, at the same time, began to possess him. Thus, when called upon to preside over Puvali, the priest brought Gailaji with him. When possessed by Gailaji, the priest's style of speech is even more markedly disjointed, his motions more abrupt and violent, than during an ordinary possession.

Puvali's domain also contains a Balaji (Hanuman) and a Shiva *lingam,* thus incorporating more of general Hinduism's powerful gods into the local complex. There are also spots on Puvali's grounds dedicated to a Sagasji, to the lingering spirit of a Muslim butcher from Sawar who was robbed and murdered in the vicinity, and to several other minor deities. Most of these just passively "take *dhūp,*" which prevents their becoming troublesome; otherwise they have no major part in the shrine's workings."

At about three o'clock every Saturday afternoon the priest, seated on the ground and reclining somewhat on the Cave Baba's fireplace, is possessed by Bhairuji acting as the direct agent of Dev Narayanji—that is, the *bhāv* of Bhairuji comes to him. While the drum beats and the pilgrims are hushed, he begins to breathe heavily and to tremble; his eyes roll about weirdly; his head lolls and jerks. Once the possession is complete, the priest as deity mounts the main platform and sits down near Dev Narayanji's colored-cushion throne, although never upon it. From there he begins summoning his pilgrims, sometimes according to ailment and sometimes according to village.

Usually the possessed priest calls for cases of mad-dog bites first, the theory being that they require the most immediate attention, but there rarely are any such cases, as it is not one of Puvali's famed specialities. Calling pilgrims by their villages,[31] the possessing god shows his awareness of who must catch the afternoon bus and who is at leisure to wait, as well as of whose cases are easily treated and whose problems demand intricate measures.

During the long afternoon curing session, the priest is always attended by several solicitous assistants and devotees. They change or adjust his turban when it becomes disheveled because of his shaking and thrashing movements. They give him whiffs of perfume and, when commanded, splash cow urine. They support him when, occasionally overwhelmed, he appears about to collapse. This will usually occur toward the end of the day when the possession may "lift" and redescend several times. The priest's most frequent muttered comment at this juncture, as the scribes of Miller's recordings discovered to their shocked amusement, is "I'll shove a stick up his mother"—a fairly serious "mother-insult" by village standards. This insult was directed, I was told, to Dev Narayanji's Mother—Sadu Mata, a lady worshipped in her own right—because the priest was enraged with the god for causing him to suffer so deeply through being possessed. In fact, the man clearly does find possession physically taxing. He often vomits repeatedly when it is over and, once home in the village, may take to his cot, groaning audibly. Sometimes he would beg Miller for Alka-Seltzer to ease his own "stomach sorrow" after having, as shrine priest, eased so many pilgrims' pains.

The priest's resort to remedies from another source is not, however, inconsistent with the practice of the deity he represents. During curing sessions I have several times heard him stating that certain afflictions are out of his range of competence. A man whose wife suffered from aching knees received this curt reply: "It is *vāyaṇ* ["wind"] and it won't be cured by me."[32] When the pilgrim persisted in begging for help, the priest speaking as deity recommended an oil massage and repeated, definitively, "It is not *our* disease." He thus dismissed the pilgrim with a denial of his

31. When he summoned Miller or me, sometimes to extract monetary commitments but often just to offer pleasant predictions of success, the possessed priest would blurt out "from America from America" (*amrīkā kā amrīkā kā*) in exactly the same fashion that he called for residents of other villages.

32. A "wind" disease would fall within the domain of Ayurvedic medicine (there was a resident practitioner in Ghatiyali). Wind is one of the three *doshas*, or humors, fundamental to Ayurvedic theory. For one description of the humors, their normal and pernicious functions, see Dash 1978:18–28.

own power—and of his responsibility—to cure this particular affliction. I have also heard him recommend to a chronic fever sufferer that he obtain malaria pills from Miller.

The pilgrims who flock to Puvali are predominantly Gujars, Minas, Malis, and others of the clean peasant castes. They also, however, include the *ṭhākur*s of nearby Sawar, a number of other Rajputs, and a fair sprinkling of Brahmans. Persons from three of Ghatiyali's caste communities stand out today as most deeply involved in the current operations at Puvali. They are Gujars, a Nath, and a Rajput, and we recall that members of the same three groups played key parts in founding, or, more accurately, renewing, the shrine as an active place of power.

Being a Gujar hero-god, Dev Narayanji is worshipped and supported largely by that caste in many villages. Devji's priests are drawn from either Gujars or Balai (weavers). It was, as we have seen, a Rajput patron-devotee who, convinced by cures and dreams, installed a new icon at Puvali with his own hand. He performed the installation, moreover, under authority from a Nath. Today a Rajput woman and a Nath man are the two outstanding participants, besides the chief priest and other Gujar *bhopā*s assisting him, in the shrine's activities. Their involvement in Puvali appears, however, to have more to do with personal history than with caste tradition.

The case of the Rajput woman Bhabhasa's long-term affiliation with Puvali and her role there present a number of anomalies to the observer of normative customs and hierarchies in Ghatiyali. As an in-married Rajput female, she putatively lives in purdah—that is, "curtained" from all public exposure. Indeed, Bhabhasa maintains the pretense of this seclusion of Rajput wives, unique among Ghatiyali's castes, in going neither to the well to draw water nor to the reservoir to bathe. However, as a devotee of Dev Narayanji, she not only regularly attended Puvali's Saturday sessions and its all-night sings but also was to be found in various village homes whenever the chief priest's *bhajan* party performed. She had made at least one long pilgrimage without her husband in the company of this Gujar priest and his retinue. Almost yearly she traveled to Pushkar fair with the same group, sleeping in the Gujar *dharmashālā* that houses the Dev Narayanji temple there.

It was rumored that Bhabhasa had an equal partnership with the Gujar priest in the shrine's considerable profits. She liked to describe her relation with him as that of sister to brother in *dharma*. In the priest's absence, Bhabhasa would sometimes assert that she was equal to him in religious knowledge, but in his company she tended to defer, at least superficially, to his status as *bhopājī*. However, Bhabhasa was indeed a healer in her own right, possessing various spells to remove aches and pains and being adept at a technique of deep stomach massage which was sometimes administered in cases of infertility, along with petitions to Devji.

One of the priest's most competent helpers at Puvali was a Nath man, son of one of the participants in the original installation who had fled from the eerie lights. This gentle, humorous, and highly articulate man acted as an intermediary between male pilgrims and possessed priest in much the same fashion as Bhabhasa did for female *jātarī*s. His role is important, for the deity often speaks elliptically and mysteriously, and pilgrims are sometimes too tongue-tied to present their petitions in a properly convincing way. The nature of this Nath's relationship with the priest and the shrine was never fully apparent to me, but it clearly involved financial as well as religious links.

The priest appreciated the Nath's role at the shrine and compensated for it, I was told, by making him interest-free loans. The Nath, who was the best lead singer in the priest's *bhajan*-party, also reaped some profits from this role, receiving donations when they performed. This man was probably in his early forties and thus far had remained childless. Although his second wife was aging, he still sustained the hope of receiving that great boon which Dev Narayanji had lavished on so many lesser devotees.

The Nath seemed to have a very realistic sense of Puvali's priest's human character, while at the same time sincerely and deeply revering and devoting himself to Dev Narayanji. Nearly illiterate but with some Hindi veneer on his Rajasthani, he was one of the first persons to shed light for me on some of Puvali's action. Explaining the distribution of grain donations, he told me in deadpan style that the small piles would be scattered for and consumed by the pigeons while the large amounts were taken and eaten by the "big pigeon"—of course the shrine priest himself.

After many months of attending Puvali's weekly and special sessions, I began to apprehend some of the separate tales lying behind the formulaic "sorrow-and-trouble" of pilgrims. Although many involved minor complaints or quests, others represented cases of severe affliction involving malevolent possession, intrafamilial jealousies and rage, occasional miracles, deep faith, and prolonged suffering. The three cases presented below are samples not intended as typical. Rather they are among those that sparked a special interest and curiosity and aroused some amount of surprise as well as pity among other pilgrims and bystanders who saw or heard of them.

Although the first two cases were both described as "crazy" (*pāgal*), they appeared to be quite different sorts of madness. One concerned a youth who had clearly been suffering some kind of seizures since early childhood, which over the years had almost wholly disabled him. His father still hoped and expected to receive a full evaluation from some deity, which would teach him the way to restore his son's mind and body. The second crazy one was an older man, also accompanied by his father, whose sudden fits of violent madness disrupted what appeared to be a hitherto fairly normal existence. What the two had in common were problematic relationships with deities. The third case, on the other hand—a woman afflicted by a malevolent, child-devouring female spirit—demonstrates a deficiency caused by a negative, lower being.

Chronic Illness and Peripatetic Faith

The following dialogue is extracted from the transcribed text of a lengthy recorded interview with the father of a young man referred to as "crazy." The father had transported this virtually incapacitated son to Puvali with some difficulty. His answers reveal the perpetual hope offered by shrines even in the face of repeated and long-term disappointments.[33]

Interviewer: And now you have come to Devji. Before this, where did you go?

Pilgrim: Many places. We have been many places. Many times we have taken him to Mavalya Mataji's place. We took him to Mataji's place.

33. Some of the places enumerated by this informant were well-known and popular curing shrines in the Ajmer-Bhilwara area; others neither I nor my research assistant were familiar with. Within this man's frame of reference, Victoria Hospital in Ajmer, a dispenser of Western medical treatments, appears hardly distinguishable from other numerous places of power which he had visited to no avail.

Interviewer: Mavalya Mataji?

Pilgrim: Yes, we took him to Kanei Mavalya Mataji. We also took him to Khotya. We also took him to Anguca Bhura Baba and to Khamor Sagasji. We also took him to Hakale Mataji, and we took him to Ajmer too.

Interviewer: To the hospital?

Pilgrim: Yes, to the hospital.

Interviewer: Victoria?

Pilgrim: Yes, to Victoria. And we took him to Jhatala Mataji, and we also took him to Runije.

Interviewer: Ram Devji's place?

Pilgrim: Yes, and we took him to Deval also. . . . And first of all we took him to Dabarela. They said that he had polio, so we took him to Dabarela.

Interviewer: First, suspecting polio, you took him to Dabarela.

Pilgrim: Yes, to Devki Nandji Maharaj. Then we wandered like that very much. We came to our Bhairuji also, and Dhanop also, and we also came to Kusayata here.

Interviewer: You came also to Kusayata? Then how did you hear about *this* Devji, that "in that place [Puvali] there is a Devji"?

Pilgrim: We heard the fame of this place in this way: "Here many crazy ones come who get better." If we had heard it previously we would have come sooner, but now . . .

Interviewer: Who told you about this place?

Pilgrim: People from our village come here.

Interviewer: From Bargav?

Pilgrim: Yes, Gujars, and they said that they saw crazy ones getting better. For this reason they received faith, and they told us.

Interviewer: They told you, "Crazy ones get better there"?

Pilgrim: Yes, they said, "There crazy ones get better. For this reason you ought to take him there." So we have brought him here. They had full faith in this place and so we also immediately thought: "We too will go."

Although this man had visited a great number of shrines during the lengthy course of his son's illness, he had, as the interview eventually revealed, invested the most hope (and money) in one particular deity: Kanei Mavalya Mataji. Although he now declared his full faith in Devji, he was clearly still involved in a relationship with this goddess, the only one whose aid he had sought repeatedly, and the only one who had any positive, albeit temporary, effect on his son's condition. Speaking of her, he tended to sound like a thwarted but still fervent lover, filled sometimes with resentment, sometimes with adoration.

Interviewer: You have taken him to so many places, but none of them have caused any change?

Pilgrim: No change came at any place, except for Mavalya Mataji. She opened his legs and made him stand. But within twelve months the legs returned to their previous condition and stayed that way, so we left off going there. But if that had not happened, at first, Mavalya Mataji caused a lot of change [for the good]. She eased his twisted body and supported his life. Since then, for five or six years, she has not even glanced at him; formerly, whatever she said, I did, but when there continued to be no change we left off going there. . . . I even held a *savāmaṇī* feast there.

Interviewer: At Mavalya Mataji's place?

Pilgrim: Yes, as she told us to do. We brought all the things and held an all-night sing. Our whole *bhajan* party went and spent the whole night.

Interviewer: All the way to her place?

Pilgrim: Yes, there we had a ceaseless all-night wake, for the entire night, and we had a *savāmaṇī* feast. Whatever she told us we did it all. . . . But later there was no difference. For seven years we went, but when there was no difference we quit going. Otherwise we would have built a new road there, for Mavalya Mataji.

The fact that the goddess first took such a promising view of the youth, but that relapse rather than greater improvements in his condition followed, sets the stage for attributing the crazy one's continued suffering to her provoked disfavor. In giving this diagnosis, Puvali's possessed priest reaffirms what was already known by the paralyzed youth's father.

Interviewer: Is it a problem of some witch or ghost?

Pilgrim: It's nothing like that, no ghost or witch. He [the possessed priest] said that it was a quarrel of this Mavalya Mataji's. Wherever we go, they say just this, that he [the crazy one] was struck by Mavalya Mataji's arrow. They say that wherever we go.

The pilgrim used several different terms during the interview to describe the goddess's negative influence on his son. In the passage just cited it is a "quarrel" (*laṛ*) and it is also an angry emanation—her "arrow" (*bāṇ*). At another point he speculated that Mavalya Mataji became angry with him for going to deities other than herself, and in this context the phrase "[her] *choṭ* fell [upon him]" was used. Now *choṭ* is a term which, according to the *RSK*, means a troublesome deterioration caused by contact with a person born under a bad astrological configuration or, alternatively, by the bad effects of contact with menstruating women.

In Ghatiyali usage, *choṭ* seems similar, in its automatic functioning, to the "evil eye" (*nazar*)[34]. However, whereas an evil eye usually weakens the too splendidly whole and healthy, *choṭ* generally falls upon healing wounds or convalescents. I have heard it used most frequently with reference to snakebites, and never in any other case in association with a deity's displeasure. The spoiling power of *choṭ* is innate and distinctly feminine.[35] The implication of its use here is that, Mavalya Mataji's jealousy having been aroused by her pilgrim's resort to other deities, some flow of negative substance originating in this goddess blighted the healing process that she herself had begun.

No startling revelations were made in this case by Puvali's Devji. Speaking through his priest, the deity declared his full "support," a very vague but comforting assertion. Essentially he told the passive pilgrim what he already knew, that he must return to a more active courtship of the goddess's favor. The actions prescribed by Devji were that Mavalya Mataji's "bath water" be administered to the youth monthly on the bright eighth—the goddess's day—and that curative "sweeping" be performed on

34. The harmful potency of the evil eye (*nazar*, or gaze) in Ghatiyali was of concern in many contexts: a jealous neighbor present during milking could cause fresh milk to curdle; a jealous glance at a new set of bangles could cause them to break; a jealous (or admiring) eye cast on a healthy child could cause it to sicken. For evil eye in rural South Asia, see Maloney 1976; Pocock 1981. For evil eye beliefs in cross-cultural and case study perspectives, see Dundes, ed., 1981; Maloney, ed., 1976.

35. After a snakebite victim's wound has been treated (the poison is sucked out by a priest of Tejaji while he is possessed by that deity), the victim usually spends several days convalescing in a temple—any temple convenient to his or her residence. The explicit reason for this, I was told, was to avoid *choṭ*: menstruating women would not even accidentally come near, as they consciously avoid temples.

this same day in Mavalya Mataji's name.[36] If this regime were followed, the god promised, "within seven months there will be some difference." The father appeared satisfied, almost elated, by this diagnosis: "In my heart it seems he told what the gods told before and I understand it fully. It is a true thing. So now we will go only to her [Mavalya Mataji]."

In this crazy one's case, shrine pilgrimage appears to be self-perpetuating and inconclusive. The son's chronic and gradually deteriorating condition is unacceptable to his father, who continues to seek for cures in every direction. He is hardly surprised or upset, however, when Devji, rather than vouchsafing a total cure, just sends him back the way he has come. One of the chief sorts of information offered at shrines is an inventory of all invisible powers involved in a case, and advice on how they may be respectively satisfied. Thus Devji's appraisal is an appropriate one. Moreover, it confirms the pilgrim's own analysis of the situation and reiterates other deities' verdicts. From his pilgrimage to Puvali the father has received a renewed will to try once more to please the difficult goddess, whose praises he blurts out even while complaining of her abandonment. For seven months at least he now has a program to follow and some hope. The priest also suggested that at the end of this stipulated period he return to Puvali, but so far as I know, he never did. This is often the case with *jātaṛīs* from afar who receive no immediate boons.

The Mad Mina from Navagao

The Mad Mina's case of craziness differs strikingly from the one just examined, in several respects. First, the crazy man himself was not a passive, voiceless invalid but a strong adult whose violent fits of madness alternated with perfectly lucid and coherent states. Second, the possessed priest was able to identify not one but three offended deities. Moreover, while accepting these explanations concerning the deities involved in his problems, the crazy Mina himself had still other insights into his own madness and its potential mitigation, deriving from household and familial dy-

36. Marriott has pointed out the two-way or circulative flow here: If the devotee will regularly drink the goddess's lowest substance (her "bath water"), then the goddess will take back from him, in the sweepings, the illness previously sent by her (personal communication).

namics. These vistas opened, perhaps therapeutically, during the shared experience of the mad man and his family at the shrine.

K, the crazy Mina from Navagao, was brought into Ghatiyali proper with his arms tightly bound to his body as his father and an accompanying cousin-brother more or less dragged him along by a rope. They had arrived on a Friday when the shrine would be deserted, and so proceeded directly to the priest's house. Seeing the emergency, the priest agreed to repair to Puvali at once and hold a special possession session that very afternoon.

During this session the deity, speaking through his priest, identified three separate causes of the man's problem:

1. K and his family had offended a *jhūjhārjī,* spirit of a deceased uncle already enshrined in their home.

2. K personally had committed a "fault" (*dosh*) against a Dev Narayanji (known as the Sandhill Devji) of his home village (Navagao) by stepping on that deity's unprotected icon while wearing shoes (apparently during a mad spell, so this was a secondary cause).

3. Puvali's Devji was annoyed with this family because of vows they recently had made to him and had not yet fulfilled. These vows—of grain, fodder, and a feast—were spoken by K's father upon the successful cure of another "mad" son (whose case when described sounded more like severe heatstroke and involved only a single, nonviolent episode). The father responded rather curtly to the deity in regard to these pledges: he would fulfill them after harvest. His tone implied that the god was being unreasonable, making demands now when he knew that the crops were not yet gathered.

K himself did not deny any of these three causalities. He certainly attributed much of his trouble to the offended uncle-deity, but he lodged the blame for that deity's displeasure with others in the household who had refused to recognize its demands, thus causing it to attack K. There was something else preying on K's mind, however, and during our interview with him he insisted on going into this matter in great detail, despite his relations' attempts to shut him up. It had to do with money: an outstanding debt of 120 rupees which K owed to a man for an ox, now dead, which the man had sold to an uncle of K's, also recently deceased, for which the uncle's son (not the cousin accompanying K at Puvali) definitively refused to pay.

Because K had taken the role of informal "co-signer" to this purchase, and because he had an enduring fictive kin relation with the creditor—a man of another village and a different caste—the burden of this debt weighed heavily on him and he seemed to associate it strongly with the origins of his madness. According to his somewhat convoluted tale, K had first become crazy and stepped on the Sandhill Devji's icon after a chance but disastrous encounter with his cousin, during which the latter had fully repudiated all responsibility for the debt. The possessed priest never mentioned this fourth problem, and it was left unresolved when K departed, but I note it here to show how the shrine may be a context for revelations of interpersonal strains. This problem of K's with humans was, moreover, analogous to and connected with some of his problems with deities. The issue of an unpaid debt was involved in Puvali's Devji's displeasure with K and his family, and the episode that offended the Sandhill Devji was precipitated by K's encounter with the defaulting cousin.

Some annotated selections from the recorded text of Friday's diagnostic possession session reveal characteristic modes of communication between deity and pilgrims. They show both an elliptical style on the part of the priest and a ready response from the pilgrims—indicative of the preestablished nature of much of the deity's pronouncements. These selections highlight the moments of judgment when the god identified the three causes of K's madness. Although I have discussed the sources of K's madness in the apparent order of their causal priority, the deity gave the least important one first, according to his own interest.

Priest possessed by Bhairuji (hereafter B): *Cet Cet! Bābā! Cet cet cet!* [These exclamations are characteristic of the possession. *Cet* means "Watch out!" and *Bābā,* I was told, is an appeal to the priest's guru, the Cave Baba, despite the fact that now he is speaking as Dev Narayanji's agent.] Yes, Brother, why did you call today?

Father of K, the crazy one (hereafter F): Grain-giver, see him, his stomach is welted, his hands are welted, for three days he has been tied with rope.

K, the crazy one (hereafter K): Milk for milk, water for water [make a true judgment], Grain-giver.

F: His whole body is scratched.

[Now the deity gives his first diagnosis, concerning the unfulfilled pledges to himself made by the madman's father.]

B: Yes, on that day, what did you say? You said a *savāmaṇī* feast.

F: What did I say? Now, listen to the whole story.

B: You said one son's *savāmaṇī* feast for me.

F: Yes.

B: I cured one son.

F: Yes.

K: Give wealth and health, Grain-giver, and I'll do it.

B: What, *hã hã hã* [a breathy sound, frequently emitted by the possessed priest], what, what did you say to me? You on that day, you brought that child to me, on that day.

F: I said a *savāmaṇī* feast.

B: And . . . ?

F: And I said bundles of fodder [offered at shrines to feed cattle, a meritorious act].

B: Yes.

F: And I said millet. But this was that one's [that is, his other son's] affair.

B: Bring the millet!

F: As I said on that very day, when my new crop comes, I will give it.

B: When the new crop comes, I will take it, *hã hã hã!*

F: Where is the millet now? and the fodder bundles also? Now from where will I get them to scatter them?

[Here the deity abruptly switches to the primary source of this family's joint troubles.]

B: The middle brother.

F: Yes.

B: Middle brother, one brother, one brother died, didn't he?

F: Yes, died.

B: Yes, his land, who is eating it? You are eating *hã hã hã hã hũ hũ hũ*. You will seat him on the well [that is, install an icon dedicated to the madman's deceased uncle on a well located in his former field].

F: Yes, we will seat him if you tell us to.

[After some further attention to this, the deity makes another abrupt shift of topic, almost as if he suddenly sees the third transgression.]

B: Yes, and look, they put their feet on the god's footprints and stood there. [At the Sandhill Devji's place in Navagao there is no platform for the icons. Thus the stone footprints representing the deity are on the ground, and apparently during a violent struggle with a relation encountered at that place, K had inadvertently stepped on this icon and also dragged his opponent upon it. The possessed priest now specifically addresses the father.] Why couldn't you grab him, why couldn't you prevent it?

F: I wasn't even there, how could I grab him?

B: Two were standing there.

F: If they were, what do I know? I was in the fields: anyone might have been there. Any neighbor, somebody or other, might have been there. This thing will be told by those who were there. [He thus washes his hands of any complicity in this insult committed by his son.]

The deity prescribed "lifting off with the *dhūp*-holder" and five circumambulations but repeatedly insisted "I will keep him half-crazy." Thus, despite passionate pleas from all concerned that the night pass peacefully, the god refused to promise this. In fact, K had to be painfully tied to a thorn tree near the shrine when his madness overcame him again around dawn.

After the possession by Dev Narayan's Bhairuji lifted, the priest questioned K a bit as to his current condition. Suddenly, however, the priest was repossessed, this time by Gailaji, the crazy deity, whose special business is madness. Gailaji did little more than rehearse the facts already established. After his influence also lifted, we all continued to sit around Puvali for an hour or so, talking with the madman and his family and listening to the priest and a few of his followers fondly reminisce about previous cases of madness cured by Dev Narayanji. Most relished in the telling were episodes involving young women whose illness manifested itself in a desperate striptease.

The following day, a Saturday, when the shrine was regularly active, we returned to Puvali too late to see the possessed priest dealing for the second time with the mad Mina. From interviewing K, however, we learned the events of the morning. He seemed perfectly lucid at this time, and told us that the main conclusions of the deity's diagnosis were the same as the previous day's: the uncle's *jhūjhārjī* was to be seated on the well, and the pledges made to Puvali on behalf of the other son, K's brother, were to be fulfilled. K complained bitterly about having been tied again, during his fit, by his father and cousin, displaying the marks on his skin from rope burns and the thorns of the tree to which he had been bound. He admitted, however, that at the time he could not feel the pain. "If one had awareness, who would scratch himself like this?"

At this point it seemed that his pilgrimage was finished and he was ready to go home, but suddenly he became crazy again, putting both his thumbs in his mouth and stretching his lips horizontally in a curious fashion, while breathing heavily. His relations hastily pushed him front and center before the deity, and the possessed priest began to shriek at him, exasperated with this unseemly new display.

> *B:* Have him bow, have him bow, *Bābā! Cet cet cet cet! Vā!* Here, have him seated, have him seated in front, yes, *Bābā!* Yes, come here, *Bābā! Cet cet cet cet! Hũ hũ hũ,* yes, come here! Bring the incense-holder here! *Cet cet cet cet!* Throw on drops [of cow urine], throw on drops!

K finally removed his hands from his face and, still clearly in the grip of a powerful wave of madness, had the following exchange with the deity:

> *K:* You are the guru, you are the guru, you are the guru!
>
> *B:* Yes, *Bābā, cet cet cet cet!*
>
> *K:* I am your cow, your cow, your cow. *Āre bāre* [exclamation of grief and pain]! I am a cow. I am a cow.

In the course of this last encounter the possessed priest extracted a final commitment from the madman and his family to offer grain and sweets at the shrine of Devji in their home village, where K had accidentally stepped on the icon. They were also instructed to make prostrations at that shrine before returning to their house and were urged to hasten on their way. The priest had repeatedly expended energy on this case, and he had now prescribed some restitution that would improve K's relations with each offended deity.

The case of the mad Mina did have a good outcome, so far as I was able to follow it. Approximately three weeks after his visit to Puvali, I attended a *melā* at the Devji shrine in Navagao, his home village. During my visit there I encountered K, looking and sounding quite normal and happy. He had just made an offering of five kilos of sweets at this home shrine, as he had promised to do while at Puvali. The grains and fodder bundles and feast on his brother's account were still due to Puvali's Devji, and the seating of the *jhūjhārjī* on the well would not take place for several months because of calendrical strictures. Nevertheless, K felt that his episode of madness was well closed.

The Sandhill Devji of Navagao. Devji's sandhill in Navagao is worth describing, for it offers a nicely contrasting example of shrine (and shrine priest) character and management. Like Puvali, the shrine at Navagao is located outside the settled village, in this case on a dunelike rise. The shrine consists simply of a large *nīm* tree beneath which are the original icons, five small stones (in lieu of Devji's usual bricks). Near these is a more recently installed icon of Devji in the form of stone footprints. It was on these footprints that K so unfortunately had placed his own. A number of spears and flagpoles presented to the god as thank-offerings are clustered near the central icons.

Answers to pilgrims' questions are determined here through the common technique of "grain-asking," and ashes of *dhūp* are dispensed for general beneficent purposes. The priest does not become possessed, however, nor are afflictions by "witches" and "ghosts" treated. The place does have two specialties: snakebites and mad-dog bites. These are cured by the method of "sweeping" with *nīm* leaves. For this treatment Devji's spears are used as conduits, and the sweeping is directed from the afflicted part to the icons. It was explained to me that the deity, without harm to himself, is able to receive the poison transmitted to him by the sweeping.

Unlike Puvali, which is neither supervised nor subsidized by Ghatiyali as a community—it might, indeed, be viewed as a form of private enterprise on the part of the priest and his entourage—the sandhill shrine of Navagao, whose population is predominantly Mina, has a management committee which keeps a tight rein on its finances. Under the committee's stipulations, the priest, a Balai from a nearby village, receives for his personal consumption only the small amounts of grain called *maṭhaṛī* designated for grain-asking, and perishable foods like yogurt or cooked treats. Larger amounts of grain, mostly from fulfilled pledges, are kept strictly separate and must, by the deity's express command, be strewn for consumption by pigeons and other wild birds. The priest receives a fixed stipend assessed from every household in Navagao at each harvest (that is, twice a year), which should amount to ten kilograms per household annually. The considerable cash offerings made at the shrine are allowed to accumulate in the hands of the management committee over the course of a full year and are then used solely to buy brown sugar. This is distributed to all the pilgrims as Devji's munificent *prasād* on the annual *melā* day. The year I attended this *melā* the largesse amounted, I was told, to twenty-five hundred rupees' worth of sugar. Dispensed by the generous handful from huge burlap bags, it was truly an impressive display.

Why, we asked the priest, were such large amounts of money thus dispersed yearly when they might be spent on building a platform and a dome for the god? The priest replied proudly that they were only following Devji's orders. Each year, by means of grain-asking, they sought his permission to build a temple or otherwise improve the place, and each year he forbade any use of the money other than for brown-sugar distribution. The priest speculated that Devji especially desired birds to have all of the grain offerings intended for them. Birds can easily peck grains out of sand, whereas other animals cannot. If there were a smooth platform on which offerings were placed, then the birds might lose their advantage. There was no question of a "big pigeon" here.

One cause of the Mad Mina K's trouble was an offense against the Sandhill Devji of his home village, but his cure was not effected until he came to Puvali's Devji, where the possessed priest revealed this offense, and others, to him. Although it is not by any means a rule, madness, possession, and other afflictions perpetrated by intrusive malignant beings or offended deities seem often best dealt with at shrines where the priest does become possessed by a god—also a situation of intrusion.

There were moments in K's session with Puvali's priest when the deity seemed directly to address the deceased uncle's spirit: "I will have you seated on the well." When he referred to the time K stepped on the icon, the deity spoke as if he had a slightly cloudy but direct vision of this critical event. He thus demonstrated two major attributes of the priest who receives a god's *bhāv:* ability to communicate directly with other powerful beings, and perception that goes well beyond ordinary human limits.

The Blemish of a Witch

In the following case descrption, Puvali's priest is dealing only secondarily with a deity, a *pattar* resulting from one of the pilgrim's three dead children. Here the primary agent of affliction is a *ḍākaṇ,* or "witch," and the priest's art must be largely directed toward beating and removing rather than cajoling and appeasing her, although he does some of each.

A woman connected with or attached to (the verb used is *lagnā*) a *ḍākaṇ* or a *meḷī* is typically a young or not-so-young wife who has a record of losing her children, whether through miscarriage, stillbirth, or precipitate infant mortality. The source of her affliction is thought to be deliberate predation by another woman—if alive, a *ḍākaṇ;* if deceased, a *meḷī.* The last is a rather technical differentiation, and I have often heard the terms used interchangeably to refer to the same case in the same context. Ordinary people tend to use the more common *ḍākaṇ;* the possessed priest, for dramatic effect, will use the more chilling *meḷī.* What is important is that the source of evil, the cruel devourer of children's livers, is not the same as the woman suffering the loss of her children, but rather an alien parasite upon that bereaved mother. Although also feminine, the witch is fully separable from her hapless victim. One witch may be held responsible for more than one woman's sorrows. A living witch is most often determined to live in a fairly distant place, and may be identified by caste but not by name. She is usually dealt with only through her victim.[37] If a woman who has lost many children can be separated

37. That witchcraft suspicions may sometimes fall, with violent results, on real persons is painfully attested to in Carstairs 1983. The murder he reports took place in the 1950s in an out-of-the-way Mewar village.

from the parasitic creature devouring her progeny, she may then bear offspring that survive and may enjoy a happy wifehood.

The case considered here was long remembered and much discussed among habitués of Puvali: first, because the afflicted woman had come all the way from a large and distant city, Kota; second, because she "played"[38] so boldly and persistently. In her case the god began by promising complete success: "I will cut out her blemish" and "I will give a son." Soon, however, he indicated that he expected the pilgrims to fulfill certain demands of his. He would effect a complete cure, not this day, but rather when they returned with "ingredients" for a pouch and an armband—the former in order to bless the woman with a child, the latter to ward off any future malevolent invasions. The initial dialogue between possessed priest and the husband of the witch-victim established the facts of the case. The woman herself, face completely covered, remained passive and silent during this exhange.

Priest possessed by Bhairuji (hereafter B): Now, what is needed? I will cut out her blemish.[39]

Husband of witch-victim (hereafter H): Yes, cut it out!

B: I will cut out the blemish, yes, and make you happy. You came for two reasons. Otherwise you have bliss in all things. You already have good lentils and bread.

H: Yes, we have good lentils and bread.

38. The actions of ghosts and witches when they possess humans are often referred to as "play," using the common verb *khelnā,* the same that is used for children's games and sports. Ghatiyalians said that deities possessing humans did not, by contrast, "play." Erndl, however, reports from Uttar Pradesh that at least the goddess's possession is regularly described as her play (1984). Another word specifically associated with divine play is *līlā,* but this is never applied to possession; it is essentially the prerogative of the high gods, who do not descend into human bodies. Dramas about divinities may be called *līlā*—for example, the famous Ram Lila and Ras Lila cycles of Rama and Krishna—whereas *khel* is sometimes used for more down-to-earth theater. (See Kinsley 1979 for one study of divine *līlā;* see Hawley 1981 and Hein 1972 for *līlā* in theatrical traditions.)

39. The word I translate as blemish here is *kāḷo,* the color black. Both noun and adjective, *kāḷo* has a range of dark meanings: black snake, opium, stigma, deceit, frightening, inauspicious. I use the English "blemish," hoping to convey the idea that the flaw or blackness of a witch is not permanently lodged in the victim.

B: The rest is all fine, but this girl-child [to the deity all women are girls] has a *meḷī* attached to her. Her stomach, hands, feet, and digestive tract hurt, and she keeps crying. Her stomach hurts and she has no offspring. This is why she came from Kota. . . .

H: Her hands and feet are hurting.

B: Look! Listen! She has pain in her ribs.

H: Grain-giver, as it appears to you, tell it that way.

B: I will not let your house be ruined. I will give you a flower [that is, a son]. A *ḍākaṇ* has been attached to her for seven years. Seven years have passed . . . and *hũ hũ*, her eyes suffer, eyes suffer, eyes suffer. During all this time that *ḍākaṇ* has kept on eating her from within. . . . So do this: bring ingredients for a pouch and also bring ingredients for an armband. Did you hear me? Good, if you bring them next Saturday, that's fine.

H: We live far away, but whatever you tell us, I'm ready to do.

B: Everything is mine! I will give a flower.

After a brief interlude during which the priest dealt with other pilgrims, the witch inhabiting the woman from Kota began to "play." First she did not speak but produced in her victim a pronounced rhythmic breathing accompanied by small vocal gasps.[40] The priest declared that he would "cause her to speak from her mouth"—force her to reveal her identity and demands. The husband was not pleased with this prospect and replied, "No, you just remove her [the witch]; what's the use in getting her to speak from the mouth? You should remove her and that's all."

The priest then spoke rather mysteriously of the dead children, perhaps deliberately to provoke the witch:

B: One child—whose?—died. One child died. There is also one *pattar*. One child—whose?—died. He is a *pattar* and will sit.

H: Will sit on the neck?

40. These sounds struck both Miller and me as sexual. The few informants we asked about this, however, appeared not to understand. Nonetheless, men watching videotapes of witches "play" occasionally snickered for some reason. In Hindu lore witches are expected to be sexually desirous as well as hungry for human flesh.

> *B:* Two went, altogether three died, three were born, but one will sit. [His meaning here is that two of the dead children's spirits have left the house, but one lingerer wishes to be worshipped as a *pattar.*]

After this reference to the children, the witch-victim, now totally in the thrall of her malign possession, became more violent in her motion and louder, if still inarticulate, in her vocalizations. The priest began to blurt out commands such as "Grab her!" "Make her bow!" "Grab her braid!" and, obviously beside himself at this challenge to his power, "Your mother's stick!"

The witch became somewhat subdued following all this commotion, and the priest commanded the woman's husband to make her sit down. The deity then directly addressed the witch:

> *B:* Yes, what do you want? Speak! *Hũ!*
>
> *Witch (hereafter W):* *Hã hã hã hã hã.*
>
> *B:* Yes, speak now! What do you want?
>
> *W:* *Hã hã hã hã hã.*
>
> *B:* Speak, what will you take? What do you want?
>
> *W:* *Hã hã ho ho ho hã hã.*

Tiring of the game, the possessed priest once more advised the couple to return on the following Saturday with all the necessary goods. Then the witch began to speak:

> *W:* Many days have gone by, for me many days have gone by.
>
> *B:* *Hã hã,* what do you want, you!
>
> *H:* [clearly agitated by this development] What is she saying! That many days have passed, yes, in giving sorrow! Let her speak from the mouth, from the mouth let her demand what she demands!
>
> *W:* *Hã hã, hã* many days, many days, many days have passed, many days have passed in demanding, *hã hã hã.*
>
> *B:* Now what do you want?
>
> *H:* Whatever you want, tell about it? Whatever you demand, demand it. What will you take?
>
> *W:* I have eaten, eaten three children. I remember I remember I ate I ate three children *hã hã hã.*

H: So now what will you take? What do you want? Take it, say it, lady.

W: I ate ate ate ate ate *hã hã.*

H: Now what do you want? You have eaten three children; those are eaten. Now will you eat me? Then what do you want? Tell, "Brother, I want this."

W: *Hã hã hã hã hã.*

H: Now whatever you want, ask for it!

W: Many days have passed, yes, many days have passed with this one falling on my back.

H: I've heard enough of "many days have passed." Now say something else.

W: What should I say? What should I say?

H: You should just demand whatever you want.

W: *Hã hã hã hã hã.*

B: *Cet cet cet cet!*

The priest had almost withdrawn during this lengthy exchange between husband and witch. When it became clear, however, that the witch would not soon fix on any demand, the priest began to instruct the husband once more on what he must bring to effect a final exorcism the following Saturday. He then attempted to turn his attention to other pilgrims, but the witch began to "play" still more violently. Instructed by the priest, now very excited himself, the husband and several other men grabbed the panting, swaying woman by her little finger and her braid, and the assistant *bhopā* applied copious cow-urine sprays. The witch emitted a final scream of pain as she was forced to prostrate herself, and then appeared to have fled the body of the collapsed woman, who feebly asked for water in a different voice. The priest also cried out, in victorious agony, as his own possession temporarily lifted.

Despite the deity's apparent triumph, the cure was not considered to be complete. Both exorcism and pouch-filling rites would be required to eliminate fully this woman's problem. In the best outcome, her deficiency would be remedied by arranging through worship that her pouch be filled with a child-to-be, the gift of Devji. The survival of a living child would be a sign of the deity's total victory over the witch. During the week the priest in his own persona promised Miller and me a dramatic witch-removal the next Saturday, but the Kota *ḍākaṇ* never returned for her pouch and armband. Whether this first treatment proved fully effective, or whether the couple simply were not convinced enough to make the long journey from Kota again, of course I cannot say.

Transactional Flows in the Context of *Jātrā*

The three cases presented above by no means exhaust the kinds of tales of woe encountered at Rajasthani shrines nor the means of counteracting sorrows offered by shrine gods and their priests. Combined with the broader discussion of well-being, however, they do provide ample material for some generalizations about the ways that pilgrims' problems are dealt with at regional shrines. Rather complex substantial flows—of foods and residues, of prayers and powers, of trust and knowledge—appear to lie at the heart of Rajasthani shrines' effectiveness. I will summarize briefly here some of those already exemplified.

Two most essential and ubiquitous complementary elements of the shrine pilgrimage complex are proofs and vows. The word commonly used by villagers to include all cures, boons, and enlightened advice (as well as punishments rapidly inflicted on scoffers or violators of some rule) is *parcyā,* or "proof." It is a significant term, different from "wonder" (*camatkār*) in that it seems to imply not just a demonstration of power but a response to human needs. The gods also have wants, however, which men can satisfy, and it is often the spoken "vows" or "pledges" (*bolārī, votanā*) pilgrims make to offer up pleasing items which convince deities to deliver proofs.[41]

A god who gives proofs, then, will receive offerings—the tangible signs of success that all these regional deities apparently covet—whether in the form of enduring buildings, rapidly consumed sacks of sugar, grain enjoyed by pigeons, or cash that fills the *bhopā*'s coffers. In K's case the first item on the deity's agenda was an unfulfilled pledge made to him by K's father. Once assured that his pilgrim was not going to default on a previous vow, he could consider new matters.

41. See Moreno 1984 for an elaborate discussion and profuse illustrations of how pilgrims very physically serve the needs of deities in Tamilnad.

Schematically, a pilgrim promises to make a certain offering if he receives a certain boon; the deity won't fulfil the prayer without the vow; the pilgrim, however, is not accountable for anything if he does not get his proof. A Sikh herbal-medicine peddler who visited Ghatiyali offered a rather similar deal. He would either sell his packets for a few rupees, their printed cost value, or—and this was generally preferred by both parties—he would leave them without payment. Whenever he returned, which might be several years later, his satisfied customers would then reward him with five or ten times the actual cost of the stuff. On the other hand, those who were not helped by his potion did not need to pay at all.

There is one important difference, however, between the peddler's system and most shrine transactions, and this lies in the factor of "faith" or "belief" (*vishvās*). While the Sikh peddler asked for no prior trust—only a willingness to experiment—worshipful belief in the god's power should be freely flowing from a pilgrim in advance. Thus the first crazy one's father stressed his newfound faith in Puvali's Devji, with whom he had not yet engaged in any complex transactions. Along with faith go the physically enacted routines of self-lowering and self-giving, such as prostrations, circumambulations, and the effort of the journey itself.

During the initial encounter between pilgrim and shrine deity, then, both sides give in unqualified fashion what they have in plenty. The pilgrim freely gives effort and faith, but restricts his investment in limited valuable goods to a token coin, a handful of grain, a tiny bottle of *ghī*, or a packet of cheap incense. The deity similarly dispenses generously its plentiful, cheap if potent waste products: bath water, ash, food-leavings, and the flow of *darshan*.

Most of the costly and elaborate offerings made by pilgrims to shrines are dependent on, and commensurate with, boons received. When prayers have been granted, then pilgrims "offer up" valuable things—unmarked, highly transformable items: money, whole grains, cloth, or premium foods. Large feasts in a deity's honor; donations of rest-house rooms or deities' implements, such as tridents, spears, and canes, are always made in the aftermath of blessings received. The gods apparently covet such demonstrations. They want what pilgrims promise to bring, and that is why they do the work of curing.

The fine offerings left by pilgrims may sometimes be compensations to the god for the dangerous and deadly things pilgrims leave at deities' places. Snake poison may be swept toward and absorbed by a deity, and the strips of cloth tied onto the body during a sickness and later removed at a shrine transfer some final remnant of the disease. When Puvali's priest exorcizes a witch, he traps it in a clay pot and buries it somewhere in the field adjacent to the shrine. Obviously deities have in varying degrees the capacity to absorb or to handle, and yet not be damaged by, bad substances and evil beings. They must be paid for taking undesirable things as well as for giving desired ones.

The flow of substances and powers between devotees and deities is not restricted to the special environment of shrines. All kinds of things continually move back and forth between home village and deity's place, sometimes more than once. For example, the coconut that is brought for pouch-filling is placed on the shrine, then bestowed on the woman to be carried home again, and finally returned to the shrine to stay in a hanging cradle-basket. A simpler example is that of deities' leftovers—whether food, ash, or bath water—that are always carried away by pilgrims.

To bring home and redistribute a god's power-imbued leavings is integral if not defining to the act of shrine pilgrimage. This humbling piece of an interview reiterates the purposeful versus the diffuse dimension of the distinction between *jātrā* and *yātrā,* the distinction that opened this chapter.

Interviewer: When you made a burnt offering with coconut, what did the priest return to you?

Pilgrim: *Prasād* of coconut and ashes.

Interviewer: What did you do with the *prasād* and ash?

Pilgrim: I ate some there and brought some here [to her home in the village].

Interviewer: What did you do with that which you brought home?

Pilgrim: I gave it to the children. If I did not do that, what would be the use of going there [to the deity's place]? I hardly went just to wander. If you know so little, why are you asking me?

Emphasis on what is brought home from a pilgrimage serves both to remind us of the concerns of the preceding chapter and to lead us into the next one. In chapter 2 it was suggested that the overarching meanings of Hindu pilgrimage involved multiple responses to death and corresponding manners of treating the dead and coping with the fact of human mortality. Journeys to regional shrines were linked with spirits of the dead who linger in the house. Such spirits are more easily contacted at shrines, and their wills learned. They may then be established and maintained in comfort in the home. If they are content, then cause for hostility toward their living kin is removed and household difficulties cease. Of the various cases related here several have directly involved pacification of such lingering spirits of dead family members.

The pervasiveness of human fertility and birth motifs within villagers' responses to death was another theme of chapter 2. At shrines fertility is sought, actively implemented, and celebrated, sometimes in direct conflict with death-dealing forces. The rage and panting of witches when they play and the ultimate replacement of evil devourer with god-given coconut as child is a dramatic enactment of birth prevailing over death. The yearning of barren women for sons, expressed in their devotional songs, is a moving, low-key rendition of the same theme.

When Puvali's priest promises to give a "flower," he means he will give a child, and the icon of a dead male-child's spirit (*pattar*), worn about the neck and worshipped, may also be called "flower." Chapter 4 follows pilgrims carrying "flowers" to sink them in the Ganges. These "flowers" are bone and ash remains gathered from the cremation pyre. As the informant just cited claimed that bringing home and distributing deities' leavings was critical to the meaningfulness of her journey, Ganges pilgrims without exception insisted that to sink flowers and return without a sealed pot of Ganges water would be an unthinkable travesty. The Ganges pilgrimage must begin and end at the village shrine of Path Mother, also known as Ganges Mother. This shrine is sung of as "overspread with flowers." In chapter 4 the exchange of bones called "flowers" for Ganges water and its subsequent celebration, beginning at the place of Path Mother, will again draw out continuities within another kind of pilgrimage of death, fertility, and birth.

4. Sinking Flowers: Ganga Ma and Peace for the Dead

Two important backgrounds in which the Ganges pilgrimage from Ghatiyali is embedded make up the first part of this chapter. These are an account of how King Bhagirath saved his ancestors by bringing the Ganges down from heaven to earth; and a description of a "form" of the river goddess who abides on the outskirts of Ghatiyali. Called Path Mother, she is worshipped before and after all journeys made to submerge the bones of dead kin in Ganges river water.

Two possible sequences of the journey itself are then described: the simplest, to Hardwar and back; alternatively and more elaborately, a circuit involving thee major crossing places: Prayag, Gaya, and Hardwar. The soteriological and social reasons for bringing Ganges Mother home to the village are considered from several angles, leading to a description of the Celebration of Ganga (Gangotsav) held by pilgrim returnees. An interpretation of this celebration is proposed, connecting it to the playful female reproductive triumph over death (see chapter 2).

The Descent of Ganges and Her Place on the Village Outskirts

The tale of the Ganges' descent to earth is well known to most villagers both literate and illiterate. Found in various Puranic sources,[1] it is available to pilgrims in numerous inexpensive Hindi pamphlet versions; I have seen one member of a pilgrim party

1. For English translations or retellings of the descent-of-Ganges story, see, for example: Darien 1978:17–19; Dimmitt and van Buitenen 1978:322–323.

read aloud to the rest from one of these booklets while passing the night at a rest house in Hardwar. More often, however, the story is told orally from memory, during or while recalling a pilgrimage; spontaneously or in response to anthropological probing. It presents a clear mythic charter for the power of Ganges water to grant release to the dead, not only to those who have peacefully passed away but even to those who have suffered a cursed and untimely demise.

When, sharing distress from the hardships of the road, I asked my chief informant on a journey to Hardwar why it was worth the trouble to take his father's bones all this way, he responded by praising the extraordinary power of the Ganges and giving an oral summary of the story of King Bhagirath. He then asked to borrow my newly purchased pamphlet to reinforce his account with the printed word. What follows here is portions of the story, translated from the Hindi pamphlet obtained in Hardwar.

> King Sagar was a very famous universal emperor in the Sun lineage. . . . He had made a resolution to perform one hundred horse sacrifices. When he had finished the ninety-ninth sacrifice and was about to do the one-hundredth, he released his horse, Dark Ear. Then Indra [king of the gods] realized that if King Sagar completed one hundred horse sacrifices, he would be able to take over Indra's throne. So Indra took the sacrificial horse to Kapil Muni's ashram and tied it there. The reason for this action was that King Sagar's lineage—because of being so huge—could only be destroyed by the curse of some seer. Kapil Muni at that time was accepted as the foremost seer, and no king possessed the strength to endure his brilliance.
>
> When King Sagar's sixty thousand sons, who had been searching for this horse, arrived at Kapil Muni's ashram, they saw the horse there and were very happy. But when they just seized the horse without giving a respectful greeting to Kapil Muni and without his permission, Kapil Muni became angered by their disrespect. At that time, full of anger, he reduced all the sons to ashes in one moment with a mere glance.
>
> Afterwards King Sagar's grandson Anshuman served Kapil Muni greatly until the seer allowed him to take back the horse with which the king's sacrifice was finally completed. So, the sacrifice was complete but the sixty thousand princes were ashes. They could not get released in any way. Anshuman asked Kapil Muni to

tell him the remedy whereby the sixty thousand sons of the king might receive release. Then Kapil Muni gave this boon: "In your third generation, from endless asceticism and effort, when the Ganges will descend to earth, then their deliverance [*uddhār*] will occur."

Anshuman tried with all his might but failed to bring Ganges to the earth. In the course of time Anshuman's son Dilip ruled the kingdom, and he also, accepting his father's order, performed great ascetic feats in order to bring Ganges, but he also remained unsuccessful.

King Dilip's son Bhagirath performed difficult ascetic feats in the Himalayan crossing place Gokan and won from Brahmaji the boon of bringing Ganges to the earth's surface. Brahmaji gave this boon to Bhagirath, but the wave of Ganges descending to the earth's surface would be violent and unbearable. How could it be done carefully?

In order to receive a means of overcoming this difficulty, King Bhagirath went to Kailash. There, having once more performed deep ascetic practice, he pleased Shiva. Then Shiva agreed to stop the flow of Ganges in his locks of hair and afterwards she would come down gently to the surface of the earth. Shiva was thus valiant and he is praised with the name of "Ganges-Holder."

Ganges descended to earth and followed King Bhagirath. . . . Bhagirath, having forced open the lower regions gave the stream of water, which had been restrained by mountain ranges, a way to flow ahead. Because of having penetrated impregnable mountains and brought Ganges to the level ground, King Bhagirath became our first engineer.[2]

Thus, breaking through the mountainous garlands, Ganges' flow became normal in Hardwar. Ganges went from here to merge in Ganga Sagar. There, merely from receiving the touch of Ganges water, King Sagar's sixty thousand sons were released. Bhagirath gave the gift of life to his forefathers and was satisfied. (*Ma Ganga* n.d.: 27–30)

This booklet, as do others like it, goes on to give in Hindi a compendium of praise verses translated from Sanskrit texts extolling to heights of hyperbole the virtues of Ganges pilgrimage, Ganges baths, and Ganges water. Regarding such claims, villagers

2. Such gratuitous analogies between mythic and modern technological or scientific realities occur frequently in popular Hindi religious tracts. Moreover, a recently established Indian journal of engineering is called after Bhagirath (I thank G. Raheja for calling this to my attention).

tend to maintain a healthy scepticism, although it coexists with a wholehearted belief in wonders. To them, however, the essence of the Ganges story is the precedent set for service to ancestors, a precedent which they follow even today. Thus a village informant wrote out in Hindi this version of the story for me, containing in a nutshell both charter and practice:

> King Sagar had sixty thousand sons, who were cursed and burned to ashes by Kapil Muni. Among the descendents of this King Sagar was King Bhagirath, who wanted to secure release for these sixty thousand forefathers. For the sake of this release he did much service for God and performed ascetic feats. God became happy and said, "Whatever you want, ask for it." Then King Bhagirath said, "I want the release of my forefather King Sagar's sixty thousand sons." Then God told him, "Wherever they were burned by the curse, in that very place where the remnants of their ashes or bones are lying, you should bring the pure river Ganges." King Bhagirath did asceticism for God and brought the Ganges from heaven to this mortal world, and thus King Sagar's sixty thousand sons' wandering souls received release.
>
> For this reason, since then, to give peace and liberation to souls, flowers and ashes are dropped in the Ganges.

In order to worship Mother Ganges, a goddess known as Pathvārī Mā̃, approximately translatable as "Path Mother," is established in Ghatiyali and most other villages of the immediate surrounding area. All the rituals at Path Mother's shrine are associated with the pilgrimage to submerge "flowers"—the postcremation remains of the dead—most often in Hardwar, Prayag, or Gaya. Between the grand descent of the Ganges to and beyond Hardwar and her presence in Ghatiyali's wayside shrine, certain direct continuities will become apparent.

The place of Path Mother for any village is located beside the road that leads roughly toward the northeast (and Hardwar), a little beyond the inhabited section but well within the area of agricultural land owned by that village. Although the shrine is most commonly referred to as Path Mother, its presiding deity is also addressed in song as "Dhārājī" (literally "honored stream," an epithet for the Ganges), "Gangā Mā̃" (Ganges Mother), and "Giyā Mā̃" (Gaya Mother, Gaya being the North Indian crossing place most strongly associated with offerings to ancestors).

Path Mother is never anthropomorphically represented. Her shrine is generally a hexagonal column, seated on a raised platform where offerings may be placed. The top of the column is depressed and contains soil in which grains are sprouted on appropriate occasions. I have seen Path Mother in five villages and in each she approximated this appearance. The form of Path Mother's shrine resembles that of Tulsī Mā̃ (Basil Mother), which is also a column, although usually four-sided, with the revered basil plant growing on top in place of sprouts. Tulsi Ma, found in Ghatiyali in the courtyard of the Niranjani (Vaishnavite) temple as well as in private courtyards, is, however, much smaller than Path Mother.

In common with other goddesses of the region, Pathvari Ma always has beneath her shrine or facing it a stone icon representing her Bhairuji (Rajasthani for Bhairava)[3]. Bhairuji as a generic title may encompass numerous deities, but Path Mother's Bhairu is particularized. He is usually addressed in song and prayer as "Ganges Bhairu" (Gangā ko Bhairū̃) or as "Banaras-dweller" (Kāshī ko vāshī). Thus, the place of Path Mother is the abode of a village goddess said to be a form of the river Ganges and attended by a Bhairuji said to reside in the distant pilgrimage center of Banaras. How do they come to be here as well as there?

While sitting near the place of Path Mother I once asked a fellow pilgrim, a literate Brahman villager, to tell me anything he could about this deity's meaning and history. Although he had

3. For a summary of Bhairava's history, mythology, and iconography, see Eck 1982:189–197. Bhairava is sometimes described in ethnographic contexts as a leader of ghosts or an incarnation of Shiva who administers punishments to ghosts (see Babb 1975:227–228; Kakar 1982:59). Rajasthani informants describe Bhairu as a part or fragment of Shiva, implying his homologous nature but intrinsically lesser status; Bhairu is a *devatā;* Shiva is *bhagvān.* One man told me that Bhairu was the son of Shiva and Prithvi, the earth. One time when Shiva spilled his semen on the ground, Bhairuji arose there.

In Rajasthan Bhairu is strongly linked to the goddess in her many forms. One person said to me, before the fatal 1980 plane crash, in which Indira Gandhi's son Sanjay was killed, "Every goddess has her Bhairuji—just as Indira has Sanjay." Further inquiry determined that this informant was stressing, not the mother-to-son aspect of the relationship, but rather the configuration of power and agency: *shakti* always needs effective workers in the world. Bhairuji is often called the "one who goes ahead" in relation to another deity, whether it be the goddess or the male Dev Narayanji. Bhairu does not seem to share Shiva's qualities of asceticism nor his penchant for meditative withdrawal. On the contrary, perhaps the most essential fact about Bhairu is his involvement in all kinds of action. See also Atal 1961 for Bhairu in Rajasthan.

none of the factual particulars, his response included one revealing statement. Gesturing toward the shrine, he said, "This very shrine, ahead, is in a crossing place; that is to say, is in the Ganges."

In the context of other Hindu conceptions of the special qualities of places manifest in pilgrimage centers and temples,[4] this is not a peculiar statement. An understanding of the presuppositions that lie behind it will illuminate the nature of Path Mother's place. Important to this understanding is a concept used in Rajasthan to relate major places of a deity to subsidiary ones. This is *dhām,* a very broad term in Hindi for "place" or "deity's place," which was, however, used in a specific limiting sense when referring to local shrines in my area of Rajasthan. A shrine is referred to as a *dhām,* or secondary place, of deity X when deity X has elsewhere his "essential" abode—the place where his icon has appeared of its own accord, without human direction. A *dhām,* in contrast to this natural or miraculous site, is understood to have a human history, whether this is remembered or forgotten.[5]

Construction of a *dhām* generally occurs when a devotee of a distant deity, wishing to have a form of that deity always near him, decides to institute its worship in a locality nearer to him. In order to do this he will bring earth, a small stone, or other power-charged substance from the original place. He may also obtain a similar icon and perform its "installation" (*sthāpanā*) at the new place. This may be done elaborately, with the help of Brahmans and Sanskrit *mantra*s, or minimally, with the combined hands and prayers of five men.

Path Mother and her Bhairuji are sometimes referred to as the *dhām* of Ganga, established by the village as a community. Thus my informant's statement means that Ganges Mother and her

4. See, for example, Beck 1976 and Eck 1982. The virtues of one pilgrimage center are often conceived of as equivalent to those of all centers; or the human body may be thought to contain all external places of power in a finer, subtler form; or, particularly relevant here, a lesser center may be believed to possess and confer on the sincere pilgrim the merits of a greater center (or all centers) when the latter are inaccessible to him.

5. I cannot say how widely this specific usage occurs. The *RSK* defines *dhām* as (1) house, (2) place, (3) god-place, (4) heaven, (5) crossing place, (6) body, (7) flame, (8) ray, (9) brightness. Morinis translates *dhāma* from Bengali usage as "sacred location." This appears to be associated there with ideas about heaven realized on earth and could therefore come within the general notion of a power secondarily established, however complete its manifestation (1984:122–138).

lively force Bhairuji exist on the village outskirts, for the sake of villagers worshipping them in that place, but their origin and source are thought of as being within a crossing place on the Ganges River. It is in the nature of a *dhām,* normally, for its power to be more restricted and less effective than that of the original. A *dhām* seems to require periodic renewal and revitalization in order for the deity or deities to continue to bestow powers and blessings there. Even though Path Mother is Ganges and her Bhairuji is Banaras-dweller, the pilgrim when bathing in the original Ganges (especially in Banaras) should remember Bhairuji and give him an "invitation" to come to the pilgrim's village, to the place of Path Mother, on the day when the pilgrim opens his Ganges water. In the course of the ritual performed on this occasion, the Brahman invokes "all chief rivers: Ganga, Sarasvati, Yamuna, Godavari" and "all oceans" to "all come here and make this pot of Ganges water pure."

Path Mother is worshipped at her shrine only in association with pilgrimage.[6] There are two major types of occasion which call for *Pathvārī pūjā*. One is pilgrims' departure for and return from nonregional crossing places, particularly where the Ganges flows and where rituals for the dead are performed: Hardwar, Prayag, Banaras, and Gaya. While it is desirable for anyone making such a pilgrimage, Path Mother's worship is absolutely essential for those taking the flowers of dead kin to sink them in the Ganges.

The other event that must be launched at the place of Path Mother is opening the sealed container of Ganges water which a pilgrim has previously brought home, taking it into the village, and eventually distributing it to assembled, feasting guests. A general term for this project is "raising the water pot." It may be performed, with more or less extravagance, as "Celebration of Ganga" (Sanskrit, *Gangotsav;* colloquially *Gangoj*) or "walking-sticks night" (*ḍangaṛī rāt*).[7] Whereas the Celebration of Ganga is

6. Path Mother is, however, worshipped in the village by women on certain festival occasions, including the morning of Calf Twelfth and the final day of Dasa Mata Puja. On these occasions she is established as a little pile of pebbles—each woman participating in the group worship must add her own to the pile. The stories of Path Mother told in conjunction with her worship during these festivals have nothing to do with pilgrimage, the Ganges, or the dead. Rather, they are primarily concerned with fate and the earned fruits of karma.

7. See Atal 1968:162–164 and Cauhan 1968:223–225 for brief references to these events in some other villages of Rajasthan.

most often held in conjunction with funeral or wedding feasts, the walking-sticks night is usually done spontaneously; whereas the former calls for invitations to a large group of relations, caste fellows, and neighbors, the latter prescriptively includes only one's pilgrim company and immediate kin. The distinction between the two is not always clear. At one event of the opening of Ganges water the host and hostess, perhaps modestly, consistently referred to the affair as a "walking-sticks night" while the several Brahman officiants and many others present declared it to be incontrovertibly a "Celebration of Ganga."

Path Mother is worshipped on similar occasions by all the "clean" castes, from Brahmans down to Minas. I have personally observed her worship and the Celebration of Ganga performed by Brahmans, Gujars, Lodas, Minas, and Kumavats, as well as by a mixed-caste group that included three Brahman subcastes, Rajputs, Carans, Kumhars, and Malis. There was little difference among these instances.[8]

The worship of Path Mother is performed by a Brahman, an expert who knows the appropriate Sanskrit lines and coaches the participants in their appropriate actions. In Ghatiyali and two other nearby villages, Path Mother's worship was always conducted by one of three Gujarati Brahmans of the Avadic subcaste, all full brothers, who have the exclusive rights to life-cycle rituals in the immediate area. In somewhat more distant villages, however, I encountered officiants of different Brahman subcastes.

The shrine of Path Mother, at least in Ghatiyali, also has a hereditary *bhopā,* or non-Brahman shrine-priest, traditionally a Mali (gardener) of the Phuleriya lineage.[9] Non-Brahman shrine priests today still perform worship and service for most local deities. In the recent past the Phuleriya Malis conducted Path Mother's worship and received gifts of clothing and cash from pilgrims. At some point, however, village patrons handed the prerogative to perform Path Mother's worship to Brahmans, and the

8. Rajput women, however, do not participate in Gangotsav as water carriers, although they may perform the worship of Path Mother jointly with their husbands. A female member of one of the service castes with hereditary ties to a Rajput household may act as a substitute for the women of that household, carrying water in the Celebration of Ganga.

9. Phuleriya Malis are considered "pure," as they do not consume liquor and meat; their traditional work is to tend flower gardens and make garlands for the gods. In Ghatiyali, Path Mother's *bhopā* lived not with the other Malis but on a street of Brahmans, and the young women of his household emulated their Brahman neighbors by dressing in saris.

bhopā's role has atrophied. Ghatiyali's gardener *bhopā* still attends the rituals at Path Mother and may assist the Brahman by performing some of the routine actions such as preparing the offering of *ghī* on smoking cow-dung. He receives the thick saltless bread offered to Bhairuji, but the money and grain go to the Brahman.

The place of Path Mother must be the last and first touch-point in the village for pilgrims to the Ganges. Although few today continue on foot down the road from the shrine as they once did, most returning to the center of town to board a bus, they must on no account reenter their homes between performing Path Mother's worship and leaving the village. In the same fashion, on their return, they should not go straight home but must proceed directly to Path Mother. Preferably, they should spend the night at her shrine, perform her worship at an auspicious hour of the morning, and only then go to their houses accompanied by the village drummer and by family, neighbors, and song.

Most of the items necessary for the worship of Path Mother are standard for any village ritual: a brass pitcher filled with well water, red powder for making auspicious dots, incense, mung beans, rice, mustard seed, betel nut, raw sugar, and multicolored string. There are also burning cow-dung cakes on which *ghī* and foodstuffs are placed as burnt offerings, separately for both Path Mother and Bhairuji. Saltless bread and soaked raw chickpeas, foods preferred by Bhairuji, are also required.

Three special items are most significant for Path Mother's worship: (1) "sprouts" (*juvārā,* usually of millet) grown both in a covered clay "vessel" (*kalash*)[10] from each pilgrim's household and on top of Path Mother herself, (2) "walking sticks" (*ḍangaṛī*), and (3) either "flowers" (*phūl,* meaning bones), which departing pilgrims wear in bright red pouches around their necks, or pots of Ganges water, which returning pilgrims bring in multicolored straw baskets.

The manipulations and meanings of these key elements are considered here briefly. Potential sprouts are present in seed form

10. The term *kalash* is used for clay waterpots, normally called *maṭkā,* when they are employed in any ritual context. I will consistently translate it as "vessel," which effects the required distinction from ordinary "pot" and also has some of the implications of *kalash* as containers of powerful substances and beings. Vessel does not, however, convey another important and linked definition of *kalash*: "crown" or "pinnacle" and thus the round, often golden orbs used to ornament the tops of temple domes (see chapter 1).

at the first *Pathvārī pūjā* and in full growth at the second; they are also planted in advance of the Celebration of Ganga. In other parts of Rajasthan, sprouting appears as an essential feature for worshipping a goddess whose shrine may be neither a form of Ganga Ma nor a place of community worship. The *RSK* gives "*panthvāriyau*: . . . that protected place where after [pilgrims have] gone on pilgrimage, wheat or millet, having been planted by the women of the house, is watered." This suggests a private shrine established just for the purpose of raising sprouts by families whose members have gone on pilgrimage.

Those who remain at home feel that if the sprouts are flourishing through their steady care, so are their pilgrim kin. The sprouts thus maintain and indicate the well-being of the journeyers. The place of Path Mother, which is the place of departure and welcome, is also the place where pilgrims are sustained within the realm of the home community. Speaking of the sprouts grown in the home vessel, one man said, "We planted them in the house so that our relations will return to our house in the same condition that they left." Thus in both locations, home and Path Mother, the sprouts give organic continuity to a carefully nourished contact between travelers and home. At the time of the returning worship of Path Mother (I was told but did not observe) some sprouts are snipped from the home vessels and mixed with sprouts snipped from the village Pathvari shrine, merging pilgrims as travelers with pilgrims as household members.

Between the first and the second worship of Path Mother, while the flowers are replaced with Ganges water and the old walking stick either returns unchanged or is replaced with a similar new item, the sprout vessels have been transformed through growth. Many of the songs special to Path Mother contain references to the sprouts, evoking in lilting poetic imagery their overdrooping greenness. The image of green blades, grown so long that they flop over, like the image of sloshing water which also pervades the songs, is a purely joyful one in desert Rajasthan. Thus the vessels with sprouts are felt to be appropriate signs of the joy experienced on the return of pilgrims. They also signify an auspicious welcome to Bhairuji and Ganges Mother, who have come to the village as honored guests along with the pilgrim company. And, as a vivid sign of new life and growth, they certainly connote fertility.

A walking stick is of course an aid for walking, and its association with journeying is not surprising. Informants, however, gave various explanations for the significance of the wooden walking sticks in the context of pilgrimage. One said that they were carried out of respect for the memory of the aged because one most often went to crossing places with the bones of one's elders. Nevertheless, the walking stick is a requisite piece of pilgrimage equipment even if the bones are those of a younger person.

Another, rather exceptionally articulate man said that the walking stick was the "companion" of the pilgrimage and the "support" of the pilgrim. He went on with further eloquence to state that it was in fact "life's companion" and quoted a popular *bhajan* in which the entire human life cycle is described as a "performance," or "show of wood" (*tamāshā lakaṛī kā*), from the infant's cradle and toys to the funeral pyre fuel. Thus the walking stick may represent the frailty and transience of the human condition. It also marks continuity between the old and the young, and between the beginning and the end of the journey. It is carried by sincere pilgrims wherever they go for worship and baths. The bones are left in the Ganges but the walking stick returns to be worshipped once more at Path Mother's shrine.[11]

Villagers taking flowers to the Ganges feel that they are carrying, not lifeless bones, but souls who are aware of everything that happens. The pilgrim wearing flowers identifies with them in a very human, bodily way. One very sensitive person on his way to Gaya kept hearing the voices of those whose flowers he was carrying, murmuring to him along the way: "We are going happily, we are going happily." When he placed the bones in the river the voices ceased.

The pilgrim obtains his sealed pot of Ganges water only after disposing of the bones in the cooling river. Although many people in fact use a common verb for "put," "drop," or "pour in" for this action, the polite Rajasthani term, consistently employed by more self-conscious speakers, is *bolāṇo*. This means "to cause to

11. Many pilgrims bring home the same walking stick with which they left. However, it is sometimes the practice to place the original in the Ganges along with the bones. A new identical stick must then be purchased and brought back home for ritual attention during the worship of Path Mother and Celebration of Ganga. The giving of yet another stick to an elderly beggar, as undertaken by Ladu Ram, seems intended to reinforce the notion of respect for the aged as well as to benefit the spirit of the deceased by performing a meritorious act in his name.

sink" and is specifically used when icons, religious story-paintings, vessels, or any "hot," charged object is submerged in water. At Hardwar the water with which pilgrims' pots are filled is taken deliberately from that portion of the river, considered to have the most powerful qualities, where bones are sunk. One may speculate that this Ganges water derives its potent qualities from the remains of those who have died and contains some transformed, substantial essence of their lives.

This living water is returned to the village, where it is eventually made available to the community at the Celebration of Ganga. While distributing Ganges water a host may wave before his guests a yak-tail whisk, normally used only on icons of the gods in temple worship. Guests are to be accepted as deities, and at this moment their divine qualities peak. A kind of immortality, both substantial and social, is transmitted to them. The funeral feast is one of the grandest of all social events, and here the group which has suffered a loss through death reincorporates the life-substance of the dead through drinking the pilgrim's gift of Ganges water.

In a women's song performed at the place of Path Mother, the myth of Ganges' descent is re-created as the pilgrim's return:

Song of Gangaji

[1] I'll milk, my Ganges Mother, the rich-milk-giving cow,
I'll milk, my Ganges Mother, the spotted cow,
I'll boil thick rice pudding.

[Refrain-a] Bhagirath brought my Gaya Mother[12] as an honored guest.
Banaras-dweller brought Jamana[13] as an honored guest.

[2] I'll cook rice, my Gaya Mother, radiant-white,
I'll cook rice, my Gaya Mother, radiant-white,
and sauce of green mung beans.

[Refrain-b] Our clan's Bhagirath brought Ganges as an honored guest.
Banaras-dweller brought Jamana as an honored guest.

12. Gaya in Bihar is strongly associated with rites for the ancestors; these will be described below.

13. Jamana is the Rajasthani pronunciation of Yamana, the river of Krishna country where most pilgrims bathe when on their way to Banaras, Prayag, and Gaya.

Here an explicit connection is confirmed between the charter established when King Bhagirath engineered the Ganges' descent via Hardwar in order to give release to his ancestors, and the present-day returning pilgrim's service to his own lineage forefathers. It is important to note that this, as well as other songs of Ganges Mother and Path Mother, praises the pilgrim, not for taking his dead kin to the Ganges but for bringing the Ganges back home with him. Moreover, just as Bhagirath must obtain the help of Shiva in order to control the power of the Ganges' flow, so the pilgrim invites Bhairuji, a "part" of Shiva, to assist at the entrance of Ganges Mother into his home. The Banaras-dweller referred to in the song is none other than Ganga's Bhairu, and Ganga's Bhairu is present at the Celebration of Ganga in possessing the women who carry vessels of water on their heads. Shiva slowed the Ganges' rush by catching her in his mass of matted hair, and the women possessed by Bhairuji carry the pots of Ganges water into the village with their own long hair significantly unbound.

The implications of these associations will be explored further in the conclusion of this chapter. For the moment it is enough to have demonstrated that the place of Path Mother is quite literally where Ganges bursts into the village and that, by effecting her entrance, the returning pilgrim is seen—in the image of King Bhagirath—as saving his ancestors. At the same time he replenishes the life of household, caste, and village, just as Mother Ganges bestows on mortals not only release but other salubrious gifts.

The Ganges Pilgrimage from Rajasthan

Two possible sequences of Ganges pilgrimage are described here, both from participatory experience. The journey which Ladu Ram, a Brahman schoolteacher, made to place his father, Mangilal's, flowers in the Ganges was of the simplest variety—an economical and hasty round trip to Hardwar and back. This pilgrimage and the subsequent Celebration of Ganga which took place on Mangilal's twelfth-day feast are briefly sketched in chapter 2. Here I add to their description considerably.

Ladu Ram, like all those who make the flower pilgrimage within twelve days after a death, had all critical rites executed with dispatch in Hardwar. If, however, flowers are saved beyond those days (or if silver flowers are later fashioned), they may be taken on a longer journey and treated to more elaborate ritual attentions in a number of crossing places. I observed this lengthened version of the flower pilgrimage during a thirty-day bus journey to Puri and back (for which see also chapter 5). A good number of the pilgrims left wearing around their necks pouches with flowers. Although the tour was not focused wholly on attentions to the dead, these pilgrims had the opportunity to perform rites on behalf of their deceased kin and ancestors at several important sites along the way. Most notably they had their heads shaved in Prayag, deposited the flowers and offered flour balls in Gaya, and on the way home secured pots of Ganges water from Hardwar. They had their names inscribed as bringers of flowers in the priests' record books at all three of these places and several others as well.

This routine is not fixed. I know of several cases, for example, when bones were placed in the confluence at Prayag. However, certain aspects of the sequence are adhered to quite firmly. When the bus owner attempted to change the order of events on our trip by making Hardwar an early stop on the way east, his pilgrim passengers would not agree to this. They insisted, first, that they must obtain pots of Ganges water from Hardwar only, and second, that they didn't want to worry about maintaining the purity of these pots over the course of the whole month-long pilgrimage. Therefore, the Hardwar stop would have to be made on the return journey.

Inexplicably, although Banaras was a major place for *darshan* and bathing by all our pilgrims, it was not—despite its fabulous reputation as giver of release—a key spot for the flower bearers. Only one, subtle act was performed there: the invitation to Bhairuji, Banaras-dweller. While bathing in Banaras, each pilgrim with flowers inwardly invited Bhairuji to attend his Celebration of Ganga, whenever it would be held back in his home village. Bhairu-from-Banaras, however, will possess the water carriers during Celebration of Ganga even after a pilgrimage like Ladu Ram's which touches only Hardwar. The invitation must be given on the banks of the Ganges, but not necessarily in Banaras itself.

Round Trip to Hardwar

The events preceding Ladu Ram's Hardwar pilgrimage were related in chapter 2. He left Ghatiyali on the morning of the fourth day following the death of his father, Mangilal, having gathered the bone and ash remains, or flowers, from the cremation ground on the third. Shortly after performing Path Mother's worship, Ladu Ram boarded the 11:30 A.M. bus to Devali. My research assistant and I accompanied him.

As we traveled we discussed the various special requirements of this journey. Ladu Ram was carrying his father's old walking stick; he contrasted its worthlessness in monetary terms with the necessity to worship it and carry it respectfully all this way. The walking stick still bore multicolored string (*lacchā*) tied on it by the pandit at Path Mother's shrine. In Hardwar Ladu Ram would put the walking stick in the Ganges along with his father's remains, he told me, and purchase two others: one to take home and one to give to a beggar in Pushkar. He said that "old people" (like his father) used canes and that he would give such a stick to another old man for the sake of the soul of his dead father. If he gave a cloth, a cane, or anything else to the poor here on earth, that thing would become available to his father's spirit. From the charities of the son, Ladu Ram, "peace" (*shānti*) and "happiness" (*sukh*) would also come to Mangilal's spirit. Waxing still more enthusiastic on the fruits of his pilgrimage, and especially of giving to the poor in crossing places, Ladu Ram concluded, still speaking of his father's soul, "He may get release; he will get everything."

Another important item that Ladu Ram was taking to Hardwar was a tiny slip of paper bearing a hand-written invitation to "God" (vaguely, *bhagvān*) to attend the funeral feast. On most festive occasions Ganeshji, the deity of auspicious beginnings, receives the first invitation. But Ganesh is neither worshipped nor invited during a period of death pollution. By "God" Ladu Ram meant Vishnu, and he told me that he would deliver this slip in Hardwar through the priest who conducted the rituals there.

Ladu Ram was not wearing shoes, but he did have on thick warm socks. He explained, after my question, that going shoeless had to do, not with any renunciation or asceticism, but with "nonviolence" (*ahimsā*). When you wear shoes, he said, you cannot avoid treading on and crushing to death small living creatures and thus committing "sin" (*pāp*). Ladu Ram added that he was going shoeless for the sake of *dharma* and that during this particular time, following his father's death, it was especially necessary for him to act in accordance with moral duty. At the Kota train station, where we had a fairly long wait, he squirmed a little and joked nervously about how crazy he must appear to other people, carrying the old walking stick and wearing a good watch but no shoes. He said, "If I were wearing the flowers on the outside" (displaying the pouch momentarily) "then everyone would understand at once." Nevertheless, he immediately tucked it away again beneath his shirt and sweater. Despite being out of sight, the flowers, embodying Mangilal's spirit, were a presence traveling with us. Ladu Ram, as anyone wearing flowers must do, invited the deceased's spirit to participate whenever he took food, drank, or urinated.

On the long, slow train-ride from Kota to Hardwar, Ladu Ram spoke at length about his family, his education, and his childhood. He seemed glad of the chance to unburden himself. He was the only surviving offspring of his parents, several siblings having died. His elder brother had passed away when Ladu Ram was very young, and, he told me now, since that time he had felt very heavily the importance of serving his parents. While still a child he was not able to do very much, but as he grew older and more capable he sought to fulfil his childhood resolutions. It was for these reasons that he was now undertaking this arduous journey. It was winter, and chilly, and there was much talk throughout the trip recalling the comforts of home and contrasting them with the journey's discomforts. The theme of hardship and peril on the "road of dharma" (*dharmarāstā*) was often evoked.[14]

Arriving at Hardwar station around 3:30 P.M., we encountered the traditional multivocal confusion of a pilgrim center terminal: *paṇḍā*s ("pilgrims' priests") seeking clients, cart-drivers seeking fares. There were no touts present for our *paṇḍā*'s house, but we knew, through advice from experienced covillagers, that we should ask for the "gourdman"—so called because of the logo on his sign, an ascetic's dry gourd water-carrier. This gourdman

14. Most villagers believe that pilgrimage imperils one's health. My research assistant found the unaccustomed cold of Uttar Pradesh unendurable and announced on the first day that if he had to stay in such a climate for a week we would have the job of depositing his flowers in the Ganges too. When I returned from this first Hardwar journey, several people made a point of telling me how tired and weak I looked. One of them later explained, when I complained that it was not pleasant to hear this, that such comments were appropriate and standard greetings for a returning pilgrim. After the long bus pilgrimage, on which I had indeed lost weight and sleep, I could hardly move through the village streets without hearing several comments on my lamentably depleted condition.

dealt with most castes of pilgrims from our area of Rajasthan. We thus contracted with a cart-driver to be delivered to the gourdman's rest house (*dharmashālā*), where the signboard indeed announced that he catered to Jaipur, Ajmer, Kekari, and Sawar. As we were residents of Aimer district and Kekari subdistrict, and Samar was our closest market town, we were well assured that we had come to the right place.

The gourdman's rest house was a place where Rajasthanis, particularly illiterate, non-Hindi speakers, might feel at home. The priests all understood the Rajasthani vernaculars and sprinkled their Uttar Pradesh Hindi with bits of them. Since much of their livelihood depends on periodic tours of Rajasthani villages to collect grain pledges made by former pilgrims, they are quite familiar with the geography, customs, and social structure of the area. At the rest house, moreover, one inevitably met people from close to home, if not actual acquaintances. We were joined on our first evening by a potter from Kota and dined with him, but there was not enough common ground to continue the companionship. The next day, however, Ladu Ram ran into a fellow schoolmaster from Sawar who had actually taught for several years, and been much respected, in Ghatiyali. This man, literate and witty, was good company, and we toured Rishikesh with him and traveled home together as far as Ajmer.

Ladu Ram, who had hoped to complete the ritual work that day, was gradually calmed and persuaded by the *paṇḍā* that his business must wait until morning. The *paṇḍā*'s conciliating talk went something like this: "As you desire; if you say in the night, then we will have to do it in the night, but I must tell you it is done in the morning, early in the day. But if you tell us to do it at midnight, then we will do it at midnight." After several rounds of protest and smooth rebuttal, Ladu Ram's final objections subsided, and the *paṇḍā,* assuring him that it was after all a good thing to spend one night in a crossing place, turned to the first formal matter.

This was to locate Ladu Ram's family in the bulky looseleaf "record books" (*pothī*) kept by Hardwar pilgrims' priests. These books were organized according to districts within Rajasthan and after that by village, caste, subcaste, and *gotra*. After several false tries, the *paṇḍā* began reading out names that did belong to Ladu Ram's relations, noting the move by one branch to another village, and the most recent entry of a pilgrimage seventeen years ago. Ladu Ram was pleased to hear this recitation, and we all agreed that hearing the names gave us full trust in the *paṇḍā*[15]

Having read out the records, the *paṇḍā* proceeded to bring them up to date, inscribing in his book all the information he could extract from Ladu Ram about marriages, births, and deaths in the extended family. He also inscribed my research assistant's name and my own as companions to the chief pilgrim, a customary practice.[16]

The *dharmashālā* was a busy place; other *paṇḍā*s, all members of one lineage, were engaged in the same activity of reading and writing names with other groups of pilgrims. This steady flow of business, they assured me, was quite normal. Seeing no other women among the groups of pilgrims at the gourdman's rest house, I asked the reason for this, having read and heard that it was not only proper but enjoined to perform pilgrimage *joṛe* ("paired") with one's spouse. The reply I received from my fellow pilgrims, with which the *paṇḍā*s concurred, was that it was indeed absolutely necessary to have your wife with you on "journeys to crossing places" (*tīrthayātrā*). If you left her behind, it was sinful and your pilgrimage would surely be fruitless and useless. However, the task of sinking flowers was not that kind of *tīrthayātrā*. It was not made for the sake of wandering, seeing the gods, or bathing. Rather, our purpose, like those of our fellow guests at the rest house, was to make flour-ball offerings to the spirits of the dead. A pilgrimage made in haste for this single purpose did not require the presence of women, who in fact could only slow you down. I learned later that this definitive response was contextualized in our particular situation at that time. Flour-ball offerings may well be made by paired couples. However, the currently fashionable practice of placing bones in the Ganges within the twelve days following a death rarely allows for the company of women, simply because there is too much business to be attended to at home.

15. See Goswamy 1966 for the importance of *paṇḍā*s' record books to scholars as well as to pilgrims.

16. Instructed by Ladu Ram and Vajendra, the *paṇḍā* recorded my presence as "Ain Roj, Angrez [English], Jomil's sister." They felt that this description, despite its factual inaccuracy, was how I would best be recognized by future generations of Ghatiyalians, and that was what mattered.

Having completed all the preliminaries and become resigned to passing the night, we were advised by the *paṇḍās* to go to Hardwar's famed bathing *ghāṭ,* Har kī Pairī ("the Lord's Stairs") and enjoy the *darshan* of twilight *āratī*—an offering of lights and prayers to the great river. After that we might come back and eat a good dinner. Our first sight of Mother Ganges at nightfall, with pilgrims' leaf-cup offerings of flowers and burning oil wicks twinkling as they floated downstream, aroused some deeper emotion in all of us. The dominant atmosphere at the *ghāṭ,* however, was of a pleasurable promenade; the crowd seemed composed mostly of bourgeois pilgrims—women in nylon saris and men in Western clothes. A scratchy cinematic rendition of *āratī* music blasted out over loudspeakers, and we soon retraced our steps to follow the *paṇḍā*'s second piece of advice and take our meal. After dinner, all suffering from the cold, we wanted nothing but to wrap up in blankets and go to sleep in our bare room.

In the complaining spirit of the moment I asked, "Why do you have to bring the flowers here anyway, when it's so much trouble?" Ladu Ram replied at this time with reference to the descent-of-Ganges story which he and Vajendra, my assistant, were able to produce orally. Immersion of bones in the Ganges, they concluded, was done to give peace to the soul, as well as "deliverance" (*uddhār,* a close synonym to *moksha*). Here in Hardwar Ladu Ram thus gave a mythic and soteriological reason for his journey, whereas on the train he had stressed service to his parents.

The next day began with tea and shaving, which was executed deftly by several barbers attending to clusters of pilgrims huddled about warming fires. Ladu Ram waited his turn, was duly tonsured, and we all headed for the river once more, accompanied by a guide from the rest house. On the way we stopped to purchase two indispensable things: pots in which to collect and carry home Ganges water, and brightly colored flowers to be used in the worship at the river. Ladu Ram spent thirty-five rupees on a fine brass waterpot with a screw-on lid. At the *ghāṭ* we went to the gourdman's designated area. There under a big umbrella sat another *paṇḍā* connected with our rest house, a vendor of *pūjā* supplies. Ladu Ram paid two and one-half rupees for "flour-ball ingredients."

Two distinct but consecutive rituals were now performed. The first was sometimes referred to as "worship of the Ganges"

(*Gangā kā pūjan*) and sometimes as "worship of the bones" (*asthi pūjan*; note the use of the Sanskrit word *asthi* for "bone" here rather than the euphemistic *phūl*).[17] This rite preceded the placing of the bones in the river and a Ganges bath. The entire action at the *ghāṭ* was sometimes subsumed under the name of the second rite—"flour-ball act" (*piṇḍa kriya*)—in which, of course, the chief accomplishment was making "flour-ball offerings" (*piṇḍadān*) to the spirit of the deceased.

Having removed his father's bones from the red pouch, Ladu Ram sat facing the *paṇḍā*, holding them in his hands. On top of them, according to the *paṇḍā*'s instructions, he put a coconut and on top of that a red flower. Ganges water was poured over all of this. On the ground in front of Ladu Ram a number of coins were laid out along with three leaf cups containing red and yellow flowers. The text of the ritual which I recorded and had transcribed is partly in a very simplified Sanskrit and partly in Hindi. The *paṇḍā* had Ladu Ram repeat after him phrases identifying himself and the time and place and stating his purpose as having brought his father's bones. Still repeating, Ladu Ram asked that his father receive a "dwelling in heaven," a "dwelling in Vaikunth" (Vaikunth being a particular named heaven), and a "true passage" (*sat gati*),[18] and that all his sins be destroyed.

The *paṇḍā* then arrived at what, for him, was the highlight of the occasion: "From Laduji's hands, for father Mangilal's satisfaction, gift of grain, gift of cow, gift of clothing, gift of utensils, feast for Brahmans," building up to a "gratuity" (*dakshiṇā*) for the *paṇḍājī*, "given joyfully, with a happy mind, for father's satisfaction." At this crucial moment he ordered us to turn off the tape recorder and repeated once more the list of desirable gifts. Ladu Ram volunteered one-half maund (twenty kilograms) of wheat to

17. For the duration of this ritual I will call the bones "bones" because real flowers figure in the action; not only I but my companions as well were several times confused as to what was meant when the *paṇḍā* instructed Ladu Ram to do something with "flowers."

18. *Gati* indicates a good outcome after death, but not necessarily an exit from *samsāra*. Its literal meaning, "the action of going from one place to another," simply implies a change of state, which might be from ghost to ancestor, as well as from bound to liberated. Although some scholars of devotional Hindi literature (for example, Allchin 1966) translate *gati* as "salvation," I will use the more literal "passage," which may be understood in context either as passage from one existence to another or out of creation altogether.

be collected in the village along with one loincloth. The *paṇḍā* waxed eloquent on the many services he was performing and demanded a cash gratuity, to be paid now. Ladu Ram settled, after some haggling, on twenty-five and a quarter rupees and, after yet more badgering, one "Brahman *bhojan*"—that is, the cost of one good meal for a *paṇḍā*.

Returning to the ritual format, Ladu Ram obediently repeating "with a happy mind," pledged these things. He then very rapidly placed the bones in the river and slid his father's walking stick in after them. He was instructed to bathe and to rinse his mouth. After bathing and dressing in dry clothes, Ladu Ram was seated once more facing the *paṇḍā* for the flour-ball offerings. Before him was a *pūjā* tray on which, arranged in a circle, were red powder, turmeric, puffed rice, and grains of wheat and rice. In the center was incense. On top of the rice a red thread was placed representing "cloth" and next to the incense was a white curled thread, the *janeū* ("sacred thread") worn by twice-born males. On a separate leaf were five *piṇḍa*s—balls made of wheat flour and water—one for each day since Mangilal's death.[19]

The *paṇḍā* greeted the gods in Sanskrit, and Ladu Ram repeated once more the date, place, his name, and prayer for his father's reaching heaven and receiving release. Water was poured onto Ladu Ram's head, and he drank three times and washed his hands. The *paṇḍā* picked up one *piṇḍa* and rolled it between his palms, then put it into Ladu Ram's hand and placed a flower on top of it. A pitcher of water was poured over the *piṇḍa* now, and the *janeū* was placed on it. Something of every item from the *pūjā* tray was also put on top of the *piṇḍa,* as well as another red flower. Ladu Ram lit incense. During all these actions the *paṇḍā* continued to recite verses, including prayers evoking worldly well-being and reminiscent of the stated goals of regional shrine pilgrimage: "Keep happiness and peace in the house, increase wealth, increase progeny, live with love."

Ladu Ram was instructed to speak the name of Ram 108 times.

19. While in the flour-ball offerings of the twelfth day (chapter 2) the *piṇḍa*s represent the new *pret* and the three preceding generations of ancestors, here they are part of the series of daily *piṇḍa* offerings prescribed to build up the body of the *pret* part by part during the days immediately following death (see Parry 1982b:84; Stevenson 1971:159–161).

Then all the major crossing places, including Mathura, Kashi, Puri, and Dwarka, were invoked as givers of release. Father Mangilal's release and true passage were again called for. Mother Ganges was asked to "destroy all sins from birth to birth," and again to "increase riches, grain, and progeny, to give peace to father's soul, to make father's deliverance, to make father's release, and to make our pilgrimage fruitful." Finally, "Victory to Ganges Mother!" was softly shouted.

Ladu Ram's brass waterpot, which had temporarily vanished, was brought out by another *paṇḍā,* already filled with Ganges water, sealed with wax, and marked with auspicious red powder. It was worshipped. Ladu Ram, as instructed by the *paṇḍā,* then held the first flour ball to his forehead and to each shoulder, from left to right. Finally he placed it, and the others as well, in the river. The *paṇḍā* told him to make three "water offerings" from his hands and to sprinkle himself with Ganges water and take three sips. Then he announced soothingly that our program was finished. We all received forehead marks from the priest under the umbrella and paid him a small amount of money.

It was at this point that we met up with the Ghatiyali schoolteacher and decided, after much debate, to do some sightseeing with him. Ladu Ram would probably have preferred to go straight home, as he was in much anxiety over the coming twelfth-day feast and all the arrangements required for its success. At the same time, however, there was a sense that it wasn't right to come all this way and not at least visit Rishikesh and Lakshman Jhula, the two most famed attractions in the area. As these sights were associated by all in our village with the Hardwar pilgrimage, people would be sure to ask us if we had viewed them; it might even be inauspicious to neglect key *darshans*. Our tour was rapid and perfunctory, but the Gita Temple and the magnificent mountain scenery did distract Ladu Ram's mind briefly from his home worries.

After this side trip, Ladu Ram completed his Hardwar business by purchasing two new walking sticks and a colored straw basket in which to carry home his sealed pot of Ganges water, We were also "given" (at one and one-quarter rupees per person) white-sugar-candy *prasād* and yellow straw garlands at the gourdman's rest house. As our dilapidated and springless bus pulled out of the

Hardwar depot, Vajendra in a low voice let out the traditional cry uttered when pilgrims leave a crossing place, proclaiming the triumph of its chief deity: "Speak Ganges Mother's victory!"

After about twenty-four hours of discomfort unmitigated by conversation, as we were all too cold and tired to engage in it and the buses too noisy in any case, Ladu Ram reached Pushkar. Pushkar is called by Rajasthanis of our area the "last crossing place" because for them it is mandatory to stop there on the way home from any Ganges pilgrimage. Hurrying from the bus stand toward the lake shore, Ladu Ram told me that, rather than seek a family or caste *paṇḍā* here, he could just as well do his business at "any old *ghāṭ-vāṭ,*" and his sole aim was to do it quickly. We proceeded, therefore, to the nearest *ghāṭ* where willing *paṇḍā*s immediately performed worship of Pushkar and worship of the pot of Ganges water on Ladu Ram's behalf. In the course of these rites Ladu Ram bathed in Pushkar Lake and then bathed his sealed pot of Ganges water with Pushkar water. The reason he gave for this was that Pushkar was the "guru of all crossing places" and the "navel of the universe." Pushkar water thus could only improve the purity of Ganges water. However, the seal was not broken on the Ganges-water pot.[20]

Ladu Ram went from the lake to have *darshan* at his "lineage seer" temple, a temple dedicated to Gautam Rishi, the chief ancestor of all Brahmans of his subcaste. On the way from this temple back to the bus stand for our return to Ajmer, he gave away the spare walking stick, but only on the second try, as one beggar refused to accept it (whether because of its inauspiciousness or its uselessness I was not able to determine).

Our pilgrimage was effectively complete now, but we had missed the last bus that would give us a connection to Ghatiyali and had to pass the night in Ajmer. Here a minor contretemps occurred which casts some light on the ambiguous status of the pilgrim who journeys within the twelve days after death, during the time of death pollution. We had been welcomed at the home of my research assistant Vajendra's wife's elder sister and her hus-

20. Zeitlyn reports that Pushkar water "is regarded as a form of lord Vishnu, the husband of Laxmi" (1983:17). Guru also generally has masculine connotations. Pushkar water may be complementary to Ganges water as male to female, a complementarity congruent with the outside-to-inside relation between the lake and the fluid sealed within a pilgrim's pot.

band, who fed us well and offered us a place to sleep. Our relaxation there, however, was suddenly interrupted by some excited conversation which I was not able to follow entirely. Collecting our belongings and rushing out the door, we were conducted by the husband to a nearby Jain rest house and obtained a room and quilts there.

After the dust settled I learned that we had unwittingly committed a very grave mistake in going to Vajendra's relations' house in the midst of this pilgrimage with flowers. We had rendered their home "bad" (*kharāb*) or "impure" (*ashuddh*). According to Ladu Ram, he and Vajendra had not been aware of this contagion and neither had our hosts. The furor had arisen only when an old neighbor woman, who paid strict attention to such matters, snooped out the reason for our presence there. Vajendra's wife's sister's husband was then forced in embarrassed fashion to hustle us on our way. The rest of our return was uneventful. Ladu Ram stored the pot of Ganges water in his home shrine; on the twelfth day after his father's death, following the worship of Path Mother, he would festively welcome Ganges Mother and Bhairuji Banaras-dweller to his house as honored guests (chapter 2).

Prayag, Gaya, Hardwar: Shaving, Flour-Ball Offerings, Water

From this version of pilgrimage with flowers in its simplest form, compressed within a three-day round trip to Hardwar, and within the twelve days immediately after a death, we turn to an account of an alternative, elaborated, and prolonged mode of removing bone remains from house to crossing place. In my experience, the longer pilgrimage was embedded in a general "Hindu *darshan* bus tour" (chapter 5). Not all the participants in the bus tour were transporting flowers, and those who were did not consider it the sole rationale for their journey. Most, in fact, described the decision to make the trip as resulting from a combination of serendipitous circumstances: acquaintances were also going, friends and relations were encouraging, cash was available, and flowers were sitting in the house.

The flower bearers were, however, prime ritual actors at several points during the pilgrimage process, beginning with the predeparture worship of Path Mother. While visiting several famed spots in Rajasthan, experiencing Krishna country, and gazing at the spectacles of Agra, those carrying flowers had no distinctive role except for required daily attentions to the needs of their charges. When we reached Prayag, our first encounter with the Ganges, the pilgrims with red pouches of bones were definitively distinguished. My original field notes record this fact almost as an afterthought: "Here [in Prayag] some had their heads shaved, the barbers screaming that it is karma and for the sake of one's parents. Those with *phūl* had their heads shaved. The others set about with great enthusiasm washing their clothes." My research assistant similarly recorded in his (Hindi) journal: "When we reached there [Prayag] many barbers came to us and one grabbed Gulab Singh [a loud, robust Rajput who, unlike Ladu Ram, always wore his red pouch prominently displayed atop a white *kurtā* and ample belly] and shaved his head and beard clear. In this way all those who had *phūl* were shaved."

Thus, following the worship of Path Mother, the first important act of the flower bearers was to be shaved in Prayag, and it is interesting that Sanskrit texts have a great deal to say on the importance of tonsure at this ancient site.[21] Our company, on the contrary, although submitting to the practiced hustle of barbers and *paṇḍās*, appeared to have only a vague acceptance of Prayag's greatness, based largely on the triple confluence of powerful waters.

Unlike the tale of the Ganges' descent to earth via Hardwar, which is common village lore, Prayag's mytho-historical virtues were not well known among our group. This was demonstrated by our *darshan* experience there. After some were shaved and all had bathed, we were loosely herded toward the fort near the riverbank, where all who were willing to pay the fifty-paisa admission fee (and this did not include everyone) went into the basement and viewed many icons of the gods. Here was the

21. Kane tells us: "The two verses quoted by most writers are 'one should tonsure the head at Prayaga, offer pindas at Gaya, made gifts in Kruksetra and should commit (religious) suicide at Benares. What is the use (or necessity) of pinda offerings at Gaya, or death in Kasi, or gifts at Kuruksetra, if one has tonsured one's head at Prayaga?'" (1953:601–602). See also the section on "shaving at a *tīrtha*" in Salomon's translation of Narayana Bhatta's "Bridge to the Three Holy Places" (1985:274–309). This includes a lengthy and elegant argument against those who claim that one should shave only at Prayag, thus confirming the preeminence of Prayag as a place to be shaved.

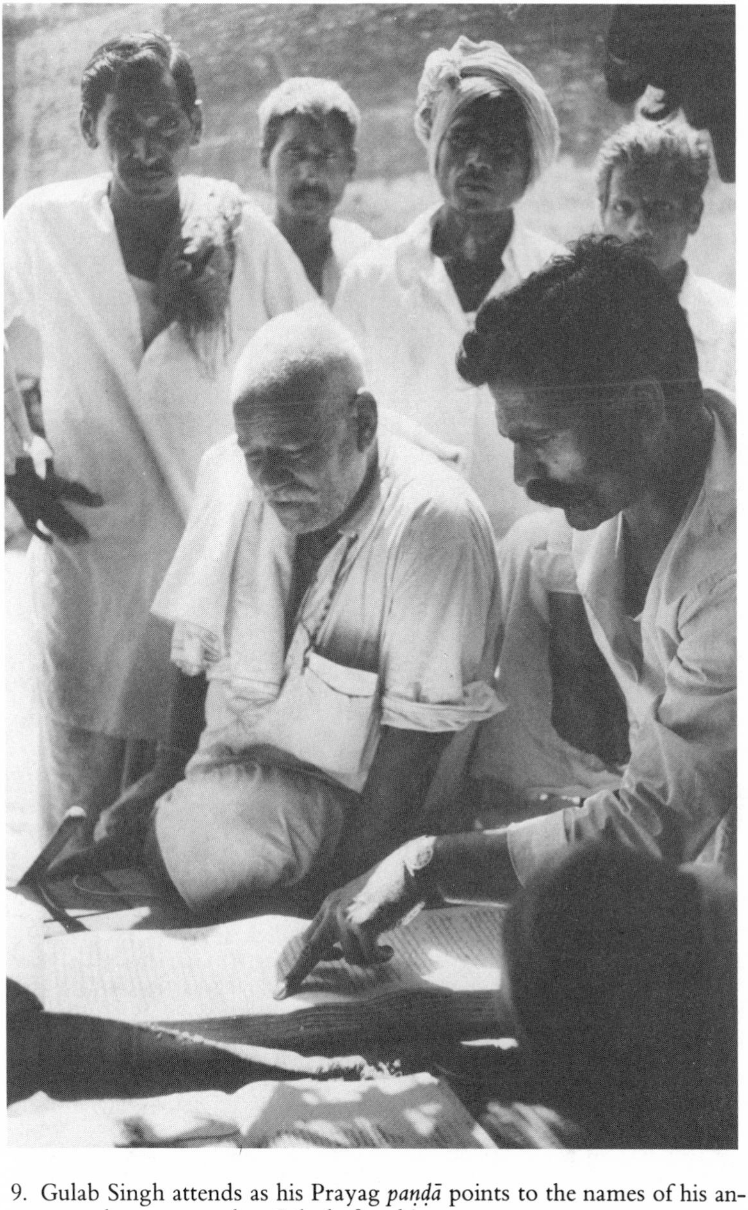

9. Gulab Singh attends as his Prayag *paṇḍā* points to the names of his ancestors who came to that *tīrtha* before him.

"Indestructible Tree" (Akshay Vaṭ), among whose roots sat Brahma, Vishnu, and Mahesh (Shiva). None of our pilgrims seemed to know or care much about this Indestructible Tree, preferring to gaze on somewhat gaudy icons of more familiar deities. Textual sources, however, locate the foundations of Prayag's glory in a mythic Akshay Vaṭ.[22]

Next to bathing near the confluence, not *darshan* but name-writing was the chief feature of our one-day stay in Prayag. Here we encountered for the first time *paṇḍā*s whose record books showed names from our pilgrims' home villages and families. All the members of our party had their own names added, and those with flowers recorded the identity of the deceased persons. The authenticity and enduring qualities of the record books were highly meaningful to the pilgrims, and everyone seemed satisfied to transact this business with the *paṇḍā*s. Some pilgrims considered sinking their flowers in the confluence at Prayag, an acceptable option, but the prevailing opinion was to wait for Gaya. Several quoted, in support of waiting, the popular saying and pun "Once in Gaya they have *gone!*" (Giyā mẽ to giyā!) referring to the theory that putting the physical remains of the dead in Gaya truly effects a permanent removal of their spirits. This theory is, however, often contradicted by experience, as we shall see.

Gaya's textual and popular fames, unlike Prayag's, were quite homologous. The story of the founding of Gaya atop the body of the prodigious demon Gayasur was both previously known to our pilgrim party and constantly reinforced during our stay in that

22. Prayag's mythic charter is much more abstract than Hardwar's. The printed pamphlet describing Prayag's "greatness" stresses an Indestructible Tree's primary significance. To the question "Why do you call Prayag the King of Crossing Places?" the wise Markandeya replies, "Believe my words, because in the great dissolution [of the universe] the Vedas and everything were hidden and only one Indestructible Tree remained behind, which is present in this very crossing place" (*Prayag Raj Mahatmya* n.d.: 3–4). In Kane there are similar claims for the tree's importance (1953:600). A popular Hindi guidebook gives an update on Prayag's Indestructible Tree which may explain its lack of preeminence today. "Previously in the underworld cave of the fort there was a dry branch buried with cloth wrapped around it, and, calling this the 'Indestructible Tree,' its *darshan* was done" (Rajiv 1979:131). Today, however, the guidebook continues, a more visible tree is available for public *darshan*. It appears that the tree, which captivated me but not my fellow pilgrims, is a recent innovation, replacing a less impressive-looking branch, but neither had any deep connection with the ancient, undissolving *Akshay Vaṭ* of Puranic lore.

crossing place. Colorful posters—called, like all the stylized diagrams of pilgrimage centers or routes, "maps"—depicting the overlay of Gaya's sacred geography on Gayasur's prone body, with the gods holding it in place, were displayed by every peddler of pilgrims' souvenir paraphernalia. Moreover, Gaya's foundational association with death and liberation was perpetually recalled, both in pilgrims' oral lore and in popular printed text.

In the first chapter of the "Story of the Greatness of Shri Gaya" (*Shri Gaya Mahatmya Katha*) the opening question is "Tell me the story of some such crossing place that is a 'giver of release' [*muktidāyak*] and from hearing whose greatness release is received." I cite the reply at some length, as it so persistently reinforces the *mukti* theme.

> The only such crossing place is Gaya. It is such a pure ground that from doing *shrādh* and *piṇḍadān* there release is obtained. Once a big powerful demon named Gayasur was produced there. On top of him the Brahmans put a *dharma*-stone and made a sacrifice. In order to make this stone motionless, Lord Vishnu, bringing a club and called by the name "Club-holder," was situated there, and then all the gods, holding the form of Phalgu [the name of the Ganges at Gaya; also called "Hidden Ganges"], settled there.
>
> Brahma after sacrificing gave to the Brahmans gifts of dwellings, jewels, gold, etcetera, and since then this city became pure.
>
> Just there ancestors always dwell and always we hope that in our lineage someone will be born who will come to this place and give *piṇḍa*s, from which act we will become released. If the son goes to Gaya and merely touches the Phalgu River, his ancestors go to dwell in heaven.
>
> In the field of Gaya, even if you offer a *piṇḍa* as small as a sesame seed, ancestors obtain an indestructible world.
>
> In the field of Gaya, by performing *piṇḍadān* for their own sakes, those without any lineage are freed from deep sins like the murder of Brahmans or the drinking of wine.
>
> In Gaya, if mere acquaintances take the name of a dead man and give *piṇḍadān,* he becomes released.
>
> In Gaya, fruit equivalent to that of ten million crossing places and a horse sacrifice is received from doing *piṇḍadān*.
>
> In Gaya, those who do *shrādh* should have no thought of death.
>
> In Gaya, even if the ancestors aren't present they immediately arrive after seeing *shrādh* performed. When going to Gaya for the sake of *piṇḍadān,* lust and anger should be renounced.

In every part of the field of Gaya, crossing places are splendidly located. Consequently, the field of Gaya is counted the first among all crossing places. (*Gaya Mahatmya Katha* n.d.:1–3).[23]

The progress of our pilgrims in Gaya was difficult from the start. We arrived, as had been calculated by the bus owner, during the annual fair of *shrāddh paksh,* or the dark half of the lunar month of Ashvin (September–October) during which "faithful offerings" (*shrāddh*) to departed kin are both most enjoined and most effective. Although it was only the fourth day of the fair, the effects of crowds and inadequate sanitary arrangements were already much in evidence. The authorities stopped our bus as it approached the city environs and injected everyone in disconcerting fashion with cholera immunizations. We were then directed to park in a designated area (Gandhi Stadium) amidst scores of other similar pilgrim-tourist buses. Our group set off at once on the long trek to the riverbank, hoping to sink our flowers and make flour-ball offerings that very day.

On the way, however, two of our women—a Rajput matron and her Daroga companion—became separated from the group and lost their way. This caused a great deal of commotion when we arrived at the river and their absence was belatedly discovered. One of the missing ladies was the wife of the same Gulab Singh mentioned above, a cantankerous and imperious Rajput with a clear leadership role among the lower-caste peasant pilgrims from

23. See Kane 1953:656–663 and Vidyarthi 1961:114–117 for English versions of the "Greatness of Gaya" translated from the *Vayu Purana*. I append here a curious piece of folklore regarding the nongreatness of Gaya, which my research assistant heard from a barber on the *ghāṭ*.

Here, one time, Sita and Rama came to offer *piṇḍa*s to Dasaratha. At this time Ram Candraji went to the bazaar to get ingredients for the *piṇḍa*s. Then the soul of Dasaratha called out, "Give me the *piṇḍa*s right now, I'm very hungry, I'm late." Hearing this, Sita, while Rama was gone, made a *piṇḍa* of clay and offered it and Dasaratha's soul went back.

When Rama came, then Sita said, "I have given the *piṇḍadān* already." Rama asked, "Who is the witness?" Sita answered, "There is a Brahman, a cow, and the river." But all three, out of self-interest, denied it. They said they knew nothing about it because they thought that if Rama offered *piṇḍadān* they too would get something.

At this time Sita gave a curse. She cursed the river, the Ganges, to flow hidden; even after much rain the water goes down to a very shallow level in just a few days. And she cursed the cow to keep on eating shit. And she cursed the Brahman: "You will always be poor and begging." So all these three things came true.

his village (the majority of the passengers). He made such a vociferous and eloquent fuss about his wife's disappearance that I turned on my tape recorder. Among his ravings, this bit of rhetoric was included: "No matter, she'll be found and if she's not found, no matter, no matter. This is Mother Ganges. I also will become an offering here; her passage will be mine also." Although most of his harangue dealt not with the soul's liberation but with the cursedness of the bus owner for not transporting the pilgrims closer to the river (an absolute impossibility given the traffic congestion and narrow streets), it is nonetheless striking that he enhanced his emotion-laden speech with the traditional notion that it is good to leave your body in a crossing place. Such a death, as an offering to Mother Ganges, would ensure passage to a better birth, heaven, or freedom.

The outcome of the mishap, however, was not so drastic: Gulab Singh's wife and her companion, having thoroughly lost their way in the bazaar, quite sensibly asked a riksha-driver to take them back to where the buses were parked, and we found them safely waiting there when we returned. Many of the other pilgrims privately speculated after this event—not the first, but the most apoplectic of Gulab Singh's outbursts—that the flowers he carried might be those of persons not at all eager to be left in a crossing place. This, others felt, could account for both his bad temper and his various troubles along the way.

The confusion resulted in a general disarray among our party that day. Some of the flower bearers were shaved once more, and here women planning to participate in the *piṇḍadān* also each gave one symbolic lock of hair to the barbers. Everyone bathed in the shallow and very unappealing water. Some of those with flowers placed them in the river, a simple and personal act unassisted by *paṇḍās*. The bones were removed from the pouch, bathed with river water, and mixed into the sandy bottom with the prayer "Be royally seated here and reach the spot of Vaikunth. We are happily sending you off."

Attending upon this solemn moment were only the pesky, untouchable scavenger children, eager to seize the coins that had been placed in the pouch along with the bones, as the pouch's entire contents were emptied now. One very old, partially deaf, and very nearsighted pilgrim from our party suffered a real indignity from these children. Preparing to put his flowers in the river, he was fumbling with the pouch string when one of the sweeper kids grabbed the pouch away from him and emptied it for him, seizing the coins and fleeing. The man was left bewildered, having lost his chance to sink his relations' remains. The same person, incidentally, had further troubles during the next day's rituals, for he put all his flour balls in the river when he should have put in only the first set of seventeen, and was thus unable to complete the series of offerings.

Not all of the pilgrims submerged flowers that day, and there was a lot of uncomfortable talk throughout the evening about the impropriety of placing one's forefathers in such a dirty place. Much of the riverbank, a short way down from the prime bathing spot but well within view and olfactory range, was given over to latrine purposes. Moreover, because of a ban on pigs within this sacred ground, the normal Indian scavenging cycle was broken and the foulness daily compounded. However, having left Prayag behind, people felt committed to Gaya, and the deed was or soon would be done. One of our most sincere and soothing Brahman pilgrim companions quoted another popular Rajasthani expression to the effect that when you take the dead to Gaya "they go and don't come back" (*jāve pache nāve*).

The next day was one of the fullest of the entire journey and certainly involved the most elaborate and lengthy ritual action. We had already connected with the *paṇḍā* for our area, and in the morning proceeded, as directed, to his house. There the usual financial haggling took place, of which I give a sampling from my tape recording, not merely for the humor but because subtle as well as crass aspects of these negotiations become apparent. Pilgrims almost universally feel that using up money at crossing places is one of the most desirable and appropriate side-effects of pilgrimage. At the same time, they are ever guarding against exploitation. The *paṇḍā*s must and do expertly play upon both these chords by arguing that their pecuniary demands present both a great bargain and a singular opportunity for meritorious largesse. It is also worth noting that Gaya was the only place we visited where the *paṇḍā*s had record books but were unwilling to take the time to find and read out the old names. Like the dirty water, this was accepted but was not pleasing to the pilgrims.

Panda (hereafter Pa): Whatever work you have to do here, death *sam-*

skāra, piṇḍadān, give me the money and we will do the work for you.

Nandalal Sharma (Brahman schoolteacher pilgrim, frequent spokesman for the others, hereafter NS): Maharaj, do it fast, we don't have much time.

Pa: All right, I'll write you down for one and one-quarter rupees.

Mangilal Gujar (young, earnest pilgrim traveling with his devout widowed mother and his father's bones, hereafter MG): Yes, but first tell us our old names. From this we will know if you are our *paṇḍā* or not. Bring your record book.

Pa: Look, you are one hundred people and I am only one, so if you have any faith in me, then whatever work you came here to do, do it. And if you don't want to do it, then go to whatever *paṇḍā* you meet in Gaya and do the work with him. If you don't have any faith in me, then go. I don't have the time. You don't have time and I don't either. Look [pointing to his assistant], he is writing names. If you want, have your name written with him. . . .

NS: Write, write!

Pa: In this place, for one and one-quarter rupees you can write just your name, but if you want to write all the details of your forefathers, then go to him [gesturing toward yet another *paṇḍā*] and he will write them all, but it will cost more money. Now, think in your mind, what is your desire, for the sake of your forefathers, what will you give?

NS: Eleven rupees.

Pa: [outraged] This is not a store! For eleven rupees only the expense of the *pūjā* will come. If you want to do *dān,* to do *dharm,* first think.

Unindentified pilgrim: You mean, all the expenses, of the *piṇḍadān* and everything are included in this?

Pa: Yes, yes yes, all is included.

Unidentified pilgrim [to NS]: All right, so make it a little more, make it twenty-one rupees.

Pa: Yes, included in this, when you return from the *piṇḍadān,* you will get garlands and *prasād.* And the *paṇḍā* who does your *piṇḍadān,* if you desire to feed him, you can give him one or two rupees. . . . Here there is no routine. If you want you can give a *lākh* of rupees. And if you are so poor, then you can just join your hands [that is, give respect but no money]. So, if someone has money he will surely give *dān,* but if he doesn't have any money, then what *dān* will he give?

Gulab Singh: So, do the writing of names.

Pa: When you tell me the names, I can write them. [addressing MG] Tell, what do you want to take and give? One hundred and one? Fifty-one? Tell, is your desire more or less? Grain, cloth, what?

MG: Within this all expenses will come, of *piṇḍadān,* name-writing, garlands, and *prasād?*

Pa: Yes.

MG: Tell, what all will come?

Pa: In all three places, *piṇḍa*s will be offered; all the ingredients of the *piṇḍa*s, flour and so forth will be given. I will send a Brahman with you and he will offer your *piṇḍa*s. And after the *piṇḍa*s, understand, you come here and I will give you a blessing and *prasād* and you go. But the Brahman who does your *piṇḍa*s, he will ask you to offer one or two rupees, and that you should give. And on the road to the crossing place, there are the crippled and lame and the beggars; you give to them as you desire. Those Brahmans who do the *piṇḍa*s, you ought to feast them.

MG: Thirty-one.

Pa: Listen to me, listen, listen! If in your heart is the desire to give one hundred rupees but before you opened your mouth some greed came, and you

10. Mehru party preparing to perform *piṇḍadān* on the beach at Gaya during *shrāddh paksh melā.*

> said less, then reflect. Why am I saying this to you? Because we are going to give this information to your mother and father whose flowers you have brought.

This was the *paṇḍā*'s final thrust and it had no perceptible effect, for the amount was settled at thirty-one rupees, and both peasants and priests appeared satisfied in the end. The chief *paṇḍā* then rapidly dispatched us to the *ghāṭ,* accompanied by a Brahman in his service who would conduct our rites. He first had all who would participate in the *piṇḍadān* ceremonies bathe and put on clean clothes. Then those who had not put their flowers in the river on the previous day without priestly assistance did so now under the *paṇḍā*'s supervision. The act, however, remained simple and rapid, the priest merely adding a few Sanskrit *mantra*s and holding the scavenger children at bay.

The *paṇḍā* then seated the participants on an unshaded sandy portion of the riverbank in two lines facing south. Countless other groups of worshippers were also seated in similar fashion and performing *piṇḍadān* up and down the *ghāṭ*. For each family who brought flowers one leaf plate was placed in front of the worshipper or worshippers. Married couples would perform the rite "joined." Mangilal Gujar and his mother, who had jointly brought his father's remains, also sat together before one plate. A child who, accompanied by his paternal grandparents, had brought his mother's flowers was seated between the old couple.

Near each leaf plate a clay cup of Ganges water was also provided, and a ragged girl appeared and sold each worshipper, for a few paise, some already very watery milk to mix into this. The *paṇḍā* then placed wheat flour, whole barley, sesame, and rice on the plates. He also made grass rings and instructed the men performing the ritual to wear them on the ring fingers of their right hands.

Each worshipper then mixed the ingredients on the plate with water from the clay pot to make a dough, from which three large *piṇḍā*s were formed. Following the *paṇḍā*'s instructions step by step, they then divided one of the three large *piṇḍā*s into seventeen small *piṇḍā*s. These seventeen *piṇḍā*s offered at Gaya differ both from those given at Hardwar and from the *piṇḍā*s of the twelfth-day rites of joining. Individually dedicated to particular ancestors, the Gaya *piṇḍā*s neither construct a body nor merge bodies for spirits of the deceased, but simply allow the living to satiate them. *Piṇḍa*s generally appear both to represent their recipients and to nourish them.[24]

Now the *paṇḍā* distributed real flowers and a sparkling mix of red powder and ground mica; he also gave out additional barley, sesame, rice, and another piece of grass. While the first set of food ingredients went to make the *piṇḍā*s, this second set would be offered to these *piṇḍā*s. Then the *paṇḍā* inscribed a square ritual space in the sandy ground in front of each pilgrim's plate.

The priest, after greeting the gods, told the pilgrims to take some flowers in their hands. (As the bone-flowers are now safely sunk in the river we can refer to real flowers without confusion.) He spoke more Sanskrit lines of praise and greeting to various deities and asked the worshippers to drop the flowers into the squares and take barley, sesame, and water in their hands. The pilgrims proceeded to repeat after him the date and their business: "In the dark half of Ashoj (same as Ashvin), my mother, father, guru,

24. During all types of *piṇḍadān* rites, the *piṇḍa*s themselves first receive offerings and then become offerings. Marriott comments that these transformations suggest that all substance is mutable and relational; that distinctions between objects, receivers, media, channels, and so forth are relative and transient (personal communication). For some interesting thoughts on *piṇḍa*s, see also Knipe 1977; O'Flaherty 1980a; Parry 1982b.

grandfather, father-in-law, all who have gone to the world of Vishnu, to all of them at this pure crossing place of Gaya I make an offering of *piṇḍās*." They then bathed all the *piṇḍās* with milky Ganges water. There followed the main body of the *piṇḍadān* rite during which the seventeen little *piṇḍās* were dedicated one by one with prayers for the various named recipients to receive heaven and release.

Each *piṇḍā* in turn was held in the hand; bathed from the milk-water pot; offered red powder, flowers, and more milk-water. The first little *piṇḍā* was dedicated to the father by all except widows, who were told to name their husbands. (Throughout the dedications, if the relative in question was still alive the pilgrims were instructed not to participate in that offering.) After naming the recipient, the *piṇḍā* was deposited in the square by pushing it from the right hand with the left thumb, an act called "making an offering of a *piṇḍā*" (*piṇḍā arpaṇ karnā*).

The second *piṇḍa* went to father's father, the third to father's father's father, the fourth to mother, the fifth to father's mother, the sixth to father's mother's mother, the seventh to mother's father, the eighth to mother's father's father, the ninth to mother's father's father's father,[25] the tenth to mother's mother, the eleventh to mother's mother's mother, the twelfth to father's brother or other "brother-relations." All the rest but one were given according to the needs and wishes of the pilgrims—for example, to father's sister, mother's sister, mother's sister's husband, and so forth. The seventeenth *piṇḍa* is a catchall dedicated as follows: "He who is forgotten, whose name we don't know, who was bitten by a snake or killed by a lion, any person who hopes that we will give him a *piṇḍa*, a friend or whoever, who was drowned in water, some *bhūt* or *pret*; his passage will be made in the crossing place of Gaya, in the spot established by Vishnu, by the grace of Vishnu, by the promise of a Brahman, may he dwell in Vaikunṭh." All the little *piṇḍas* were now in the square, and they were bathed once more as a group and offered flowers, barley, sesame seed, as well as sandalwood and incense supplied by the *paṇḍā*.

The pilgrims were instructed to pick up one of these already

25. When I made inquiries as to why there should be a special *piṇḍa* for the maternal great-great-grandfather but not for any other ancestors of his generation, I was simply told that sometimes the others did receive them and that "it depends on the Brahman."

dedicated small *piṇḍa*s and to salute it by touching it to their shoulders and forehead, praying to the ancestors: "Hey, Fathers, dwell in heaven, dwell in Gaya, keep the body free of disease, fulfil the mind's desires, increase our wealth and sons. Victory to Mother and Father!" They then set the *piṇḍa* back down with the rest, took water in their hands, released the water, and joined their hands in respectful salute to the *piṇḍa*s. Next they gently "shook" all the small *piṇḍā*s with both their hands, picked them all up, and got to their feet.

The *paṇḍā* told them to go to the river and "cause [the *piṇḍa*s] to flow." He added, "A Brahman [that is, a different one] will go with you and speak *mantra*s and as you desire you can give him *dān.*" Everyone held their small *piṇḍa*s and stood in the shallow river facing the new Brahman and the east. They spoke *mantra*s after him, the meaning of which approximated "In this pure crossing place of Gaya, dwell, stay here." They put their *piṇḍa*s into the water, splashed their heads with water, and saluted the river. The river *paṇḍā* then entreated them with the usual eloquence to commit themselves to offering "Brahman feasts"; "Don't look in one another's directions or talk with each other or think, because he gives four *ānnā*s [one-quarter rupee] I will too, but just give from your desire." After they offered small amounts, he gave them a blessing: "You will be wealthy; you will have many sons."

Now the pilgrims picked up their leaf plates containing the two large *piṇḍa*s and remaining *pūjā* ingredients, and they proceeded to the nearby Vishnu temple for the second series of *piṇḍadān,* which was in most ways identical with the first. Thus they made seventeen *piṇḍa*s out of the second of the three large *piṇḍa*s and dedicated them as before. Whereas in the first series Ganges Mother had been called upon as "witness," here the witness was Vishnu. When all the dedications were completed, the pilgrims deposited their seventeen *piṇḍa*s in a round pit surrounded by a silver fence and directly facing the temple's main Vishnu icon. No different *paṇḍā* assisted at this juncture or asked for more money as at the river, but the pilgrims did each drop a ten-paisa coin into the pit along with the seventeen *piṇḍa*s. Then they circumambulated the pit, took *darshan* of Lord Vishnu, and received *prasād* of flowers and basil leaf from the temple priest.

The *paṇḍā* reassembled his charges and led them, still carrying the leaf plate with its remaining contents, including the final large *piṇḍa,* to the place of Gaya's own "Indestructible Tree," actually a far more impressive specimen than the one in the basement of the Prayag fort. It was not a banyan but a *beḷ* tree, normally deciduous, that was said never to shed its leaves. The tree was covered with scraps of cloth tied on by pilgrims, and an assortment of stone icons nestled among its magnificent roots. It resembled, in fact, trees found at Rajasthani shrines, but the pilgrims were too hot and exhausted to appreciate this touch of home.

Here a final set of seventeen small *piṇḍa*s was offered in the same way as before. After the dedications, which the *paṇḍā* was by now spewing out with incredible speed, the pilgrims placed all their *piṇḍa*s along with a small coin offering, emptied their leaf plates, and thankfully abandoned them at the Indestructible Tree's ample roots. They then circumambulated the tree, and its attendant priest gave them each a blessing by patting their shoulders. The *paṇḍā* who had seen us through these rites from the beginning then asked for, and received without resistance, a small amount of cash from each exhausted worshipper or set of worshippers. We now returned to the house where we had written the names in the morning, rapidly acquired sugar *prasād,* straw garlands, and more blessings from the chief *paṇḍā* there, and retraced our steps, with many a sigh of relief, to the bus.

The pilgrims were famished and complained a great deal about the length and complexity of the day's work and the sun's fierceness. Moreover, they were none too sure that good results of this elaborate, expensive, and enervating procedure were assured. Many felt troubled that they had asked their forefathers to abide in such a dirty place. Mangilal Gujar, the young and ardent pilgrim mentioned above, stood out as the only one to express satisfaction with Gaya but dissatisfaction with the rites for what he felt to be their overly hasty quality. He stated his intention of having silver flowers fashioned and returning to Gaya, joined with his wife, to spend three entire days doing *piṇḍadān* for his father properly. He was considered a braggart by the rest, who felt, on the contrary, that they had had more than enough; that they had paid an exorbitant price to suffer through a largely incomprehensible ritual which might or might not be effective in granting peace to the spirits of the dead.

What remained of this day we spent as tourists in Bodhgaya, the Buddhist monument a few kilometers away. In interviews conducted several days later, when I asked people to tell the highlights of their journey thus far, many recalled a modern, gold-domed Buddhist temple of Bodhgaya as a favorite sight, but none mentioned Gaya itself or the *piṇḍadān* in listing their best memories.

For the remainder of the journey to Puri and during the three pleasant days spent there no special actions distinguished the flower carriers—now released from the burden of constant attention to their charges—from the rest of the party. The next place where they had particular business was Hardwar, which we reached on our return loop a number of days later. Because these pilgrims had already been shaved, had sunk their flowers, and had offered *piṇḍa*s, they had far less to do in Hardwar than had Ladu Ram.

Most had their names written at the house of the gourdman, although a few dealt with other caste-specific *paṇḍā*s from other rest houses. The next vital task was to acquire a pot of Ganges water. These were purchased in the Hardwar market and formally filled, sealed, and worshipped during Ganga *pūjā* when the pilgrims also bathed. Each made a cash offering of eleven and one-quarter rupees and also a pledge of five or ten kilograms of grain payable upon the *paṇḍā*'s arrival in their home villages. After completing the rituals at the *ghāṭ*, on the way back to the bus the pilgrims purchased colored baskets in which to carry their new Ganges-water pots, garlands, and *prasād*. Many expressed approbation for Hardwar as a clean and beautiful place, a good place to bathe that was not filthy like Gaya. Some openly regretted not having kept the flowers and placed them here, where they might truly be expected to remain happily.

We arrived several days later in Pushkar, the last crossing place. Here among our whole company a general sense of homecoming prevailed, and along with this was an awareness of imminent separation. There was a general dispersal of our party to different bathing *ghāṭ*s, different rest houses, different *paṇḍā*s. This was due largely, of course, to the organization of Pushkar priestcraft along caste lines—at least for Rajasthanis—but it was also a consequence of being on familiar ground and savoring it. People no longer felt like strangers, needing to keep together for comfort and security. Most had been here before, and even those who had not were at home linguistically and culturally. Everyone bathed, but not all felt it necessary to engage the *paṇḍā*s' services. Most of the flower carriers, however, performed Pushkar worship, rinsing their pots of Ganges water with Pushkar water just as Ladu Ram had done.

11. Mehru's Path Mother with sleeping pilgrims; baskets containing pots of Ganges water and walking sticks are set on Path Mother's platform.

The bus arrived in Mehru, the home village of the majority of pilgrims, in an atmosphere of joyful reunion. Everyone had returned in more or less good health; the completed pilgrimage was considered "successful" (*saphal,* literally "fruitful"). The pilgrims greeted their families and were received by them with many demonstrations of affection and continuous excited chatter. The bus departed after its passengers—satisfied customers now—garlanded the owner, the driver, and the mechanic, handsomely tipping the latter two. Although relatives carried the travelers' belongings home, the pilgrim company could not disperse or return to their houses that night. Instead they moved in clusters, accompanied by friends and relations, to the place of Path Mother. They were brought food from their houses, and later a *bhajan* party came from the village and sang well into the night, although a nightlong singing session was not held. Eventually all nonpilgrims returned to their homes, and the returnees made their last camp at the place of Path Mother.

The next morning's events were noted by my research assistant while I devoted myself to photography, in all the confusion of multiple worship and crowding spectators. As it conveys the flavor and something of the disorder, I present his description here, translated from his Hindi diary.

12. Mehru; welcome with sprouts for returning pilgrims at the time of Path Mother's worship.

The pilgrims got up at about 6:00 A.M. Their families brought tea from the village, and after drinking it everyone bathed in the water reservoir [across the road from Path Mother] or at a nearby step-well. Women came from the different households of the pilgrims in twos and threes carrying pots to water Path Mother and bathe Bhairuji. Later, at about 8:30 A.M., women came in groups, singing, some carrying on their heads the vessels with sprouts [carefully tended at home throughout the thirty-day interval between Pathvari *pūjā*s and now overflowing through every hole with green grasses], some carrying trays of items for the worship. They were accompanied by the drummer.

The pandit had set the auspicious time for the ritual at 9:10 A.M. Before beginning, all the walking sticks were placed in one pile, leaning against Path Mother. The separate *pūjā* trays were placed on Path Mother's platform. Each contained saltless bread with oil and soaked raw chickpeas [Bhairuji's two favorite foods], red powder, incense, multicolored string, mung beans, raw sugar, rice, mustard seeds, a pitcher of water, and a coconut.

Pilgrims sat facing Pathvari. The pandit took red powder from one of the trays and mixed it with water and applied it to Bhairuji. He then put a thin sheet of sparkling metal foil on Bhairuji. The pandit tied multicolored string on each walking stick. The pandit knotted the couples together, placing a five-paisa coin in each knot. An offering of *ghī* on smouldering cow-dung coals was placed before Bhairuji.

Incense was lit for Path Mother. Some pilgrims also offered incense at this time to their individual pots of Ganges water by lighting two sticks and placing them on top of the unopened basket. Auspicious string was tied on the vessels with sprouts.

The pandit, speaking Sanskrit *mantra*s, put water in the right hand of all the worshippers for "releasing a resolution" [*samkalp choṛnā*]. Each pilgrim took some of this water and put it on his own head. The pandit, continuing to speak *mantra*s, put a few grains into their hands. Then each pilgrim gave an offering of water and grain in Bhairuji's direction. The pandit put more water in each person's hand, and added red powder to it. All threw this toward Bhairuji as another offering. The pandit then added raw sugar to Bhairuji's *dhūp*. Then he made a *svastik* on Path Mother with red powder and attached multicolored string to it.

The pandit told his assistants, two other Brahmans, to collect two rupees from each pilgrim at this time. Then, everyone took his pot of Ganges water out of the basket, tied auspicious string around it, and marked it with a dot of red powder. All released resolutions with water over the pot. Then the pandit handed each pilgrim the brass pitcher from that pilgrim's own tray, with a coconut set on top. Holding the pitcher in both hands, they touched the coconut to their left shoulder, their right shoulder, and their forehead in greeting. [This identical action was previously performed at Path Mother with the pouch of bones and at Gaya with the *piṇḍas*.]

The pandit put red dots on all the worshippers' foreheads. Then he collected the saltless bread from all the trays and placed it before Bhairuji. The chickpeas were also set before Bhairuji.[26]

The pandit spoke more *mantras*, and the pilgrims stood up, each with his palms pressed together, praying to Path Mother. They were seated again, and women of the pilgrims' families [ideally the man's sister or someone standing in that relation to him] performed *āratī* to them.

The ritual action was finished with the *āratī*. Then the pilgrims received gifts of cloth from their families: turbans were wound around the heads of the men, and bright new wraps around the women. Blouse-cloths and towels were also given as less expensive gifts to women and men. The women carrying vessels with sprouts replaced them on their heads and circumambulated Path Mother seven times, and so did some of the pilgrims. Finally, accompanied by bagpipes and the drummer, all went into the village to view the god at the central temple of Four-Arms. Having bowed here and having offered one and one-quarter rupees, the pilgrims separated, and each family returned to their own house to eat a good meal and distribute the mementos of their journey [such as *prasād* of white-sugar candy, garlands of yellow straw, small framed pictures of the gods, copper rings with the name of Ram, and so forth].

This closure at Path Mother, as we know, is not the full closure of the journey with flowers. That occurs only at the Celebration of Ganga when the sealed pot is opened and the water consumed. I now consider the meanings of this full cycle, both for spirits of the dead who are transported to crossing places and for the living who bring home the various fruits of their pilgrimage.

26. While the bread was left at the shrine, presumably for Path Mother's *bhopā* to collect, the chickpeas were distributed as Bhairuji's *prasād* along the way as worshippers and onlookers returned to the village.

Why Sink Flowers? No Wandering-Turning for the Ghost-Soul

During my first pilgrimage to Hardwar with Ladu Ram, my research assistant and I conducted an extensive taped interview with one of the *paṇḍās* at the gourdman's rest house. In the course of our exchange I tried to discover if, according to his views, rituals performed for the dead in Hardwar ensured release (*moksha, mukti*) from the perpetual flux of rebirth and redeath (*samsāra*) for the spirit of the person on whose behalf they were executed. Here is a fragment of this conversation:

Paṇḍā (hereafter Pa):	[from flour-ball offerings] a human womb is experienced.
Interviewer:	Yes, but you said that *moksha* . . .
Vajendra (my research assistant, a Ghatiyali Brahman by now very familiar with my peculiar interests and viewpoint; hereafter V):	Perhaps *moksha* is like this, I mean, that birth is not taken again, that one is let loose from the eighty-four [*lākh* of rebirths, the proverbial cycle]. It is said, if another birth is taken, then *moksha* is not complete.
I:	Yes.
V:	But, if he takes birth again and again, then he must experience the eighty-four [*lākh*] of births.
Pa:	Yes, mankind must experience them.
I:	So, when flour-ball offerings are given, then are there more births, or does *moksha* . . .
V:	She means, doesn't *moksha* happen after flour-ball offerings?
Pa:	[irritated] Why shouldn't *moksha* happen?
V:	But, if he still, again and again, takes new birth?
Pa:	[exasperated] But yes, he will take birth.
V:	So, so, he hardly receives *moksha*. What is called *moksha?*

Pa: This we call *moksha:* peace for the soul, that the spirit of man does not wander [*baṭaknā*].

V: Good.

Pa: This is called *moksha.*

V: The ghost-soul does not wander.

Pa: Yes, in [the condition of] the ghost-soul [there is] no wandering-turning.

V: Good.

Having steeped myself in philosophical and poetic definitions of *moksha* before coming to the field (see Rose 1978) I was attempting to elicit a distinction or even an opposition between release and rebirth which I had learned from texts. For in India's classical philosophical systems, as well as much of the literate Hindu religious tradition, *moksha* means to cease taking births altogether. When teaching others or being taught higher ideas through the kind of learned discussion called "knowledge-talk" (*gyān-carcā*), villagers indeed recognize such a distinction (witness Vajendra's ability to articulate it). Often, however, the two concepts are merged pragmatically as they are in the *paṇḍā*'s statements. Thus *moksha* comes to mean a liberation from the state of hovering, malevolent, and disembodied ghosthood in order to take a new birth—preferably a human birth. Or, in similar fashion, *moksha* may be interpreted as departure from the scenes of one's previous life to dwell in "heaven" (*svarg*), "paradise" (*Vaikunṭh*), or "father realm" (*pitṛlok*)—all seen as temporary way stations en route to another human body.

The Hardwar *paṇḍā* whose opinions reflected those of his clients forced on me the popular definition of *moksha* as "peace for the soul" in the negative sense of "no wandering." *Moksha* as peace opposes not the recycling of deceased persons' spirits on the wheel of *samsāra* but the trapped condition of lingering ghosts. Such ghostly spirits, because of excessive attachment to objects or interests in the places of their most recent births, remain near those places and at best may be served as minor deities and exercise such deities' powers. Thus, according to the most commonly held and stated concepts of villagers, and of the *paṇḍā,* the liberated soul—the one achieving *moksha*—cycles smoothly from human rebirth to human rebirth while the unliberated soul remains stuck along the way.

At this very juncture the conversation was led by the *paṇḍā* toward possession by ghosts and the problems caused by them. He described the case of one of his clients from Rajasthan, a woman possessed by the ghost of her mother-in-law, who had jumped down a well. The ghost began to speak, through the daughter-in-law, at the moment the *paṇḍā* sprinkled the latter with Ganges water and the flour-ball offerings for the dead woman were set before her. The ghost identified herself and when asked, "What do you want?" replied, "By force these people caused me to fall into the well. Since then my soul is wandering-turning. My passage has not happened. Now you cause my passage." The spirit of the dead woman had directly implored the *paṇḍā* for release from her wretched (and destructive) condition of lingering ghost. In his view, the rituals performed at Hardwar had allowed her to relinquish unhappy attachments to an unsatisfactory life cut off by an untimely, violent death and to proceed to a new human birth.

This *paṇḍā* and his fellows, with a growing enthusaism to further my understandings, recommended highly and then obtained for my perusal a recent issue of the popular magazine *Satya Katha*, or "True Stories." This volume contained an article involving Hardwar *paṇḍā*s, Rajasthani pilgrims, and the liberation of an ancestral spirit. Entitled "Release from a Serpent Birth" (Sarp Yoni se Mukti), it is pertinent here. Although the case it presents is unusual and amazing, the tale nicely dramatizes some cultural premises generally underlying the pilgrimage with flowers. I translate portions verbatim and summarize others, as is indicated by brackets.

Release from a Serpent Birth

In April of 1974 the Kumbha Mela was taking place in Hardwar. From all corners of India, thousands of persons were arriving to take Kumbha baths.

Ramdev Didavana from the district of Nagaur in Rajasthan, with his wife, his sister, and her daughter Gauri, also arrived there. It was his second pilgrimage to Hardwar. One year before, in 1973, he had come with his family to Hardwar in order to put the silver bones of one of his ancestors in the Ganges.

[But the chief *paṇḍā* being absent at the time, Ganges worship was not performed.]

This time when Ramdev reached his *paṇḍā* Pandit Mohanji's office, there was quite a crowd of clients there, and the *paṇḍā*'s agent, Bhagavant Ram, was looking for the clients' names in the record books.

[The agent remembered Ramdev and advised him to come the next day to meet Pandit Mohanji.]

On the next day, Ramdev met Pandit Mohanji, and after touching his feet, spoke. "Panditji, last year I asked the junior panditji the names of my forefathers, and he was not able to tell them. Now would you please look in your record books and tell the names of my forefathers."

Having asked Ramdev the names of his father and grandfather, village and district, Mohanji searched through his book for quite a long time. Then he said, "It seems as if none of your forefathers ever came to Hardwar."

"How can that be, Maharaj?" Ramdev said. "Please look one time more, carefully."

Then Mohanji took out a very old book and looked, and this time he found written the names of Didavana. He read these names, and Ramdev listened but said, "Hearing these names it seems to me that none are of my forefathers, but I don't really know. But when our *pitarjī* tells me, then I will accept it."

Hearing about this *"pitarjī"* Mohanji was somewhat surprised and said, "What do you mean by *'pitarjī'?*"

Hearing Mohanji's question, Ramdev began to open his bag, and Mohanji watched with curiosity to see which *pitarjī* he might be taking out from his bag. Ramdev's wife, his sister, and her daugther Gauri were seated at his side.

Ramdev slowly opened the bag, and from its mouth a snake raised its hood and began to sway. Seeing this, Mohanji was frightened, jumped back, and said, "Watch out! Close the bag at once!"

"Don't be afraid, Panditji," Ramdev said. "This is our *pitarjī*. He will not bite our own people."

"No, no!" Still trembling, Mohanji spoke: "How can this be some *pitarjī?* You close the bag."

"No, no, Panditji. He will not bite." This time Ramdev's wife, laughing, spoke. "This is our *pitarjī*. Don't get upset. Until today he has bitten neither us nor anyone else."

[The pandit was still frightened, but Ramdev took the snake from his bag.]

When Ramdev took the snake out of the bag, it performed a circumambulation of the throne on which Mohanji was sitting. Then it circumambulated the stand on which the old record book lay. Mohanji's soul was not happy, and Ramdev again and again reassured him. "Panditji, really don't be afraid. You just watch him silently. He will not hurt anyone."

In the end, finishing his tour, the snake stopped in front of the record book with his hood raised, as if he wanted to hear something.

"Panditji," Ramdev said, "now you read some of the names of the Didavanas."

Mohanji, with a dry throat, pausing again and again, began to read the names loudly. Just as he mentioned the name Govardhan, the snake laid his hood on the volume as if he had become peaceful and gone to sleep.

"Panditji," Ramdev spoke up happily, "now it is firm. This is the name of our ancestor, whom you see before you in the form of a snake."

[Ramdev allowed the snake to slide back in the bag and responded to Mohanji's excited inquiries by telling the following story:]

"After I was married my line did not increase. I was alone in my family. Whatever work I did, in order to support myself, I always sustained losses. In this way my troubles were ever growing.

"Some years ago, snakes began to appear in my house. At the beginning, in one week or ten days one or two snakes came out. Then little by little, faster and faster, they came out in greater numbers. At one time it was like this: in one day five or six snakes might appear. Dying of fear, our condition was very bad. In the day we could not relax and in the night we could not sleep. And if sometimes we dozed off then we saw snakes in dreams. But there was this benefit: until today no snake ever bit any person of the household."

[A series of diviners and experts failed to solve Ramdev's snake problem. Eventually, a *bhopā* determined that the largest and oldest of the snakes was an ancestor "experiencing a snake birth" and the family then duly honored this *pitarjī* and offered it milk.]

"That very night, *pitarjī* came in a dream and gave me an order: I must have his silver flowers made and go to Hardwar and scatter them there and perform *piṇḍadān*. Then he would be released from the snake birth.

"From that day, *pitarjī* began to live in our house and no other snakes appeared. At the same time another thing happened. I began to profit from my labors, and the worldly conditions of the household, in very few days, became comfortable. Now whatever work I do, I do it after obtaining *pitarjī*'s approval. This approval he gives me by coming in dreams.

"Last year, just as *pitarjī* ordered, I brought him to Hardwar and here I scattered his silver flowers and gave *piṇḍadān*. Then I went to Gayaji and there I did *piṇḍadān* again.

"A few months ago, *pitarjī* gave me the order in a dream to go to Hardwar at the full *kumbh* [during the Kumbha Mela] and perform the worship of the Ganges. Then I must go to Badrinath and perform *piṇḍadān* there. After this he will receive release from the snake birth."

[The *paṇḍā* advised Ramdev to go to Badrinath now and return to Hardwar when the *melā* crowds had abated. He promised that then he would perform Ganges worship on Ramdev's behalf. Ramdev acted accordingly, and in due course the rite was under way.]

At the time of this worship, *pitarjī*, coiled, hood raised, saw and listened to everything with attention.

When the other people doing *pūjā* at Brahmakund saw a coiled-up snake peacefully sitting and watching, their surprise knew no bounds. A crowd of people came, and all were curious to know how such a strange snake came to be who, forgetting his own nature, was so attentively gazing at the worship.

The full *pūjā* took two and one-half hours. After it was finished, Mohanji told all the family to take a Ganges bath. Before putting his foot in the Ganges, Ramdev said to his *pitarjī*, "Please come, *pitarjī*."

On this request from Ramdev, the snake circumambulated Mohanji. Then he slid into that very tray where the remains of the worship ingredients were lying, and began to turn about. His body became smeared with the worship ingredients. Then he preceded Ramdev into the Ganges.

Ramdev remained beside the bank, but the snake went into the fast current and began to flow with it in midstream. Seeing this, Ramdev cried out, "*Pitarjī, pitarjī!* Come back or else you will be washed away."

Hearing this, his *pitarjī* came swimming toward the shore. But then he just raised his hood over the water and lowered it again, three times, as if he were bidding farewell to all. Then he returned to the fast current and began to move away with it.

Seeing this, Ramdev ran along the bank of the Ganges crying, "*Pitarjī, pitarjī*, come back! Come back!"

But *pitarjī* got farther and farther away until he was out of eyesight. Then Ramdev, sitting with his wife and sister on the shore, lamenting, began to cry, as if some dear one of his had been washed away in the stream.

Ramdev sat with his family for some time on Har ki Pairi, hoping that perhaps his *pitarjī* would come back. But *pitarjī* did not come back again. Perhaps now he had received release from his snake birth. (Harsha 1980:156–160, 205–207)

This story displays an idealized vision of the release for the dead obtainable at crossing places. Its appeal for the *paṇḍās* was understandable, as it confirmed the effectiveness of their work. To recapitulate, an ancestor, or "father," who is trapped in an undesirable body makes himself known to living descendants. First he shocks them into recognizing his presence. Later, after they enlist the assistance of a *bhopā,* he becomes able to communicate with them directly, through dreams. He helps them to prosperity in their lives and at the same time instructs them as to how they may help him to obtain a better existence. While his serpent body might be understood as a low rebirth due to bad karma, it could also be interpreted as indicating his status as a lineage deity. The lingering spirits of the dead who eventually become such household deities (*pattar* and *jhūjhār* in Ghatiyali and environs) often take the form of snakes, appearing to their living kin in dreams to demand recognition.

Whatever the case, the snake-ancestor's behavior is exemplary, and the outcome of the pilgrimage with silver flowers and the worship of the Ganges is exactly as it should be. The story thus validates the direct impact on spirits of the deceased from sinking their flowers in the Ganges. The snake gives a wonderful pantomime demonstration of how unseen ancestors may hear and acknowledge the *paṇḍā*'s recitation of their names, show all due respect to Brahman officiants, actively partake of worship ingredients, and ultimately depart with decorum, presumably for a better existence. The *pitarjī*'s release is specified as release from a snake birth and does not necessarily imply a release from earthly cycles of birth and death. But whatever the course of his passage, Ramdev's *pitarjī* came to the crossing place voluntarily and would not turn back from his flow toward liberation—in the very current of Mother Ganges—even when entreated to stay by loving and grieving family members.

In the experience of villagers, however, things are not always so simple. Spirits of the dead, most especially those who have revealed themselves as household deities, are not easy to leave in a crossing place. In fact, *pattar* and *jhūjhārjī* often refuse to go and may manifest their refusal in various ways (chapter 2). Some even agree to go and then change their minds.

Following the return from the bus pilgrimage described above, one such household deity evidenced its failure to receive release in striking fashion. After the morning worship of Path Mother, while the pilgrims and their families were returning to the center of the village with song and drum, a daughter-in-law of one pilgrim's household began to show the same signs of possession that women do when bringing home Ganges water at the Celebration of Ganga.

Everyone agreed that this was not supposed to happen. Possession by Ganga's Bhairu is desirable and acceptable on the occasion of Gangotsav, but now no Ganges water had been opened, and this woman was carrying a vessel containing only earth and the sprouts that had been tended in her house during the pilgrim's absence. Her uncle explained in a resigned tone that it was not Bhairuji at all who was possessing her but a *pattar.* This particular *pattar,* a brother's son but "just like a son" to our fellow pilgrim, had been entering the woman's body over the course of more than five years. His bones had been taken to the Ganges in hopes that he would receive peace and stay there. But it was clear now that he had declined this opportunity of release.

Our informant speculated that the reason for this might well be the nasty filth at the riverbank in Gaya where the bones were placed. He also confessed that, while the *pattar*'s approval for the journey had been obtained, they had used only the less direct grain-pick method. They had not consulted the *pattar*'s *bhāv,* fearing, he implied, a distinct refusal. In any case, it was clear now that this household lingerer had returned to the village and to the body of the woman whom he had formerly possessed. The *pattar* was not likely to be less respected for this perseverance.

If one major incentive for making the pilgrimage with flowers is to satisfy, pacify, and remove the spirits of dead kin, another distinct but complementary benefit is to bring home power-charged Ganges water and perform the festive rituals that confirm the water's incorporation into the village. Regarding this return aspect of the pilgrimage to Ganga Ma, informants often phrase their motivational concerns in terms of social transactions. They say, for example, that they go "to repay the debt of a morsel"—that is, to engage in reciprocal feasting incumbent upon and among returnees. Or they say that they go to escape the inevitable scorn that falls upon those who *don't* treat their ancestors to this dutiful journey. Both the social obligations fulfilled by Ganges pilgrimage and the subtler exchanges of power manifest in them are evident in the context of the return Celebration of Ganga.

Why Sink Flowers? Bringing It All Back Home

Every person questioned agreed that to sink flowers at a crossing place in the Ganges and return to the village without a sealed pot of Ganges river water would be wholly meaningless and futile. I tried to provoke informants on this by asking questions such as, "Well, what if you didn't, then what?" and the results were uniform. In the first place, it was unthinkable, and in the second place, if anyone were to commit such folly, their whole journey would have been for nothing. These emphatic responses were particularly striking when elicited from persons who, earlier in the same interview, had denied that any benefit other than "seeing the land" accrued to pilgrims in any case. What then could be lost by neglecting to bring home water? The answer to this will emerge through an examination, first, of some answers to the question of "Why sink flowers?" and second, of the Celebration of Ganga. On that occasion, referred to as an honored guest, the river of crossing places is welcomed into the village, and a feast is held by the pilgrim who brought her back with him.

Several informants, most of them male, all of whom had personally made the pilgrimage with flowers, very emphatically denied any reason for it other than acquiescence to social pressures. Here is how one old man of the Mali caste put it:

Interviewer: The way people take flowers and perform *piṇḍadān*—why do they do this?

Pilgrim: I don't know. Our forefathers did it, so we also do it. Even better than this is to take your mother and father there when they are alive and cause them to bathe. Yes, to bring the flowers, what use is it? If when they are living you don't cause them to bathe, after they die, what is the use? The flowers are a pretext. He himself [the son] is enjoying his trip. And, if he doesn't do this then others say, "Hey, your forefathers are lying here, so drop them in Gangaji."

Interviewer: So people only go for the sake of their reputation?

Pilgrim: Yes, for their reputation.

Another interviewee, again an aged male but of the Nath caste,[27] expressed this perspective even more bluntly in an interview conducted without my being present by my assistant, Bhoju.

Pilgrim: Suppose you, Bhoju, did not take your mother and father, then what would they [your caste-fellows] do to you? Nobody could do anything. But, whereas now they say [praisefully], "Oh, Bhoju is like this; Bhoju is like this," then, if your mother and father died and you did not take them, they would say [insultingly], "Oh that Bhoju, that son-of-a-cock-eater, he did not take them." Nothing else at all is in it. That's it, Bhoju, I see nothing else in this [practice of going to crossing places], no other reason for it. . . . If you don't do it, people will taunt you, like this: "Which Ganga-Gaumati have you dumped your mother and father in anyway?" Because of this kind of taunting, people die [expend all their resources]. So for this reason, everyone takes their mother and father to Ganga-Gaumati and they all become destitute.

A third man, another elderly Mali, spoke in the same vein, contrasting true *dharma,* which could better be performed in the course of ordinary life, to the false, or socially pretentious, *dharma* of pilgrimage.

Pilgrim: Journeys to crossing places are right here.

Interviewer: How do you mean?

Pilgrim: Serve your mother and father greatly. Afterwards, if you desire to go to a crossing place, then go, but if not, no matter. Ganga and Gaumati are right here. If, while

27. Given the Nath caste's alternative and potent means of securing release for the deceased (Hing Laj Ma Puja; see chapter 2), a Nath informant might be expected to place less stock in sinking flowers. However, members of several other peasant castes expressed similar skepticism toward the soteriological benefits of the pilgrimage with flowers.

he [one's father] is alive you don't give him bread, then what use is it to drop his flowers after he's dead. . . . And as for feasts, they are the debt of a morsel. If we don't hold feasts, people speak ill of us. If it weren't for this, who would hold them? If someone doesn't hold a feast, then people say; "Your father died and you didn't even offer up a spark."

Interviewer: Suppose a person has not served his parents in their lifetimes, after they die why does he get the desire to take them to a crossing place?

Pilgrim: It's a mistake.

Pilgrim's son (who has been listening silently): If someone's mother and father are not satisfied here, then where is the advantage in taking them there?

The taunting received by those who do not sink flowers is clearly standardized. Even the same obscene insult—"son-of-a-cock-eater"—was cited by several separate informants in this context, and it is one I never encountered in any other. A man of the Gujar caste, however, went on from reasons of public pressure to articulate other rationales for the pilgrimage also touched on in the preceding statements. These included the fulfillment of duty toward one's mother and father—traditionally conceptualized as one of the three debts which every man ideally pays to his superiors in a single lifetime[28]—as well as the obligation to hold return feasts, a kind of community debt based on reciprocity. Finally, he suggested the achievement of a more diffuse release, which he saw as a logical result of fulfilling biomoral obligations. These comments were made in the course of a discussion about why people prefer to take flowers to the Ganges rather than to some more accessible crossing place in Rajasthan, such as Pushkar.

28. The three debts, according to Manu, are "to the great sages, to the manes, and to the gods" (Buhler 1969:169). The debt to the sages is fulfilled by studying the Vedas, to the ancestors by begetting sons, and to the gods by offering sacrifices (Buhler 1969:205). According to informants, the reason for begetting sons is that they may perform *shrāddha,* or "faithful offerings," on behalf of the ancestors. From this derives the interpretation that performing *shrāddha* in pilgrimage centers in fact fulfills the debt to the forefathers. In the idea of this debt, concern with procreation and attentions to the dead are once again closely linked. For the debt to the ancestors, see also L. Dumont 1980.

Pilgrim: People will say, "Oh you son-of-a-cock-eater, have you dropped your forefathers in Ganga-Gaumati? What kind of work, like causing prostitutes to dance, have you done? [How have you squandered your money?] Several generations of flowers are lying here, and have you dropped them in Gangaji?" There [at the Ganges] the tradition will be fulfilled; the debt [*karj*] will be finished. When we drop them in Hardwar, in the Ganges, we feel that our debt [*urṇ*] is acquitted—that debt which from our soul we owe to our mother and father is acquitted. This is the reason for going to Hardwar; if not, you might as well put them in Pushkar.

Interviewer: The debt we owe our mother and father is paid in full?

Pilgrim: Yes, it is paid in full, and the penalty [*daṇḍ*] of the caste, that also is settled. We hold a feast and this settles the penalty of the caste. [Feasting is owed to those caste-fellows who have feasted you.] If there is a man of good fortune in our lineage, he does this work, as it says in the song: "A well-fated one of the lineage has come to take you to Gangaji." This means, in the lineage a fortunate person has come who is going to take the flowers of his lineage and bring Ganges Mother to the village. . . . We go there for *dharma,* so *moksha* also happens. It is a matter of here and there. From rinsing the bones, the debt is acquitted.[29] At God's door, surely some fruit or other is received.

This man's answers encompass a range of reasons for the journey with flowers, from response to community pressure to intrafamilial morality to consequent improvement of the inner, subtle self. A similar interplay of inner and outer reasons and attitudes underlying Ganges pilgrimage appears in the following conversation with a married couple of the Kumavat caste.[30] When I talked with them on the last day of the bus pilgrimage, they were already planning and anticipating their Celebration of Ganga.

Interviewer: Did you give an invitation to Bhairuji in Banaras?

Wife (hereafter W): Yes, we gave one in all the places. We gave them

29. He used the word "bones" rather than the usual euphemistic "flowers." Moreoever, the verb I have translated "rinse" is none of the several polite terms normally employed for sinking flowers but rather that commonly used for rinsing laundry by sloshing it about in the water.

30. Kumavats are potters who don't make pots but are predominantly landowning agriculturalists. This couple's Gangotsav is described below.

all invitations: "Please grace our house." At all the crossing places we gave invitations: "Come all! Come all!" Back in the village people say, "Where have you dropped the flowers? In what Gayaji have you dropped the flowers?" [a version of the usual taunt to which she can now reply proudly] but I have put my son's wife in Gayaji. And I said this to Gayaji, "You also please come."

Interviewer: But when will she come?

W: When I hold a feast . . . at that time she will come. . . . But this is on my mind. My son, whose wife died, after Dev Uṭhaṇī Gyāras [Gods-Getting-Up Eleventh][31] we will bring a second wife for him and we will hold the walking-stick celebration at that time. This is on my mind.

Interviewer: When someone dies, why do we put their flowers in Hardwar or Gayaji?

Husband (hereafter H): It is an old custom.

W: Our ancestors did it and for this reason so do we. And if we don't do this work, don't take them to Hardwar, then the [other] village people will taunt us: "You have put them in what Gayaji? You have put them in what Hardwar?" For this reason we do it.

Interviewer: Do you have this belief, that after sinking them in Gayaji or Hardwar they will obtain *moksha?*

H: The belief is there, but no certain knowledge. But people say it is so, that release comes from sinking in Hardwar or Gaya.

W: Those who don't want to go, even so, if you offer them *piṇḍa*s in Gaya they have to go. So we took our son's wife also and sank her in Gaya. And as long as she was alive she gave me only

31. Dev Uṭhaṇī Gyāras falls on the bright eleventh of Kartik (October-November). Four months before this, on Dev Sovaṇī Gyāras (Gods Going-to-Sleep Eleventh, which falls on the bright eleventh of Asharh [June–July]), all the deities are said to fall asleep or to descend to the underworld. Between these dates no weddings may be performed. This period could hardly be described, however, as one of ritual inactivity, as several of the year's more important festivals take place within its span.

comfort. And since she died she has not even come to me once in a dream. She died one and one-half years ago. And when I sank the flowers in Gaya, I said, with my hands joined [in respect and supplication], "When you were alive you gave me comfort; in this same way now give comfort."

H: Look, it is the world's belief; the world accepts it but no one receives a written receipt. You have the *piṇḍa*s offered, but you don't get a receipt stating, "I received the *piṇḍa*s." If someone's mother and father die, and he does the rituals for twelve days and gives the Brahman a cow, grain, a rope, and a pitcher, he gives these; but he does not receive a written letter from his mother and father: "The cow that you gave, we are drinking its milk. We are eating the grain and we are drinking from the well with the rope and the pitcher." If you know of anyone who received such a written letter, tell me.

A contrast is apparent here between the wife's more simple and sincere belief in the efficacy of her pilgrimage and the husband's more restrained, somewhat skeptical approach. He later, apart from his wife, firmly denied inviting any deities from crossing places to attend his feast and declared himself unimpressed with the whole notion. Nevertheless, on the day of his celebration he declared the *bhāv* to be authentic.

From the wife's comments the most immediate reason for their pilgrimage at this time emerged: they wanted to pacify the spirit of their son's first wife before bringing a second wife into the house. Thus they had brought the first wife's flowers to Gaya, around the neck of her eight-year-old son. By this means, and a very elaborate Celebration of Ganga, they thought to appease and remove her, forever. They also, of course, found an opportunity to display their not insignificant financial means and their elevated values. Considering their low-middle-caste rank, this couple was unusually concerned with performing rather ostentatious *dharma*.

These interview samples indicate something of the range of goals and the interweaving of gross and subtle, public and private, selfish and selfless reasons for the pilgrimage with flowers. In summary, those mentioned include: to maintain reputation and honor (avoiding taunts); to pay a "debt" (*udhār, daṇḍ*) to the community by reciprocating feasts; to pay a "debt" (*karj, urṇ*) established by *dharma* with respect to parents and ancestors; to remove spirits of the dead from the house (of both those who go readily and those whose departure is problematic); to help these spirits of dead kin to achieve peace or release; to benefit one's lineage by bringing Ganges Mother home. All these stated motivational strains mingle in the ritual action and play of the Celebration of Ganga. Although interviewees clearly did not consider fertility concerns a direct or appropriate reason for sinking flowers (as, by contrast, such concerns were for shrine pilgrimage), Gangotsav's rites and pageantry refer explicitly in several ways to auspicious reproduction. Among these references are the imagery of sprouts, water, and coconut pieces in the pouch, as well as the verses of some women's songs that accompany Celebration of Ganga. The role of Bhairuji is also, I will argue, of fertilizing significance.

The Celebration of Ganga held by the Kumavats who went on pilgrimage to pave the way for a replacement daughter-in-law's arrival in their household was the only opening of Ganges water that I observed which was not held in conjunction with a twelfth-day funeral feast. If flowers are not transported within the twelve days immediately following a death, not only may they be kept in the home for an indefinite period until an opportunity for pilgrimage arises, but the water brought back after they are taken may also then be stored until a special occasion demands or justifies its opening.[32] The majority of my fellow pilgrims were thus in no hurry to "raise" their pots, except for these Kumavats.

About three months after our return from the pilgrimage to Puri, my research assistant and I received a hand-delivered invitation—a scrap of paper accompanied by the traditional grains of yellow rice—summoning us to an opening of Ganges water to be held by our fellow pilgrim Harzi Kumavat in his home village of Piplaj. When we reached Piplaj around 6:00 P.M. on the evening before that designated as Celebration of Ganga, we found quite

32. I heard several wondrous stories about pots of Ganges water that had been placed within a wall and plastered over for security. A new generation in the house might not know the exact location of the pot but would know of its existence. Once they made the decision to hold Gangotsav and began to search for the water, a small stream would come trickling out through the plastered wall of its own accord, indicating the hiding place. When the pot was retrieved, its seal, needless to say, would still be intact.

elaborate arrangements in Harzi's clearly prosperous home. Several Brahman pandits were at work on a Sanskritic fire-oblation rite, and the ornate wooden chariot of the deity Thakurji, brought from Piplaj's Four-Arms Temple, was lodged in Harzi's courtyard beneath a festive canopy. Shortly after our arrival *āratī* was performed for Thakurji by the temple priest, who had accompanied his god's icon. By this time, Bhoju and I were thoroughly mystified: a postpilgrimage celebration to our knowledge never required fire oblations, and the presence of the temple god was even more puzzling. We were soon illuminated by our proud hosts. Harzi was holding his Celebration of Ganga along with the marriage of a pipal tree, growing in his yard, to the deity Thakurji. Five years previously, we learned, he had wed his basil plant to Thakurji. At that time he had also celebrated the marriages of his three daughters. Now he wished to sponsor the pipal's union as well. Along with this "daughter" he was offering a dowry of goods and land whose profits would go into the Four-Arms treasury. Unspoken here but nonetheless obvious was the fait accompli of Harzi's son's new wife, who had already quietly taken up residence in the house.

The impressiveness of all this rather showy business was somewhat marred by a great deal of quarreling over minor amounts of money, resulting in the cancellation of a scheduled twenty-four-hour *Ramayana* reading and the nonparticipation of an expected *bhajan* party. Even so, the "wedding" was held in a fairly grand fashion, and the Celebration of Ganga involved the usual songs, frolic, and festivity. It is noteworthy that the context of wedding versus funeral feast does virtually nothing to change the format of the events at Path Mother's shrine and on the road home. Thus, although the Gangotsav preparations and actions were somewhat mingled with the wedding business, they proceeded in a fashion almost identical to that already described in chapter 2 for a funeral feast day. I can therefore treat Gangotsav's action summarily.

In the night the usual invitation was given at the place of Path Mother by women of the house who desired to be possessed by Bhairuji. On this occasion, however, they actually called to him out loud. Although the pandit assured us that the fire-oblation rite was connected only with the wedding and had nothing to do with the Celebration of Ganga, nonetheless in its course the sealed pot of Ganges water was offered cloth and tied with multicolored string. Moreover, during the actual wedding ceremony when the couple (icon and tree) were knotted together, the multicolored string used for this purpose was run deliberately over a Shiva *lingam* covered with purple cloth and seated in a brass pot, and I was told that this was "because Shiva always has the Ganges in his hair." This indicated that the power of Ganges, flowing down through Shiva's "ascetic-erotic" presence (see O'Flaherty 1973), was especially invoked for the benefit of the marital union.

Immediately following the conclusion of the wedding rites, Harzi carried his pilgrim's basket containing the Ganges-water pot and his walking stick to the place of Path Mother. A woman of his household came bearing a vessel with sprouts, and five other women brought vessels to receive Ganges water. The worship ingredients were identical with those already described for the worship of Path Mother, as was the course of the ritual. Harzi was joined with his wife, and their grandson (the one whose mother had died and who had worn the flowers on our pilgrimage) was seated between them. Although a child, he actually held the position of chief mourner.

After the worship of Path Mother and her Bhairuji, the pot of Ganges water was taken from its basket and placed on the *pūjā* tray; rice was strewn over it, and it was bathed with water and tied with multicolored string. The Brahman pierced it, first watered Path Mother's sprouts, and then distributed a little water into each of the five waiting vessels. Harzi's sister performed *āratī,* and the vessels were placed on the heads of the women who had invited Bhairuji. Harzi received gifts of cloth from his wife's relations at this juncture.

The women with vessels circumambulated Path Mother and headed back toward Harzi's home. Only one of the five became possessed, and she was pacified and guided to the house by Harzi, who was sweeping the ground with his turban, bowing, and offering coconut pieces, which were placed in her pouch in the usual fashion. In the doorway she fell to her knees but rose and entered after being ofered *dhūp*. When the vessel was taken from her head, a little water spilled out, and she seemed to stiffen and then swooned. She was quickly revived with a few ceremonial "sprinkles" from the pot of undiluted Ganges water.

After this the feast food (*lapsī-puṛī*—cracked wheat and raw-sugar pudding with fried bread, served with watery but fiery hot potato curry) was offered to the deities present: Thakurji, Tulsi Mother, the pipal tree bride, and Harzi's other household gods. The guests were served next. Harzi told us that a little of the remaining Ganges water would be sprinkled on the food in the big cooking pots and the rest distributed among the guests as they sat in eating lines. He expressed his conviction that the *bhāv* that day was from the Ganges and no other place, but also said that it wouldn't matter if no *bhāv* came—the Ganges water still reached the house and could be served to the guests.[33]

Harzi Kumavat's Gangotsav was integrated into an unusual and ostentatious performance. The pandit who conducted the marriage of the pipal tree to Thakurji said that "among one hundred or one thousand only one or two persons have done [such work]. This is the road of 'merit' [*puṇya*] and nothing else at all." Harzi himself had the usual reaction when we asked him what "fruit" he might receive from this day's activities: "God knows." When further pressed, however, he was able to articulate at least some of his inner motivations rather effectively.

> Who knows? This is the debt [*udhār*] of my previous birth. This I can't say: what is the benefit or what isn't. [Harzi used benefit consistently although Bhoju and I in our questions used fruit.] I know and think that this—what is received—is the earning of a previous birth. Benefit? Look, when I was young I was very poor, I wasn't even married, and after I was married my mother and father died, so I was in much trouble. Now I am spending, and from spending no lack is coming. It is God's grace. People who don't do this work are just the same as I am.

Consistent with his stance during the pilgrimage, Harzi never alluded to the new daughter-in-law as in any way connected with his expensive and meritorious ritual undertakings; that was his wife's mundane concern. What he did express, however, was the conviction that his religious expenditures were somehow linked to

33. I witnessed Gangoj perhaps a dozen times, and only once did the *bhāv* totally fail to come. This occasion marked a particularly unhappy death—a young woman who had died in pregnancy, leaving behind four small children. Her funeral rites were performed meticulously and elaborately because it was felt that she was very likely to become a lingering ghost. A *bhajan* party was called at great expense all the way from Jaipur, and a much-reputed pandit was imported from a nearby town to read the *Garuda Purana*. However, people explained to me that it would not have been proper for the *bhāv* to come, as it was not an occasion for happiness and revelry (nor perhaps for evoking fertility).

his continued prosperity; equally strong was his denial of anything other than predetermined karmic causality for his good works. It is a rare person who would not thus disclaim any notion of deserving fruit or benefit that may result from undertakings such as a Ganges pilgrimage or "religious gifting" (*dān*), including the gift of a daughter, whether vegetable or animal, in marriage. The ideology expressed by peasants on this subject is very like the *Gita*'s in that acts are performed for their intrinsic worthiness and fruits are left "in God's hands." Here lies the major difference between pilgrimage to local shrines frankly made to wangle boons from the lesser deities, and pilgrimage to crossing places—that is, the difference between the ideologies of *jātrā* and *yātrā* in the broadest sense. Nonetheless, the Ganges pilgrimage process viewed as a whole, from departure through return celebration, does display certain motifs of fruitfulness. In the attempt to grasp this largely unspoken intentionality, women's songs once more provide sources of cultural meaning.

There exists a rather limited corpus called "songs of Gangaji" or "songs of Pathvari Ma" with a comparably limited context of performance. Some are sung on the way to and at the place of Path Mother, while others are special to the entrance of Ganges water into the village and explicitly aimed at stimulating the women carrying vessels to receive the *bhāv* of Ganga's Bhairu and to act, once possessed, in the expected ways.

Richest in ritual imagery among Path Mother's songs is this one, usually sung on the way to or during that goddess's worship. Both returned pilgrims and those who have stayed behind will sing it, but the song appears to be, from the viewpoint of the latter, a welcome to homecomers.

Song of Path Mother 1

[1] Today my Gaya-dweller has come to the outskirts,[34]
Today my Gaya-dweller has come to the outskirts,
come showing a basket, O my Gaya Mother,
Dharaji's water overflows.
He came swaying-splashing, swaying-splashing, swaying-splashing,
swinging baskets on his shoulders,
in his hands a walking stick.

34. The word I translate as "outskirts" is *kānkaṛ*; it refers to the outer, uninhabited limits of village land.

In the outskirts we'll greet him with green sprouted grasses,
at Pathvari we'll celebrate,
at Pathvari we'll welcome him with vessels,
And we'll cover Pathvari with flowers.

[2] Today my Gaya-dweller has come into the garden,
Today my Gaya-dweller has come to Pathvari.
He had Pathvari's worship done, O my Gaya Mother,
Dharaji's water overflows.
He came swaying-splashing, swaying-splashing, swaying-splashing,
swinging baskets on his shoulders,
in his hands a walking stick.
In the garden we'll greet him with green sprouted grasses,
at Pathvari we'll celebrate,
at Pathvari we'll welcome him with vessels,
And we'll cover Pathvari with flowers.

[3] Today my Gaya-dweller has entered the gateway,
Today my Gaya-dweller has crossed over the threshold.
He was fanned with eighty-four whisks, O my Ganga Mother,
Dharaji's water overflows.
He came swaying-splashing, swaying-splashing, swaying-splashing,
swinging baskets on his shoulders,
in his hands a walking stick.

[4] Today my Gaya-dweller has come onto the porch,
Today my Gaya-dweller has come into the storeroom,[35]
as happy as a flowering vine, O my Ganga Mother,
Dharaji's water overflows.
He came swaying-splashing, swaying-splashing, swaying-splashing,
swinging baskets on his shoulders,
in his hands a walking stick.

The identity of the "Gaya-dweller" (*Giyā-vāsī*) in this song is meaningfully ambiguous. Pictured is the returning pilgrim, carrying his basket replete with abundant Ganges water and his characteristic walking stick. But a pilgrim cannot really be a crossing-place-dweller, and thus the song actually addresses Mother

35. By "storeroom" I translate *auvaryā*, always described as a dark, windowless, inner room. It may be the place where the water vessel is set after removing it from the *bhāv*'s head; its womb-like quality should reinforce the interpretation that follows.

Ganges herself and her Bhairuji, whose most common epithet is "Banaras-dweller" (*Kāshī ko vāshī*). It might in fact be understood as positing an identity among the three. Returning pilgrims are traditionally greeted as deities, and their footdust is taken by elders and superiors.[36]

The most persistently repeated image in this song is that of bountiful Ganges water. It overflows from the pilgrim's basket, splashing like ocean waves, and this despite the fact that the container in a homecoming pilgrim's basket is actually always sealed and must remain sealed until Gangotsav. The overflowing of water occurs, of course, only then when the swaying *bhāv* drenches herself from the covered but not sealed clay vessel. Thus, although ostensibly addressing a returning male pilgrim, the song's most powerful imagery evokes the dramatic, homeward progression of the female *bhāv*. It may, however, be sung at the time of the worship of Path Mother when no water is opened, as well as at the Celebration of Ganga.

Other songs of Path Mother or Ganges Mother have for their main content the recitation of delicious treats to be prepared and offered to returning pilgrims and the deities that accompany them. Such promises of rich treats may appear in women's songs for almost any deity (for example the Song of Jhujharji 1 in chapter 2). One such song, notable for its rousing chorus, will suffice here. Although its words fete Ganges Mother and address Rama, this piece is most often performed during Bhairuji's possession of the water-carrying women.[37]

36. Based on the shoulder-basket image, a few informants indentified the returning pilgrim described in this song with Shravan Kumar, the legendary devoted son who attempted to carry his living but blind parents to Banaras in a pair of shoulder baskets and who is, in village tradition, worshipped as an ideal brother on the day of Raksha Bandhan ("Tying On Protection"). This holiday, more commonly known as Rakhi (the term for the decorative wristbands that play such an important part in the festival) arrives on the full-moon day of the month of Shravan (July–August). On this day the stylized image of Shravan Kumar with his two big shoulder baskets is drawn on the wall beside the doorway of every home and then worshipped. A similar picture may be drawn in the home of a returning pilgrim. The association of the song image of shoulder baskets full of water, and the story and wall picture with shoulder baskets containing parents, supports an interpretation (to be developed below) of the Ganges pilgrimage as an exchange of ancestors' remains and souls for fertilizing Ganges water; of flowers (bones) for flowers (sons).

37. The unity of Ganges Mother and her Bhairuji is similar to that of Dev Narayanji and his Bhairu at Puvali ka Devji's shrine described in chapter 3. In both

Song of Path Mother 2

[Refrain] Shout, shout, city people,
Shout victory to Ganga Ma!

[1] Yes, O Rama, I will give you a high seat.
Shout victory to Ganga Ma!

[2] O Rama, the strong cow gives rich milk;
O Rama, I'll cook thick rice pudding.

[3] O Rama, I'll roll out lovely oil-bread;
O Rama, I'll cook thick rice pudding.

[4] O Rama, I'll boil bright rice;
O Rama, I'll add sugar by the handful.

[5] O Rama, I'll form firm round sweets;
O Rama, thirty or thirty-two treats.

[6] O Rama, I'll set out a handsome pitcher;
O Rama, the pitcher is filled with Ganges water.

Whereas the preceding songs are considered songs of Ganges Mother in the form of Path Mother, the following four are of Bhairuji. The first of these actually serves to summon and then addresses Bhairu's *bhāv* and is performed only on the return from Path Mother's shrine after the women have placed vessels with Ganges water on their heads. It has a special, intoxicating, typically eight-beat rhythm, usually accompanied by the drum, which is thought both to induce and to sustain possession. The *bhāv*'s apparently erratic but actually patterned and predictable actions on the way home from Path Mother's shrine are simultaneously described and provoked by the verses. The possessed women themselves do not sing or utter any intelligible sounds, but they sway and gasp or pant rhythmically. The verses vary, but the following compilation, taken from numerous recordings and eliminating countless repetitions, includes a good sampling of them. The first verse given here is the usual opening for this song; otherwise the order is not fixed.

---

cases the possessing agent is said to be Bhairuji, but the possession is regarded by worshippers in many ways as coming from the major deity—Mother Ganges or Devji. An "O Rama" like this one is often explained by villagers as a harmonic or rhythmic device.

Song of Ganga's Bhairu 1

[1] Golden Pathvari, O Mother, green sprouted grasses;
Green sprouted grasses, O Mother, sprouts drooping down.

[2] The watering-maid is clever, O Ganga's Bhairu,
clever, O Kashi-dweller;
Drink a cup of raw milk.

[3] On all four sides of Pathvari plays that Ganga's Bhairu,
plays that Kashi-dweller;
Drink a cup of raw milk.

[4] He demands a sack of coconuts, that Ganga's Bhairu,
demands, that Kashi-dweller;
Drink a cup of raw milk.

[5] Dodging in the lanes plays Ganga's Bhairu,
plays Kashi-dweller;
Drink a cup of raw milk.

[6] If you are true, turn back,[38] Ganga's Bhairu,
turn back, Kashi-dweller;
Drink a cup of raw milk.

[7] If you are true, kneel down, Ganga's Bhairu,
kneel down, Kashi-dweller;
Drink a cup of raw milk.

[8] In the square rejoices that Ganga's Bhairu,
rejoices that Kashi-dweller;
Drink a cup of raw milk.

[9] A great number of sons were born too, O Ganga's Bhairu,
were born, Kashi-dweller;
Drink a cup of raw milk.

The last verse here, reminiscent of the favorite joke of Calf Twelfth—"lots of babies will be born" (chapter 2)—is perhaps the most explicit statement in my data of the fertility concerns expressed on the occasion of Celebration of Ganga.[39] However, the nature of women's relation to Bhairuji, a deity who often bestows children, is portrayed in several songs as mutually seductive. The

38. The idea here is that the "true" *bhāv* will not docilely walk to the house but will always act in a contrary fashion.

39. Ganges water is, however, a source of fertility in other Rajasthani lore. See Saran 1978:35–37 for one story of miraculous pregnancy following its consumption.

following is the least explicit in this sense, but it does establish a dialogue pattern that may be seen as more flirtatious in the next example. Like the first song of Path Mother, it primarily depicts a progression and procession of celebration from the village outskirts to the inside of a home. The logical order—from outskirts to home—in which the verses are presented is not necessarily the way they are sung, which appears from numerous recordings to be quite random, as does the correlation of locale with caste.

Song of Ganga's Bhairu 2

[1] Barber-girl, your house is on the road,
mine is a hut beneath the *nīm*.[40]
Kashi-dweller will come and be jubilant on the village outskirts.

[2] Merchant-girl, your house is in the lanes,
mine is a hut beneath the *nīm*.
Kashi-dweller will come and joke on the village outskirts.
On the road the dust will fly,
and on the village outskirts there'll be celebration.

[3] Gardener-girl, your house is in the lanes,
mine is a hut beneath the *nīm*.
Ganga's Bhairu will come and be jubilant on the village outskirts.

[4] Potter-girl, your house is in the lanes,
mine is a hut beneat the *nīm*.
Kashi-dweller will come and be jubilant at Pathvari.

[5] Drummer-girl, your house is in the lanes,
mine is a hut beneath the *nīm*.
Ganga's Bhairu will come and be jubilant in the gateway.

[6] Brahman-girl, your house is in the lanes,
mine is a hut beneath the *nīm*.
Kashi-dweller will come and be jubilant in your house.

Striking here, as well as in the following song of Ganga's Bhairu, is the series of different caste names with which each verse is repeated. Path Mother is said to belong to the whole village and to no particular caste. As one informant put it: "No one can say that he has personal authority over her, because, with the excep-

40. Bhairuji shrines are often located beneath *nīm* trees, and *nīm* leaves are a suitable offering to that deity.

tion of Bhangis [Harijans], all the castes go: Rajputs, Banyas, Brahmans, and so forth. She belongs to the whole village, and not to any single community." These songs confirm this. Although usually sung on an occasion dominated by a single caste (of the celebrant), they nonetheless incorporate many caste names. The next refers not only to various castes but to some of their characteristic services. It has a definite erotic undertone that is in keeping with Bhairuji's reputation in village lore as a womanizer, and is revealing of the erotic-procreative content of the whole Path Mother and Ganges-water ritual complex.

Song of Ganga's Bhairu 3

[Refrain] You made me lose sleep, lose sleep, O Bhairu,
You got me excited.
I brought my companions here with care, O
Kashi-dweller,
I brought them, O Ganga's Bhairu.

[1] I'm a Brahman's daughter, you are Ganga's Bhairu.
If you say so, I'll bring a blanket and a mattress,
O Kashi-dweller
I'll bring them, O Ganga's Bhairu.

[2] I'm a Potter's daughter, you are Ganga's Bhairu.
If you say so, I'll bring a double set of pots,
O Kashi-dweller,
I'll bring them, O Ganga's Bhairu.

[3] I'm a Gardener's daughter, you are Ganga's Bhairu.
If you say so, I'll bring flower-garlands,
O Kashi-dweller,
I'll bring them, O Ganga's Bhairu.

[4] I'm a Servant's daughter, you are Ganga's Bhairu.
If you say so, I'll fan you,
O Kashi-dweller,
I'll fan you, O Ganga's Bhairu.

[The song may continue, mentioning other caste names and appropriate gifts or services.]

In village talk it is common to allude to women's unfulfilled sexual desires by speaking of their insomnia. This song of Bhairuji thus rather explicitly poses a sexual attraction, a longing if not a consummation, between female devotee and masculine deity. With no attempt to probe the complex history of Bhairu's mythology, some of his relevant character traits may be briefly mentioned here. Above all he is an instrumental, grossly active deity. He is also markedly unpaired, unattached. While the women of Rajasthan sing many romantic songs about the pairs of Shiva and Parvati, Sita and Rama, Radha and Krishna, Bhairuji has no mate and appears to be a kind of midnight rambler. He comes to his female devotees' houses in the dead of night and tries by various ruses to persuade them to let him in. If they do not, he sometimes curses them. He is attractive, seductive, and a little dangerous, like lightning and thunder as evoked in the next song. Although addressed to Kala-Gora Bhairu[41] rather than Kashi-dweller, this song was in fact recorded at the place of Path Mother, not during Gangotsav but on a night when a group of pilgrims returned.

Song of Kala-Gora Bhairu

[Refrain] Bhairu, on your head a cap is sparkling:
What do I think? Lightning flashes, my Kala-Gora Bhairu.
Bhairu, on your waist silver bells are ringing:
What do I think? It is Lord Inder's thunder, my
Kala-Gora Bhairu.

[1] Bhairu, on the road to Inder's throne a Brahman girl
is calling,
my Kala-Gora Bhairu;
That Brahman girl is calling,
my very juicy[42] Bhairu.

[The same words repeat substituting, in my recording, the following caste names: Gardener, Wine seller, Washerwoman, Potter, and Rajput.]

The outspoken final line of the first song of Bhairuji and the flirtatious dialogues of the second, third, and fourth point to an interpretation of Gangotsav's pageantry as reproductive. This in-

41. Kālā-Gorā translates as "black-fair." Often represented as two figures, identical except for their complexions and instruments, Kala-Gora Bhairu may be addressed in song and *bhajan* as a single being. See Carstairs 1961:73 for a "Black Bhaironji" who is "notorious for making free with men's wives."

42. "Very juicy" is a literal translation of *gaṇā rasīlā*. It may connect both to the rain imagery of the song and to semen.

terpretation leads back to themes stressed in the last part of chapter 2: the transformation of death into life through fertility expressed in women's play. The colorful and festive atmosphere of Gangotsav, difficult to convey in black and white, has much to do with female exuberance. But here—as is not the case on Calf Twelfth—exuberant women happily tolerate the close proximity of males.

For a big feast, guests will be invited from as many as twenty or thirty villages in the area, and such occasions are prime opportunities among the young for flirtation and the formation of other more serious liaisons. Crowds of pretty girls, clustered in companionable groups, are dressed in their best and brightest red and yellow and vivid turquoise clothing, their wraps decorated with spangles stitched in whorl, star, or flower designs. All wear heavy silver ornaments on their ankles, necks, and arms, and shiny *lākh* bangles studded with rhinestones. Aggressively they surge and push in the area surrounding the *bhāv*s—those women carrying pots of Ganges water on their heads and possessed by Kashidweller—singing encouragement and delight. The women participating as *bhāv*s, although they retain their modesty by keeping their faces hidden, become the center of public attention. They may, and indeed should, act in balky, teasing, demanding ways unbecoming to women, and are not to be criticized for such deportment. Quite the contrary, they are reverently placated and honored as deities, for they are vehicles of Bhairuji; like Bhairu's source, Lord Shiva, they bear on the heads the force of Ganges Mother's arrival in the "world of mortality" (*mṛtyulok*).

The decorous ritual at Path Mother's shrine is performed by a Brahman male for the benefit of a male worshipper (preferably joined with his mate). But it is women who plant and water the sprouts, sing the songs of Path Mother and Bhairuji, invite Kashidweller to possess them, place the pots of Ganges water on their heads, receive the *bhāv* of Bhairuji, and indulge in his teasing play. Calf Twelfth's "jokes" involved females' appropriation of male goat play—billy goats' mating cries and postures. Possession on Gangotsav is similarly of a transsexual nature: women become the ultramale deity Bhairuji. As on Calf Twelfth, the predicted result is the birth of sons. Moreover, the *bhāv* moves forward, ultimately, only when coconut pieces are placed in her pouch, recalling the shrine rite of pouch-filling with a coconut in order to induce conception.

Thus the transformation from death to life, effected through the exchange of flowers for Ganges water, is consummated at Gangotsav in a sexually tinged performance motivated by fertility concerns. Women's innate power might be represented by clay waterpots, carried sedately in everyday fashion. But when he possesses the water-carrying women, Bhairuji's juicy masculinity sets them in rhythmic motion and soaks their garments. The water is delivered to the house of the celebrant—and placed in the dark, inner room—charged with the immediate, loosened, available potency of union between Bhairu and the possessed woman, as well as with Ganges Mother's boundless life force. At the feast which soon follows, this water is consumed by all the assembled caste-fellows of the deceased.

Some informants hold that the *bhāv* of Gangotsav is truly Bhairuji's, invited by pilgrims at the Ganges and brought home as an honored guest who will bring general well-being (including fertility) to the celebrant's household. Others, and this is not an uncommon opinion, say that in this decadent age the gods hardly bother to visit human habitations. The action of Gangotsav, they declare, is merely the sport, the play, the intoxication of women for their own amusement.

Whatever people may say—and we have seen how skeptical they are about the fruits of Ganges pilgrimage in general—they nonetheless choose to perform both the journey to sink flowers and the return celebration if they have or can scrape together the wherewithal. All the interviewees cited—even those who declared its meaninglessness in no uncertain terms—were either doing or had done the pilgrimage with flowers and had performed or planned to perform the Celebration of Ganga.

While stated motivations for the pilgrimage with flowers range from fulfillment of social and biomoral debts to securing release for the spirits of the dead, and unstated motivations have been suggested in terms of communal fertility and regeneration, the rationale for pilgrimage *without* flowers is far less penetrable. In a superficial light, the *darshan* pilgrimage is often frankly treated as wandering for selfish if harmless pleasure: *ghūmnā*. Yet it is also claimed to be a journey toward knowledge and freedom, partaking of the bliss of soul-cleansing waters and countless viewings of the great gods. Negatively, the indiscriminate wandering of pilgrims from crossing place to crossing place may be equated with the benighted, wasteful, and condemned sojourning of ghosts: *baṭhaknā*. Better than outer journeying, say unlettered housewives as well as esoteric teachers, is the inner pilgrimage. Within the self, subtle knowledge, real release, unlimited *darshan* may be found. The following chapter will look at some conceptions of outer and inner journeys and their fruits.

5. Sweeping the Road Ahead: The Hindu *Darshan* Bus Tour

Two round trips, traversing measurable and immeasurable spaces, lie ahead. The first journey is a loop, from Mehru village in land-locked Rajasthan to the Lord Jagdish[1] of Puri and the sea—and back. The second is a conceptual exploration of equally circular passages: between inner and outer deity, inner and outer devotion, inner and outer wandering. Through these two peregrinations I investigate in two ways the rationale of *yātrā*s made neither particularly to obtain boons nor to sink the bones of the dead: first, descriptively, by telling the story of one trip; second, interpretively, by attempting to elucidate pilgrims' motivations for and understandings of such human journeys to divine powers.

In the two preceding chapters I have shown how the articulated desires of pilgrims traveling to regional shrines, and to the Ganges with flowers, are closely linked to their aspirations within this current life cycle, and acutely tuned to social and domestic pressures. Here, in dealing with still a third style of *yātrā,* and continuing to draw largely on interview statements and texts from oral tradition, the focus is on another set of values. These are connected, although most often indirectly, with the life aim of *moksha* in the sense of total liberation.

Another way of construing *moksha,* as "peace" (*shānti*) for the dead, in the context of sinking flowers, was considered in the preceding chapter. During the *darshan yātrā,* however, I believe that *moksha* is understood as the highest human aim: union with God, perfect realization of the identity of soul and supreme being, final release from *samsāra*'s flux. Evidence that bus tour pilgrims had

1. No one among Ghaityalians nor any of my fellow pilgrims ever used the name Jagannath to refer to the Lord at Puri. Everyone said "Jagdish," and throughout these pages I follow the local custom.

such a set of meanings in mind is in part their staunch denials of hoping to attain this *moksha.* A peaceful death with appropriate rites, which does not result in lingering as an unhappy ghost, is, on the contrary, an explicit aspiration held by most persons.

Many pilgrims conceive of the "road of *dharma*" (*dharmarāstā,* a common term for the pilgrim's way) not as directly approaching the higher, ineffable *moksha,* nor far less as gaining it, but at least as preparing for it. Everyone accepts as given that a supreme deity resides not only beyond all beings but within each. If a person can divest himself of excess belongings—both goods and mental or emotional attachments—he may come nearer to uncovering or realizing the deity within himself. This realization of an inner divinity should lead to freedom from all remaining personal involvements in the world of flux. For many this reduced, yogic mode of being is something to practice in old age. A majority of the pilgrims on my bus to Puri, and many others on similar trips (especially those who are not transporting flowers) were in their sixties and seventies. Some spoke explicitly of this trip as a major break in their ways of living. After they returned they would devote themselves single-mindedly to praising God.

Pilgrimage helps to loosen all kinds of bonds, but not because the waters of *tīrtha*s cleanse the results of bad deeds from men's souls; not one person among my informants evinced any trust in such reputed powers of *tīrtha* baths.[2] Rather, pilgrimage helps because the cumulative effect of being removed from daily routines and attachments at home, of taking many powerful *darshan*s of the gods, of voluntarily enduring hardships on the road, and above all of putting out money both for the sake of these experiences (the initial fare) and during them (the constant drain of rupees and paisa into the outstretched hands of *paṇḍā*s and beggars) is decidedly good for the soul. The effect is one of lightening: the returning pilgrim should be thinner and poorer. The bodily rigors suf-

2. Indeed, informants universally scoffed at this proposition. I should add, however, that although they maintained no belief in the soul-cleansing power of baths in crossing places, they nevertheless bathed methodically in every one that we visited no matter how unattractive or polluted the appearance of the water. Moreover, not to avail oneself of the opportunity to bathe in crossing places was considered improper conduct. Having seen two corpses floating in the river at Prayag, I became squeamish and did not want to bathe there. I was chastised for this reluctance by my fellow pilgrims. They were decidedly uncomfortable with the thought that one could be on this famed shore and not go in the water.

fered, the repeated exposure to divinities, and the charities practiced while journeying to foreign lands all contribute to reaching an inner, subtle goal, which is, everyone knows, unreachable through journeys on the earth.

Before going to the field, drawing mostly on texts translated from Sanskrit, I considered some apparent "irresolutions" in Hindu thought related to pilgrimage (Rose 1978). One of the grandest of these, rendered here in its simplest, starkest form, is that according to received authority—lawbooks (*dharmashāstra*s), the epic *Mahabharata,* and numerous *Purana*s—bathing at crossing places is the easy, cheap, democratic alternative to difficult, expensive, elitist sacrifice. *Tīrtha* baths, all these texts assure, obliterate even the most heinous sins and bring every imaginable boon, from health and wealth to heaven and release. However, according to the same texts in different moods, bathing in crossing places is patently useless, especially for sinners. Not futile washings of the outer body, but only cleansing in "real" fords—inner truth, meditation, devotion—should be the conditions of the truly fruitful human journey.

For example, P. V. Kane tells us in his digest of lawbooks that, according to the *Lingapurana* and the *Skandapurana,* "Even if a man be a sinner or a rogue or irreligious he becomes free from all sins if he goes to Avimukta (Banaras)" (1953:630). Moreover, the *Mahabharata* states: "If a person, after committing a hundred bad deeds, sprinkles himself with Ganges (water), the waters of the Ganges burn all of them as fire burns fuel" (Kane 1953:586). However, another digester cites the *Skandapurana* as declaring this:

> A man who is impure, slanderous, cruel, a hypocrite, and attached to sense-objects, though bathed in all the *tīrtha*s, remains sinful and impure. A man does not become pure by getting rid of bodily impurities; but when mental impurities are abandoned, then he becomes immaculate within. Fish are born and die in the waters (of *tīrtha*s); and they do not go to heaven, for the impurities of their minds are not purified. . . . He goes to the supreme path, who bathes in that *tīrtha* of the mind, which is purified by meditation, whose water is knowledge, and which wipes away passion, sins and impurities." (Salomon 1985:206–207)

And the *Mahabharata*'s "Tour of the Sacred Fords" is prefaced with similar statements on the primary value of inner morality as a prerequisite to attaining the fruits of external pilgrimage (1976:373).[3]

Precisely the same apparent conundrums were to be found in my largely unlettered informants' responses to questions about the purpose and value of *tīrthayātrā* as they practiced it. In the second part of this chapter I attempt to set forth the ideology, the premises, both of journeying and of not-journeying, from the villagers' point of view—no longer regarding these as exotically paradoxical, ambivalent, or irresolute. Simultaneous understandings—pilgrimage is ascetic versus pilgrimage is self-indulgent; pilgrimage brings every goodness versus pilgrimage is quite fruitless—form the fundamental and essentially stable ground of belief among the peasant journeyers with whom I discussed these issues.

Journey to Jagdish

The circumstances of my participation in a month-long bus pilgrimage from Rajasthan to Puri, Orissa, and a condensed account of the tour itself, are presented here.[4] Following this narration is a consideration of the highlights and meanings of our journey to the East, to the Lord of the Universe and to the sea, which was also, of course, a round trip beginning and ending at Path Mother's shrine outside the village of Mehru.

My joining Mehru's pilgrim company was fortuitous and quite sudden. Having long wished for a chance to participate with villagers in a bus pilgrimage, I had eventually given up hope of finding such an opportunity. Ghatiyalians were happy to tell me about their past excursions, but no one happened to be embarking on another during the period of my residence. Many said that because of the poor rains (two years running) and subsequent scant harvests, no one could afford such an enterprise. Pilgrimage is, af-

3. Religious revolutionaries or reformers like the Sikh founder Guru Nanak also find the concept of inner *tīrtha*s helpful in their rhetoric. Thus, Guru Nanak proclaims: "The true *tīrath* is the divine Name; it is inner contemplation of the word and it is true knowledge (*jnān*). The Guru's *jnān* is the true *tīrath* where every day is an auspicious day" (cited in McLeod 1968:211–212).

4. Copious notes, recordings, and a full photographic record may someday be developed into a complete study of this journey. For current aims, however, it does not seem "fruitful" to relate all the details. In the account that follows, then, I give essential background data and attempt to convey the journey's flavors and meanings for its participants.

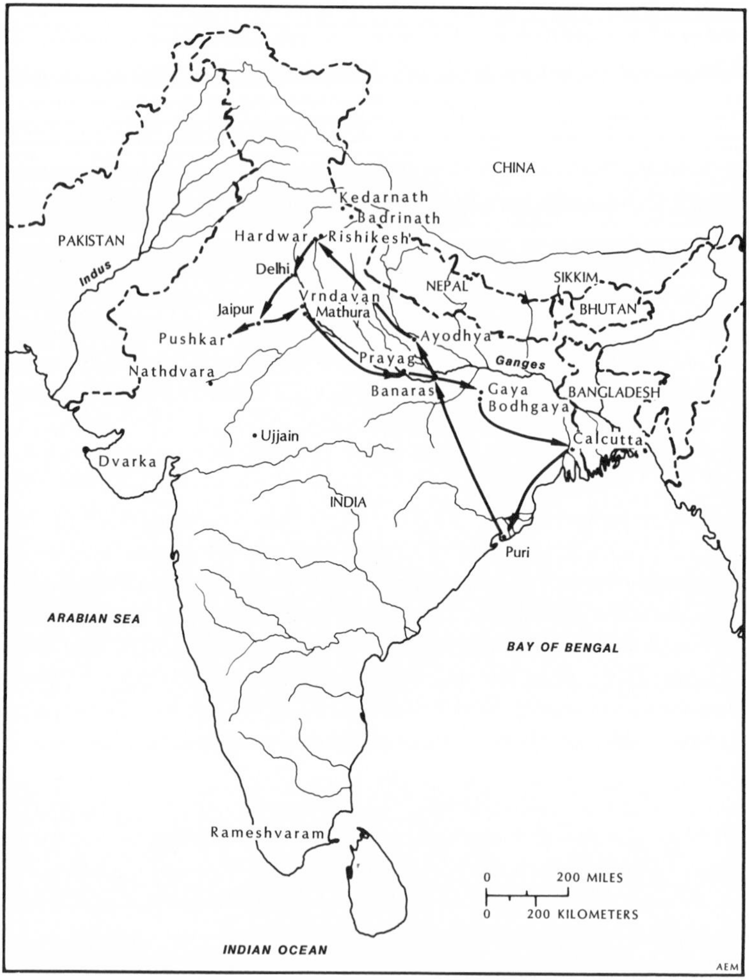

Map 3. India, showing some major *tīrtha*s and stops on the *darshan* tour route.

ter all, as the popular phrase has it, the "rice pudding of money"—that is, however delectable and highly esteemed, it is not an everyday matter but an occasional luxury. Rice pudding is only made and savored when there is a surplus of milk; *tīrthayātrā* and the attendant pleasures of seeing other lands require a surplus of cash.

About one year after my arrival in the village, when I was resigned to experiencing only Hardwar and many regional trips, I learned that the priest of the Niranjani temple, the Brahman Gam Shyamji, was about to leave on a *darshan* tour. Distant kin to the bus owner, who for reasons of his own was treating numerous relations to a free ride on this particular trip, Gam Shyamji spoke with enthusiasm of their plans to visit all the major North Indian shrines.

I gleaned this much information on the morning of September 18, 1980. At about dusk of that same day my research assistant, Bhoju, and I biked to Sawar, the nearby market-town where the bus owner lived. We sought him out and eagerly inquired about the details of the trip. Except for his dozen or so relatives, he told us, the remaining passengers were a company recruited from the village of Mehru, not far from Sawar. As is often the case, the pilgrims had been signed up by a covillager acting as agent for the bus owner. It so happened that the agent in Mehru, Nandalal Sharma, a retired schoolteacher, was yet another distant kinsman to the bus owner's family. Nandalal and his wife would also ride as pilgrims on the tour.

The bus owner at first would hear nothing of our joining the trip: No seats were left and he was already overloaded. Several persons would be sitting on backless straw stools in the aisle. He was also worried about trouble with the police if he took a foreigner. When assured again and again that Bhoju and I would gladly sit on stools and that I had a valid passport and visa, his refusals softened somewhat. When it appeared that I had in my purse the full cash amount to cover both our fares, he relented in earnest and began to think where he might borrow two more stools. We told him we would join the bus the next day in Mehru. The Mehru company was scheduled, he had informed us, to perform Path Mother's worship in the early morning, and the bus would collect them around noon.

Thus I learned of the trip on the morning of the eighteenth, reserved my "seat" that evening, packed well into the night, and breathlessly left Ghatiyali at dawn. Bhoju and I stowed our bags at the tea stall in Sawar and careened on rented cycles over sandy, thorny, bumpy paths to reach Mehru, auspiciously enough, just a few minutes before the precise, astrologically determined time set for the worship of Pathvari Ma. We rushed to her spot, directed by frankly staring villagers, just as women from pilgrims' households, with vessels for sprouts on their heads, were themselves more decorously arriving, walking in clusters and singing songs of the Ganges. (The worship of Path Mother and all activities of the pilgrimage involving flowers—the bones of dead kin—are treated in chapter 4.)

At Path Mother's shrine we encountered many who would be our constant companions over the next month and went through the inevitable introductions with them. The Mehru folk, although a mixed-caste group, had a self-conscious cohesiveness derived from their identification with a single home village; they said as much. Several had marriage connections with Ghatiyali, and Bhoju and I were welcomed among them with ready acceptance, along with inquiries as to the well-being of daughters living in our village. As it turned out, some of the passengers, in addition to the bus owner's family, were also not from Mehru. In the first place, there were two Mehrus, one large and one subsidiary settlement at some distance from the first. A few pilgrims came from the latter. There was also a Gujar couple from Sawar (who tuined out miraculously enough to stand in the relation of "father's sister" and "father's sister's husband" to Bhoju). Harzi Kumavat and his wife and grandson came from Piplaj—a fair distance from Mehru, but they had relations among the Mehru Kumavats. Certainly, the essential division within our company, and the most important social fact throughout the journey, was the distinction between town Brahmans and Mehru peasants.

Counting Bhoju, the bus driver, his helper, and myself, our full number was sixty-three adults and four children. The caste breakdown for adults was as follows: there were fifteen Brahmans related to the bus owner of whom twelve were immediate family members, all literate town-dwellers. The remaining three were Gam Shyamji (the only Ghatiyalian besides Bhoju and me) and Nandalal Sharma, the schoolmaster who had organized the Mehru company, along with his wife. The dozen town Brahmans included Suresh, nephew of the bus owner, a young man who was acting "bus-master" for this trip. None of this group of town Brahmans had flowers (Nandalal Sharma and Gam Shyamji did, however), and all claimed that they were going "for the sake of wandering" (*ghūmne ke lie*). They participated in bathing, *darshan,* and some worship, but none of them had *piṇḍadān* performed in

Gaya. They made a point of keeping themselves quite separate from the "peasants," including the Brahman peasants, despite the fact that we were all *yātrā* brothers and sisters now.

The rest of the adults in our party consisted of seven other Brahmans, of various subcastes different from the bus owner's; two Rajputs; four Caran Rajputs (that is, Carans or "royal bards" with large landholdings); seven Darogas (traditionally servants of the Rajputs, several on this trip still acting in that capacity); six Kumavats (farming potters); five Lodas (one of several farming castes in the area); five Gujars (traditionally cowherds; Bhoju, his "aunt" and "uncle" from Sawar, and a widow and her grown son from Mehru); five Malis (gardeners); two Kumhars (potting potters); one Damami (royal drummer), a widower; one Hada Rajput (actually a kind of Daroga), a widow. This totals sixty adults. The driver, his troubleshooter cum mechanic, and I completed the company, bringing the total of adult passengers to sixty-three, although I believe the bus was licensed for no more than fifty-five.

Needless to say, in a group as mixed as this one, all was not perfect harmony, and the fact that we were sharing a pilgrimage did not act as a leveler of rank.[5] The educated town-dwellers formed a distinct front-of-the-bus elite. Among themselves they referred to the Mehru folk as the "British Battalion" or simply "Angrez" ("English"), because the peasants were in their eyes awkward and stupid like the English. Nandalal Sharma with a foot in both parties played his mediating role rather ineffectively. His town kin did not appear to respect him greatly, and the peasants obviously didn't trust him. The role of spokesman for the Mehru folk went to Gulab Singh, the sole Rajput man, an imposing and bellicose person who received deference, especially from peasants, potters, and Darogas.

5. See E. V. Daniel 1984:245–287 and I. Karve 1962 for other participatory accounts of Hindu pilgrimage in Tamilnad and Maharashtra respectively. During Daniel's pilgrimage intercaste barriers were effectively dissolved by dissolving the existence of separate identities among the pilgrims. Every member of the group shed even his name, assuming that of the deity, thus radically affirming the oneness of devotees before and with the Lord. In Karve's company there was no intercaste dining, and she was troubled by this persistent maintenance of separateness and rank. The only time my pilgrim company all sat down to dine together, rather than around separate cookstoves, was when we feasted on *prasād* in Puri. I noticed that the pilgrims seated themselves according to caste. When I asked about the appropriateness of this on the road of *dharma,* everyone assured me that it was a matter of "feeling" and a hardly a matter of *jāti*.

Two other personalities who stood out among our company were quickly given nicknames by the literate wits. One, Kalyan Singh Caran, was an aged landlord well over seventy—tall, heavyset, and hard-of-hearing as well as nearsighted. Quite intrepid about crossing the road and making his own way through crowds, he frequently wandered in the wrong direction. He was soon dubbed Sikandar ("Alexander the Great"). Sikandar often did present a comical sight, but when I interviewed him at length I found that far from being a dotard, he possessed a penetrating mind and ample self-respect. Then there was Cand Bai, clothed in prescriptive widow's drabbery which always looked soiled and rumpled, who could hold her own among men in religious "knowledge-talk." She received the half-ironic, half-admiring title of Mira, after the legendary princess-renouncer-poet devotee of Lord Krishna, whose name and deeds are common currency all over Rajasthan.

While all but three of the town Brahmans were in their twenties and thirties, the peasants, with a few exceptions, were of the grandparental generation. There were eighteen couples among our company, so that slightly over 50 percent of the pilgrims were making the ideal pilgrimage—that is, going to *tīrtha*s joined with their lifelong mates. Indeed, several gave this—the opportunity to travel as a pair—as the explicit reason for their present journey. Those who were not coupled more often than not had some kind of kin or intimate connection with at least one other pilgrim. For example, there were a mother and son; a mother-in-law accompanying her daughter and daughter's husband; a widowed younger brother's wife traveling with her husband's elder brother and his wife; a young Daroga woman who had come without any of her family in order to attend the wife of Gulab Singh as a "lady's companion." The old Damami and "Mira," each without previous connections among the company, were definite exceptions to the norm.

The bus-master Suresh, responsible for daily scheduling, complained frequently that the peasants, the "British Battalion," cared only for "bread, water, and pissing." It did indeed seem that a disproportionate amount of talk and energy was spent on these needs and on when, how long, how often we should halt to accommodate them. Of course, many of the passengers were aged and a number of them had never traveled before, so it was not wholly unreasonable that they were greatly concerned with maintaining their creature comforts.

Everyone except for Bhoju and me had kerosene stoves, fuel, and staple food supplies. Time had to be allotted for the preparation of morning tea and at least one hot meal a day, usually a midday repast. The evening meal was most often made of cold leftovers from the first. A campsite or cooksite had to have plenty of water for bathing, washing, cooking. For an overnight stop the pilgrims required a reasonably secluded area where they could relieve themselves in the predawn hour when they customarily arose. It was their strong preference for open-air sanitary arrangements over closed latrines, as well as a fear of having their "pockets cut" while they were asleep by thieves said to lurk in traditional rest houses, which made them insist on bedding down around petrol pumps for most of our nights on the road. They would rather sleep under glaring fluorescent tube-lights, in a dank atmosphere of grease and gasoline, but with open fields behind, than in dimly illuminated rest-house rooms equipped with cubicle latrines that often reeked.

Of the total of thirty nights spent on the road, only the two in Puri, one in Hardwar, and one in Pushkar were spent indoors in *dharmashālā*s. The rest were largely passed at petrol pumps, although we also camped on the concrete porch of a Bihar schoolhouse; in the sands of a park near Bodhgaya where a band with an amplifier played half the night; beside the road at the Uttar Pradesh–Rajasthan border, where we were treated to the perpetual roaring of trucks; and, without choice because of the *melā* crowds, at the unutterably filthy bus stand of Gaya.

When not preoccupied with the mundane details of food and sanitation, or the ever-resurgent quarrels over seat allocation, the pilgrims did tell wonderful stories of the gods and sing devotional songs. Women more often than men, but not exclusively, would break into song, usually in the morning when spirits were always higher, or sometimes to pass the time during a breakdown or flat-tire change. The morning series of songs for the gods always included Ganeshji and Surya Raj, the Sun King. These might then be followed by songs of Rama, of Radha and Krishna, of Gangaji or Badrinath.

Although dedicated to the gods, these women's songs are very simple and homey, both in terms of the devotion they express and in their portrayal of the deities themselves. The most popular song of the Sun King is voiced by a woman who says that each day she never touches food until she has had the *darshan* of the sun. If she can't see him from her own courtyard, then she climbs up on her neighbor's roof. Another addresses the Sun King's father, King Kasan, telling him, as if he might be unaware, "Get up, Father, wake your child, he's not a child but an *avatār*."

The most favored song of Ganesh praised the fat elephant god's appearance attended by his two wives, Riddhi and Siddhi. Thus, its refrain goes, "Ganapat looks lovely with his two women, two women; your beauty so rich with two women; Gajanandji looks good with two women." The verses describe the services these women perform for him: "One woman fills and brings his water pitcher, the other woman readies his bath"; or "One woman brings his ornaments, the other woman readies the whisk."

Some songs were not about the gods but about the process of pilgrimage itself. The following is a charming example of this genre. It probably uses the names Radha and Rama just as typical village names rather than in reference to the deities, as the mythic Radha and Rama are never coupled.

Song of Pilgrimage

Hey Radha, there's a company going to Ganga;
Let's both make the journey, Oh Lord,
Let's go paired on pilgrimage, Oh Lord.

Hey Radha, your husband's father is going too;
How will you praise God? Oh Lord.

Hey Ramji, I will join both my hands to husband's father;
With my mouth I will praise God, Oh Lord,
In my heart I will praise God, Oh Lord.

Hey Radha, there's a company going to Ganga;
Let's both make the journey, Oh Lord,
Let's go paired on pilgrimage, Oh Lord.

Hey Radha, your husband's mother is going too;
How will you praise God? Oh Lord.

Hey Ramji, I will press both of husband's mother's feet;
With my mouth I will praise God, Oh Lord,
In my heart I will praise God, Oh Lord.

Hey Radha, this company's going to Jagdish;
Let's both make the journey, Oh Lord,
Let's go paired on pilgrimage, Oh Lord.

Hey Radha, the people of Mehru are with this group;
How will you praise God? Oh Lord.

Hey Ramji, I will veil my face slightly;
With my mouth I will praise God, Oh Lord,
In my heart I will praise God, Oh Lord.

Hey Radha, this company's going to Badrinath;
Let's both make the journey, Oh Lord,
Let's go paired on pilgrimage, Oh Lord.

Hey Radha, Ainn-bai is with this group;
How will you praise God? Oh Lord.

Hey Ramji, I will veil my face slightly;
With my mouth I will praise God, Oh Lord,
In my heart I will praise God, Oh Lord.

This song suggests some particularly feminine attitudes toward the pilgrimage experience. To go "paired" with one's husband is both inviting and embarrassing. But superior both to the thrill and to the shame of this unaccustomed public exposure as a couple is the praise of God. God's *bhajan* in this context means songs from the mouth and constant devotion in the heart. The presence of in-laws, neighbors, or anthropologists cannot inhibit this true devotional emotion and its expression.

Every evening approximately around the time of sunset an *āratī* in praise of Jagdish was sung by almost everyone on the bus. Suresh would switch on a small electric bulb located beneath the several deities' icons that graced the dashboard, and light a couple of sticks of incense. Above this "shrine," inscribed in broad calligraphic strokes extending across the width of the front windshield, was the motto "Lord make your journey fruitful" (Īshvar āpkī yātrā saphal karẽ).

The Jagdish *āratī,* far from being unique to the Puri pilgrimage, is sung in most Vaishnava temples in the villages of our area. The first verse, however, recorded on the pilgrimage, contains a single word change as noted.

Āratī of Jagdish

[Refrain] OM Victory to Lord Jagdish!
Sovereign, Victory to Lord Jagdish!
Master, Victory to Lord Jagdish!

[1] Those who go receive fruit[6]
And a trouble-free mind, Master,
Happiness, prosperity come into the home;
the body's sufferings are removed.

[2] Your are my mother and father,
To what other shelter might I go? Master,
Without you there is no other;
on whom might I hope?

[3] You're the complete supreme soul,
You're the inner master, Master,
Beyond creation, supreme Lord,
you're everyone's master.

[4] You're an ocean of compassion
Caring for all, Master,
I am the servant, you the master;
have mercy O King!

[5] You are unknowable,
Husband of all creatures, Master,
How can I with my base intellect
deserve your pity?

[6] Brother of the poor, sorrow-defeater, Sovereign,
You're my ruling Lord, Master,
Extend your hand, Sovereign;
I am standing at your door.

[7] Erase poisonous thoughts,
Defeat sin, Master,
Increase faith and devotion and
the service of the saints.

[8] My body, mind, and wealth are yours,
How can I make an offering to you, Master,

6. This line as sung on the bus—"jyo jāve phal pāve"—seems to imply "those who go [on a pilgrimage to Jagdish] receive fruit." In the village it is usually rendered "jyo dhāve phal pāve"—meaning "those who praise him receive fruit."

When nothing's left
that's mine.

The *āratī*'s content is less playful and less rustic than that of women's devotional songs. At its core is the magisterial omnipotence of the Lord of the Universe contrasted to the lowly adoration of his devotee. Although ordinary people rarely speak with such poetic eloquence, the prayer-song does seem to convey accurately the real humility that peasant worshippers feel before the mighty gods. No one would argue or bargain with Jagdish as he might with Dev Narayanji, Bhairu, or Jaipal. In closing, the *āratī* states a deeply felt urge to surrender all to the supreme deity. Perhaps not unwittingly, the *paṇḍā* at the Puri *dharmashālā* led our company in a rousing rendition of Jagdish's *āratī* just before soliciting donations.

Most major pilgrimage centers along the popular route we followed have highly organized and highly aggressive priesthoods, whose members control to a large degree the circulation and actions of peasant pilgrims within their domain. Indeed, they often board the bus uninvited at the outskirts of a *tīrtha* town and do not part company from the group until final donations are extracted at the end of their visit to that place. Peasants are naturally ambivalent toward these *paṇḍā*s and their machinations. On the one hand, they are genuinely glad to be guided, for they would otherwise have little idea of what to do. On the other hand, in a kind of stubborn reaction against *paṇḍa*s' acquisitiveness, the pilgrims would often demand the cheapest and briefest package of *darshan* and *pūjā*.

Sometimes the *paṇḍā*s went too far in their aggressive behavior; they might then be roundly abused, as when Kalyan Singhji summed up his opinions of the priests in Calcutta: "Don't ask about the *paṇḍā*s. Seeing the condition of the *paṇḍā*s, there is no desire to do a *yātrā*. Those sister-fuckers, they would tear my clothes! Those ones from cunts, those ones with protruding teeth! If everyone knew that *paṇḍā*s were like this, then no one would come on a pilgrimage. Everyone would think, we should not come to *tīrtha*s." Nevertheless, every informant including this man insisted that the nature of the priests who received their offerings in no way spoiled the meritorious nature of such gifts.

13. On the pilgrims' road; women relax and take the opportunity to dry a skirt during a bus breakdown.

The flour-ball offerings made at Gaya and related activities in Prayag and Hardwar (all described in chapter 4) were the only complex rituals in which our pilgrims engaged. For the rest, it was bathing, temple viewing, gifts to priests and beggars, and occasional perfunctory *pūjā*s, undertaken by couples on the bathing *ghāṭ*s. The town Brahmans tended to take advantage of more opportunities to sight-see than did the older, slower, poorer, and less adventurous peasant crowd. Although I preferred to stay with the peasants, considering them the "real" pilgrims, if there was a steep hill to climb or a rupee to pay, I had often to leave them sitting near the bus and accompany the Brahmans.

The essential conviction that the Lord is within, or wherever you find him, often inspired people, when things were going badly, to devalue the very enterprise in which they were currently engaged. Gam Shyamji often yearned for his much-beloved black stone icon of Niranjani back home in Ghatiyali. "I miss God," he would enunciate with deep feeling even as he enjoyed the *darshan*s of Hinduism's most renowned and powerful images.

Concern with auspiciousness was pervasive among all the *darshan* bus passengers—peasants and Brahmans alike. When we suffered numerous breakdowns and got stuck in the mud several times in flood-ridden Uttar Pradesh between Agra and Allahabad, there were several hypotheses advanced as to the cause of these troubles. A number of the men blamed it on some women, known to be menstruating, who had washed their skirts and dried them heedlessly on top of the bus. The women did not subscribe to this theory, but many blamed themselves for singing the Sun King's song before Ganeshji's one morning. Ganeshji is not pleased unless he is first.

Suresh, the young bus-master, was convinced that someone among our company was under bad astrological influences. Rather sheepishly, given his pretensions to citified sophistication, he tied an old shoe as a "charm" to the front of the bus, reciting a spell intended to draw malevolent powers into the shoe rather than into the vehicle itself. Our troubles seemed to clear up soon afterward, but on that same day the women were particularly attentive to Ganeshji, so no one could be sure whose remedy had made the difference.

Of the major sites visited on the outbound route up to Puri, the first three stops were all in Rajasthan (as were, symmetrically enough, the journey's last three). Each had its distinctive qualities. East of Ajmer is the district of Savai Madhapur to which we went first in order to visit the historic fort of Ranathambaur. For the pilgrims this stop was Ranathambaur Ganeshji, for it was not the monumental fort with its concentric walls and enormous gates that drew us, but a small temple of Ganeshji located within them. Considered to house the greatest Ganeshji in all of Rajasthan, this temple is the first stop for most major bus *yātrās* departing from our area, just as Pushkar is the last for those returning. Ganeshji is the god of auspicious beginnings. If Path Mother's initial worship secures a safe return, Ganeshji is prayed to for success and well-being along the way.

The next stop was Galtaji, outside of Jaipur, a place of natural beauty where waterfalls poured into tiered pools. Men bathed in the upper pool, and women below, explicitly in the runoff from the men's baths. There was a temple of Rama near the bathing spot, but only a few of our company went inside to take *darshan;* the thing to do at Galtaji was bathe. The distance from this picturesque outdoor scene to the dim and vaguely demonic setting of Mehndipur Balaji's temple complex is not nearly so great as the contrast between the two places.

Sudhir Kakar has richly described the approach to and atmosphere of Mehndipur Balaji (1982:53–56). Although situated on a small street in town rather than in the midst of village fields, Mehndipur Balaji's operations are in many ways similar to Puvali ka Devji's (see chapter 3). In recent years this place of Hanuman and Bhairuji has gained great fame—again, like Puvali, largely because of the success of a charismatic *bhopā*. It now attracts extraregional pilgrims as well as Rajasthanis by the hundreds. The place's specialty is exorcism of recalcitrant ghosts and witches.[7]

This was the single exorcistic shrine visited by our tour bus, the only one belonging to an active healing tradition where deities speak through human bodies and grapple with malevolent beings.

7. Kakar 1982:68–81 gives an interpretation of the exorcism process at Mehndipur as therapy, with a few fragmentary but interesting case histories.

In keeping with the nature of a *darshan* bus tour, our visit to Mehndipur was properly for *darshan* only. Indeed, when some of the peasants showed an inclination to sit down and soak up the spellbinding atmosphere (*bhajan*-singing was under way, and many clients swayed and panted and trembled under the influence of their possessive spirits) Suresh abruptly hustled his charges outside. He then ordered everyone to return to the bus at once.

Suresh justified his peremptory interference by alluding to the reputed contagion of possession in this place. If somebody else's ghost or witch took a notion to "play" in one of his passengers, or even worse, if any of them had their own spirit that became aroused, Suresh feared he would then be obliged to keep his whole party waiting there until the episode was finished. That might easily be a matter of days. Our pilgrims found his motives reasonable and docilely returned to the bus. We soon pulled out of Mehndipur and continued almost nonstop into the night and into the heart of Krishna country, once more traversing a distance whose meaning can hardly be gauged kilometrically.

Throughout Vrndavan, Mathura, and Gokul we were manipulated by expert *paṇḍās*, but even their outrageous demands and high-pressure techniques could not spoil the simple pleasures of being in the land of Krishna's childhood. Indeed, they probably enhanced it, for as J. S. Hawley tells us in his monograph on Vrndavan, the "simple aim" of the *paṇḍās* "is to connect the place with the story, and to assure their charges that they are retracing Krishna's steps. . . . At every spot there is something the pilgrims can to do solidify the connection" (1981:35).

Thus we were enjoined to rest where Krishna's father had rested in his desperate flight to save the divine babe from an evil, child-slaughtering uncle. The happiest exclamations were aroused by pretty *darshan* tableaux which recalled villagers' own experiences. Women sympathized with Krishna's mother on her childbirth couch and cooed over baby Krishna's draining poison from the breast of a demoness: "Look, see how God is sucking!" Another favorite was a pond where the infant Krishna's soiled clothing had been washed. People explicitly mentioned the Lord's "shit" in this context as if it enhanced the pool with very special charms. Although most of our company was highly frugal and abstemious when it came to purchasing food, everyone bought and ate half-kilos of expensive milk sweets in Gokul, saying, "We should eat them because God does."

Toward the monuments of human rather than divine exploits that they encountered in Agra, pilgrims had a different attitude. Although the Taj Mahal and Red Fort certainly elicited much wonder and tongue-clicking, the Rajasthani peasants were not overawed. Several made remarks to the effect that "these stones are all that's left—the people who built this thought they needed it but they died like everyone. We all die." Their appreciation for Agra's glories, then, was pervaded by a kind of cynicism toward the ponderous residue of human lives, which contrasted greatly with their recent veneration of Lord Krishna's subtle traces.

Following Agra was a long and difficult passage through flooded Uttar Pradesh to Prayag. From Prayag we took a side trip to Citrakut on whose peaceful and clean riverbank the epic poet Tulsidas was said to have had the *darshan* of Lord Ram. Here those who were willing both to pay the boatman and to struggle up the hills were rewarded with magnificent vistas and moving visions of the gods. In these very hills Rama and Sita were said to have dwelt in simple sylvan splendor during their forest exile, and one of the shrines we visited was called Sita's Kitchen. The effort of the climb prompted several participants to remark on the greater value of foot pilgrimage, a sentiment rarely heard during the bus trip.

Our next camp was just outside Banaras, and we pulled into the "City of Light" shortly after dawn. After several false turns the driver eventually found his way to the parking area near Vishvanath Gali, the heart of Varanasi for all pilgrims and tourists. A brief dispute ensued as our party hovered uncertainly near the bus, between those who wanted tea first and those who felt that bathing should precede all consumption. The tea drinkers won, and soon afterwards *paṇḍās* took over, parceling us among themselves into three parties. We were then led to the river to bathe and were taken on a whirlwind tour of central Kashi's most famed temples. Few could later distinctly recall any of these. My own impressions—a blur of shining icons, masses of red and orange and yellow flower offerings, hastily mumbled *pūjās*, and coins plunked down to punctuate each divine viewing—were shared by many. We were soon on the road again with Gaya our next destination (see chapter 4).

From Gaya we reached Calcutta, an experience encapsuled in my field notes as follows:

> In and out of Calcutta very rapidly indeed, as the minute we got there policemen like leeches were jumping on the bus and demanding money because of the overload. No ticket, just a straight bribe; no receipt. One took twenty, one took over a hundred, the third took I think thirty-five rupees. Suresh was fed up and [after the temple and the zoo] put ten of us in taxis and got the hell out of town. The Kali Temple was like a scene out of *narak* [a place of afterdeath tortures in Hindu cosmology], the screaming demands and clawing hands of the *paṇḍās* as if the bloodthirsty soul of the goddess had infested them with some perverted transformation of her energy. Saw her, Kali, and fled. Saw one priest prying coins out of the curled fingers of our old Caran [poor Alexander the Great] who wanted to throw them himself onto the icon. Our own *prasād* (of flowers, sweets, *pampalo* [a seedy grapefruit-like item] and cucumber) was also snatched hastily and none returned with proper temple courtesy. Poor Gam Shyamji just keeps praising Ghatiyali and wishing he were back in the Niranjani temple with his *bhagvān*. After that the zoo was a real retreat.

From Calcutta we came to Puri, the end point, the high-water mark of our *yātrā*. There everyone relaxed, enjoyed sleeping indoors in *dharmashālā* rooms with electric ceiling fans and water taps, eating sweet meals of temple *mahāprasād,* and most of all, the encounter with the sea:

Interviewer: What is the greatest *tīrtha*?
Pilgrim: Jagdish.
Interviewer: How is it that Jagdish is the greatest?
Pilgrim: Because the ocean is so huge.

All the Rajasthani pilgrims I knew who had made the Puri bus *yātrā,* whether in connection with sinking flowers or just to wander, thought of the ocean as a highlight of their journey. This includes pilgrims recalling trips twenty years past, as well as those who accompanied me to Puri in 1980. While some spoke of having the ocean's *darshan,* just as they might of a deity or a saint, the most common phrase for the experience of the sea was "taking

14. Taking waves; tangled bodies in the surf after morning ocean worship at Puri.

waves" (*lahar lenā*). *Darshan,* for all its interactive connotations, does not really convey what happens in the water. The word *lahar,* or "wave," has a range of meanings that includes all kinds of extraordinary pleasure. Among its definitions in the *RSK* are these: "mind's enjoyment," "intoxication," "emotional love," "grace," and "bliss."

Supervised by the "fishermen" of Puri beach who play the part of lifeguards in their distinctive conical caps, pilgrims threw themselves into the waves with remarkable abandon and togetherness. If Victor Turner's general vision of pilgrimage as "liminoid" and "antistructural" is anywhere directly pertinent to Rajasthanis' journeys, it is here on the beach at Puri.[8] During their extended frolic in the waves our pilgrim company did appear to enjoy "joyful ludic communitas" (Turner 1978:37). In this regard it is perhaps not facetious to cite an English-language pamphlet pur-

8. For Victor Turner's major statements about pilgrimage, communitas, liminality, and liminoidness, see his "Pilgrimages as Social Processes" (1974:166–230); "'Liminal' to 'Liminoid,' in Play, Flow and Ritual" (1979:11–59); "Death and the Dead in the Pilgrimage Process" (1979:121–142); and Turner and Turner's "Pilgrimage as a Liminoid Phenomenon" (1978:1–39).

chased at Puri and published "on behalf of Shri Jagannath Temple Managing Committee": "A dip in the sacred sea brings in broadness of mind doing away with all meanness" (*Shri Khetra Parichaya* 1976:7). This is certainly part of what Turner means by "communitas" and part of what the pilgrims experienced.

The women at least had anticipated their surrender to the ocean, having heard much about the force of the waves from friends who had previously made the trip. Among other things, they were aware beforehand that their ocean bath would involve a loss of customary modesty. These women were quite used to bathing in their clothes and changing into dry ones with dextrous ease, never displaying an unseemly inch of flesh. But they had been warned that the ocean waters were not as calm as village tanks or gently flowing rivers. Always, both at home in Ghatiyali and on the road, Rajasthani women had teased me for wearing underpants, basically a garment appropriate only to schoolgirls in knee-length skirts. But several confided to me as we neared Puri, "Ah, when we reach the ocean waves, then we too should put on underpants like you." Of course, none of them did, nor did anyone become embarrassingly exposed in the water, at least not long enough for it to matter. Nonetheless, part of the waves' attraction was a potential for self-abandonment that included for women a disarrangement of their normally modest dress.

The breakers were very strong with a heavy undertow, and clothing was twisted, tangled, and plastered to bodies. In the excitement, confusion, and dangerous thrill of the waves, couples who usually barely glanced at one another (standard public etiquette for husband and wife in rural Rajasthan) held hands tightly. Even unconnected persons of different sexes tumbled about together in the churning foam and sand.

The sticky salty aftermath of the ocean bath, necessitating still another rinse and change of clothing back at the *dharmashālā,* also made it stand out as unique in peoples' thoughts. Moreover, this beach was the single experience of the entire journey which almost every member of our company sought to repeat. No one went back to the temple on our second day in Puri for another look at the Lord Jagdish; all repaired, as if by silent consensus, to the ocean shore. No one repeated the perfunctory "ocean worship" that had preceded the previous day's bathing. They had returned purely to play in the salt waves.

In contrast to universal emphasis on the ocean as a prime moment of the *yātrā,* only a few persons interviewed mentioned the famed *darshan* of Jagdish and his companion icons with their truncated limbs as particularly profound or impressive. I myself was not allowed to enter the temple, but my wait outside did not last long. When I asked Gam Shyamji how it was to view Jagdish he shrugged and muttered, "Well, God is God." Perhaps, always considerate, he wanted to console me. It is also true, however, that these Hindus had seen countless icons in their lives, but only one sea.

Other aspects of Puri which people did consistently discuss and recall were the meals of *prasād* served at the *dharmashālā* and the subsequent donations of cash and pledged grain made by all pilgrims. Our first day in Puri began with worship of the ocean and bathing, followed by a visit to the main temple of Lord Jagdish. Then a full meal including rice pudding was served to the entire company as the Lord's *prasād.* Rest and other temples followed, and a second meal, this one with sweet fried pancakes, another dish esteemed and relished by Rajasthanis.

That night all our company was called together to hear the head *paṇḍā* tell the story of the greatness of Puri. In sonorous tones and simple, clearly enunciated Hindi, he gave us the essential origin legend of the wooden icons of Jagannath, Balabhadra, and Subhadra.[9] He then described the place of Puri within India's major sets of pilgrimage centers: the seven "cities" (*purī*) and the four "established spots" (*dhām*). He told how each crossing place made unique demands on a pilgrim's devotion. He reminded us, not so subtly, that we had now, twice, satiated ourselves on quality meals of *mahāprasād*—cooked food from the Lord's kitchens. Finally he got to the heart of the matter.

> Who sent it from the temple? The committee-*vāle.* Why did they send it? Because you are God's guests. You are devotees. You came to do God's pilgrimage. You came a distance of seven hundred and fifty *kosh.* For this reason *prasād* was sent for you. And if you do something before you leave, then when others will come, they also

9. The origin story of the Jagannath temple, approximately as the *paṇḍā* told it, is found in English in the pamphlet *Visit Puri* (1977:8–11). The myth and history of Puri's gods have been given extensive scholarly consideration in Eschmann, Kulke, and Tripathi, eds., 1978. Two articles by Marglin (1981, 1982) analyze the relation between temple rituals and myth in Puri.

15. Puri *paṇḍā* tells pilgrims the story of the greatness of Puri and Jagdish.

> will be served. What others have given, you received. What you will give before leaving will be received by others.
>
> In the same way as the sun pulls water from the earth, and from this comes rain, then water reaches the earth and the rivers and canals are filled, and from this agriculture is possible; it is a circle.
>
> For this reason *prasād* came and the chief work inside Jagannathji is the offering of *aṭkā*. . . . What is *aṭkā?* The gift which you will make at God's crossing place. *Aṭkā,* its name is *aṭkā*. Where is this offered? Every day four maunds of lentils, rice, and vegetables are offered to God as food-to-enjoy. After being offered as food-to-enjoy, this *prasād* is available to all. . . . From giving to all, God is happy. Your desires will be fulfilled and your pilgrimage will be fulfilled.
>
> For this reason, for the grain-gift, whatever you give, these gentlemen have come from the temple with a receipt book. So you give your gift and take a receipt.

The *paṇḍā*'s rhetoric, with its hydraulic metaphor, was brilliant. Although the pilgrims did not meet his highest expectations, our party certainly did make bigger cash gifts and grain pledges in Puri than they had elsewhere, including Gaya. Taking waves and giving *dān* go together, perhaps. Loosening and emptying are

16. Puri *paṇḍā* negotiates with pilgrims for cash offerings and grain pledges.

17. The *darshan* tour bus, journey's end; posing, *from left to right:* Suresh, the bus-master; his paternal aunt; the author; the driver; the mechanic.

both vital to pilgrims' progress, especially if it is toward any kind of release.

From Puri to Ayodhya we drove almost three full days without any stops other than those occasioned by human or mechanical necessities. There was a sense of homeward-boundness and anticlimax, a lot of squabbling, and much fond reminiscing about the fun of the waves. After Ayodhya our return route included Garh Mukteshvar, Hardwar and Rishikesh, Delhi, Amer Fort, Jaipur city, Diggi, and Pushkar—the place of the "last bath."[10] An afternoon and night were spent in Ajmer, for shopping and the movies only, and then we returned, at last, to Mehru. Throughout the entire return lap of the journey several of the older pilgrims were feeling ill, suffering fevers and stomach problems. Many were weary of *darshans* and homesick for family left behind.

Rather than narrate this homeward journey, during which little of extraordinary interest occurred, I turn now to the motivations for and meaning of this third distinct style of journeying—pilgrimage for its own sake, for wandering, for merit, for cleansing, or for *moksha*. How do participants conceive of its fruitfulness or fruitlessness in connection with the aims of human life?

Sweeping the Road Ahead

In gathering pilgrims' views on *tirthayātrā's* ineffable fruits, the questioner's role was one of persistent probing, and this should be kept in mind. *Paṇḍās* did frequently use the concept of "fruits" and the terms *moksha* and *mukti* in ritual contexts, including prayers which pilgrims were asked to repeat mechanically. No one, however, among unlettered villagers, produced the latter terms spontaneously in ordinary discourse, and few liked to talk about their motivations as oriented toward any specific desirable results.

My standard questions, then, about "What are the fruits of crossing places?" and "Do you get *moksha?*" usually jarred upon people. Everyone responded strongly to them, however, one way or another. The first impulse was almost invariably a shrug and a

10. See chapter 4 for a description of a "last bath" in Pushkar. For Pushkar's cosmological meanings and sociological functionings, Zeitlyn's unpublished dissertation (1986) is the best source.

denial—to fruits: "Oh, what is received?" to *moksha:* "Oh, it's all in God's hands!" Some persons, however, were willing to go beyond these blockades and explore the subjects more deeply.

Perhaps the most concise yet suggestive interpretation came from "Mira," the widowed Hada Rajput who was practiced in "knowledge-talk" and spent most of her time in devotions. After a long discussion she finally summed up the relation between pilgrimage and ultimate liberation in this way: "Sweeping the road ahead, then, Brother, *moksha* happens well." Mira clarified the "road ahead" as future lives. According to her view, meritorious activities such as pilgrimage help you on the way toward better births in which, no doubt, you may attain release. *Moksha* is thus a very distant goal indeed, and pilgrimage more a means of clearing the path than narrowing the distance.

How is this sweeping effected? From other responses to my probings one firmly positive aspect of pilgrimage emerges clearly: giving away, using up, spending money. Some believe that this giving is causally conducive to *moksha*; others just know it's a good thing but continue to deny all higher fruits to the pilgrimage process. Along with this general agreement on the virtues of giving went a full consensus on the uselessness of bathing.

An unsophisticated, aged Mehru Brahman, traveling paired with his almost equally aged spouse, first answered my general question about *tīrthaphal* ("the fruits of crossing places") with unusual expansiveness, saying that God gives everything to pilgrims and listing the usual components of worldly happiness: wealth, health, and sons. When I then asked if *moksha* were included among these limitless boons a pilgrim might expect, his response was totally negative.

Pilgrim: *Moksha* does not happen.

Interviewer: From going to crossing places, *moksha* does not happen?

Pilgrim: No, no, it's a false matter. From what does *moksha* come? From his own hand, God's, that's from whom. It does not come from wandering. Whatever you give, in whatever place give it. From this comes *moksha*. What kind of *dharma* is dirtying the water? But *dharma* is giving-and-taking.

The opposition this informant posits while discussing *moksha*—of useless bathing versus the virtues of "giving-and-taking"—was a common valuation among peasant pilgrims, with, however, the stress laid on giving.

The old Damami pilgrim, who had clearly spent more thought on the matter than most, stated explicitly that the reason for doing pilgrimage was to spend money on the road of *dharma*. When, however, I asked him whether *moksha* might be expected, he responsed in exactly the same fashion as the Brahman, by jumping to a denial of the use of traveling and bathing in respect to that high aim. "Uh uh! Nothing will be received. 'Why do you search for me, fool, I am here near you' [he is speaking as God would to a deluded pilgrim]. If one's heart is clean then, put water in the kneading-platter and bathe and it is equal to the Ganges." My research assistant then produced a rhymed saying of identical import: "man cangā to kaṭhautī mẽ Gangā" (mind is clean, then Ganges is in the kneading-platter). Now the *kaṭhautī* is a very humble vessel, traditionally made of wood and used for the everyday work of mixing bread dough. All its implications are thus of the unextraordinary, unexotic, and homey, in direct contradistinction to the glamour of pilgrimage.

If, however, it is absurd to count *moksha* as a fruit of pilgrimage, only a few informants wholly denied that *tīrthayātrā* produces some merit. Most located the source of this "merit" (*puṇya*) or *dharma*—like the Brahman and the Damami—squarely in the realm of expenditures. Thus a Mali couple's opinions on the subject of why people go on *yātrā*s were as follows:

Husband: Well, the money collects; for this reason we do pilgrimages.

Wife: Yes, it is a pretext made for spending money. From this pretext, *dharma* emerges. Yes, and sin and sorrow all depart.

It is interesting to note that she appears to view the expenditure as automatically meritorious, almost in the way texts may praise bathing. In choosing to go on pilgrimage, people place themselves in a situation where, willy-nilly, money will go for religious gifting as it never would at home.

Some informants considered not only that money was dispensed more copiously in the course of a pilgrimage, but that the quality of gifting itself was improved in the environment of a crossing place. Another Mali and former participant in a Puri bus *yātrā* answered questions to this effect:

Interviewer: What fruit is received from pilgrimage?

Pilgrim: God knows.

Interviewer: But what do you think in your soul, what belief do you have?

Pilgrim: *Dharma*'s money emerges. It is given to *paṇḍās*, to the crippled.

Interviewer: But if we make religious gifts at home or at crossing places, what is the difference?

Pilgrim: The gifts we give here remain here, but the gifts we give there reach God.

The same person denounced the notion that baths at crossing places are of the slightest efficacy.

Interviewer: But there is a belief that from bathing in crossing places all sin will be washed away.

Pilgrim: No one has such belief.

Interviewer: There is no belief that from bathing in the Ganges one becomes pure.

Pilgrim: No, no one becomes pure. It was begun by our forefathers and we on this pretext go to see the cities.

This man's statements contain a vivid contrast between the worth of gifting in pilgrimage centers and the worthlessness of bathing. While the former offers a way of approaching God through selfless charities, the latter is a mere self-serving pretext for sightseeing. Many others agreed with this appraisal of the absolute uselessness of bathing for cleansing the soul. One woman said that sins were blacker than the soot on the underside of a griddle: "That blackness doesn't open." Another spoke of sin as "stains" that no amount of washing could ever remove.

The idea that gifting is far more efficacious than bathing was also shared by many, as was the notion that gifts made at crossing places may be channeled directly toward God. One interviewee, whose Puri journey was also several years past, confessed to having had an intention to exploit this special access. He went on the pilgrimage, he said, hoping to get the boon of a male child for his only son, as so many go to the lesser, wonder-working gods of Rajasthan. As he explained it, "I went with this 'wrong desire' [*lālac*]." The *RSK* specifically defines *lālac* as the desire to have something for improper reasons. The former pilgrim continued:

> I thought to myself, I should take the flowers of the old man and old woman [his parents] and go all the way to Lord Jagdish [although the flowers, of course, were sunk in Gaya]. I thought, perhaps Lord Jagdish would look in our direction also and if God looks in our direction it is good. . . . If it costs one hundred or two hundred, one thousand or two thousand, that's what it costs. And if in that stream of merit my Lord may gaze. . . .

This man's rather complex thought was, it would seem, that his expenditures on the pilgrimage and for the sake of *dharma* would create a kind of stream or flow between him and God which might just work both ways. That is, on the same path along which his money flowed to God in the special setting of crossing places, God's grace might be channeled back to him and bring the fervently desired child. It didn't happen, however, which is perhaps why he used the pejorative *lālac* for his desire, and why he bluntly denied any fruit coming from the practice of pilgrimage, speaking throughout the interview with scathing cynicism.

In general, although there is certainly a range of opinions, the worth of pilgrimage in terms of *dharma*—that is, beyond the readily acknowledged enjoyment of wandering and seeing—does seem to boil down to using financial resources in a way that is qualitatively different from anything possible in the village. Most of the Sanskrit texts on the fruits of crossing places claim that gifts made in *tīrthasthān* bring many times more merit than the same gifts made at home.[11] The views maintained by villagers thus demonstrate a continuity with these classical teachings.

Here the essential role of the grasping *paṇḍās*, whether they grasp by crude physical assault, as in Calcutta's Kali temple, or artfully with fine rhetoric, as in the Puri *dharmashālā*, becomes evident. It is not easy for peasants to spend money, especially for

11. See, for example, Kane 1953:600–601 and Salomon 1985:446 for the increased worth of gifts made in *tīrtha*s. A panel chaired by Raheja at the 1986 meeting of the Association for Asian Studies in Chicago explored various perspectives on the gift in Hindu and Buddhist traditions. In a contribution to that panel (A. Gold 1986) I discussed in greater depth than I do here both textual and popular ideas about the increased value of gift-giving in *tīrtha*s. There I attempted, in preliminary fashion, to relate these ideas to Raheja's persuasive arguments for *dāna* as a transfer of inauspiciousness away from the donor to an appropriate vessel (1985). See also Khare 1976 and Vatuk and Vatuk 1976 for some other observations on gift-giving in Hindu society.

selfless reasons. But on pilgrimage they constantly encounter *paṇḍās* and beggars who forcefully persuade them to loosen their purse strings, although they may struggle against it. However unpleasant the process itself may be, there is a residual satisfaction in knowing that the money has gone for *dharma*.

Giving in the village is not as good, some said, because even if it is giving to Brahmans or temples, it is inevitably a calculated, calibrated transaction. If not made for tangible return or to repay past obligation, then it will surely be for reputation or "name" (*nām*). I was told again and again that hidden or anonymous gifting was the best, and yet in the village it seemed few could resist announcing their charities. Whether it was a rupee's offering announced during a religious drama or several thousand rupees for a *dharmashālā* room, there was always a name shouted or inscribed along with the amount of money. But on the pilgrimage road, although one might get receipts from the *paṇḍās* at a few large institutions, many small donations to temples, to beggars, and to priests would be made daily without any record and without anyone's certain knowledge. The intransitive verbal form "emerges" (*nikalnā, kaṛbo*)—meaning to come out, appear, or emerge like snakes from their holes or like rashes on the skin—was usually used to describe this emission of cash. Here lay the greatest merit-producing virtue of pilgrimage, and here if anywhere was the potential for increasing chances of release in some distant future.[12]

A solitary respondent among my interviewees did claim to expect immediate salvation on her journey. This was another widow, the Gujar woman traveling with her grown son. She gave this atypical response to my standard question about the fruits of crossing places: "I don't need any fruit. That which I will receive is the deliverance of my body-soul. What is the need for fruit? This pilgrimage is done and from this my body-soul's deliverance will be."

12. Egnor has poetically described giving as a technique of reducing the heavy substance of the person in order to arrive at light and emptiness. She writes: "Giving and not taking is the higher way. A sign of giving is a decrease of one's own substance. . . . Reduction of substance, hard substance, useless substance, can be seen to result in an increase of cleanness and power" (1978:56). The congruence between the notion of giving as emptying and refining expressed in Egnor's exposition of a Tamil guru's teaching and Rajasthani peasants' views is striking. Inden's (1976) discussion of making gifts to higher-ranking beings as a way of transformation or transmutation producing superior fruits is also relevant here.

Significantly enough, this woman found the whole concept of fruit opposed to that of deliverance. Her stance is consistent with the devotional approach of the *Gita*: fruits are to be surrendered to God, and liberation is a by-product of selfless devotion, quite beyond causality. The woman was not claiming that her body-soul would be delivered as a result of her pilgrimage experience, but spontaneously, as part of it. Thus she insists on the possibility of release almost in the same vein that other pilgrims deny it. A disjunction between the supreme life aim and earned fruit is sustained.

Further understandings of the subtle benefits of pilgrimage may be explored by considering, first, the resonance of *tīrtha*s in popular metaphor, and second, the esoteric internalization of journeying. I take for my primary texts a well-loved women's song that finds all pilgrimage baths in the *darshan* of Rama, and a Nath *nirguṇa bhajan* advising humans that all crossing places are located in the body-soul and they should therefore perform *darshan* within and eschew outer travels.

One source of inner transformation as a spontaneous fruit of pilgrimage experience is a special kind of *darshan*—a vision depending on inner devotion as much as outer images. The following women's song, considered to be a "song of Ganges Mother," may be sung during Path Mother's worship and Celebration of Ganga, as well as in the course of any journeys that involve the Ganges River. It is very popular among village women of our area, and I recorded it frequently both in Ghatiyali and on the Puri bus. Deceptively simple, it renders a complex sentiment with brevity and conviction.

Ram's Golden Chariot

On Ganga's bank a golden chariot's come, O Ram,
On the Great Stream's bank a golden chariot's come.
    Let's go, O my girlfriends, to see the chariot
    Where Lord Ram's enthroned, O Ram.
Seeing Ramji's face we have bathed in all the fords, O Ram,
Seeing Ramji's face we have bathed in all the fords, O Ram,
Bathed in the Ganges at Gomati, body-souls uplifted at Badari,
    O Ram.

[The song repeats, substituting "on Jamana's bank" and "on Pushkar's bank" in the opening line.]

This song's message is a variant on a theme already discussed: the worth and worthlessness of visiting crossing places or "fords" (an alternative translation of *tīrtha,* which I used in the song for the sake of rhythm). Here, the worth is found not in meritorious expenditures but rather in *darshan.* But *darshan,* as portrayed in the song, is not the temple-confined and regulated viewing of a magnificent icon, however power-imbued. Rather, it is a hierophany, the perception of a divine and radiant presence. There is a sense of joyful immanence as well as urgency. The presence is not stationary, like temple gods, but in passage. The chariot has just arrived and may well depart momentarily.

The song conveys a definite hierarchical valuation of *darshan* as superior to bathing at crossing places. All the virtues of bathing are contained in the vision of Ram: "Rāmjī ro mukhaṛo dekhtā cyārõ tīrth nāyā." The first verb, "seeing," (*dekhtā*), is a present participle; the second, "bathed" (*nāyā*), a completed past. Thus, seeing God's face is to have bathed in all fords. Bathing in fords is a good thing, but seeing Ram accomplishes instantaneously the fruits of all baths.[13]

In the song's final line, the subsumption of pilgrimage baths to *darshan* is carried further: "Bathed in the Ganges at Gomati, body-soul uplifted at Badari." The results of seeing Ram's face, then, are particularly extended to include the most exalted and difficult-to-attain of pilgrimage sites—mountain places, source places of the divine river Ganges—rarely visited but greatly esteemed by Rajasthanis. Even these are comprehended, experienced, accomplished in the divine vision. The encounter with divinity is conceived as transformative, in the way that *tīrtha* baths are supposed to be, but, everyone declares, are not. Thus the body-soul is improved, kept from decay, uplifted (all possible translations of the term *sudharī*) in this *darshan* bath.

But this is hardly an antiwandering song, for where is the radiant deity found? Where does hierophany occur? On the bank of the Ganges, on the bank of the Jamuna, on Lake Pushkar's shore. These are all great *tīrtha*s, and it is at these places that Ram's golden chariot is encountered. This is after all a song of Ganges

13. Much in the same fashion, texts praising baths may claim that a drop of Ganges water accomplishes everything that a hundred horse sacrifices or a lifetime of ascetic practice accomplishes. Such hyperbolic statements are common coin in Hindu literature.

Mother and not a song of Ram, according to the village women's own system of classification, which employs both categories. Its message, then, is twofold: to view a deity is a much greater transformative experience than bathing in any crossing place, but the divine presence is to be found *at* crossing places. This is a way of reconciling mechanical and devotional approaches to the fruits of pilgrimage.

In suggesting that devotion to a radiant god "with qualities" effects a salubrious bathing of the unitary body-soul, far more powerful than that brought about by superficial rinsing in the waters of crossing places, the song approves pilgrimage so long as the goal of encountering divinity is mainained. Yet it also leaves open the possibility that journeys are unnecessary. Gam Shyamji, yearning for Niranjani's black marble icon, or Madhu Mali, singing of Ghatiyali's *cār dhām,* both expressed aspects of this understanding. Sohan, my friend and sometime cook, responded to the question "Is God found in *tīrtha*s?" by tapping her chest and saying with an indulgent smile, as to a child, "No, God is in this jug." The clay jug is a common metaphor for the fragile body as container of an imperishable soul.

A *nirguṇ bhajan* performed by Ghatiyali's Nath-led singing party takes a far stronger position against external journeying. Rhetorically posing the question "What Is Outside Wandering?" in its refrain, the *bhajan* employs the term *baṭaknā*—a verb associated with the miseries of lost souls. Yet the reference is to visiting *tīrtha*s—a wandering usually denoted by *ghūmnā* with its connotations of pleasurable aimlessness. The one who wanders (*baṭaknā*) is trapped in a maze, condemned to futile, circular motion like a ghost; but the one who wanders (*ghūmnā*) is irresponsible and free, like a holy man. The *bhajan* then answers itself, predisposed by the pejorative weight of *baṭaknā,* with a statement that effectively denies the value of all external pilgrimage: "Sixty-eight fords are right here, see them. Take *darshan* in the body-soul."

The verses go on to pose homologies between external crossing places or enshrined deities and locations within the human body: Jagdish is in the *jāng* (thigh); Kedar—referring to the Himalayan shrine of Kedarnath—is in the *kamar* (waist); Chatrapati—a royal title of Lord Vishnu—is in the *chātī* (chest). As is evident from these examples, the identification of outer with inner *tīrtha*s is based on sound homologies. There is at least an alliterative relation between each name of deity or crossing place and its bodily equivalent in the hymn. Yet the message of this hymn is not heard merely as an extended geographic-microcosmic pun.[14] As it is summed up in writing by my Nath assistant, the teaching is both straightforward and mysterious: "Hey Human! You should obtain full knowledge of your own body. Within this 'body-shaped-like-a-soul' (*ātmā-rūpī-sharīr*) exist all crossing places."

Concepts of inner pilgrimage in terms of virtue and purity of mind—briefly discussed in this chapter's opening—are standard accompaniments to pilgrimage propaganda. In Sanskrit texts (and their simple Hindi versions) outer journeys may be lauded while foundations in the primary necessity for inner truth are retained. Popular devotional poets of both *nirguṇ* and *saguṇ* traditions, as well as reformist leaders—from the early South Indian Virashaiva saints through the Arya Samaj's founder, Dayanad Sarasvati—all totally disparaged external pilgrimage rituals. Yet despite their rejection of the practice, they appropriated the vigor of pilgrimage imagery to their own purposes.[15] Even Kabir's legendary insistence on *not* dying in Kashi, as much as it was a denial of vain external hopes of salvation, can be seen as a dramatic co-opting through inversion of pilgrimage ideology.

Rajasthani villagers' strong skepticism over the worth of superficial bathing—its reduction to "dirtying the water"—is not at all out of line, then, with received wisdom in many streams of Hindu tradition. The Nath *bhajan,* however, rather than referring to diffuse preferences for ideas of inner morality or devotion probably

14. Sounds have both inherent meaning and power in Indian tradition. A Hindu ethno-linguistics would be far from Saussurean.

15. Sarasvati, for example, writes: "*Tīrtha* is that by means of which the ocean of misery is crossed: In other words, I hold that *tīrtha*s are good works such as speaking the truth, acquisition of knowledge, society of the wise and good. . . . *No places or water of rivers are tīrtha*s [italics his]" (cited in Yadav, ed., 1976:60). Paltu Das, an eighteenth-century Hindi *sant* who lived in the North Indian pilgrimage center of Ayodhya, declared in his verses the full futility of external worship and pilgrimage—valuing instead the words of the guru in his heart: "I won't take my final rest at Kashi / Or take the pilgrim's walk around the town. / Should I reach Prayag, I won't go to the bathing place, / Nor will I sacrifice myself to Jagganath at Puri. / . . . Sadhu, I'll abandon all God's names / to take the one my guru gave" (cited in D. Gold 1988). Ramanujan's translations of twelfth-century South Indian saints' devotional verses reveal simple scorn for external religion: "With a whole temple / in this body / where's the need / for another?" (1973:153).

derives from specific yogic practices: techniques of directing the breath along subtle channels to nexes of inner concentration.[16]

Most villagers, of course, know nothing of such esoteric practices, except perhaps as awe-inspiring rumors. But the notion of a "body-shaped-like-a-soul" is not alien to the common person's way of thought. An understanding of the human body as microcosm is popularly held and can readily accommodate a homology, such as the one posed by this *bhajan,* between specific sites within the body and on the earth. Moreover, as informants sometimes told me, nothing is outside that was not previously inside—giving priority to the inner as source of substance and power. Their ground for this assertion was a prevailing image of creation itself emerging from within, a village version of the cosmic-egg motif.[17] Most Ghatiyalians, then, accept the antiwandering *bhajan*'s message as consonant with cosmic realities.

The same persons who accept the premise that everything outside is also and primarily within, are clearly not discouraged from making pilgrimages. Such knowledge rarely impedes external actions, although it may console those whose outer journeys and rites have brought disappointment. This chapter, which began with reference to textual irresolutions regarding the moral value of journeying as totally efficacious and totally useless, closes with similarly construed tensions between external ritual and inner devotion or discipline. Such ambivalences—in the literal sense of mobile valuations—are deeply rooted in and expressive of Hindu tradition. On the *darshan* bus tour temple viewing, river bathing,

16. There exists in esoteric yoga a teaching in which the adept may direct his breath to particular parts of the body. This is spoken of as an inner pilgrimage whose vast fruits, for the yogic technician, may be harvested without any regard for external, behavioral virtues. The *Yoga Darshana Upanishad* tells us: "Your sins will be washed away, whether you have made love with your wife or even with your own daughter, if you carry out the pilgrimages within your own body from one *tīrtha* to another" (cited in Varenne 1976:211). See also Eliade 1969, 1975 on the internalization of ritual in yoga, and Morinis 1984:282–299 for an interpretation of Hindu pilgrimage in relation to concepts of homologies between macrocosm and microcosm.

17. For the cosmic egg, see Dimmitt and van Buitenen 1978:32. The creation tale I recorded from a caste genealogist of the Gujars who visited Ghatiyali during my residence there told of the egg being made from the body-grime of Spotless-Shapeless and nourished into growth—until it cracked in two—in the hands of a primeval goddess. Brahma, Vishnu, and Shiva then emerged from the shell, whose top half became the sky and its lower half the earth.

and brahmanical rites often seemed to be the least meaningful parts of the journey to participants. Many felt at heart that it was their inner resolution to go and the outer hardship and expense endured as signs of that resolution which validated whatever fruits, gross or subtle, they did or did not hope to attain in this life or future lives.

6. Conclusion: What Is Outside Wandering?

This book attempts to answer the question "What is outside wandering?" not as the Nath *bhajan* poses it, rhetorically and didactically, but as the anthropologist creates it, literally and evocatively. I have gathered up and then surrendered the fruits of my own fieldwork pilgrimage, a process that has certainly involved some sorting, ordering, polishing, paring, and trimming of these fruits. The results are composed of fact and flavor, ritual paraphernalia and chorused or antiphonal voices, data recorded, experiences felt, inspiration, and intuition. In conclusion I reconsider the process of composition and review some of the concepts on which it reflects. I recapitulate styles of journeying and reemphasize the nature and significance of returns.

Stephen Tyler, in his contribution to an anthology concerned with the art of ethnographic writing, suggests that a postmodern ethnography (which doesn't yet exist) would be, among other things, "an evocation of quotidian experience, a palpable reality that uses everyday speech to suggest what is ineffable, not through abstraction but by means of the concrete" (1986:136). Such has been my enterprise here, to a large extent. But it is not Tyler (read two years after the bulk of this work was completed) whose sensibilities I emulate; rather it is India itself.[1] To suggest what is ineffable by means of the concrete is a dominant Hindu process.

The infinite profusion of name and form, icon and story that makes Hindu tradition so dense yet permeable is neither solely

1. It is probaly not irrelevant that Tyler's own early fieldwork and ethnographic writings were based in South Asia.

crude trappings nor delusive trap (although sometimes spoken of as both by those who know it from within). Rather, these are manifestations of a reality understood as fluctuating, of power understood as transmutable from gross to subtle forms and back, and of supreme deities who choose to play.[2] "It's one single illusion" (*ek hī māyā hai*) was a statement I tired of hearing from villagers in response to questions that sought, for example, discrimination among powerful beings in ways meaningless to my patient friends and neighbors. If I asked "What is the difference between Lakshmi and Dasa Mata?" or "What is Dev Narayanji's relation to Vishnu?" I might be thus wisely and summarily silenced.

The concrete, however, is not at all so glibly subsumed in the ineffable in practice as it may be in discourse. If Dasa Mata is the same as Lakshmi, and both are forms of the one Goddess, Dasa Mata's stories and ten-knotted yellow string, her handful of grains, her special days, and her specific domestic blessings make her worship unique. And the same woman who could refer me to "one *māyā*" could also elaborate instructively on Dasa Mata's required routines, which she personally fulfilled with meticulous care.

A Hindu world view would seem to be composed of such multiple, shifting perspectives, ever approximating but never realizing the whole. In the preceding chapters I have presented and interpreted the attitudes and experiences of Rajasthani villagers as pilgrims. No doubt the results may be characterized as a fragmentary fantasy of reality (Tyler 1986), even as they display elements of well-documented and properly grueling ethnographic research. But the reality they fantasize is understood, in any case, as fanciful (O'Flaherty 1984).

Within four arbitrary if logically nested settings—intellectual and indological inquiries, personal crises and adjustments, social-cultural-historical location, and popular religious practice—I have described three kinds of pilgrimage and have shown their interlacing with ideas about death and birth grouped into four configura-

2. See S. Daniel for an elegant demonstration of how the concept *līlā* (divine play) is a "culturally patterned mode for ordering the multiplicity of the Hindu world view" (1983:59). See also Egnor 1978:174, and 1988 and Ramanujan 1980 for related perceptions of South Asian thought processes. Other appreciations of the interplay among realities—gross, subtle, and/or illusory—are found in Waghorne and Cutler, eds., 1985, and O'Flaherty 1984, a particularly spellbinding and mind-stretching account.

tions. The ethnosociological aspirations that guided this project were for congruence between my interpretations and indigenous perceptions. I knew that really I could neither share nor replicate native visions (Geertz 1976). But by retaining indigenous categories and heeding indigenous exegesis I sought not to violate those visions.

I answered the question "What is outside wandering?" with a detailed description of three patterns in pilgrims' journeys and motivations. Travels to the shrines of regional gods are often explicitly instrumental, and most pilgrims' motives, generalized as sorrows and troubles of the perishable body (often caused by dissatisfied spirits of the dead), are straightforward enough. Although some make these journeys out of devotional affiliation, for the sake of pressing down pebbles, this shelter relationship almost always has its source in boons previously received, work previously accomplished. The value of such journeys is questioned only in terms of efficacy. Do the deities deliver what is asked of them? If one doesn't, another may do so.

The Ganges pilgrimage to submerge bones is avowedly made to satisfy public opinion as much as to improve the condition of ancestral spirits. Such a show will be derided as useless if attentions are paid to the spirits of recently deceased persons when no care was taken for their comforts while they were alive. Yet all villagers who can raise the cash perform the flower pilgrimage with compunction. And the flow of Ganges water back to the village, which always follows the transportation of bones away from it, occasions communal celebration evoking vitality and fertility.

Journeys made to wander are imbued with the greatest ambivalence, probably because their highest potential fruit is, by definition, unseekable and unclaimable. Yet despite the certainty that, for those with inner devotion and clean minds, Ganges flows in the kneading-platter, these *darshan* tours are increasingly popular among Rajasthani peasants today. For there is also a conviction, simply but eloquently expressed in the song of Ram's golden chariot, that pilgrimage to crossing places may put humans where divine beneficence and even release—the final uplifting of the spirit beyond mortality and natality—are more readily approached.

The grouping into three kinds of journeys—for work, to sink flowers, and for wandering—reflects in fact one categorization of journeying (but not the only one) held by villagers. The *jātrā/yātrā* distinction discussed in chapter 2 omits "sinking flowers" as a distinct category of trip. Indeed, the latter category was infrequently produced spontaneously in discussions of *yātrā*. Nonetheless, when asked, everyone agreed it was different from journeys just for wandering—obviously so, since it had a definite purpose. Still less could it be equated or merged with visits to the local goddesses and gods for boons.

Some pilgrims' paths that I shared with villagers are not described here. I attended Pushkar Mela with a number of Ghatiyalians in the fall of 1979; participated with Miller, two priests, and a devotee of Dev Narayanji in a remarkable journey through that deity's mythic geography in the early spring of 1980; attended Ujjain's Kumbha Mela in the company of my Rajput landlady, the Gujar priest of Puvali ka Devji, and several of his henchmen during the hot season of that year; and just as the monsoon rains were breaking undertook my own journey, by hired jeep and in the company of three friends and assistants-cum-*jātarīs*, to a number of important shrines in Ajmer, Bundi, and Kota districts.

Certainly participation in these journeys contributed to my overall understandings of pilgrimage; why exclude them from this account? Two of these, since they were initiated by foreigners, might easily be dispensed with as somehow "inauthentic." But the omission here of *melā* pilgrimages needs some further explanation. Perhaps they don't fit into my scheme? In fact, I would argue that they do fit, but not quite as nicely as those I've chosen to exemplify it.

Melā journeys, where the site is a *tīrtha*, as are Pushkar and Ujjain,[3] come within the third motivational complex: for *darshan*, baths, and wandering (and for health, heaven, and release in pamphlet promises). Central to these *melā*s' establishment and continued flourishing existence is the idea that certain astrological condi-

3. Besides the famed great *melā*s held at pan-Hindu *tīrtha*s, innumerable lesser fairs take place at regional and local shrines in Rajasthan and throughout India. Puvali ka Devji had two each year, and Ghatiyali's Tejaji shrine also was the scene of an annual fair which attracted visitors from many surrounding villages. I attended these and many other local *melā*s, usually in the company of folks seeking amusement rather than the grace of the gods—whether as boons or as shelter. For a vivid description of some regional *melā*s in Rajasthan, see Erdman 1985:59–68; see also *Census of India* 1961.

tions make certain baths at certain moments extraordinarily auspicious. These premises are ancient and enduring. Both the full moon of Kartik at Pushkar and the Kumbha *melā*s in their four rotating sites are chartered in the *Mahabharata* and *Puranas* as extraordinary chances to harvest infinite rewards from a *tīrtha* bath.[4]

Villagers, however, don't understand much about the exact nature of these extremely auspicious baths nor about the benefits to be had from taking them. Many indeed say that a pilgrim who goes for love of the gods and not for amusement of the mind does not go at *melā* time. For *melā*s, if they offer intangible accumulated potencies of divine power, present an array of vital, sensual distractions concentrated in one location that is equally awesome. At both Pushkar and the Kumbha *melās,* so much was happening in the way of cultural performances—plays, epic recitations, all-night singing of *bhajans,* sermons, puppet shows, and endless expanses of fascinating, seductive markets—that my companions had as little time or patience for answering questions as I had for asking them. Whereas the Puri bus pilgrimage afforded plenty of leisurely hours, on and off the bus, to interview and contemplate, the *melā*s were temporal whirlwinds and conceptual whirlpools. These trips left me dazzled by an overdose of impressions, frazzled through having my attention split so many ways, and baffled in my attempts to elicit from participants coherent interpretations of the meaning of such *yātrā*s.

My strongest memory of Pushkar Fair is of being pulled all over town at 4:00 A.M. on the full-moon night by a female companion whose guidance I had sought for the climactic bathing experience at dawn. She was looking for a secluded place to relieve herself before the auspicious moment for entering the water, and we were actually late in arriving at the *ghāṭ*s because of her urgent belief that before a *tīrtha* bath one must empty the bowels. Thus I spent Kartik Purnima's prime moment on the edge of a reeking field dotted with shadowy squatters.

*Melā*s can also be difficult environments for a foreigner attempting participant observation fieldwork. At the Ujjain Kumbha my five fellow pilgrims were as disconcerted as I was by

4. For Kumbha Mela, see Lal 1961:229, and Roy and Devi 1955. The virtues of a Kartik Purnima bath at Pushkar are proclaimed in the *Mahabharata* 1976, 2:374–375, and the *melā* taking place on this auspicious occasion is also described in *Census of India* 1961:77–80 and Narasimhachary 1977.

the attentions our small company received from the naked, ash-covered renouncers who—accustomed to encounters with hippies—kept greeting me with expansive gestures and intimate remarks and offering me their hashish pipes. My companions had come expressly to take advantage of the unique opportunity afforded by the fair to have *darshan* of these holy men, assembled once every four years from their mountain and forest retreats and perpetual wanderings. But villagers' concept of taking *darshan* did not include attracting special notice from, or having verbal exchanges with, the godlike objects of their gazes. After all, these were power-filled, potentially dangerous, and notoriously capricious characters. My group was sufficiently upset by the whole experience of touring the Kumbha *melā* with a foreigner to cut short their trip by two days and several temples on my account. And I confess that my attempts to dissuade them were weak.

Clearly a selective process was at work when I chose to represent the third kind of journeying by the Puri bus pilgrimage and excluded *melā* experiences from all descriptive consideration in the body of this book. The differences between journeys to *melā*s and journeys to crossing places at ordinary times are highlighted in the vernacular portion of Ghatiyali's wedding rites. Among the promises made by the wife to her husband is a pledge not to go about wantonly with girlfriends to *melā*s. For his part the husband promises his bride not to make *tīrthayātrā*s without her. These two promises are not really reciprocal. For her, the vow to eschew *melā*s is a vow to avoid public display of herself and her charms, and ensuing temptations to stray. *Melā*s—especially regional fairs, but that would include Pushkar for Ghatiyalians—are prime set tings for flirtation. The man's promise, however, means that he will not deny his wife participation in the subtle benefits of pilgrimage as meritorious action; that he will share the higher fruits of journeying with his ritual half-body. Perhaps one explanation for my omission of *melā*s would be to say that, like a good Rajasthani wife, I have foregone their diversions and distractions and chosen not to stray from the path of *dharma*.

If the three kinds of pilgrimage described in this book are fairly closely aligned with Ghatiyalians' own categories of journeying, the four responses to mortality are somewhat less definitive. I never in fact asked informants to produce a list of all the things that can happen to the soul after death. Instead I said, "Tell me about *jhūjhārjī*" or "How do you get *moksha*?" In the natural course of conversation or unstructured interviews, however, one such topic quite often led to another.

Comprehensive cosmological systematizations are certainly available in Hindu tradition—in the *Garuda Purana,* for example. But for villagers whose domestic and soteriological concerns make several understandings of death simultaneously germane in various contexts of their lives, *Garuda Purana* is one source of knowledge among many. The shrine priest who talks to spirits is another; the pandit who invokes the gods and ancestors with his Sanskrit *mantra*s is another; the Nath guru with his mysterious spells and his affinity for graveyards is another. Just as world-creation and world-destruction happen many times in many ways in Hindu myth,[5] so do the soul's passages through births and deaths in Hindu cosmologies.

As for the set of attitudes and practices which I call a fourth response to mortality—a complex involving sexuality and female power—some of it came from folklore and ritual. Calf Twelfth's rites, dances, jokes, and worshipful stories strongly suggested that life-affirming sexuality on the part of women offered a bountiful replenishing of the human community faced with death's losses. This specific analysis, however, reinforced poetically the cumulative precipitate of almost two years spent among a population who cared obsessively about getting children by means of processes divine and organic.

The associations, as I have cautiously called them, between ways of understanding and dealing with the consequences of death, and pilgrimage and its aims, were at least sometimes on the evident, observable surface: pilgrims' concern with ghosts, bones, and the road ahead supported such contiguities. I suggested that the focus on reproduction had more to do with home than with journeying. This is true even when that focus is an acknowledged component of the pilgrimage process. The coconut from pouch-filling must be taken home; the Ganges water, obtained after sinking flowers, is joyfully carried by women toward the dark inner chamber of the house.

While my explications of lingering spirits, ancestors, and release were based on specific ritual attentions to particular spirits of the dead in certain conditions of existence, the fourth complex of

5. For varieties of Hindu creation, thematically sorted in different ways, see Dimmitt and van Buitenen 1978:16–58 and O'Flaherty 1975:25–55.

values made no clear references to life after death. However, it seemed obliquely connected with the concept of rebirth or transmigration of souls—the Hindu tenet best known in the West but least stressed, it would seem, in village traditions.

Practices connected with notions of rebirth have appeared in these pages, but they only highlight the vagaries surrounding the concept. For example, the idea that eating an ancestral *piṇḍa* helps a woman to conceive a child suggests an immediacy of rebirth and a recycling of spirits in the same human lineage. But the mark observed in the flour placed on the site of death during cremation may indicate immanent birth as an animal. And the very common reference to the necessity to wander through eighty-four *lākh* of nonhuman births before entering another human womb expands the possibilities and time scale much further and in dizzying fashion.

The relative underemphasis on rebirth does not imply disbelief in the process but rather reflects the uncertainties of its mechanisms and chronology. Above all, rebirth is less relevant to villagers because there are no channels of communication and exchange with the reborn as there are with ghosts and ancestors. It is, however, on rebirth and redeath that the flux of *samsāra* is premised. Except for release, all other outcomes of death are temporary conditions leading to birth and death again.

Just as cyclical natality and mortality underlie other concepts of death, so the fertility motif in village religion, with its playful and serious, bawdy and esoteric expressions, seems to penetrate most aspects of religious life. Here it has been highlighted sporadically. Shrine pilgrimage for pouch-filling or impregnation was described at some length in chapter 3. The flowering garden, the family with children, the fertile womb were shown to be vital factors in the more general well-being sought at shrines. Satisfied ancestors (*pitṛ*) as well as pacified lingering spirits of the dead (*pattar* and *jhūjhārjī*) are all understood as having some authority to inhibit or permit births within their lineages. And birth is also a way of satisfying ancestral spirits, fulfilling the moral debt owed to them. Gangotsav, the closing rite of a pilgrimage to sink flowers, was analyzed in chapter 4 as being permeated with reproductive imagery.

The journey to wander suits the close of the householder life stage (although by no means is its accomplishment restricted to the aged). On a *darshan yātrā,* although traveling "paired" is highly valued, sexual intercourse is definitively proscribed. The life aim of release, associated with aimless pilgrimage, opposes sexuality and family bonds, although even here procreative mysteries sometimes image or express higher ones. Such journeys may at times be viewed as ways of transmuting or refining sexual interests and energies. The legendary King Gopi Cand was caused by his guru to go on a *cār dhām yātrā* carrying a tray of fire on his head in order to make him a firm, literally a "cooked," disciple. This was his guru's way of preparing him for the ultimate ordeal of his renunciation: to part from his queen by calling her "Mother" (a conflation so painful that, despite his firing by pilgrimage, he almost fails to accomplish it).

Most pilgrims returning from *tīrtha*s, unlike Gopi Cand, need to rejoin, rather than finally part with, loved ones. The night spent at Path Mother's place, the welcome by women with songs and with vessels lush with sprouts, the sharing out of *prasād* and other souvenirs, all serve to reestablish connections between pilgrims and their village world, even as these customs recognize and honor the changes wrought by journeying. The fruitfulness of most outside wanderings ultimately does rest in return—whether it is to a state of health and harmony, a lineage blessed with sons and unafflicted by restless spirits of the dead, or a knowledge of divinity within that brings the human spirit closer to release from round-trip cycles.

Glossary

āratī	Auspicious (clockwise) circling of a tray with worship ingredients before a deity (usually at sunrise and twilight) or before the chief worshipper who has just completed a ritual (usually by a "sister"); also refers to a prayer recited or sung on such occasions. Elsewhere in India *āratī* is often defined as "waving lights" because that which is circled auspiciously will be a burning lamp or lamps. In Rajasthan, although a wick lamp may be present, it is not the defining feature of *āratī*.
ātmā	Soul; self.
ātmā-rūpī-jīv	Spirit in the shape of a soul; the transmigrating self.
ātmā-rūpī-sharīr	Body in the shape of a soul; the perishable body as microcosm.
avatār	Descended incarnation; most frequently refers to the God Vishnu's births in various bodies for various purposes.
baṭaknā	To wander fruitlessly, lost, as a ghost.
bhabhūt	Ashes of burnt offerings made on cow-dung coals; Rajasthani for *vibhūti,* deriving from a term for God meaning omnipresent, all-powerful.
bhagvān	God, the Lord in an unspecified sense; may also be term of address or reference for a particular male divinity.
bhaktī	Devotion; devotional love; a way of approaching God defined in opposition to ritual, to knowledge, to asceticism.

bhāv A person possessed by a deity; the phenomenon of a deity possessing a person; also existence, emotion, essence.

bhāvārth Essential, deep or hidden meaning (as of an esoteric song or story).

bhopā Shrine-priest; non-Brahman priest.

cār dhām Four established places, pilgrims' goals; traditionally Badrinath in the north, Puri in the east, Dwarka in the west, and Rameshvar in the south.

caraṇāmṛt Foot-nectar; water used to wash icons (or the feet of a living guru); a powerful substance with curative properties, distributed to devotees who may drink it, apply it to their bodies, or carry it home in bottles.

ḍākaṇ "Witch"; a malevolent female capable of intruding into the bodies of other women, causing them physical distress, and "eating the livers" of their unborn children.

dān Gift given, frequently in ritual circumstances, to priest or temple; a selfless gift associated with acquiring religious merit and removing sin.

ḍangaṛī Pilgrim's walking stick.

ḍangaṛī rāt Walking-sticks night; an all-night celebration following a pilgrim's return, during which he feasts his pilgrimage companions and close kin.

darshan Auspicious sight of a powerful icon or living being; *darshan* is not "done" but "taken" and conveys a sense of power and blessings flowing in through the eyes (as well as prayers and devotion flowing out).

deva Deity, divinity.

devasthān Deity's place; a shrine.

devī-devatā Goddesses-and-gods; collective term often used for lesser, local deities in opposition to, for example, Shiva or Vishnu or Durga.

dhām Established deity's place; in Rajasthan often has the connotation of a secondary place whose powers are derivative from another.

dharma Biomoral duty; righteousness; coherence; one of the four human aims (see *purushārth*).

dharmarāstā Road of *dharma;* pilgrims' road.

dharmashālā Rest house for pilgrims.

dhūp Smouldering cow-dung coals on which *ghī* and other food substances are burned as offerings to deities and other powers. In Hindi *dhūp* may refer to incense, but in Rajasthan it is meaningfully differentiated from commercially produced, perfumed incense sticks.

Gangoj; Gangotsav Celebration of Ganges water; a festive event in which a pilgrim opens the Ganges water he or she has brought home, usually from Hardwar, in a sealed container, and eventually distributes it to guests.

gati Passage, from one condition to another; motion, movement. *Gati* is often used to refer to liberation after death, either from a ghost state or from all life cycles.

ghāṭ Riverbank or lakeside bathing place.

ghī Clarified butter, a ubiquitous food and ritual substance.

ghūmnā To wander aimlessly but pleasurably.

gotra Lineage; name shared by descendants of a single ancestor; exogamous kin category.

gṛhastha Householder; a man in the second stage of life, associated with marriage, child-rearing, money-earning, and sacrificial ritual.

gyān-carcā Knowledge-talk; informal conversations on deep religious subjects, often held when a known expert is present, or during interludes between singing esoteric, difficult-to-interpret hymns.

jāgaraṇ All-night session devoted to singing worshipful songs; literally "wake" but without the funeral implications, as such sessions may precede not only rites for the dead but weddings, house construction, enshrinement of deities, feasts dedicated to shrine gods, and many other events.

jāti Birth-group; here translated as caste.

jātrā Pilgrimage, any journey (in Rajasthani).

jātarī Pilgrim, traveler (in Rajasthani).

jholī Pouch, pocket, sack; a recepticle formed in a woman's wrap.

jholī bharnā Pouch-filling; ritual impregnation performed at shrines to help women conceive.

jhūjhārjī Deity deriving from the spirit of a warrior killed in battle or any married adult who has met an untimely death; such spirits usually reveal themselves through dream or divination as desiring worship.

jīv Live-essence; spirit.

joṛe Paired, joined; describes the union of husband and wife for ritual purposes, including pilgrimage made as a couple.

juvārā Green sprouted grasses, usually of millet, planted for ritual use.

kalash Crowning orb, sometimes gold-covered, on top of a temple; also, a round clay pot in which a deity is installed, sprouts are planted, or pure water is carried on ritual occasions—here translated "vessel."

kālī yuga The fourth, most degenerate era in Hindu chronology; the present; a ready explanation for the failings of men and gods.

kayā Unitary body-soul; the perishable body united with a surviving soul.

kismat Fate, destiny.

lākh 10,000; also lac, a resinous substance used to make colorful bangles.

lingam Phallus; a stone icon of Lord Shiva's erect phallus, the form in which he is most commonly worshipped.

mahātmya Greatness, glory; used for oral and printed descriptions of the special histories and qualities of pilgrimage centers.

man Human mind, but not so valued as its English counterpart; considered wayward, and easily deluded.

mandīr Temple.

mantra Powerful syllables from Sanskrit used in fire oblations, meditation, exorcism.

mantra-tantra Verbal spells; refers to incomprehensible, magical incantations.

maṭhaṛī Grains piled on a Rajasthani deity's shrine-platform and kept separate from other categories of grain-offerings; frequently used for grain-pick divination.

māyā Illusion; the nature of the created world.

māyājāl Net of illusion; the snaring attractions of the world.

melā Religious fair, frequently combining carnival, market, and devotional atmosphere and activities.

meḷī "Witch" (see *ḍākaṇ*) without a living body, whose intrusions are consequently more dangerous and more difficult to remove.

moksha Release—from any bonds, but specifically from the bondage of cycles of rebirth and redeath, that is from *samsāra*.

mukti Release (variant of *moksha*).

nīm A kind of tree whose branches and bitter leaves are used, both medicinally and in worship, as purifying agents.

nirguṇa Without qualities; a way of describing God as formless, partless, having neither character nor history.

nirguṇa bhajan Devotional hymn praising the Lord without qualities.

nirguṇa bhaktī Devotion to the Lord without qualities.

oṛhnī Wrap; a cloth worn by Rajasthani women over their skirts and blouses. It is tucked into the skirt, wrapped around the waist, and pulled up over shoulders and head.

paṇḍā Pilgrims' priest; Bramans who live in pilgrimage centers and hold, as inherited family tradition, the rights to perform rituals for pilgrims.

panth	Path; a religious teaching; a group whose members follow a certain teaching, sharing its particular practices.
pāp	Sin, in the sense of major transgressions.
pāp dūr karnā	To remove sin.
pār karnā	To cross over, to take to the other side; used for liberation of an indeterminate nature, like *gati*. That is, the other side may be the other side of an immediate difficulty, a whirlpool; or it may be the other side of existence.
parcyā	Proof; manifestation of a deity's power.
pattar	Spirit of a deceased, unmarried male—usually a child—enshrined in a silver or gold neck-medallion.
phal	Fruit; good results of action.
phūl	Flower; bones of the dead; child in the womb.
phūl boḷāṇo	To submerge bones, ritually, in pure water.
piṇḍa	Flour ball (or rice ball) used in various kinds of offerings made to spirits of recently deceased persons, as well as to ancestral spirits.
piṇḍadān	Offerings of *piṇḍa*s.
pitṛ	Father, ancestor; spirits of deceased relations who have left the ghost state and the home environment but have not yet been reborn or released.
pitṛlok	Ancestor-world; the realm where ancestral spirits exist.
prasād	Favor, grace, blessed leavings from offerings made to a deity and returned to the worshipper.
pret	Ghost; disembodied human spirit.
pret-ātmā	Ghost-soul; spirit of newly deceased person while it lingers near the house, or any lingering spirit.
pūjā	Worship; ritual offerings and attentions given to deities.
puṇya	Merit that accrues from selfless acts or acts in accordance with *dharma*.
purushārtha	Human aim, end, or goal. There are traditionally four *purushārtha*s: *moksha, kāmā, artha,* and *dharma* (release, desire, gain, and biomoral duty).

rāti jagā — Night-awake; all-night singing session held by women, usually to honor or appease one or more deities.

saguṇa — With qualities; a way of describing God as personified, mythologized.

saguṇa bhajan — Hymn praising and describing God with qualities.

saguṇa bhaktī — Devotion to God with qualities.

samādhi — Advanced state of meditation where there is no awareness of surroundings; meditation until death; the stone monuments commemorating sites where advanced religious adepts took "living *samādhi*"; any renouncer's tomb.

samsāra — World of flux; endless cycles of rebirth and redeath that are the nature of all existence this side of release; sometimes, the family.

samskāra — Polishing, moulding, impression; hence, (a) life-cycle rite; (b) residues both good and bad left on the self from former births.

sannyāsa — Renunciation; the condition of having left the world, died to family and caste, given up all possessions.

sannyāsī — World-renouncer.

saphal — Successful; literally, with fruit.

sapiṇḍī shrāddha kriyā — Action of faithful offerings that unite *piṇḍa*s; refers to the rites held twelve days (or months) after death in which the spirit of a recently deceased person is joined with three generations of ancestors.

satī — True wife who burns herself on her husband's funeral pyre; the act of doing this.

Satī Mā̃ — Goddess deriving from the spirit of a woman who by commiting *satī* ended her life, virtuously but abruptly.

savā — One and one-quarter; a number frequently used in the amounts offered at shrine rituals.

savāmaṇī — Feast, usually prepared and served at a shrine in fulfillment of a vow; made from one and one-quarter maunds (approximately fifty kilos) of wheat flour and corresponding quantities of ingredients for a spicy sauce dish and generally a simple sweet as well.

shakti Power, energy, the Goddess as power.

shānti Peace, calm; can refer to the condition of a human spirit satiated by appropriate funeral rites and willing to leave the scenes of its former life.

sharīr Perishable body.

sharm Modesty or shame, felt or affected by women in the presence of husbands, elder male in-laws, and male strangers.

shrāddha Faithful offerings to spirits of dead kin as ancestors.

ṭhākur Local ruler, village lord, name of God.

tīrtha Ford, crossing place, pilgrimage center.

tīrthayātrā Journey to pilgrimage center.

uddhār Deliverance; generally used as equivalent to *moksha* or *mukti* but carries stronger devotional connotations of a divine deliverer's agency.

yātrā Pilgrimage, any journey.

References

Allchin, F. R., trans. 1966. *Vinaya-Patrikā (The Petition to Rām),* by Tulsī Dās. London: George Allen and Unwin.

Atal, Yogesh. 1961. "The Cult of Bheru in a Mewar Village and Its Vicinage." In *Aspects of Religion in Indian Society,* edited by L. P. Vidyarthi. Meerut: Kedar Nath Ram Nath.

———. 1968. *The Changing Frontiers of Caste.* Delhi: National Publishing House.

Babb, Lawrence A. 1975. *The Divine Hierarchy.* New York: Columbia University Press.

———. 1982. "Glancing: Visual Interaction in Hinduism." *Journal of Anthropological Research* 37: 387–401.

Bahl, Kali Caran. 1972. "On the Present State of Modern Rajasthani Grammar." *Parampara* 33–34:1–76.

———. 1980. *A Structural Grammar of Modern Rajasthani.* Jodhpur: Rajasthani Shodh Sansthan.

Bauman, Richard. 1977. *Verbal Art as Performance.* Prospect Heights, Ill.: Waveland Press.

Beck, Brenda. 1976. "The Symbolic Merger of Body, Space and Cosmos in Hindu Tamil Nadu." *Contributions to Indian Sociology* (N.S.) 10(2): 213–243.

Bhagavād Gītā. 1973. Translated by R. C. Zaehner. London: Oxford University Press.

Bharati, Agehananda. 1963. "Pilgrimage in the Indian Tradition." *History of Religions* 3:135–167.

———. 1970. "Pilgrimage Sites and Indian Civilization." In *Chapters in Indian Civilization,* edited by J. W. Elder. Dubuque, Iowa: Kendell/Hunt.

Bhardwaj, Surinder M. 1973. *Hindu Places of Pilgrimage in India: A Study in Cultural Geography.* Berkeley and Los Angeles: University of California Press.

Binford, Mira R. 1976. "Mixing in the Color of Ram of Ranuja." In *Hinduism: New Essays in the History of Religions,* edited by B. L. Smith. Leiden: E. J. Brill.

Bishnoi, Sonaram. 1979. *Bābā Rāmdev Sambandhī Loka-Sāhitya* (Folk Literature Connected with Ramdevji). Jodhpur: Usha Publishing House.

Bloch, Maurice, and Jonathan Parry. 1982. "Introduction: Death and the Regeneration of Life." In *Death and the Regeneration of Life,* edited by Maurice Bloch and Jonathan Parry. Cambridge: Cambridge University Press.

Bouillier, Véronique. 1979. *Naître Renonçant: Une Caste de Sannyāsi Villageois au Népal Central.* Nanterre: Laboratoire d'Ethnologie.

Briggs, George W. 1973. *Gorakhnath and the Kanphata Yogis.* Delhi: Motilal Banarsidass.

Buhler, Georg, trans. 1969. *The Laws of Manu.* New York: Dover Publications.

Carstairs, G. Morris. 1961. "Patterns of Religious Observances in Three Villages of Rajasthan." In *Aspects of Religion in Indian Society,* edited by L. P. Vidyarthi. Meerut: Kedar Nath Ram Nath.

———. 1975. *The Twice-Born: A Study of a Community of High-Caste Hindus.* Bloomington: Indiana University Press.

———. 1983. *Death of a Witch: A Village in North India 1950–1981.* London: Hutchinson.

Census of India. 1961. "Rajasthan: Fairs and Festivals." Volume XIV, Part 7-B.

Chakravarti, Anand. 1975. *Contradiction and Change: Emerging Patterns of Authority in a Rajasthan Village.* Delhi: Oxford University Press.

Chaturvedi, Mahendra, and B. N. Tiwari, eds. 1979. *A Practical Hindi-English Dictionary.* New Delhi: National Publishing House.

Chauhan, Brij Raj. 1967. *A Rajasthan Village.* New Delhi: Vir Publishing House.

Clifford, James. 1983. "Power and Dialogue in Ethnography: Marcel Griaule's Initiation." In *Observers Observed,* edited by George W. Stocking. Madison: University of Wisconsin Press.

Clifford, James, and George E. Marcus, eds. 1986. *Writing Culture: The Poetics and Politics of Ethnography.* Berkeley and Los Angeles: University of California Press.

Cohn, B. S., and McKim Marriott. 1958. "Networks and Centres in the Integration of Indian Civilisation." *Journal of Social Research* 1(1): 1–9.

Crooke, W. 1924. "Hinglaj." *Encyclopedia of Religion and Ethics,* 6:715–716. New York: Charles Scribner's Sons.

Daniel, E. Valentine. 1983. "Karma Divined in a Ritual Capsule." In *Karma: An Anthropological Inquiry,* edited by C. F. Keyes and E. V. Daniel. Berkeley and Los Angeles: University of California Press.

———. 1984. *Fluid Signs: Being a Person the Tamil Way.* Berkeley and Los Angeles: University of California Press.

Daniel, Sheryl B. 1980. "Marriage in Tamil Culture: The Problem of Conflicting 'Models.'" In *The Powers of Tamil Women,* edited by Susan S. Wadley. Syracuse, N.Y.: Maxwell School of Citizenship and Public Affairs.

———. 1983."The Tool Box Approach of the Tamil to the Issues of Moral Responsibility and Human Destiny." In *Karma: An Anthropological Inquiry,* edited by C. F. Keyes and E. V. Daniel. Berkeley and Los Angeles: University of California Press.

Darian, Steven G, 1978. *The Ganges in Myth and History*. Honolulu: The University Press of Hawaii.

Das, Veena. 1977. *Structure and Cognition: Aspects of Hindu Caste and Ritual*. Delhi: Oxford University Press.

———. 1979. "Reflections on the Social Construction of Adulthood." In *Identity and Adulthood,* edited by Sudhir Kakar. Delhi: Oxford University Press.

Dasgupta, Shashibhusan. 1969. *Obscure Religious Cults*. Calcutta: Firma K. L. Mukhopadhyay.

Dash, Vaidya Bhagvan. 1978. *Fundamentals of Ayurvedic Medicine*. Delhi: Bansal and Company.

Devereux, George. 1967. *From Anxiety to Method in the Behavioral Sciences*. The Hague: Mouton.

Dimmitt, Cornelia, and J. A. B. van Buitenen, eds. and trans. 1978. *Classical Hindu Mythology*. Philadelphia: Temple University Press.

Dimock, Edward C. 1966. *The Place of the Hidden Moon*. Chicago: University of Chicago Press.

Dumont, Jean-Paul. 1978. *The Headman and I*. Austin: University of Texas Press.

Dumont, Louis. 1960. "World Renunciation in Indian Religions." *Contributions to Indian Sociology* 4:33–62.

———. 1965. "The Functional Equivalents of the Individual." *Contributions to Indian Sociology* 8:89–99.

———. 1972. *Homo Hierarchicus*. London: Paladin.

———. 1980."La Dette vis-à-vis les Ancêtres et la Catégorie de Sapiṇḍa." *Purusartha* 4:15–38.

———. 1983. "A Modified View of Our Origins: The Christian Beginnings of Modern Individualism." *Contributions to Indian Sociology* (N.S.) 17(1): 1–26.

Dundes, Alan, ed. 1981. *The Evil Eye: A Folklore Casebook*. New York: Garland Publishing.

Dwyer, Kevin. 1977. "The Dialogic of Anthropology." *Dialectical Anthropology* 2:143–151.

———. 1982. *Moroccan Dialogues: Anthropology in Question*. Baltimore:

Johns Hopkins University Press.
Eck, Diana L. 1981a. *Darśan: Seeing the Divine Image in India.* Chambersburg, Pa.: Anima Books.
———. 1981b. "India's Tīrthas: 'Crossings' in Sacred Geography." *History of Religions* 20(4): 323–344.
———. 1982. *Banaras: City of Light.* New York: Alfred A. Knopf.
Egnor, Margaret T. 1978. "The Sacred Spell and other Conceptions of Life in Tamil Culture." Ph.D. dissertation, Department of Anthropology, University of Chicago.
———. 1988. "Ambiguity in the Oral Exegesis of a Sacred Text: *Tirukkōvaiyār.*" *Cultural Anthropology.*
Eliade, Mircea. 1969. *Yoga: Immortality and Freedom.* Princeton: Princeton University Press.
———. 1975. *Patanjali and Yoga.* New York: Shocken Books.
Erdman, Joan L. 1985. *Patrons and Performers in Rajasthan.* Delhi: Chanakya Publications.
Erndl, Kathleen. 1984. "The Play of the Goddess: Possession and Performance in the Panjabi Cult of Seranvali." Paper presented at the Conference on South Asia, Madison, Wisconsin.
Eschmann, Ann C., Hermann Kulke, and Gaya C. Tripathi, eds. 1978. *The Cult of Jagannath and the Regional Tradition of Orissa.* New Delhi: Manohar.
Fabian, Johannes. 1983. *Time and the Other: How Anthropology Makes Its Object.* New York: Columbia University Press.
Garuḍa Purāṇa. 1911. (Saroddhāra) Translated by Ernest Wood and S. V. Subrahmanyam. *The Sacred Books of the Hindus,* vol. 9. Allahabad: Indian Press.
———. 1968. Translated by Manmatha Nath Dutt Shastri. Varanasi: Chowkhamba Sanskrit Series Office.
———. 1979. Ancient Indian Tradition and Mythology Series, vols. 12, 13, 14. Delhi: Motilal Banarsidass.
———. n.d. Edited by Shriyut P. Ramji Sharma. Allahabad: Shri Durga Pustak Bhandar.
Gayā Mahātmya Kathā (Story of the Greatness of Gaya). Gaya: Kailash Pustakalay.
Geertz, Clifford. 1976. "'From a Native's Point of View': On the Nature of Anthropological Understanding." In *Meaning in Anthropology,* edited by K. H. Basso and H. A. Selby. Albuquerque: University of New Mexico Press.
Gold, Ann Grodzins. 1982. *Village Families in Story and Song: An Approach Through Women's Oral Tradition in Rajasthan.* Indiakit Series, Outreach Educational Project, South Asia Language and Area Center, University of Chicago.

———. 1984. "Life Aims and Fruitful Journeys: The Ways of Rajasthani Pilgrims." Ph.D. dissertation, Department of Anthropology, University of Chicago.

———. 1986. "Dharma's Money Emerges: The Value of Giving Gifts at Pilgrimage Centers." Paper presented at the Annual Meeting of the Association for Asian Studies, Chicago.

———. 1987a. "What Do the *Jātarīs* Ask? Intraregional Pilgrimage in Rajasthan." In *The Idea of Rajasthan: Explorations in Regional Identity,* edited by Karine Schomer et al. Unpublished manuscript.

———. 1987b. "Sexuality, Fertility, and Erotic Imagination in Rajasthani Women's Songs." Unpublished manuscript.

Gold, Daniel. 1987. *The Lord as Guru: Hindi Sants in North Indian Tradition.* New York: Oxford University Press.

———. 1988. *Comprehending the Guru: Towards a Grammar of Religious Perception.* Decatur, Ga.: Scholars Press.

Gold, Daniel, and Ann Grodzins Gold. 1984. "The Fate of the Householder Nath." *History of Religions* 24(2): 113–132.

Goswamy, B. N. 1966. "The Records Kept by Priests at Centers of Pilgrimage as a Source of Social and Economic History." *Indian Economic and Social History Review* 3(2): 174–184.

Grierson, George A. 1878. "The Song of Manik Chandra." *Journal of the Asiatic Society of Bengal* 47:135–238.

———. 1885. "Two Versions of the Song of Gopi Cand." *Journal of the Royal Asiatic Society of Bengal* 54:35–55.

Gupta, Dau Dayal. 1979. *Durgā-Mahimā* (Glory of Durga). Delhi: Pustak Mahal.

Gupta, Giri Raj. 1974. *Marriage, Religion, and Society: Pattern of Change in an Indian Village.* Delhi: Vikas Publishing House.

Hansen, Kathryn. 1986. "Navtanki Chapbooks: Written Traditions of a Folk Form." *The India Magazine* (January): 65–72.

Harsha, Vinod. 1980. "Sarp Yoni se Mukti" (Release from a Serpent Birth). *Satyakathā,* pp. 155–160; 205–207.

Hawley, John Stratton. 1981. *At Play with Krishna: Pilgrimage Dramas from Brindavan.* Princeton: Princeton University Press.

———. 1984. *Sūr Dās: Poet, Singer, Saint.* Seattle: University of Washington Press.

Heesterman, J. C. 1985. *The Inner Conflict of Tradition.* Chicago: *University of Chicago Press.*

Hein, Norvin. 1972. *The Miracle Plays of Mathura.* New Haven: Yale University Press.

Hess, Linda. 1983a. *The Bījak of Kabir.* Berkeley, Calif.: North Point Press.

———. 1983b. "The Cow Is Sucking at the Calf's Teat: Kabir's Upside-down Language." *History of Religions* 22(4): 313–337.

Hitchcock, John T. 1959. "The Idea of the Martial Rajput." In *Traditional India: Structure and Change,* edited by Milton Singer. Philadelphia: American Folklore Society.

Inden, Ronald B. 1976. *Marriage and Rank in Bengali Culture.* Berkeley and Los Angeles: University of California Press.

Inden, Ronald B., and Ralph W. Nicholas. 1977. *Kinship in Bengali Culture.* Chicago: University of Chicago Press.

Jinavijaya, Shri Muni. 1966. "Introduction." In *Rajasthan Through the Ages* 1:2–23. Bikaner: Rajasthan State Archives.

Jindel, Rajendra. 1976. *Culture of a Sacred Town.* Bombay: Popular Prakashan.

Joshi, Om Prakash. 1976. *Painted Folklore and Folklore Painters of India.* Delhi: Concept Publishing Company.

Kakar, Sudhir. 1978. *The Inner World: A Psycho-analytic Study of Childhood and Society in India.* Delhi: Oxford University Press.

———. 1982. *Shamans, Mystics, and Doctors: A Psychological Inquiry into India and Its Healing Traditions.* New York: Alfred A. Knopf.

Kane, P. V. 1953. *History of Dharmaśāstra.* Vol. 4. Poona: Bhandarkar Oriental Research Institute.

Karve, Irawati. 1962. "On the Road: A Maharashtrian Pilgrimage." *Journal of Asian Studies* 22:13–29.

Kaushik, Meena. 1976. "The Symbolic Representation of Death." *Contributions to Indian Sociology* (N.S.) 10(2): 265–292.

Khare, R. S. 1976. "Prayers and Prestations: Two Homologous Systems in Northern India." In *The New Wind,* edited by K. A. David. The Hague: Mouton.

Kinsley, David R. 1979. *The Divine Player: A Study of Kṛṣṇa Līlā.* Delhi: Motilal Banarsidass.

Knipe, David. 1977. "*Sapiṇḍikaraṇa:* The Hindu Rite of Entry into Heaven." In *Religious Encounters with Death,* edited by F. Reynolds and E. H. Waugh. University Park: Pennsylvania State University Press.

Kolenda, Pauline. 1964. "Religious Anxiety and Hindu Fate." In *Religion in South Asia,* edited by Edward J. Harper. Seattle: University of Washington Press.

———. 1982. "Pox and the Terror of Childlessness: Images and Ideas of the Smallpox Goddess in a North Indian Village." In *Mother Worship,* edited by James J. Preston. Chapel Hill: University of North Carolina Press.

Kothari, Komal. 1982. "The Shrine: An Expression of Social Needs." In *Gods of the Byways.* Oxford: Museum of Modern Art.

Lal, Kanwar. 1961. *Holy Cities of India.* Delhi: Asia Press.

Lalas, Sitaram. 1962–1978. *Rājasthānī Sabad Kos.* 9 vols. Jodhpur: Rajasthani Shodh Sansthan.

Lévi-Strauss, Claude. 1974. *Tristes Tropiques*. New York: Atheneum.
Lodrick, Deryck. 1987. "Rajasthan: Region, Myth, or Reality?" In *The Idea of Rajasthan: Explorations in Regional Identity*, edited by Karine Schomer et al. Unpublished manuscript.
McGregor, Ronald S. 1973. *Nanddas: The Round Dance of Krishna and Uddhav's Message*. London: Luzac and Company.
McLeod, W. H. 1968. *Guru Nanak and the Sikh Religion*. Delhi: Oxford University Press.
Madan, T. N. 1982. "The Ideology of the Householder." In *Way of Life: King, Householder, Renouncer*, edited by T. N. Madan.
Madan, T. N., ed. 1982. *Way of Life: King, Householder, Renouncer*. New Delhi: Vikas Publishing House.
Mā̃ Gangā (Ganges Mother). n.d. Hardwar: Harbhajan Singh and Sons.
Mahābhārata. 1976. Translated and edited by J. A. B. van Buitenen. Vol. 2. Chicago: University of Chicago Press.
Mahapatra, Piyush Kanti. 1971. "The Nath Cult of Bengal." *Folklore* 12(10): 376–396.
Maloney, Clarence. 1976. "Don't Say 'Pretty Baby' Lest You Zap it with Your Eye: The Evil Eye in South Asia." In *The Evil Eye*, edited by Clarence Maloney.
Maloney, Clarence, ed. 1976. *The Evil Eye*. New York: Columbia University Press.
Marglin, Frederique Apffel. 1981. "Kings and Wives: The Separation of Status and Royal Power." In *Way of Life: King, Householder, Renouncer*, edited by T. N. Madan. New Delhi: Vikas Publishing House.
———. 1982. "Types of Sexual Union and Their Implicit Meanings." In *The Divine Consort: Radha and the Goddesses of India*, edited by J. S. Hawley and D. M. Wulff. Berkeley, Calif.: Berkeley Religious Studies Series.
Marriott, McKim. 1976a. "Hindu Transactions: Diversity without Dualism." In *Transaction and Meaning: Directions in the Anthropology of Exchange and Symbolic Behavior*, edited by Bruce Kapferer. Philadelphia: ISHI Publications.
———. 1976b. "Interpreting Indian Society: A Monistic Alternative to Dumont's Dualism." *Journal of Asian Studies* 36(1): 189–195.
———. 1980. "The Open Hindu Person and Interpersonal Fluidity." Paper presented at the Annual Meeting of the Association for Asian Studies, Washington, D.C.
Marriott, McKim, and Ronald B. Inden. 1976. "Toward an Ethnosociology of South Asian Caste Systems." In *The New Wind*, edited by K. A. David. The Hague: Mouton.
———. 1979. "Caste Systems." *Encyclopaedia Britannica, Macropaedia,* 3 (15th ed.): 982–991.
Mathur, Jivanlal. 1977. *Bṛj-Bāvanī*. Sawar: Mani Raj Singh.

Miller, Joseph C. 1980. "Current Investigations in the Genre of Rajasthani *Paṛ* Painting Recitations." In *Early Hindi Devotional Literature in Current Research,* edited by Winand M. Callewaert. New Delhi: Impex India.
Monier-Williams, Sir Monier. 1899. *A Sanskrit-English Dictionary.* Oxford: Clarendon Press.
Moreno Arcas, Manuel. 1984. "Murugan, a God of Healing Poisons: The Physics of Worship in a South Indian Center for Pilgrimage." Ph.D. dissertation, Department of Anthropology, University of Chicago.
Moreno Aracas, Manuel, and McKim Marriott. 1981. "The Physics of a South Indian Pilgrimage." Paper presented at the Conference on South Asia, Madison, Wisconsin.
Morinis, E. Alan. 1984. *Pilgrimage in the Hindu Tradition: A Case Study of West Bengal.* Delhi: Oxford University Press.
Narasimhachary, M. 1977. "Pushkara—a Bathing Festival." *Vivekananda Kendra Patrika* 6(1): 121–133.
Narayanan, Vasudha. 1985. "Arcāvatāra: On Earth as He Is in Heaven." In *Gods of Flesh, Gods of Stone: The Embodiment of Divinity in India,* edited by J. P. Waghorne and N. Cutler. Chambersburg, Pa.: Anima Publications.
Nicholas, Ralph. 1982. "*Śrāddha,* Impurity, and Relations between the Living and the Dead." In *Way of Life: King, Householder, Renouncer,* edited by T. N. Madan. New Delhi: Vikas Publishing House.
O'Flaherty, Wendy D. 1973. *Asceticism and Eroticism in the Mythology of Śiva.* London: Oxford University Press.
———. 1975. *Hindu Myths.* Middlesex, England: Penguin Books.
———. 1980a. "Karma and Rebirth in the Vedas and Puranas." In *Karma and Rebirth in Classical Indian Traditions,* edited by Wendy D. O'Flaherty. Berkeley and Los Angeles: University of California Press.
———. 1980b. *Women, Androgynes, and Other Mythical Beasts.* Chicago: University of Chicago Press.
———. 1984. *Dreams, Illusion, and Other Realities.* Chicago: University of Chicago Press.
———. 1986. "Sexual Doubles and Sexual Masquerades: The Structures of Sex Symbols." University Lecture, in Religion. Tempe: Arizona State University, Dept. of Religious Studies.
Pandey, Raj Bali. 1969. *Hindu Samskāras.* Delhi: Motilal Banarsidass.
Parry, Jonathan. 1980. "Ghosts, Greed, and Sin: The Occupational Identity of the Benares Funeral Priests." *Man* 15:88–111.
———. 1982a. "Death and Cosmogony in Kashi." In *Way of Life: King, Householder, Renouncer,* edited by T. N. Madan. New Delhi: Vikas Publishing House.
———. 1982b. "Sacrificial Death and the Necrophagous Ascetic." In *Death and the Regeneration of Life,* edited by Maurice Bloch and Jonathan Parry. Cambridge: Cambridge University Press.

Pfaffenberger, Bryan. 1982. *Caste in Tamil Culture: The Religious Foundations of Sudra Domination in Tamil Sri Lanka.* Syracuse, N.Y.: Maxwell School of Citizenship and Public Affairs.

Plunkett, Frances T. 1973. "Royal Marriages in Rajasthan." *Contributions to Indian Sociology* 7:64–80.

Pocock, D. F. 1981. "The Evil Eye: Envy and Greed Among the Patidars of Central Gujarat." In *The Evil Eye: A Folklore Casebook,* edited by Alan Dundes. New York: Garland Publishing.

Prayāg Rāj Mahātmya (The Greatness of King Prayag). n.d. Allahabad: Shri Durga Pustak Bhandar.

Rabinow, Paul. 1977. *Reflections on Fieldwork in Morocco.* Berkeley and Los Angeles: University of California Press.

Raheja, Gloria G. 1985. "Kinship, Caste, and Auspiciousness in Pahansu." Ph.D. dissertation, Department of Anthropology, University of Chicago.

Rajiv, Rajendra Kumar. 1979. *Hamāre Pūjya Tīrtha* (Our Worshipped Crossing Places). Delhi: Pustak Mahal.

Ramanujan, A. K. 1970. *The Interior Landscape: Love Poems from a Classical Tamil Anthology.* London: Peter Owen.

———. 1973. *Speaking of Śiva.* Baltimore: Penguin Books.

———. 1980. "Is There an Indian Way of Thinking?" Paper presented at the ACLS-SSRC Joint Committee on South Asia–sponsored "Person in South Asia" Workshop, Chicago.

Rangaswami Aiyangar, K. V. 1942. "Introduction." In *Tīrtha-vivecana-kāṇḍa of Kṛtyakalpataru of Bhaṭṭa Lakṣmīdhara,* vol. 8, edited by K. V. Rangaswami Aiyangar. Baroda: Oriental Institute.

Riesman, Paul. 1977. *Freedom in Fulani Social Life.* Chicago: University of Chicago Press.

Rose, Ann Grodzins. 1978. "*Mokṣa:* The Fourth Human Pursuit as a Value in Hindu Culture." M.A. thesis, Department of Anthropology, University of Chicago.

Rosin, R. T. 1983. "Notes on Dread and the Supernatural in Indian Society." *Man in India* 63(2): 115–140.

Roy, D. K., and I. Devi. 1955. *Kumbha: India's Ageless Festival.* Bombay: Bharatiya Vidya Bhavan.

Rudolph, Lloyd I., and Susanne H. Rudolph. 1984. *Essays on Rajputana: Reflections on History, Culture, and Administration.* New Delhi: Concept Publishing Company.

Salomon, Richard, ed. and trans. 1985. *The Bridge to the Three Holy Cities: The Sāmānya-praghaṭṭaka of Nārāyaṇa Bhaṭṭa's Tristhalīsetu.* Delhi: Motilal Banarsidass.

Saran, Richard Davis. 1978. "Conquest and Colonization: Rajputs and Vasis in Middle Period Marvar." Ph.D. dissertation, Department of History, University of Michigan.

Saraswati, Baidyanath. 1975. *Kashi: Myth and Reality of a Classical Cultural*

Tradition. Simla: Indian Institute of Advanced Study.

Sarda, Har Bilas. 1911. *Ajmer: Historical and Descriptive*. Ajmer: Scottish Mission Industries Company.

Schneider, David M. 1968. *American Kinship: A Cultural Account*. Englewood Cliffs, N.J.: Prentice-Hall.

———. 1976. "Notes toward a Theory of Culture." In *Meaning in Anthropology*, edited by K. H. Basso and H. A. Selby. Albuquerque: University of New Mexico Press.

———. 1977. "Kinship, Nationality, and Religion in American Culture: Toward a Definition of Kinship." In *Symbolic Anthropology*, edited by J. L. Dolgin, D. S. Kemnitzer, and D. M. Schneider. New York: Columbia University Press.

Schomer, Karine, et al., eds. 1987. *The Idea of Rajasthan: Explorations in Religious Identity*. Unpublished manuscript.

Schomer, Karine, and W. H. McLeod, eds. 1987. *The Sant Tradition of India*. Berkeley, Calif.: Graduate Theological Union.

Shrī Kṣhetra Parichaya (Introduction to an Auspicious Ground). 1976. Puri: Shri P. Tripathy on behalf of Shri Jagannath Temple Managing Committee.

Singer, Milton. 1972. *When a Great Tradition Modernizes*. New York: Praeger Publishers.

———. 1984. *Man's Glassy Essence: Explorations in Semiotic Anthropology*. Bloomington: Indiana University Press.

Singh, Hiramani. n.d. *Vrat aur Tyauhār* (Fasts and Festivals). Allahabad: Shri Durga Pustak Bhandar.

Sircar, D. C. 1973. *The Śākta Pīṭhas*. Delhi: Motilal Banarsidass.

Smith, John D. 1977. "The Singer or the Song? A Reassessment of Lord's 'Oral Theory.'" *Man* (N.S.) 12:141–153.

———. 1979. "Metre and Text in Western India." *Bulletin of the School of Oriental and African Studies, University of London* 42(2): 347–357.

Srivastava, S. L. 1974. *Folk Culture and Oral Tradition*. New Delhi: Abhinav Publications.

Stanley, John M. 1977. "Special Time, Special Power: The Fluidity of Power in a Popular Hindu Festival." *Journal of Asian Studies* 37(1): 27–43.

Steed, Gital P. 1972. "Notes on an Approach to a Study of Personality Formation in a Hindu Village in Gujarat." In *Village India*, edited by McKim Marriott. Chicago: University of Chicago Press.

Stern, Henri. 1977. "Power in Traditional India: Territory, Caste, and Kinship in Rajasthan." In *Realm and Region in Traditional India*, edited by Richard G. Fox. New Delhi: Vikas Publishing House.

Stevenson, Mrs. Sinclair. 1971. *The Rites of the Twice-Born*. New Delhi: Oriental Books Reprint Corporation.

Tedlock, Dennis. 1983. *The Spoken Word and the Work of Interpretation.* Philadelphia: University of Pennsylvania Press.

Temple, R. C. 1962. *The Legends of the Punjab.* 3 vols. Patiala: Language Department, Punjab.

Tod, James. 1978. *Annals and Antiquities of Rajasthan.* 2 vols. New Delhi: M. N. Publishers.

Turner, Victor. 1974. *Dramas, Fields, and Metaphors: Symbolic Action in Human Society.* Ithaca, N.Y.: Cornell University Press.

———. 1979. *Process, Performance, and Pilgrimage: A Study in Comparative Symbology.* New Delhi: Concept Publishing Company.

Turner, Victor, and Edith Turner. 1978. *Image and Pilgrimage in Christian Culture.* New York: Columbia University Press.

Tyler, Stephen A. 1986. "Post-Modern Ethnography: From Document of the Occult to Occult Document." In *Writing Culture,* edited by James Clifford and George E. Marcus. Berkeley and Los Angeles: University of California Press.

Varenne, Jean. 1976. *Yoga and the Hindu Tradition.* Chicago: University of Chicago Press.

Vatuk, Sylvia. 1981. "Cultural Conceptions of Aging and Family Relationships in a Delhi Village." Paper presented at Second Workshop on the Person in South Asia: Life Courses and Family Relationships in Alternative Psychologies of South Asia, Chicago.

Vatuk, Ved Prakash, and Sylvia Vatuk. 1976. "The Social Context of Gift Exchange." In *Family and Social Change in Modern India,* edited by Giri Raj Gupta. New Delhi: Vikas Publishing House.

Vaudeville, Charlotte. 1974. *Kabir.* Oxford: Oxford University Press.

———. 1975. "Pandharpur, the City of Saints." In *Structural Approaches to South India Studies,* edited by H. M. Buck and G. E. Yocum. Chambersburg, Pa.: Wilson Books.

———. 1976. "Braj, Lost and Found." *Indo-Iranian Journal* 18:195–213.

Vidyarthi, L. P. 1961. *The Sacred Complex in Hindu Gaya.* Bombay: Asia Publishing House.

Vidyarthi, L. P., B. N. Saraswati, and Makhan Jha. 1979. *The Sacred Complex of Kashi.* Delhi: Concept.

Visit Puri. 1977. Puri: Shri Jagannath Temple Managing Committee.

Wadley, Susan S. 1975. *Shakti: Power in the Conceptual Structure of Karimpur Religion.* Chicago: Department of Anthropology, University of Chicago Studies in Anthropology Series, No. 2.

Waghorne, Joanne P., and Norman Cutler, eds. 1985. *Gods of Flesh, Gods of Stone: The Embodiment of Divinity in India.* Chambersburg, Pa.: Anima Publications.

Woodroffe, John, trans. 1964. *The Serpent Power.* Madras: Ganesh and Company.

Yadav, K. C., ed. 1976. *Autobiography of Dayanand Saraswati*. New Delhi: Manohar.

Zeitlyn, Sushila. 1983. "Death and the Subordination of Women." Seminar paper, London School of Economics.

———. 1986. "Sacrifice and the Sacred in a Hindu Tirtha: The Case of Pushkar India." Ph.D. dissertation, London School of Economics and Political Science.

Ziegler, Norman. 1973. "Action, Power, and Service in Rajasthani Culture: A Social History of the Rajputs of Middle Period Rajasthan." Ph.D. dissertation, Department of History, University of Chicago.

———. 1976. "The Seventeenth Century Chronicles of Marvar: A Study of the Evolution and Use of Oral Tradition in Western India." *History in Africa: A Journal of Method* 3:127–153.

———. 1978. "Some Notes on Rajput Loyalties during the Mughal Period." In *Kingship and Authority in South Asia,* edited by J. F. Richards. Madison: Center for South Asian Studies, University of Wisconsin.

INDEX